The
Labor
Law
Source
Book

THE LABOR LAW SOURCE BOOK

TEXTS OF TWENTY FEDERAL LABOR LAWS

Robert M. Schwartz, Editor

work
rights
press

CAMBRIDGE, MASSACHUSETTS

The Labor Law Source Book
Editorial matter only copyright © 1999 by Work Rights Press
Printed in the United States of America
ISBN 0-945902-07-7
Library of Congress Catalog Card Number: 98-61811

Work Rights Press
Box 391887
Cambridge, Massachusetts 02139
Telephone: 1-800-576-4552

Also available from Work Rights Press:
  The Legal Rights of Union Stewards
  How to Win Past Practice Grievances
  The FMLA Handbook

See. p. 291 for ordering information.

Table of Contents

Preface

THIS BOOK contains the text of twenty important federal labor laws amended as of July 1, 1999.

The nutshells describing each law were prepared by the editor.

Federal laws are contained in an official series called the U.S. Code which is divided by subject matter into titles and sections.

The first ten laws in this book are from Title 29 of the U.S. Code. Other laws are from Titles 5, 8, 38, 40, 41, 42, and 45. The North American Agreement on Labor Cooperation, an agreement between the United States, Mexico, and Canada, is not a part of the U.S. Code.

Citations to federal laws begin with the title number and end with the section number. The symbol § is used for section. For example, 29 U.S.C. §154 refers to section 154 of Title 29 of the U.S. Code.

July, 1999

Chronology

THE **Railway Labor Act (RLA)** (1926) was the first federal legislation to protect workers' rights to form unions. Initially confined to the railway industry, the RLA was expanded in 1936 to cover the airline industry as well.

The **Davis-Bacon Act** (1931) orders contractors on federally financed construction projects to pay wage rates equal to those prevailing in local construction trades.

The **Norris-LaGuardia Anti-Injunction Act** (1932) limits the ability of federal judges to issue injunctions against workers and unions involved in labor disputes.

The **National Labor Relations Act (NLRA)** (1935), also known as the Wagner Act, is the broadest U.S. labor relations law. The NLRA guarantees organizing and bargaining rights to workers and unions in the private sector.

The **Walsh-Healey Government Contracts Act** (1936) requires companies that supply goods to the federal government to pay wages according to a schedule set by the Secretary of Labor.

The **Fair Labor Standards Act (FLSA)** (1938) creates a national minimum wage, mandates overtime pay, and restricts child labor.

The **Labor Management Relations Act (LMRA)** (1947), also known as the Taft-Hartley Act, amended the NLRA.

The **Labor-Management Reporting and Disclosure Act (LMRDA)** (1959), also known as the Landrum-Griffin Act, establishes democratic rights for union members and creates rules for union elections.

Title VII of the Civil Rights Act of 1964 forbids employers and unions from discriminating on the basis of race, color, gender, nationality, or religion.

The **Age Discrimination in Employment Act (ADEA)** (1967) extends anti-discrimination protections to workers age forty and older.

The **Occupational Safety and Health Act** (1970) requires employers to provide safe and healthy workplaces.

The **Federal Service Labor-Management Relations Act** (1978) extends collective bargaining rights to federal employees.

The **Consolidated Omnibus Budget Reconciliation Act (COBRA)** (1986) allows employees to stay in employer health plans following layoffs, discharges, and resignations.

The **Immigration Reform and Control Act (IRCA)** (1986) prohibits both the employment of unauthorized aliens and discrimination based on citizenship status.

The **Employee Polygraph Protection Act** (1988) restricts employers' use of lie detector tests.

The **Worker Adjustment and Retraining Notification Act (WARN)** (1988) requires employers to notify workers sixty days before a plant closing or large layoff.

The **Drug-Free Workplace Act** (1988) orders federal contractors to conduct employee anti-drug programs.

The **Americans with Disabilities Act (ADA)** (1990) requires employers to offer reasonable accommodations to qualified disabled employees and bans discrimination against such workers.

The **Family and Medical Leave Act (FMLA)** (1993) allows workers time off each year due to serious health conditions or to care for a newborn or newly adopted child.

The **North American Agreement on Labor Cooperation** (1993) sets out labor law standards for Mexico, Canada, and the United States to supplement the North American Free Trade Agreement (NAFTA).

The **Uniformed Services Employment and Reemployment Rights Act (USERRA)** (1994) guarantees reemployment when persons leave military service and prohibits discrimination against employees who need time off to satisfy military training obligations.

Norris-LaGuardia Anti-Injunction Act

U.S. Code, Title 29, Sections 101 to 115

Sec.

NORRIS-LAGUARDIA IN A NUTSHELL

Enacted: 1932

Purpose: To limit the ability of federal judges to issue injunctions in labor disputes

Sec. 101. Issuance of restraining orders and injunctions; limitation; public policy

No court of the United States, as defined in this chapter, shall have jurisdiction to issue any restraining order or temporary or permanent injunction in a case involving or growing out of a labor dispute, except in a strict conformity with the provisions of this chapter; nor shall any such restraining order or temporary or permanent injunction be issued contrary to the public policy declared in this chapter.

Sec. 102. Public policy in labor matters declared

In the interpretation of this chapter and in determining the jurisdiction and authority of the courts of the United States, as such jurisdiction and authority are defined and limited in this chapter, the public policy of the United States is declared as follows:

Whereas under prevailing economic conditions, developed with the aid of governmental authority for owners of property to organize in the corporate and other forms of ownership association, the individual unorganized worker is commonly helpless to exercise actual liberty of contract and to protect his freedom of labor, and thereby to obtain acceptable terms and conditions of employment, wherefore, though he should be free to decline to associate

[1]

with his fellows, it is necessary that he have full freedom of association, self-organization, and designation of representatives of his own choosing, to negotiate the terms and conditions of his employment, and that he shall be free from the interference, restraint, or coercion of employers of labor, or their agents, in the designation of such representatives or in self-organization or in other concerted activities for the purpose of collective bargaining or other mutual aid or protection; therefore, the following definitions of and limitations upon the jurisdiction and authority of the courts of the United States are enacted.

Sec. 103. Nonenforceability of undertakings in conflict with public policy; "yellow dog" contracts

Any undertaking or promise, such as is described in this section, or any other undertaking or promise in conflict with the public policy declared in section 102 of this title, is declared to be contrary to the public policy of the United States, shall not be enforceable in any court of the United States and shall not afford any basis for the granting of legal or equitable relief by any such court, including specifically the following:

Every undertaking or promise hereafter made, whether written or oral, express or implied, constituting or contained in any contract or agreement of hiring or employment between any individual, firm, company, association, or corporation, and any employee or prospective employee of the same, whereby

(a) Either party to such contract or agreement undertakes or promises not to join, become, or remain a member of any labor organization or of any employer organization; or

(b) Either party to such contract or agreement undertakes or promises that he will withdraw from an employment relation in the event that he joins, becomes, or remains a member of any labor organization or of any employer organization.

Sec. 104. Enumeration of specific acts not subject to restraining orders or injunctions

No court of the United States shall have jurisdiction to issue any restraining order or temporary or permanent injunction in any case involving or growing out of any labor dispute to prohibit any person or persons participating or interested in

such dispute (as these terms are herein defined) from doing, whether singly or in concert, any of the following acts:

(a) Ceasing or refusing to perform any work or to remain in any relation of employment;

(b) Becoming or remaining a member of any labor organization or of any employer organization, regardless of any such undertaking or promise as is described in section 103 of this title;

(c) Paying or giving to, or withholding from, any person participating or interested in such labor dispute, any strike or unemployment benefits or insurance, or other moneys or things of value;

(d) By all lawful means aiding any person participating or interested in any labor dispute who is being proceeded against in, or is prosecuting, any action or suit in any court of the United States or of any State;

(e) Giving publicity to the existence of, or the facts involved in, any labor dispute, whether by advertising, speaking, patrolling, or by any other method not involving fraud or violence;

(f) Assembling peaceably to act or to organize to act in promotion of their interests in a labor dispute;

(g) Advising or notifying any person of an intention to do any of the acts heretofore specified;

(h) Agreeing with other persons to do or not to do any of the acts heretofore specified; and

(i) Advising, urging, or otherwise causing or inducing without fraud or violence the acts heretofore specified, regardless of any such undertaking or promise as is described in section 103 of this title.

Sec. 105. Doing in concert of certain acts as constituting unlawful combination or conspiracy subjecting person to injunctive remedies

No court of the United States shall have jurisdiction to issue a restraining order or temporary or permanent injunction upon the ground that any of the persons participating or interested in a labor dispute constitute or are engaged in an unlawful combination or conspiracy because of the doing in concert of the acts enumerated in section 104 of this title.

Sec. 106. Responsibility of officers and members of associations or their organizations for unlawful acts of individual officers, members, and agents

No officer or member of any association or organization, and no association or organization participating or interested in a labor dispute, shall be held responsible or liable in any court of the United States for the unlawful acts of individual officers, members, or agents, except upon clear proof of actual participation in, or actual authorization of, such acts, or of ratification of such acts after actual knowledge thereof.

Sec. 107. Issuance of injunctions in labor disputes; hearing; findings of court; notice to affected persons; temporary restraining order; undertakings

No court of the United States shall have jurisdiction to issue a temporary or permanent injunction in any case involving or growing out of a labor dispute, as defined in this chapter, except after hearing the testimony of witnesses in open court (with opportunity for cross-examination) in support of the allegations of a complaint made under oath, and testimony in opposition thereto, if offered, and except after findings of fact by the court, to the effect —

(a) That unlawful acts have been threatened and will be committed unless restrained or have been committed and will be continued unless restrained, but no injunction or temporary restraining order shall be issued on account of any threat or unlawful act excepting against the person or persons, association, or organization making the threat or committing the unlawful act or actually authorizing or ratifying the same after actual knowledge thereof;

(b) That substantial and irreparable injury to complainant's property will follow;

(c) That as to each item of relief granted greater injury will be inflicted upon complainant by the denial of relief then will be inflicted upon defendants by the granting of relief;

(d) That complainant has no adequate remedy at law; and

(e) That the public officers charged with the duty to protect complainant's property are unable or unwilling to furnish adequate protection.

Such hearing shall be held after due and personal notice thereof has been given, in such manner as the court shall direct, to all known persons against whom relief is sought, and also to the chief of those public officials of the county and city within which the unlawful acts have been threatened or committed charged with the duty to protect complainant's property: *Provided, however,* That if a complainant shall also allege that, unless a temporary restraining order shall be issued without notice, a substantial and irreparable injury to complainant's property will be unavoidable, such a temporary restraining order may be issued upon testimony under oath, sufficient, if sustained, to justify the court in issuing a temporary injunction upon a hearing after notice. Such a temporary restraining order shall be effective for no longer than five days and shall become void at the expiration of said five days. No temporary restraining order or temporary injunction shall be issued except on condition that complainant shall first file an undertaking with adequate security in an amount to be fixed by the court sufficient to recompense those enjoined for any loss, expense, or damage caused by the improvident or erroneous issuance of such order or injunction, including all reasonable costs (together with a reasonable attorney's fee) and expense of defense against the order or against the granting of any injunctive relief sought in the same proceeding and subsequently denied by the court.

The undertaking mentioned in this section shall be understood to signify an agreement entered into by the complainant and the surety upon which a decree may be rendered in the same suit or proceeding against said complainant and surety, upon a hearing to assess damages of which hearing complainant and surety shall have reasonable notice, the said complainant and surety submitting themselves to the jurisdiction of the court for that purpose. But nothing in this section contained shall deprive any party having a claim or cause of action under or upon such undertaking from electing to pursue his ordinary remedy by suit at law or in equity.

Sec. 108. Noncompliance with obligations involved in labor disputes or failure to settle by negotiation or arbitration as preventing injunctive relief

No restraining order or injunctive relief shall be granted to any complainant who has failed to comply with any obligation imposed by law which is involved in the labor dispute in question, or who has failed to make every reasonable effort to settle such dispute either by negotiation or with the aid of any available governmental machinery of mediation or voluntary arbitration.

Sec. 109. Granting of restraining order or injunction as dependent on previous findings of fact; limitation on prohibitions included in restraining orders and injunctions

No restraining order or temporary or permanent injunction shall be granted in a case involving or growing out of a labor dispute, except on the basis of findings of fact made and filed by the court in the record of the case prior to the issuance of such restraining order or injunction; and every restraining order or injunction granted in a case involving or growing out of a labor dispute shall include only a prohibition of such specific act or acts as may be expressly complained of in the bill of complaint or petition filed in such case and as shall be expressly included in said findings of fact made and filed by the court as provided in this chapter.

Sec. 110. Review by court of appeals of issuance or denial of temporary injunctions; record

Whenever any court of the United States shall issue or deny any temporary injunction in a case involving or growing out of a labor dispute, the court shall, upon the request of any party to the proceedings and on his filing the usual bond for costs, forthwith certify as in ordinary cases the record of the case to the court of appeals for its review. Upon the filing of such record in the court of appeals, the appeal shall be heard and the temporary injunctive order affirmed, modified, or set aside expeditiously.

Sec. 111, 112. Repealed

Sec. 113. Definitions of terms and words used in chapter

When used in this chapter, and for the purposes of this chapter —

(a) A case shall be held to involve or to grow out of a labor dispute when the case involves persons who are engaged in the same industry, trade, craft, or occupation; or have direct or indirect interests therein; or who are employees of the same employer; or who are members of the same or an affiliated organization of employers or employees; whether such dispute is (1) between one or more employers or associations of employers and one or more employees or associations of employees; (2) between one or more employers or associations of employers and one or more employers or associations of employers; or (3) between one or more employees or associations of employees and one or more employees or associations of employees; or when the case involves any conflicting or competing interests in a "labor dispute" (as defined in this section) of "persons participating or interested" therein (as defined in this section).

(b) A person or association shall be held to be a person participating or interested in a labor dispute if relief is sought against him or it, and if he or it is engaged in the same industry, trade, craft, or occupation in which such dispute occurs, or has a direct or indirect interest therein, or is a member, officer, or agent of any association composed in whole or in part of employers or employees engaged in such industry, trade, craft, or occupation.

(c) The term "labor dispute" includes any controversy concerning terms or conditions of employment, or concerning the association or representation of persons in negotiating, fixing, maintaining, changing, or seeking to arrange terms or conditions of employment, regardless of whether or not the disputants stand in the proximate relation of employer and employee.

(d) The term "court of the United States" means any court of the United States whose jurisdiction has been or may be conferred or defined or limited by Act of Congress, including the courts of the District of Columbia.

Sec. 114. Separability

If any provision of this chapter or the application thereof to any person or circumstance is held unconstitutional or otherwise invalid, the remaining provisions of this chapter and the application of such provisions to other persons or circumstances shall not be affected thereby.

Sec. 115. Repeal of conflicting acts

All acts and parts of acts in conflict with the provisions of this chapter are repealed.

National Labor Relations Act
(including sections added by the Labor Management Relations Act)

U.S. Code, Title 29, Sections 141 to 187
(Original section numbers in italics)

NLRA IN A NUTSHELL

Enacted: 1935

Purpose: To guarantee employees the right to organize unions and to require employers to bargain with unions

Coverage: Private sector employers and employees (with certain exclusions)

Responsible agency: National Labor Relations Board

Sec. 141. Short title; Congressional declaration of purpose and policy *[Sec. 1]*

(a) This chapter may be cited as the "Labor Management Relations Act, 1947".

(b) Industrial strife which interferes with the normal flow of commerce and with the full production of articles and commodities for commerce, can be avoided or substantially minimized if employers, employees, and labor organizations each recognize under law one another's legitimate rights in their relations with each other, and above all recognize under law that neither party has any right in its relations with any other to engage in acts or practices which jeopardize the public health, safety, or interest.

It is the purpose and policy of this chapter, in order to promote the full flow of commerce, to prescribe the legitimate rights of both employees and employers in their relations affecting commerce, to provide orderly and peaceful procedures for preventing the interference by either with the legitimate rights of the other, to protect the rights of individual employees in their relations with labor organizations whose activities affect commerce, to define and proscribe practices on the part of labor and management which affect commerce and are inimical to the general welfare, and to protect the rights of the public in connection with labor disputes affecting commerce.

Sec. 142. Definitions *[Sec. 501]*

When used in this chapter —

(1) The term "industry affecting commerce" means any industry or activity in commerce or in which a labor dispute would burden or obstruct commerce or tend to burden or obstruct commerce or the free flow of commerce.

(2) The term "strike" includes any strike or other concerted stoppage of work by employees (including a stoppage by reason of the expiration of a collective-bargaining agreement) and any concerted slowdown or other concerted interruption of operations by employees.

(3) The terms "commerce", "labor disputes", "employer", "employee", "labor organization", "representative", "person", and "supervisor" shall have the same meaning as when used in subchapter II of this chapter.

Sec. 143. Saving provisions *[Sec. 502]*

Nothing in this chapter shall be construed to require an individual employee to render labor or service without his consent, nor shall anything in this chapter be construed to make the quitting of his labor by an individual employee an illegal act; nor shall any court issue any process to compel the performance by an individual employee of such labor or service, without his consent; nor shall the quitting of labor by an employee or employees in good faith because of abnormally dangerous conditions for work at the place of employment of such employee or employees be deemed a strike under this chapter.

Sec. 144. Separability *[Sec. 503]*

If any provision of this chapter, or the application of such provision to any person or circumstance, shall be held invalid, the remainder of this chapter, or the application of such provision to persons or circumstances other than those as to which it is held invalid, shall not be affected thereby.

Sec. 151. Findings and declaration of policy *[Sec. 1]*

The denial by some employers of the right of employees to organize and the refusal by some employers to accept the procedure of collective bargaining lead to strikes and other forms of industrial strife or unrest, which have the intent or the necessary effect of burdening or obstructing commerce by (a) impairing the efficiency, safety, or operation of the instrumentalities of commerce; (b) occurring in the current of commerce; (c) materially affecting, restraining, or controlling the flow of raw materials or manufactured or processed goods from or into the channels of commerce, or the prices of such materials or goods in commerce; or (d) causing diminution of employment and wages in such volume as substantially to impair or disrupt the market for goods flowing from or into the channels of commerce.

The inequality of bargaining power between employees who do not possess full freedom of association or actual liberty of contract, and employers who are organized in the corporate or other forms of ownership association substantially burdens and affects the flow of commerce, and tends to aggravate recurrent business depressions, by depressing wage rates and the purchasing power of wage earners in industry and by preventing the stabilization of competitive wage rates and working conditions within and between industries.

Experience has proved that protection by law of the right of employees to organize and bargain collectively safeguards commerce from injury, impairment, or interruption, and promotes the flow of commerce by removing certain recognized sources of industrial strife and unrest, by encouraging practices fundamental to the friendly adjustment of industrial disputes arising out of differences as to wages, hours, or other working conditions, and by restoring equality of bargaining power between employers and employees.

Experience has further demonstrated that certain practices by some labor organizations, their officers, and members have the intent or the necessary effect of burdening or obstructing commerce by preventing the free flow of goods in such commerce through strikes and other forms of industrial unrest or through concerted activities which impair the interest of the public in the free flow of such commerce. The elimination of such practices is a necessary condition to the assurance of the rights herein guaranteed.

It is declared hereby to be the policy of the United States to eliminate the causes of certain substantial obstructions to the free flow of commerce and to mitigate and eliminate these obstructions when they have occurred by encouraging the practice and procedure of collective bargaining and by protecting the exercise by workers of full freedom of association, self-organization, and designation of representatives of their own choosing, for the purpose of negotiating the terms and conditions of their employment or other mutual aid or protection.

Sec. 152. Definitions *[Sec. 2]*

When used in this subchapter —

(1) The term "person" includes one or more individuals, labor organizations, partnerships, associations, corporations, legal representatives, trustees, trustees in cases under Title 11, or receivers.

(2) The term "employer" includes any person acting as an agent of an employer, directly or indirectly, but shall not include the United States or any wholly owned Government corporation, or any Federal Reserve Bank, or any State or

political subdivision thereof, or any person subject to the Railway Labor Act (45 U.S.C. §151 et seq.), as amended from time to time, or any labor organization (other than when acting as an employer), or anyone acting in the capacity of officer or agent of such labor organization.

(3) The term "employee" shall include any employee, and shall not be limited to the employees of a particular employer, unless this subchapter explicitly states otherwise, and shall include any individual whose work has ceased as a consequence of, or in connection with, any current labor dispute or because of any unfair labor practice, and who has not obtained any other regular and substantially equivalent employment, but shall not include any individual employed as an agricultural laborer, or in the domestic service of any family or person at his home, or any individual employed by his parent or spouse, or any individual having the status of an independent contractor, or any individual employed as a supervisor, or any individual employed by an employer subject to the Railway Labor Act (45 U.S.C. 151 et seq.), as amended from time to time, or by any other person who is not an employer as herein defined.

(4) The term "representatives" includes any individual or labor organization.

(5) The term "labor organization" means any organization of any kind, or any agency or employee representation committee or plan, in which employees participate and which exists for the purpose, in whole or in part, of dealing with employers concerning grievances, labor disputes, wages, rates of pay, hours of employment, or conditions of work.

(6) The term "commerce" means trade, traffic, commerce, transportation, or communication among the several States, or between the District of Columbia or any Territory of the United States and any State or other Territory, or between any foreign country and any State, Territory, or the District of Columbia, or within the District of Columbia or any Territory, or between points in the same State but through any other State or any Territory or the District of Columbia or any foreign country.

(7) The term "affecting commerce" means in commerce, or burdening or obstructing commerce or the free flow of commerce, or having

led or tending to lead to a labor dispute burdening or obstructing commerce or the free flow of commerce.

(8) The term "unfair labor practice" means any unfair labor practice listed in section 158 of this title.

(9) The term "labor dispute" includes any controversy concerning terms, tenure or conditions of employment, or concerning the association or representation of persons in negotiating, fixing, maintaining, changing, or seeking to arrange terms or conditions of employment, regardless of whether the disputants stand in the proximate relation of employer and employee.

(10) The term "National Labor Relations Board" means the National Labor Relations Board provided for in section 153 of this title.

(11) The term "supervisor" means any individual having authority, in the interest of the employer, to hire, transfer, suspend, lay off, recall, promote, discharge, assign, reward, or discipline other employees, or responsibly to direct them, or to adjust their grievances, or effectively to recommend such action, if in connection with the foregoing the exercise of such authority is not of a merely routine or clerical nature, but requires the use of independent judgment.

(12) The term "professional employee" means —

(a) any employee engaged in work (i) predominantly intellectual and varied in character as opposed to routine mental, manual, mechanical, or physical work; (ii) involving the consistent exercise of discretion and judgment in its performance; (iii) of such a character that the output produced or the result accomplished cannot be standardized in relation to a given period of time; (iv) requiring knowledge of an advanced type in a field of science or learning customarily acquired by a prolonged course of specialized intellectual instruction and study in an institution of higher learning or a hospital, as distinguished from a general academic education or from an apprenticeship or from training in the performance of routine mental, manual, or physical processes; or

(b) any employee, who (i) has completed the courses of specialized intellectual instruction and study described in clause (iv) of paragraph (a), and (ii) is performing related work under the supervision of a professional person to qualify himself to become a professional employee as defined in paragraph (a).

(13) In determining whether any person is acting as an "agent" of another person so as to make such other person responsible for his acts, the question of whether the specific acts performed were actually authorized or subsequently ratified shall not be controlling.

(14) The term "health care institution" shall include any hospital, convalescent hospital, health maintenance organization, health clinic, nursing home, extended care facility, or other institution devoted to the care of sick, infirm, or aged person.

Sec. 153. National Labor Relations Board *[Sec. 3]*

(a) Creation, composition, appointment, and tenure; Chairman; removal of members

The National Labor Relations Board (hereinafter called the "Board") created by this subchapter prior to its amendment by the Labor Management Relations Act, 1947 (29 U.S.C. §141 et seq.), is continued as an agency of the United States, except that the Board shall consist of five instead of three members, appointed by the President by and with the advice and consent of the Senate. Of the two additional members so provided for, one shall be appointed for a term of five years and the other for a term of two years. Their successors, and the successors of the other members, shall be appointed for terms of five years each, excepting that any individual chosen to fill a vacancy shall be appointed only for the unexpired term of the member whom he shall succeed. The President shall designate one member to serve as Chairman of the Board. Any member of the Board may be removed by the President, upon notice and hearing, for neglect of duty or malfeasance in office, but for no other cause.

(b) Delegation of powers to members and regional directors; review and stay of actions of regional directors; quorum; seal

The Board is authorized to delegate to any group of three or more members any or all of the powers which it may itself exercise. The Board is also authorized to delegate to its regional directors its powers under section 159 of this title to determine the unit appropriate for the purpose of collective bargaining, to investigate and provide for hearings, and determine whether a question of representation exists, and to direct an election or take a secret ballot under subsection (c) or (e) of section 159 of this title and certify the results thereof, except that upon the filing of a request therefor with the Board by any interested person, the Board may review any action of a regional director delegated to him under this paragraph, but such a review shall not, unless specifically ordered by the Board, operate as a stay of any action taken by the regional director. A vacancy in the Board shall not impair the right of the remaining members to exercise all of the powers of the Board, and three members of the Board shall, at all times, constitute a quorum of the Board, except that two members shall constitute a quorum of any group designated pursuant to the first sentence hereof. The Board shall have an official seal which shall be judicially noticed.

(c) Annual reports to Congress and the President

The Board shall at the close of each fiscal year make a report in writing to Congress and to the President summarizing significant case activities and operations for that fiscal year.

(d) General Counsel; appointment and tenure; powers and duties; vacancy

There shall be a General Counsel of the Board who shall be appointed by the President, by and with the advice and consent of the Senate, for a term of four years. The General Counsel of the Board shall exercise general supervision over all attorneys employed by the Board (other than administrative law judges and legal assistants to Board members) and over the officers and employees in the regional offices. He shall have final authority, on behalf of the Board, in respect of the investigation of charges and issuance of complaints under section 160 of this title, and in respect of the prosecution of such complaints before the Board, and shall have such other duties as the Board may prescribe or as may be provided by law. In case of a vacancy in the office of the General Counsel the President is authorized to designate the officer or employee who shall act as General Counsel during such vacancy, but no person or persons so designated shall so act (1) for more than forty days when the Congress is in session unless a nomination to fill such vacancy shall have been submitted to the Senate, or (2) after the adjournment sine die of the session of the Senate in which such nomination was submitted.

Sec. 154. National Labor Relations Board; eligibility for reappointment; officers and employees; payment of expenses [Sec. 4]

(a) Each member of the Board and the General Counsel of the Board shall be eligible for reappointment, and shall not engage in any other business, vocation, or employment. The Board shall appoint an executive secretary, and such attorneys, examiners, and regional directors, and such other employees as it may from time to time find necessary for the proper performance of its duties. The Board may not employ any attorneys for the purpose of reviewing transcripts of hearings or preparing drafts of opinions except that any attorney employed for assignment as a legal assistant to any Board member may for such Board member review such transcripts and prepare such drafts. No administrative law judge's report shall be reviewed, either before or after its publication, by any person other than a member of the Board or his legal assistant, and no administrative law judge shall advise or consult with the Board with respect to exceptions taken to his findings, rulings, or recommendations. The Board may establish or utilize such regional, local, or other agencies, and utilize such voluntary and uncompensated services, as may from time to time be needed. Attorneys appointed under this section may, at the direction of the Board, appear for and represent the Board in any case in court. Nothing in this subchapter shall be construed to authorize the Board to appoint individuals for the purpose of conciliation or mediation, or for economic analysis.

(b) All of the expenses of the Board, including all necessary traveling and subsistence expenses outside the District of Columbia incurred by the members or employees of the Board under its orders, shall be allowed and paid on the presentation of itemized vouchers therefore approved by the Board or by any individual it designates for that purpose.

Sec. 155. National Labor Relations Board; principal office, conducting inquiries throughout country; participation in decisions or inquiries conducted by member [Sec. 5]

The principal office of the Board shall be in the District of Columbia, but it may meet and exercise any or all of its powers at any other place. The Board may, by one or more of its members or by such agents or agencies as it may designate, prosecute any inquiry necessary to its functions in any part of the United States. A member who participates in such an inquiry shall not be disqualified from subsequently participating in a decision of the Board in the same case.

Sec. 156. Rules and regulations [Sec. 6]

The Board shall have authority from time to time to make, amend, and rescind, in the manner prescribed by subchapter II of chapter 5 of Title 5, such rules and regulations as may be necessary to carry out the provisions of this subchapter.

Sec. 157. Right of employees as to organization, collective bargaining, etc. [Sec. 7]

Employees shall have the right to self-organization, to form, join, or assist labor organizations, to bargain collectively through representatives of their own choosing, and to engage in other concerted activities for the purpose of collective bargaining or other mutual aid or protection, and shall also have the right to refrain from any or all of such activities except to the extent that such right may be affected by an agreement requiring membership in a labor organization as a condition of employment as authorized in section 158(a)(3) of this title.

Sec. 158. Unfair labor practices [Sec. 8]

(a) Unfair labor practices by employer

It shall be an unfair labor practice for an employer —

(1) to interfere with, restrain, or coerce employees in the exercise of the rights guaranteed in section 157 of this title;

(2) to dominate or interfere with the formation or administration of any labor organization or contribute financial or other support to it: *Provided*, That subject to rules and regulations made and published by the Board pursuant to section 156 of this title, an employer shall not be prohibited from permitting employees to confer with him during working hours without loss of time or pay;

(3) by discrimination in regard to hire or tenure of employment or any term or condition of employment to encourage or discourage

membership in any labor organization: *Provided*, That nothing in this subchapter, or in any other statute of the United States, shall preclude an employer from making an agreement with a labor organization (not established, maintained, or assisted by any action defined in this subsection as an unfair labor practice) to require as a condition of employment membership therein on or after the thirtieth day following the beginning of such employment or the effective date of such agreement, whichever is the later, (i) if such labor organization is the representative of the employees as provided in section 159(a) of this title, in the appropriate collective-bargaining unit covered by such agreement when made, and (ii) unless following an election held as provided in section 159(e) of this title within one year preceding the effective date of such agreement, the Board shall have certified that at least a majority of the employees eligible to vote in such election have voted to rescind the authority of such labor organization to make such an agreement: *Provided further*, That no employer shall justify any discrimination against an employee for nonmembership in a labor organization (A) if he has reasonable grounds for believing that such membership was not available to the employee on the same terms and conditions generally applicable to other members, or (B) if he has reasonable grounds for believing that membership was denied or terminated for reasons other than the failure of the employee to tender the periodic dues and the initiation fees uniformly required as a condition of acquiring or retaining membership;

(4) to discharge or otherwise discriminate against an employee because he has filed charges or given testimony under this subchapter; (5) to refuse to bargain collectively with the representatives of his employees, subject to the provisions of section 159(a) of this title.

(5) to refuse to bargain collectively with the representatives of his employees, subject to the provisions of Section 159(a) of this title.

(b) Unfair labor practices by labor organization

It shall be an unfair labor practice for a labor organization or its agents —

(1) to restrain or coerce (A) employees in the exercise of the rights guaranteed in section 157 of this title: *Provided*, That this paragraph shall not impair the right of a labor organization to prescribe its own rules with respect to the acquisition or retention of membership therein; or (B) an employer in the selection of his representatives for the purposes of collective bargaining or the adjustment of grievances;

(2) to cause or attempt to cause an employer to discriminate against an employee in violation of subsection (a)(3) of this section or to discriminate against an employee with respect to whom membership in such organization has been denied or terminated on some ground other than his failure to tender the periodic dues and the initiation fees uniformly required as a condition of acquiring or retaining membership;

(3) to refuse to bargain collectively with an employer, provided it is the representative of his employees subject to the provisions of section 159(a) of this title;

(4) (i) to engage in, or to induce or encourage any individual employed by any person engaged in commerce or in an industry affecting commerce to engage in, a strike or a refusal in the course of his employment to use, manufacture, process, transport, or otherwise handle or work on any goods, articles, materials, or commodities or to perform any services; or (ii) to threaten, coerce, or restrain any person engaged in commerce or in an industry affecting commerce, where in either case an object thereof is —

(A) forcing or requiring any employer or selfemployed person to join any labor or employer organization or to enter into any agreement which is prohibited by subsection (e) of this section;

(B) forcing or requiring any person to cease using, selling, handling, transporting, or otherwise dealing in the products of any other producer, processor, or manufacturer, or to cease doing business with any other person, or forcing or requiring any other employer to recognize or bargain with a labor organization as the representative of his employees unless such labor organization has been certified as the representative of such employees under the provisions of section 159 of this title: *Provided*, That nothing contained in this clause (B) shall be construed to make unlawful, where not otherwise unlawful, any primary strike or primary picketing;

(C) forcing or requiring any employer to recognize or bargain with a particular labor organization as the representative of his employees if another labor organization has been certified as the representative of such employees under the provisions of section 159 of this title;

(D) forcing or requiring any employer to assign particular work to employees in a particular labor organization or in a particular trade, craft, or class rather than to employees in another labor organization or in another trade, craft, or class, unless such employer is failing to conform to an order or certification of the Board determining the bargaining representative for employees performing such work:

Provided, That nothing contained in this subsection shall be construed to make unlawful a refusal by any person to enter upon the premises of any employer (other than his own employer), if the employees of such employer are engaged in a strike ratified or approved by a representative of such employees whom such employer is required to recognize under this subchapter: *Provided further*, That for the purposes of this paragraph (4) only, nothing contained in such paragraph shall be construed to prohibit publicity, other than picketing, for the purpose of truthfully advising the public, including consumers and members of a labor organization, that a product or products are produced by an employer with whom the labor organization has a primary dispute and are distributed by another employer, as long as such publicity does not have an effect of inducing any individual employed by any person other than the primary employer in the course of his employment to refuse to pick up, deliver, or transport any goods, or not to perform any services, at the establishment of the employer engaged in such distribution;

(5) to require of employees covered by an agreement authorized under subsection (a)(3) of this section the payment, as a condition precedent to becoming a member of such organization, of a fee in an amount which the Board finds excessive or discriminatory under all the circumstances. In making such a finding, the Board shall consider, among other relevant factors, the prac-

tices and customs of labor organizations in the particular industry, and the wages currently paid to the employees affected;

(6) to cause or attempt to cause an employer to pay or deliver or agree to pay or deliver any money or other thing of value, in the nature of an exaction, for services which are not performed or not to be performed; and

(7) to picket or cause to be picketed, or threaten to picket or cause to be picketed, any employer where an object thereof is forcing or requiring an employer to recognize or bargain with a labor organization as the representative of his employees, or forcing or requiring the employees of an employer to accept or select such labor organization as their collective bargaining representative, unless such labor organization is currently certified as the representative of such employees:

(A) where the employer has lawfully recognized in accordance with this subchapter any other labor organization and a question concerning representation may not appropriately be raised under section 159(c) of this title,

(B) where within the preceding twelve months a valid election under section 159(c) of this title has been conducted, or

(C) where such picketing has been conducted without a petition under section 159(c) of this title being filed within a reasonable period of time not to exceed thirty days from the commencement of such picketing: *Provided*, That when such a petition has been filed the Board shall forthwith, without regard to the provisions of section 159(c)(1) of this title or the absence of a showing of a substantial interest on the part of the labor organization, direct an election in such unit as the Board finds to be appropriate and shall certify the results thereof: *Provided further*, That nothing in this subparagraph (C) shall be construed to prohibit any picketing or other publicity for the purpose of truthfully advising the public (including consumers) that an employer does not employ members of, or have a contract with, a labor organization, unless an effect of such picketing is to induce any individual employed by any other person in the course of his employment, not to pick up, deliver or transport any goods or not to perform any services.

Nothing in this paragraph (7) shall be construed to permit any act which would otherwise be an unfair labor practice under this subsection.

(c) Expression of views without threat of reprisal or force or promise of benefit

The expressing of any views, argument, or opinion, or the dissemination thereof, whether in written, printed, graphic, or visual form, shall not constitute or be evidence of an unfair labor practice under any of the provisions of this subchapter, if such expression contains no threat of reprisal or force or promise of benefit.

(d) Obligation to bargain collectively

For the purposes of this section, to bargain collectively is the performance of the mutual obligation of the employer and the representative of the employees to meet at reasonable times and confer in good faith with respect to wages, hours, and other terms and conditions of employment, or the negotiation of an agreement, or any question arising thereunder, and the execution of a written contract incorporating any agreement reached if requested by either party, but such obligation does not compel either party to agree to a proposal or require the making of a concession: *Provided,* That where there is in effect a collective-bargaining contract covering employees in an industry affecting commerce, the duty to bargain collectively shall also mean that no party to such contract shall terminate or modify such contract, unless the party desiring such termination or modification —

(1) serves a written notice upon the other party to the contract of the proposed termination or modification sixty days prior to the expiration date thereof, or in the event such contract contains no expiration date, sixty days prior to the time it is proposed to make such termination or modification;

(2) offers to meet and confer with the other party for the purpose of negotiating a new contract or a contract containing the proposed modifications;

(3) notifies the Federal Mediation and Conciliation Service within thirty days after such notice of the existence of a dispute, and simultaneously therewith notifies any State or Territorial agency established to mediate and conciliate disputes within the State or Territory where the dispute occurred, provided no agreement has been reached by that time; and

(4) continues in full force and effect, without resorting to strike or lock-out, all the terms and conditions of the existing contract for a period of sixty days after such notice is given or until the expiration date of such contract, whichever occurs later:

The duties imposed upon employers, employees, and labor organizations by paragraphs (2) to (4) of this subsection shall become inapplicable upon an intervening certification of the Board, under which the labor organization or individual, which is a party to the contract, has been superseded as or ceased to be the representative of the employees subject to the provisions of section 159(a) of this title, and the duties so imposed shall not be construed as requiring either party to discuss or agree to any modification of the terms and conditions contained in a contract for a fixed period, if such modification is to become effective before such terms and conditions can be reopened under the provisions of the contract. Any employee who engages in a strike within any notice period specified in this subsection, or who engages in any strike within the appropriate period specified in subsection (g) of this section, shall lose his status as an employee of the employer engaged in the particular labor dispute, for the purposes of sections 158, 159, and 160 of this title, but such loss of status for such employee shall terminate if and when he is reemployed by such employer. Whenever the collective bargaining involves employees of a health care institution, the provisions of this subsection shall be modified as follows:

(A) The notice of paragraph (1) of this subsection shall be ninety days; the notice of paragraph (3) of this subsection shall be sixty days; and the contract period of paragraph (4) of this subsection shall be ninety days.

(B) Where the bargaining is for an initial agreement following certification or recognition, at least thirty days' notice of the existence of a dispute shall be given by the labor organization to the agencies set forth in paragraph (3) of this subsection.

(C) After notice is given to the Federal Mediation and Conciliation Service under either clause (A) or (B) of this sentence, the Service shall promptly communicate with the parties and use its best efforts, by mediation and conciliation, to bring them to agreement. The parties shall participate fully and promptly in such meetings as may be undertaken by the Service for the purpose of aiding in a settlement of the dispute.

(e) Enforceability of contract or agreement to boycott any other employer; exception

It shall be an unfair labor practice for any labor organization and any employer to enter into any contract or agreement, express or implied, whereby such employer ceases or refrains or agrees to cease or refrain from handling, using, selling, transporting or otherwise dealing in any of the products of any other employer, or to cease doing business with any other person, and any contract or agreement entered into heretofore or hereafter containing such an agreement shall be to such extent unenforcible and void: *Provided,* That nothing in this subsection shall apply to an agreement between a labor organization and an employer in the construction industry relating to the contracting or subcontracting of work to be done at the site of the construction, alteration, painting, or repair of a building, structure, or other work: *Provided further,* That for the purposes of this subsection and subsection (b)(4)(B) of this section the terms "any employer", "any person engaged in commerce or an industry affecting commerce", and "any person" when used in relation to the terms "any other producer, processor, or manufacturer", "any other employer", or "any other person" shall not include persons in the relation of a jobber, manufacturer, contractor, or subcontractor working on the goods or premises of the jobber or manufacturer or performing parts of an integrated process of production in the apparel and clothing industry: *Provided further,* That nothing in this subchapter shall prohibit the enforcement of any agreement which is within the foregoing exception.

(f) Agreement covering employees in the building and construction industry

It shall not be an unfair labor practice under subsections (a) and (b) of this section for an employer engaged primarily in the building and construction industry to make an agreement covering employees engaged (or who, upon their employment, will be engaged) in the building and construction industry with a labor organization of which building and construction employees are members (not established, maintained, or assisted by any action defined in subsection (a) of this section as an unfair labor practice) because (1) the majority status of such labor organization has not been established under the provisions of section 159 of this title prior to the making of such agreement, or (2) such agreement requires as a condition of employment, membership in such labor organization after the seventh day following the beginning of such employment or the effective date of the agreement, whichever is later, or (3) such agreement requires the employer to notify such labor organization of opportunities for employment with such employer, or gives such labor organization an opportunity to refer qualified applicants for such employment, or (4) such agreement specifies minimum training or experience qualifications for employment or provides for priority in opportunities for employment based upon length of service with such employer, in the industry or in the particular geographical area: *Provided,* That nothing in this subsection shall set aside the final proviso to subsection (a)(3) of this section: *Provided further,* That any agreement which would be invalid, but for clause (1) of this subsection, shall not be a bar to a petition filed pursuant to section 159(c) or 159(e) of this title.

(g) Notification of intention to strike or picket at any health care institution

A labor organization before engaging in any strike, picketing, or other concerted refusal to work at any health care institution shall, not less than ten days prior to such action, notify the institution in writing and the Federal Mediation and Conciliation Service of that intention, except that in the case of bargaining for an initial agreement following certification or recognition the notice required by this subsection shall not be given until the expiration of the period specified in clause (B) of the last sentence of subsection (d) of this section. The notice shall state the date and time that such action will commence. The notice, once given, may be extended by the written agreement of both parties.

Sec. 158a. Providing facilities for operations of Federal Credit Unions

Provision by an employer of facilities for the operations of a Federal Credit Union on the premises of such employer shall not be deemed to be intimidation, coercion, interference, restraint or discrimination within the provisions of sections 157 and 158 of this title, or acts amendatory thereof.

Sec. 159. Representatives and elections [Sec. 9]

(a) Exclusive representatives; employees' adjustment of grievances directly with employer

Representatives designated or selected for the purposes of collective bargaining by the majority of the employees in a unit appropriate for such purposes, shall be the exclusive representatives of all the employees in such unit for the purposes of collective bargaining in respect to rates of pay, wages, hours of employment, or other conditions of employment: *Provided,* That any individual employee or a group of employees shall have the right at any time to present grievances to their employer and to have such grievances adjusted, without the intervention of the bargaining representative, as long as the adjustment is not inconsistent with the terms of a collective-bargaining contract or agreement then in effect: *Provided further,* That the bargaining representative has been given opportunity to be present at such adjustment.

(b) Determination of bargaining unit by Board

The Board shall decide in each case whether, in order to assure to employees the fullest freedom in exercising the rights guaranteed by this subchapter, the unit appropriate for the purposes of collective bargaining shall be the employer unit, craft unit, plant unit, or subdivision thereof: *Provided,* That the Board shall not (1) decide that any unit is appropriate for such purposes if such unit includes both professional employees and employees who are not professional employees unless a majority of such professional employees vote for inclusion in such unit; or (2) decide that any craft unit is inappropriate for such purposes on the ground that a different unit has been established by a prior Board determination, unless a majority of the employees in the proposed craft unit vote against separate representation or (3) decide that any unit is appropriate for such purposes if it includes, together with other employees, any individual employed as a guard to enforce against employees and other persons rules to protect property of the employer or to protect the safety of persons on the employer's premises; but no labor organization shall be certified as the representative of employees in a bargaining unit of guards if such organization admits to membership, or is affiliated directly or indirectly with an organization which admits to membership, employees other than guards.

(c) Hearings on questions affecting commerce; rules and regulations

(1) Whenever a petition shall have been filed, in accordance with such regulations as may be prescribed by the Board —

(A) by an employee or group of employees or any individual or labor organization acting in their behalf alleging that a substantial number of employees (i) wish to be represented for collective bargaining and that their employer declines to recognize their representative as the representative defined in subsection (a) of this section, or (ii) assert that the individual or labor organization, which has been certified or is being currently recognized by their employer as the bargaining representative, is no longer a representative as defined in subsection (a) of this section; or

(B) by an employer, alleging that one or more individuals or labor organizations have presented to him a claim to be recognized as the representative defined in subsection (a) of this section;

the Board shall investigate such petition and if it has reasonable cause to believe that a question of representation affecting commerce exists shall provide for an appropriate hearing upon due notice. Such hearing may be conducted by an officer or employee of the regional office, who shall not make any recommendations with respect thereto. If the Board finds upon the record of such hearing that such a question of representation exists, it shall direct an election by secret ballot and shall certify the results thereof.

(2) In determining whether or not a question of representation affecting commerce exists, the same regulations and rules of decision shall apply irrespective of the identity of the persons filing the petition or the kind of relief sought and in no case shall the Board deny a labor organization a place on the ballot by reason of an order with respect to such labor organization or its predecessor not issued in conformity with section 160(c) of this title.

(3) No election shall be directed in any bargaining unit or any subdivision within which in the preceding twelve-month period, a valid election shall have been held. Employees engaged in an economic strike who are not entitled to reinstatement shall be eligible to vote under such regulations as the Board shall find are consistent with the purposes and provisions of this subchapter in any election conducted within twelve months after the commencement of the strike. In any election where none of the choices on the ballot receives a majority, a run-off shall be conducted, the ballot providing for a selection between the two choices receiving the largest and second largest number of valid votes cast in the election.

(4) Nothing in this section shall be construed to prohibit the waiving of hearings by stipulation for the purpose of a consent election in conformity with regulations and rules of decision of the Board.

(5) In determining whether a unit is appropriate for the purposes specified in subsection (b) of this section the extent to which the employees have organized shall not be controlling.

(d) Petition for enforcement or review; transcript

Whenever an order of the Board made pursuant to section 160(c) of this title is based in whole or in part upon facts certified following an investigation pursuant to subsection (c) of this section and there is a petition for the enforcement or review of such order, such certification and the record of such investigation shall be included in the transcript of the entire record required to be filed under subsection (e) or (f) of section 160 of this title, and thereupon the decree of the court enforcing, modifying, or setting aside in whole or in part the order of the Board shall be made and entered upon the pleadings, testimony, and proceedings set forth in such transcript.

(e) Secret ballot; limitation of elections

(1) Upon the filing with the Board, by 30 per centum or more of the employees in a bargaining unit covered by an agreement between their employer and a labor organization made pursuant to section 158(a)(3) of this title, of a petition alleging they desire that such authority be rescinded, the Board shall take a secret ballot of the employees in such unit and certify the results thereof to such labor organization and to the employer.

(2) No election shall be conducted pursuant to this subsection in any bargaining unit or any subdivision within which, in the preceding twelve-month period, a valid election shall have been held.

Sec. 160. Prevention of unfair labor practices
[Sec. 10]

(a) Powers of Board generally

The Board is empowered, as hereinafter provided, to prevent any person from engaging in any unfair labor practice (listed in section 158 of this title) affecting commerce. This power shall not be affected by any other means of adjustment or prevention that has been or may be established by agreement, law, or otherwise: *Provided,* That the Board is empowered by agreement with any agency of any State or Territory to cede to such agency jurisdiction over any cases in any industry (other than mining, manufacturing, communications, and transportation except where predominantly local in character) even though such cases may involve labor disputes affecting commerce, unless the provision of the State or Territorial statute applicable to the determination of such cases by such agency is inconsistent with the corresponding provision of this subchapter or has received a construction inconsistent therewith.

(b) Complaint and notice of hearing; answer; court rules of evidence inapplicable

Whenever it is charged that any person has engaged in or is engaging in any such unfair labor practice, the Board, or any agent or agency designated by the Board for such purposes, shall have power to issue and cause to be served upon such person a complaint stating the charges in that respect, and containing a notice of hearing before the Board or a member thereof, or before a designated agent or agency, at a place therein fixed, not less than five days after the serving of said complaint: *Provided,* That no complaint shall issue based upon any unfair labor practice occurring more than six months prior to the filing of the charge with the Board and the service of a copy thereof upon the person against whom such charge is made, unless the person aggrieved thereby was prevented from filing such charge by reason of service in the armed forces, in which event the six-month period shall be computed from the day of his discharge. Any such complaint may be amended by the member, agent, or agency conducting the hearing or the Board in its discretion at any time prior to the issuance of an order based thereon. The person so complained of shall have the right to file an answer to the original or amended complaint and to appear in person or otherwise and give testimony at the place and time fixed in the complaint. In the discretion of the member, agent, or agency conducting the hearing or the Board, any other person may be allowed to intervene in the said proceeding and to present testimony. Any such proceeding shall, so far as practicable, be conducted in accordance with the rules of evidence applicable in the district courts of the United States under the rules of civil procedure for the district courts of the United States, adopted by the Supreme Court of the United States pursuant to section 2072 of Title 28.

(c) Reduction of testimony to writing; findings and orders of Board

The testimony taken by such member, agent, or agency or the Board shall be reduced to writing and filed with the Board. Thereafter, in its discretion, the Board upon notice may take further testimony or hear argument. If upon the preponderance of the testimony taken the Board shall be of the opinion that any person named in the complaint has engaged in or is engaging in any such unfair labor practice, then the Board shall state its findings of fact and shall issue and cause to be served on such person an order requiring such person to cease and desist from such unfair labor practice, and to take such affirmative action including reinstatement of employees with or without back pay, as will effectuate the policies of this subchapter: *Provided*, That where an order directs reinstatement of an employee, back pay may be required of the employer or labor organization, as the case may be, responsible for the discrimination suffered by him: *And provided further*, That in determining whether a complaint shall issue alleging a violation of subsection (a)(1) or (a)(2) of section 158 of this title, and in deciding such cases, the same regulations and rules of decision shall apply irrespective of whether or not the labor organization affected is affiliated with a labor organization national or international in scope. Such order may further require such person to

make reports from time to time showing the extent to which it has complied with the order. If upon the preponderance of the testimony taken the Board shall not be of the opinion that the person named in the complaint has engaged in or is engaging in any such unfair labor practice, then the Board shall state its findings of fact and shall issue an order dismissing the said complaint. No order of the Board shall require the reinstatement of any individual as an employee who has been suspended or discharged, or the payment to him of any back pay, if such individual was suspended or discharged for cause. In case the evidence is presented before a member of the Board, or before an administrative law judge or judges thereof, such member, or such judge or judges as the case may be, shall issue and cause to be served on the parties to the proceeding a proposed report, together with a recommended order, which shall be filed with the Board, and if no exceptions are filed within twenty days after service thereof upon such parties, or within such further period as the Board may authorize, such recommended order shall become the order of the Board and become effective as therein prescribed.

(d) Modification of findings or orders prior to filing record in court

Until the record in a case shall have been filed in a court, as hereinafter provided, the Board may at any time upon reasonable notice and in such manner as it shall deem proper, modify or set aside, in whole or in part, any finding or order made or issued by it.

(e) Petition to court for enforcement of order; proceedings; review of judgment

The Board shall have power to petition any court of appeals of the United States, or if all the courts of appeals to which application may be made are in vacation, any district court of the United States, within any circuit or district, respectively, wherein the unfair labor practice in question occurred or wherein such person resides or transacts business, for the enforcement of such order and for appropriate temporary relief or restraining order, and shall file in the court the record in the proceedings, as provided in section 2112 of Title 28. Upon the filing of such petition, the court shall cause notice thereof to be served upon such person, and thereupon shall have jurisdiction of the proceeding and of the question determined therein, and shall have power to grant such temporary relief or restraining order as it deems just and proper, and to make and enter a decree enforcing, modifying and enforcing as so modified, or setting aside in whole or in part the order of the Board. No objection that has not been urged before the Board, its member, agent, or agency, shall be considered by the court, unless the failure or neglect to urge such objection shall be excused because of extraordinary circumstances. The findings of the Board with respect to questions of fact if supported by substantial evidence on the record considered as a whole shall be conclusive. If either party shall apply to the court for leave to adduce additional evidence and shall show to the satisfaction of the court that such additional evidence is material and that there were reasonable grounds for the failure to adduce such evidence in the hearing before the Board, its member, agent, or agency, the court may order such additional evidence to be taken before the Board, its member, agent, or agency, and to be made a part of the record. The Board may modify its findings as to the facts, or make new findings by reason of additional evidence so taken and filed, and it shall file such modified or new findings, which findings with respect to questions of fact if supported by substantial evidence on the record considered as a whole shall be conclusive, and shall file its recommendations, if any, for the modification or setting aside of its original order. Upon the filing of the record with it the jurisdiction of the court shall be exclusive and its judgment and decree shall be final, except that the same shall be subject to review by the appropriate United States court of appeals if application was made to the district court as hereinabove provided, and by the Supreme Court of the United States upon writ of certiorari or certification as provided in section 1254 of Title 28.

(f) Review of final order of Board on petition to court

Any person aggrieved by a final order of the Board granting or denying in whole or in part the relief sought may obtain a review of such order in any United States court of appeals in the circuit wherein the unfair labor practice in question was alleged to have been engaged in or wherein such person resides or transacts business, or in the United States Court of Appeals for the District of Columbia, by filing in such a court a written peti-

tion praying that the order of the Board be modified or set aside. A copy of such petition shall be forthwith transmitted by the clerk of the court to the Board, and thereupon the aggrieved party shall file in the court the record in the proceeding, certified by the Board, as provided in section 2112 of Title 28. Upon the filing of such petition, the court shall proceed in the same manner as in the case of an application by the Board under subsection (e) of this section, and shall have the same jurisdiction to grant to the Board such temporary relief or restraining order as it deems just and proper, and in like manner to make and enter a decree enforcing, modifying, and enforcing as so modified, or setting aside in whole or in part the order of the Board; the findings of the Board with respect to questions of fact if supported by substantial evidence on the record considered as a whole shall in like manner be conclusive.

(g) Institution of court proceedings as stay of Board's order

The commencement of proceedings under subsection (e) or (f) of this section shall not, unless specifically ordered by the court, operate as a stay of the Board's order.

(h) Jurisdiction of courts unaffected by limitations prescribed in chapter 6 of this title

When granting appropriate temporary relief or a restraining order, or making and entering a decree enforcing, modifying, and enforcing as so modified or setting aside in whole or in part an order of the Board, as provided in this section, the jurisdiction of courts sitting in equity shall not be limited by chapter 6 of this title.

(i) Repealed

(j) Injunctions

The Board shall have power, upon issuance of a complaint as provided in subsection (b) of this section charging that any person has engaged in or is engaging in an unfair labor practice, to petition any United States district court, within any district wherein the unfair labor practice in question is alleged to have occurred or wherein such person resides or transacts business, for appropriate temporary relief or restraining order. Upon the filing of any such petition the court shall cause notice thereof to be served upon such person, and thereupon shall have jurisdiction to grant to the Board such temporary relief or restraining order as it deems just and proper.

(k) Hearings on jurisdictional strikes

Whenever it is charged that any person has engaged in an unfair labor practice within the meaning of paragraph (4)(D) of section 158(b) of this title, the Board is empowered and directed to hear and determine the dispute out of which such unfair labor practice shall have arisen, unless, within ten days after notice that such charge has been filed, the parties to such dispute submit to the Board satisfactory evidence that they have adjusted, or agreed upon methods for the voluntary adjustment of, the dispute. Upon compliance by the parties to the dispute with the decision of the Board or upon such voluntary adjustment of the dispute, such charge shall be dismissed.

(*l*) Boycotts and strikes to force recognition of uncertified labor organizations; injunctions; notice; service of process

Whenever it is charged that any person has engaged in an unfair labor practice within the meaning of paragraph (4)(A), (B), or (C) of section 158(b) of this title, or section 158(e) of this title or section 158(b)(7) of this title, the preliminary investigation of such charge shall be made forthwith and given priority over all other cases except cases of like character in the office where it is filed or to which it is referred. If, after such investigation, the officer or regional attorney to whom the matter may be referred has reasonable cause to believe such charge is true and that a complaint should issue, he shall, on behalf of the Board, petition any United States district court within any district where the unfair labor practice in question has occurred, is alleged to have occurred, or wherein such person resides or transacts business, for appropriate injunctive relief pending the final adjudication of the Board with respect to such matter. Upon the filing of any such petition the district court shall have jurisdiction to grant such injunctive relief or temporary restraining order as it deems just and proper, notwithstanding any other provision of law: *Provided further*, That no temporary restraining order shall be issued without notice unless a petition alleges that substantial and irreparable injury to the charging party will be unavoidable and such temporary restraining order shall be effective for no longer

than five days and will become void at the expiration of such period: *Provided further*, That such officer or regional attorney shall not apply for any restraining order under section 158(b)(7) of this title if a charge against the employer under section 158(a)(2) of this title has been filed and after the preliminary investigation, he has reasonable cause to believe that such charge is true and that a complaint should issue. Upon filing of any such petition the courts shall cause notice thereof to be served upon any person involved in the charge and such person, including the charging party, shall be given an opportunity to appear by counsel and present any relevant testimony: *Provided further*, That for the purposes of this subsection district courts shall be deemed to have jurisdiction of a labor organization (1) in the district in which such organization maintains its principal office, or (2) in any district in which its duly authorized officers or agents are engaged in promoting or protecting the interests of employee members. The service of legal process upon such officer or agent shall constitute service upon the labor organization and make such organization a party to the suit. In situations where such relief is appropriate the procedure specified herein shall apply to charges with respect to section 158(b)(4)(D) of this title.

(m) Priority of cases

Whenever it is charged that any person has engaged in an unfair labor practice within the meaning of subsection (a)(3) or (b)(2) of section 158 of this title, such charge shall be given priority over all other cases except cases of like character in the office where it is filed or to which it is referred and cases given priority under subsection (*l*) of this section.

Sec. 161. Investigatory powers of Board *[Sec. 11]*

For the purpose of all hearings and investigations, which, in the opinion of the Board, are necessary and proper for the exercise of the powers vested in it by sections 159 and 160 of this title —

(1) Documentary evidence; summoning witnesses and taking testimony

The Board, or its duly authorized agents or agencies, shall at all reasonable times have access to, for the purpose of examination, and the right to copy any evidence of any person being investigated or proceeded against that relates to any matter under investigation or in question. The Board, or any member thereof, shall upon application of any party to such proceedings, forthwith issue to such party subpenas requiring the attendance and testimony of witnesses or the production of any evidence in such proceedings or investigation requested in such application. Within five days after the service of a subpena on any person requiring the production of any evidence in his possession or under his control, such person may petition the Board to revoke, and the Board shall revoke, such subpena if in its opinion the evidence whose production is required does not relate to any matter under investigation, or any matter in question in such proceedings, or if in its opinion such subpena does not describe with sufficient particularity the evidence whose production is required. Any member of the Board, or any agent or agency designated by the Board for such purposes, may administer oaths and affirmations, examine witnesses, and receive evidence. Such attendance of witnesses and the production of such evidence may be required from any place in the United States or any Territory or possession thereof, at any designated place of hearing.

(2) Court aid in compelling production of evidence and attendance of witnesses

In case of contumacy or refusal to obey a subpena issued to any person, any district court of the United States or the United States courts of any Territory or possession, within the jurisdiction of which the inquiry is carried on or within the jurisdiction of which said person guilty of contumacy or refusal to obey is found or resides or transacts business, upon application by the Board shall have jurisdiction to issue to such person an order requiring such person to appear before the Board, its member, agent, or agency, there to produce evidence if so ordered, or there to give testimony touching the matter under investigation or in question; and any failure to obey such order of the court may be punished by said court as a contempt thereof.

(3) Repealed

(4) Process, service and return; fees of witnesses

Complaints, orders, and other process and papers of the Board, its member, agent, or agency, may be served either personally or by registered or certified mail or by telegraph or by leaving a copy thereof at the principal office or place of business of the person required to be served. The verified return by the individual so serving the same setting forth the manner of such service shall be proof of the same, and the return post office receipt or telegraph receipt therefore when registered or certified and mailed or when telegraphed as aforesaid shall be proof of service of the same. Witnesses summoned before the Board, its member, agent, or agency, shall be paid the same fees and mileage that are paid witnesses in the courts of the United States, and witnesses whose depositions are taken and the persons taking the same shall severally be entitled to the same fees as are paid for like services in the courts of the United States.

(5) Process, where served

All process of any court to which application may be made under this subchapter may be served in the judicial district wherein the defendant or other person required to be served resides or may be found.

(6) Information and assistance from departments

The several departments and agencies of the Government, when directed by the President, shall furnish the Board, upon its request, all records, papers, and information in their possession relating to any matter before the Board.

Sec. 162. Offenses and penalties *[Sec. 12]*

Any person who shall willfully resist, prevent, impede, or interfere with any member of the Board or any of its agents or agencies in the performance of duties pursuant to this subchapter shall be punished by a fine of not more than $5,000 or by imprisonment for not more than one year, or both.

Sec. 163. Right to strike preserved *[Sec. 13]*

Nothing in this subchapter, except as specifically provided for herein, shall be construed so as either to interfere with or impede or diminish in any way the right to strike, or to affect the limitations or qualifications on that right.

Sec. 164. Construction of provisions *[Sec. 14]*

(a) Supervisors as union members

Nothing herein shall prohibit any individual employed as a supervisor from becoming or remaining a member of a labor organization, but no employer subject to this subchapter shall be compelled to deem individuals defined herein as supervisors as employees for the purpose of any law, either national or local, relating to collective bargaining.

(b) Agreements requiring union membership in violation of State law

Nothing in this subchapter shall be construed as authorizing the execution or application of agreements requiring membership in a labor organization as a condition of employment in any State or Territory in which such execution or application is prohibited by State or Territorial law.

(c) Power of Board to decline jurisdiction of labor disputes; assertion of jurisdiction by State and Territorial courts

(1) The Board, in its discretion, may, by rule of decision or by published rules adopted pursuant to subchapter II of chapter 5 of Title 5, decline to assert jurisdiction over any labor dispute involving any class or category of employers, where, in the opinion of the Board, the effect of such labor dispute on commerce is not sufficiently substantial to warrant the exercise of its jurisdiction: *Provided,* That the Board shall not decline to assert jurisdiction over any labor dispute over which it would assert jurisdiction under the standards prevailing upon August 1, 1959.

(2) Nothing in this subchapter shall be deemed to prevent or bar any agency or the courts of any State or Territory (including the Commonwealth of Puerto Rico, Guam, and the Virgin Islands), from assuming and asserting jurisdiction over labor disputes over which the Board declines, pursuant to paragraph (1) of this subsection, to assert jurisdiction.

Sec. 165. Conflict of laws *[Sec. 15]*

Wherever the application of the provisions of section 272 of chapter 10 of the Act entitled "An Act to establish a uniform system of bankruptcy throughout the United States", approved July 1, 1898, and Acts amendatory thereof and supplementary thereto

(U.S.C., Title 11, sec. 672), conflicts with the application of the provisions of this subchapter, this subchapter shall prevail: *Provided,* That in any situation where the provisions of this subchapter cannot be validly enforced, the provisions of such other Acts shall remain in full force and effect.

Sec. 166. Separability *[Sec. 16]*

If any provision of this subchapter, or the application of such provision to any person or circumstances, shall be held invalid, the remainder of this subchapter, or the application of such provision to persons or circumstances other than those as to which it is held invalid, shall not be affected thereby.

Sec. 167. Short title of subchapter *[Sec. 17]*

This subchapter may be cited as the "National Labor Relations Act".

Sec. 168. Validation of certificates and other Board actions *[Sec. 18]*

No petition entertained, no investigation made, no election held, and no certification issued by the National Labor Relations Board, under any of the provisions of section 159 of this title, shall be invalid by reason of the failure of the Congress of Industrial Organizations to have complied with the requirements of section 159(f), (g), or (h) of this title prior to December 22, 1949, or by reason of the failure of the American Federation of Labor to have complied with the provisions of section 159(f), (g), or (h) of this title prior to November 7, 1947: *Provided,* That no liability shall be imposed under any provision of this chapter upon any person for failure to honor any election or certificate referred to above, prior to October 22, 1951: *Provided, however,* That this proviso shall not have the effect of setting aside or in any way affecting judgments or decrees heretofore entered under section 160(e) or (f) of this title and which have become final.

Sec. 169. Employees with religious convictions; payment of dues and fees *[Sec. 19]*

Any employee who is a member of and adheres to established and traditional tenets or teachings of a bona fide religion, body, or sect which has historically held conscientious objections to joining or financially supporting labor organizations shall not be required to join or financially support any labor organization as a condition of employment; except that such employee may be required in a contract between such employees' employer and a labor organization in lieu of periodic dues and initiation fees, to pay sums equal to such dues and initiation fees to a nonreligious, nonlabor organization charitable fund exempt from taxation under section 501(c)(3) of Title 26, chosen by such employee from a list of at least three such funds, designated in such contract or if the contract fails to designate such funds, then to any such fund chosen by the employee. If such employee who holds conscientious objections pursuant to this section requests the labor organization to use the grievance-arbitration procedure on the employee's behalf, the labor organization is authorized to charge the employee for the reasonable cost of using such procedure.

Sec. 171. Declaration of purpose and policy *[Sec. 201]*

It is the policy of the United States that —

(a) sound and stable industrial peace and the advancement of the general welfare, health, and safety of the Nation and of the best interests of employers and employees can most satisfactorily be secured by the settlement of issues between employers and employees through the processes of conference and collective bargaining between employers and the representatives of their employees;

(b) the settlement of issues between employers and employees through collective bargaining may be advanced by making available full and adequate governmental facilities for conciliation, mediation, and voluntary arbitration to aid and encourage employers and the representatives of their employees to reach and maintain agreements concerning rates of pay, hours, and working conditions, and to make all reasonable efforts to settle their differences by mutual agreement reached through conferences and collective bargaining or by such methods as may be provided for in any applicable agreement for the settlement of disputes; and

(c) certain controversies which arise between parties to collective-bargaining agreements may be avoided or minimized by making available full and adequate governmental facilities for furnishing assistance to employers and the representatives of their employees in formulating for inclusion within such agreements provision for adequate notice of any proposed changes in the terms of such agreements, for the final adjustment of grievances or questions regarding the application or interpretation of such agreements, and other provisions designed to prevent the subsequent arising of such controversies.

Sec. 172. Federal Mediation and Conciliation Service *[Sec. 202]*

(a) Creation; appointment of Director

There is created an independent agency to be known as the Federal Mediation and Conciliation Service (herein referred to as the "Service", except that for sixty days after June 23, 1947, such term shall refer to the Conciliation Service of the Department of Labor). The Service shall be under the direction of a Federal Mediation and Conciliation Director (hereinafter referred to as the "Director"), who shall be appointed by the President by and with the advice and consent of the Senate. The Director shall not engage in any other business, vocation, or employment.

(b) Appointment of officers and employees; expenditures for supplies, facilities, and services

The Director is authorized, subject to the civil service laws, to appoint such clerical and other personnel as may be necessary for the execution of the functions of the Service, and shall fix their compensation in accordance with chapter 51 and subchapter III of chapter 53 of Title 5, and may, without regard to the provisions of the civil service laws, appoint such conciliators and mediators as may be necessary to carry out the functions of the Service. The Director is authorized to make such expenditures for supplies, facilities, and services as he deems necessary. Such expenditures shall be allowed and paid upon presentation of itemized vouchers therefor approved by the Director or by any employee designated by him for that purpose.

(c) Principal and regional offices; delegation of authority by Director; annual report to Congress

The principal office of the Service shall be in the District of Columbia, but the Director may establish regional offices convenient to localities in which labor controversies are likely to arise. The Director may by order, subject to revocation at any time, delegate any authority and discretion conferred upon him by this chapter to any regional director, or other officer or employee of the Service. The Director may establish suitable procedures for cooperation with State and local mediation agencies. The Director shall make an annual report in writing to Congress at the end of the fiscal year.

(d) Transfer of all mediation and conciliation services to Service; effective date; pending proceedings unaffected

All mediation and conciliation functions of the Secretary of Labor or the United States Conciliation Service under section 51 of this title, and all functions of the United States Conciliation Service under any other law are transferred to the Federal Mediation and Conciliation Service, together with the personnel and records of the United States Conciliation Service. Such transfer shall take effect upon the sixtieth day after June 23, 1947. Such transfer shall not affect any proceedings pending before the United States Conciliation Service or any certification, order, rule, or regulation theretofore made by it or by the Secretary of Labor. The Director and the Service shall not be subject in any way to the jurisdiction or authority of the Secretary of Labor or any official or division of the Department of Labor.

Sec. 173. Functions of Service *[Sec. 203]*

(a) Settlement of disputes through conciliation and mediation

It shall be the duty of the Service, in order to prevent or minimize interruptions of the free flow of commerce growing out of labor disputes, to assist parties to labor disputes in industries affecting commerce to settle such disputes through conciliation and mediation.

(b) Intervention on motion of Service or request of parties; avoidance of mediation of minor disputes

The Service may proffer its services in any labor dispute in any industry affecting commerce, either upon its own motion or upon the request of one or more of the parties to the dispute, whenever in its judgment such dispute threatens to cause a substantial interruption of commerce. The Director and the Service are directed to avoid attempting to mediate disputes which would have only a minor

effect on interstate commerce if State or other conciliation services are available to the parties. Whenever the Service does proffer its services in any dispute, it shall be the duty of the Service promptly to put itself in communication with the parties and to use its best efforts, by mediation and conciliation, to bring them to agreement.

(c) Settlement of disputes by other means upon failure of conciliation

If the Director is not able to bring the parties to agreement by conciliation within a reasonable time, he shall seek to induce the parties voluntarily to seek other means of settling the dispute without resort to strike, lock-out, or other coercion, including submission to the employees in the bargaining unit of the employer's last offer of settlement for approval or rejection in a secret ballot. The failure or refusal of either party to agree to any procedure suggested by the Director shall not be deemed a violation of any duty or obligation imposed by this chapter.

(d) Use of conciliation and mediation services as last resort

Final adjustment by a method agreed upon by the parties is declared to be the desirable method for settlement of grievance disputes arising over the application or interpretation of an existing collective-bargaining agreement. The Service is directed to make its conciliation and mediation services available in the settlement of such grievance disputes only as a last resort and in exceptional cases.

(e) Encouragement and support of establishment and operation of joint labor management activities conducted by committees

The Service is authorized and directed to encourage and support the establishment and operation of joint labor management activities conducted by plant, area, and industrywide committees designed to improve labor management relationships, job security and organizational effectiveness, in accordance with the provisions of section 175a of this title.

(f) Use of alternative means of dispute resolution procedures; assignment of neutrals and arbitrators

The Service may make its services available to Federal agencies to aid in the resolution of disputes under the provisions of subchapter IV of chapter 5 of Title 5. Functions performed by the Service may include assisting parties to disputes related to administrative programs, training persons in skills and procedures employed in alternative means of dispute resolution, and furnishing officers and employees of the Service to act as neutrals. Only officers and employees who are qualified in accordance with section 573 of Title 5 may be assigned to act as neutrals. The Service shall consult with the agency designated by, or the interagency committee designated or established by, the President under Section 573 of Title 5 in maintaining rosters of neutrals and arbitrators, and to adopt such procedures and rules as are necessary to carry out the services authorized in this subsection.

Sec. 174. Co-equal obligations of employees, their representatives, and management to minimize labor disputes *[Sec. 204]*

(a) In order to prevent or minimize interruptions of the free flow of commerce growing out of labor disputes, employers and employees and their representatives, in any industry affecting commerce, shall —

(1) exert every reasonable effort to make and maintain agreements concerning rates of pay, hours, and working conditions, including provision for adequate notice of any proposed change in the terms of such agreements;

(2) whenever a dispute arises over the terms or application of a collective-bargaining agreement and a conference is requested by a party or prospective party thereto, arrange promptly for such a conference to be held and endeavor in such conference to settle such dispute expeditiously; and

(3) in case such dispute is not settled by conference, participate fully and promptly in such meetings as may be undertaken by the Service under this chapter for the purpose of aiding in a settlement of the dispute.

Sec. 175. National Labor-Management Panel; creation and composition; appointment, tenure, and compensation; duties *[Sec. 205]*

(a) There is created a National Labor-Management Panel which shall be composed of twelve members appointed by the President, six of whom shall be selected from among persons outstanding in the field of management and six of whom shall be selected from among persons outstanding in the field of labor. Each member shall hold office for a term of three years, except that any member appointed to fill a vacancy occurring prior to the expiration of the term for which his predecessor was appointed shall be appointed for the remainder of such term, and the terms of office of the members first taking office shall expire, as designated by the President at the time of appointment, four at the end of the first year, four at the end of the second year, and four at the end of the third year after the date of appointment. Members of the panel, when serving on business of the panel, shall be paid compensation at the rate of $25 per day, and shall also be entitled to receive an allowance for actual and necessary travel and subsistence expenses while so serving away from their places of residence.

(b) It shall be the duty of the panel, at the request of the Director, to advise in the avoidance of industrial controversies and the manner in which mediation and voluntary adjustment shall be administered, particularly with reference to controversies affecting the general welfare of the country.

Sec. 175a. Assistance to plant, area, and industry-wide labor management committees *[Sec. 205A]*

(a) Establishment and operation of plant, area, and industrywide committees

(1) The Service is authorized and directed to provide assistance in the establishment and operation of plant, area and industrywide labor management committees which —

(A) have been organized jointly by employers and labor organizations representing employees in that plant, area, or industry; and

(B) are established for the purpose of improving labor management relationships, job security, organizational effectiveness, enhancing economic development or involving workers in decisions affecting their jobs including improving communication with respect to subjects of mutual interest and concern.

(2) The Service is authorized and directed to enter into contracts and to make grants, where necessary or appropriate, to fulfill its responsibilities under this section.

(b) Restrictions on grants, contracts, or other assistance

(1) No grant may be made, no contract may be entered into and no other assistance may be provided under the provisions of this section to a plant labor management committee unless the employees in that plant are represented by a labor organization and there is in effect at that plant a collective bargaining agreement.

(2) No grant may be made, no contract may be entered into and no other assistance may be provided under the provisions of this section to an area or industrywide labor management committee unless its participants include any labor organizations certified or recognized as the representative of the employees of an employer participating in such committee. Nothing in this clause shall prohibit participation in an area or industry-wide committee by an employer whose employees are not represented by a labor organization.

(3) No grant may be made under the provisions of this section to any labor management committee which the Service finds to have as one of its purposes the discouragement of the exercise of rights contained in section 157 of this title, or the interference with collective bargaining in any plant, or industry.

(c) Establishment of office

The Service shall carry out the provisions of this section through an office established for that purpose.

(d) Authorization of appropriations

There are authorized to be appropriated to carry out the provisions of this section $10,000,000 for the fiscal year 1979, and such sums as may be necessary thereafter.

Sec. 176. National emergencies; appointment of board of inquiry by President; report; contents; filing with Service *[Sec. 206]*

Whenever in the opinion of the President of the United States, a threatened or actual strike or lockout affecting an entire industry or a substantial part thereof engaged in trade, commerce, transportation, transmission, or communication among the several States or with foreign nations, or engaged in the production of goods for commerce, will, if permitted to occur or to continue, imperil the national health or safety, he may appoint a board of inquiry to inquire into the issues involved in the dispute and to make a written report to him within such time as he shall prescribe. Such report shall include a statement of the facts with respect to the dispute, including each party's statement of its position but shall not contain any recommendations. The President shall file a copy of such report with the Service and shall make its contents available to the public.

Sec. 177. Board of inquiry *[Sec. 207]*

(a) Composition

A board of inquiry shall be composed of a chairman and such other members as the President shall determine, and shall have power to sit and act in any place within the United States and to conduct such hearings either in public or in private, as it may deem necessary or proper, to ascertain the facts with respect to the causes and circumstances of the dispute.

(b) Compensation

Members of a board of inquiry shall receive compensation at the rate of $50 for each day actually spent by them in the work of the board, together with necessary travel and subsistence expenses.

(c) Powers of discovery

For the purpose of any hearing or inquiry conducted by any board appointed under this title, the provisions of sections 49 and 50 of Title 15 (relating to the attendance of witnesses and the production of books, papers, and documents) are made applicable to the powers and duties of such board.

Sec. 178. Injunctions during national emergency *[Sec. 208]*

(a) Petition to district court by Attorney General on direction of President

Upon receiving a report from a board of inquiry the President may direct the Attorney General to petition any district court of the United States having jurisdiction of the parties to enjoin such strike or lock-out or the continuing thereof, and if the court finds that such threatened or actual strike or lock-out —

(i) affects an entire industry or a substantial part thereof engaged in trade, commerce, transportation, transmission, or communication among the several States or with foreign nations, or engaged in the production of goods for commerce; and

(ii) if permitted to occur or to continue, will imperil the national health or safety, it shall have jurisdiction to enjoin any such strike or lockout, or the continuing thereof, and to make such other orders as may be appropriate.

(b) Inapplicability of chapter 6

In any case, the provisions of chapter 6 of this title shall not be applicable.

(c) Review of orders

The order or orders of the court shall be subject to review by the appropriate United States court of appeals and by the Supreme Court upon writ of certiorari or certification as provided in section 1254 of Title 28.

Sec. 179. Injunctions during national emergency; adjustment efforts by parties during injunction period *[Sec. 209]*

(a) Assistance of Service; acceptance of Service's proposed settlement

Whenever a district court has issued an order under section 178 of this title enjoining acts or practices which imperil or threaten to imperil the national health or safety, it shall be the duty of the parties to the labor dispute giving rise to such order to make every effort to adjust and settle their differences, with the assistance of the Service created by this chapter. Neither party shall be under any duty to accept, in whole or in part, any proposal of settlement made by the Service.

(b) Reconvening of board of inquiry; report by board; contents; secret ballot of employees by National Labor Relations Board; certification of results to Attorney General

Upon the issuance of such order, the President shall reconvene the board of inquiry which has previously reported with respect to the dispute. At the end of a sixty-day period (unless the dispute has been settled by that time), the board of inquiry shall report to the President the current position of the parties and the efforts which have been made for settlement, and shall include a statement by each party of its position and a statement of the employer's last offer of settlement. The President

shall make such report available to the public. The National Labor Relations Board, within the succeeding fifteen days, shall take a secret ballot of the employees of each employer involved in the dispute on the question of whether they wish to accept the final offer of settlement made by their employer as stated by him and shall certify the results thereof to the Attorney General within five days thereafter.

Sec. 180. Discharge of injunction upon certification of results of election or settlement; report to Congress *[Sec. 210]*

Upon the certification of the results of such ballot or upon a settlement being reached, whichever happens sooner, the Attorney General shall move the court to discharge the injunction, which motion shall then be granted and the injunction discharged. When such motion is granted, the President shall submit to the Congress a full and comprehensive report of the proceedings, including the findings of the board of inquiry and the ballot taken by the National Labor Relations Board, together with such recommendations as he may see fit to make for consideration and appropriate action.

Sec. 181. Compilation of collective bargaining agreements, etc.; use of data *[Sec. 211]*

(a) For the guidance and information of interested representatives of employers, employees, and the general public, the Bureau of Labor Statistics of the Department of Labor shall maintain a file of copies of all available collective bargaining agreements and other available agreements and actions thereunder settling or adjusting labor disputes. Such file shall be open to inspection under appropriate conditions prescribed by the Secretary of Labor, except that no specific information submitted in confidence shall be disclosed.

(b) The Bureau of Labor Statistics in the Department of labor is authorized to furnish upon request of the Service, or employers, employees, or their representatives, all available data and factual information which may aid in the settlement of any labor dispute, except that no specific information submitted in confidence shall be disclosed.

Sec. 182. Exemption of Railway Labor Act from subchapter *[Sec. 212]*

The provisions of this subchapter shall not be applicable with respect to any matter which is subject to the provisions of the Railway Labor Act (45 U.S.C. 151 et seq.), as amended from time to time.

Sec. 183. Conciliation of labor disputes in the health care industry *[Sec. 213]*

(a) Establishment of Boards of Inquiry; membership

If, in the opinion of the Director of the Federal Mediation and Conciliation Service, a threatened or actual strike or lockout affecting a health care institution will, if permitted to occur or to continue, substantially interrupt the delivery of health care in the locality concerned, the Director may further assist in the resolution of the impasse by establishing within 30 days after the notice to the Federal Mediation and Conciliation Service under clause (A) of the last sentence of section 158(d) of this title (which is required by clause (3) of such section 158(d) of this title), or within 10 days after the notice under clause (B), an impartial Board of Inquiry to investigate the issues involved in the dispute and to make a written report thereon to the parties within fifteen (15) days after the establishment of such a Board. The written report shall contain the findings of fact together with the Board's recommendations for settling the dispute, with the objective of achieving a prompt, peaceful and just settlement of the dispute. Each such Board shall be composed of such number of individuals as the Director may deem desirable. No member appointed under this section shall have any interest or involvement in the health care institutions or the employee organizations involved in the dispute.

(b) Compensation of members of Boards of Inquiry

(1) Members of any board established under this section who are otherwise employed by the Federal Government shall serve without compensation but shall be reimbursed for travel, subsistence, and other necessary expenses incurred by them in carrying out its duties under this section.

(2) Members of any board established under this section who are not subject to paragraph (1) shall receive compensation at a rate prescribed by the Director but not to exceed the daily rate prescribed for GS-18 of the General Schedule under section 5332 of Title 5, including travel for each day they are engaged in the performance of their duties under this section and shall be entitled to reimbursement for travel, subsistence, and other

necessary expenses incurred by them in carrying out their duties under this section.

(c) Maintenance of status quo

After the establishment of a board under subsection (a) of this section and for 15 days after any such board has issued its report, no change in the status quo in effect prior to the expiration of the contract in the case of negotiations for a contract renewal, or in effect prior to the time of the impasse in the case of an initial beginning negotiation, except by agreement, shall be made by the parties to the controversy.

(d) Authorization of appropriations

There are authorized to be appropriated such sums as may be necessary to carry out the provisions of this section.

Sec. 185. Suits by and against labor organizations *[Sec. 301]*

(a) Venue, amount, and citizenship

Suits for violation of contracts between an employer and a labor organization representing employees in an industry affecting commerce as defined in this chapter, or between any such labor organizations, may be brought in any district court of the United States having jurisdiction of the parties, without respect to the amount in controversy or without regard to the citizenship of the parties.

(b) Responsibility for acts of agent; entity for purposes of suit; enforcement of money judgments

Any labor organization which represents employees in an industry affecting commerce as defined in this chapter and any employer whose activities affect commerce as defined in this chapter shall be bound by the acts of its agents. Any such labor organization may sue or be sued as an entity and in behalf of the employees whom it represents in the courts of the United States. Any money judgment against a labor organization in a district court of the United States shall be enforceable only against the organization as an entity and against its assets, and shall not be enforceable against any individual member or his assets.

(c) Jurisdiction

For the purposes of actions and proceedings by or against labor organizations in the district courts of the United States, district courts shall be deemed to have jurisdiction of a labor organization (1) in the district in which such organization maintains its principal office, or (2) in any district in which its duly authorized officers or agents are engaged in representing or acting for employee members.

(d) Service of process

The service of summons, subpena, or other legal process of any court of the United States upon an officer or agent of a labor organization, in his capacity as such, shall constitute service upon the labor organization.

(e) Determination of question of agency

For the purposes of this section, in determining whether any person is acting as an "agent" of another person so as to make such other person responsible for his acts, the question of whether the specific acts performed were actually authorized or subsequently ratified shall not be controlling.

Sec. 186. Restrictions on financial transactions
[Sec. 302]

(a) Payment or lending, etc., of money by employer or agent to employees, representatives, or labor organizations

It shall be unlawful for any employer or association of employers or any person who acts as a labor relations expert, adviser, or consultant to an employer or who acts in the interest of an employer to pay, lend, or deliver, or agree to pay, lend, or deliver, any money or other thing of value —

(1) to any representative of any of his employees who are employed in an industry affecting commerce; or

(2) to any labor organization, or any officer or employee thereof, which represents, seeks to represent, or would admit to membership, any of the employees of such employer who are employed in an industry affecting commerce; or

(3) to any employee or group or committee of employees of such employer employed in an industry affecting commerce in excess of their normal compensation for the purpose of causing such employee or group or committee directly or indirectly to influence any other employees in the exercise of the right to organize and bargain collectively through representatives of their own choosing; or

(4) to any officer or employee of a labor organization engaged in an industry affecting commerce with intent to influence him in respect to any of his actions, decisions, or duties as a representative of employees or as such officer or employee of such labor organization.

(b) Request, demand, etc., for money or other thing of value

(1) It shall be unlawful for any person to request, demand, receive, or accept, or agree to receive or accept, any payment, loan, or delivery of any money or other thing of value prohibited by subsection (a) of this section.

(2) It shall be unlawful for any labor organization, or for any person acting as an officer, agent, representative, or employee of such labor organization, to demand or accept from the operator of any motor vehicle (as defined in section 13102 of Title 49) employed in the transportation of property in commerce, or the employer of any such operator, any money or other thing of value payable to such organization or to an officer, agent, representative or employee thereof as a fee or charge for the unloading, or in connection with the unloading, of the cargo of such vehicle: *Provided,* That nothing in this paragraph shall be construed to make unlawful any payment by an employer to any of his employees as compensation for their services as employees.

(c) Exceptions

The provisions of this section shall not be applicable (1) in respect to any money or other thing of value payable by an employer to any of his employees whose established duties include acting openly for such employer in matters of labor relations or personnel administration or to any representative of his employees, or to any officer or employee of a labor organization, who is also an employee or former employee of such employer, as compensation for, or by reason of, his service as an employee of such employer; (2) with respect to the payment or delivery of any money or other thing of value in satisfaction of a judgment of any court or a decision or award of an arbitrator or impartial chairman or in compromise, adjustment, settlement, or release of any claim, complaint, grievance, or dispute in the absence of fraud or duress; (3) with respect to the sale or purchase of an article or commodity at the prevailing market price in the regular course of business; (4) with respect to money deducted from the wages of employees in payment of membership dues in a labor organization: *Provided,* That the employer has received from each employee, on whose account such deductions are made, a written assignment which shall not be irrevocable for a period of more than one year, or beyond the termination date of the applicable collective agreement, whichever occurs sooner; (5) with respect to money or other thing of value paid to a trust fund established by such representative, for the sole and exclusive benefit of the employees of such employer, and their families and dependents (or of such employees, families, and dependents jointly with the employees of other employers making similar payments, and their families and dependents): *Provided,* That (A) such payments are held in trust for the purpose of paying, either from principal or income or both, for the benefit of employees, their families and dependents, for medical or hospital care, pensions on retirement or death of employees, compensation for injuries or illness resulting from occupational activity or insurance to provide any of the foregoing, or unemployment benefits or life insurance, disability and sickness insurance, or accident insurance; (B) the detailed basis on which such payments are to be made is specified in a written agreement with the employer, and employees and employers are equally represented in the administration of such fund, together with such neutral persons as the representatives of the employers and the representatives of employees may agree upon and in the event the employer and employee groups deadlock on the administration of such fund and there are no neutral persons empowered to break such deadlock, such agreement provides that the two groups shall agree on an impartial umpire to decide such dispute, or in event of their failure to agree within a reasonable length of time, an impartial umpire to decide such dispute shall, on petition of either group, be appointed by the district court of the United States for the district where the trust fund has its principal office, and shall also contain provisions for an annual audit of the trust fund, a statement of the results of which shall be available for inspection by interested persons at the principal office of the trust fund and at such other places as may be designated in such written agreement; and (C) such payments as are intended to be used for the purpose of providing pensions or annuities for employees are made to a separate trust which provides that the funds held therein cannot be used for any purpose other than paying such pensions or annuities; (6) with respect to money or other thing of value paid by any employer to a trust fund established by such representative for the purpose of pooled vacation, holiday, severance or similar benefits, or defraying costs of apprenticeship or other training programs: *Provided,* That the requirements of clause (B) of the proviso to clause (5) of this subsection shall apply to such trust funds; (7) with respect to money or other thing of value paid by any employer to a pooled or individual trust fund established by such representative for the purpose of (A) scholarships for the benefit of employees, their families, and dependents for study at educational institutions, (B) child care centers for preschool and school age dependents of employees, or(C) financial assistance for employee housing: *Provided,* That no labor organization or employer shall be required to bargain on the establishment of any such trust fund, and refusal to do so shall not constitute an unfair labor practice: *Provided further,* That the requirements of clause (B) of the proviso to clause (5) of this subsection shall apply to such trust funds; (8) with respect to money or any other thing of value paid by any employer to a trust fund established by such representative for the purpose of defraying the costs of legal services for employees, their families, and dependents for counsel or plan of their choice: *Provided,* That the requirements of clause (B) of the proviso to clause (5) of this subsection shall apply to such trust funds: *Provided further,* That no such legal services shall be furnished:(A) to initiate any proceeding directed (i) against any such employer or its officers or agents except in workman's compensation cases, or (ii) against such labor organization, or its parent or subordinate bodies, or their officers or agents, or (iii) against any other employer or labor organization, or their officers or agents, in any matter arising under subchapter II of this chapter or this chapter; and (B) in any proceeding where a labor organization would be prohibited from defraying the costs of legal services by the provisions of the Labor-Management Reporting and Disclosure Act of 1959 (29 U.S.C. §401 et seq.); or (9) with respect to money or other things of value paid by an employer to a plant, area or industrywide labor management committee established for one or more of the purposes set forth in section 5(b) of the Labor Management Cooperation Act of 1978.

(d) Penalties for violations

(1) Any person who participates in a transaction involving a payment, loan, or delivery of money or other thing of value to a labor organization in payment of membership dues or to a joint labor-management trust fund as defined by clause (B) of the proviso to clause (5) of subsection (c) of this section or to a plant, area, or industry-wide labor-management committee that is received and used by such labor organization, trust fund, or committee, which transaction does not satisfy all the applicable requirements of subsections (c)(4) through (c)(9) of this section, and willfully and with intent to benefit himself or to benefit other persons he knows are not permitted to receive a payment, loan, money, or other thing of value under subsections (c)(4) through (c)(9) violates this subsection, shall, upon conviction thereof, be guilty of a felony and be subject to a fine of not more than $15,000, or imprisoned for not more than five years, or both; but if the value of the amount of money or thing of value involved in any violation of the provisions of this section does not exceed $1,000, such person shall be guilty of a misdemeanor and be subject to a fine of not more than $10,000, or imprisoned for not more than one year, or both.

(2) Except for violations involving transactions covered by subsection (d)(1) of this section, any person who willfully violates this section shall, upon conviction thereof, be guilty of a felony and be subject to a fine of not more than $15,000, or imprisoned for not more than five years, or both; but if the value of the amount of money or thing of value involved in any violation of the provisions of this section does not exceed $1,000, such person shall be guilty of a misdemeanor and be subject to a fine of not more than $10,000, or imprisoned for not more than one year, or both.

(e) Jurisdiction of courts

The district courts of the United States and the United States courts of the Territories and possessions shall have jurisdiction, for cause shown, and subject to the provisions of section 381 of Title 28 (relating to notice to opposite party) to restrain violations of this section, without regard to the provisions of section 17 of Title 15 and section 52 of this title, and the provisions of chapter 6 of this title.

(f) Effective date of provisions

This section shall not apply to any contract in force on June 23, 1947, until the expiration of such contract, or until July 1, 1948, whichever first occurs.

(g) Contributions to trust funds

Compliance with the restrictions contained in subsection (c)(5)(B) of this section upon contributions to trust funds, otherwise lawful, shall not be applicable to contributions to such trust funds established by collective agreement prior to January 1, 1946, nor shall subsection (c)(5)(A) of this section be construed as prohibiting contributions to such trust funds if prior to January 1, 1947, such funds contained provisions for pooled vacation benefits.

Sec. 187. Unlawful activities or conduct; right to sue; jurisdiction; limitations; damages
[Sec. 303]

(a) It shall be unlawful, for the purpose of this section only, in an industry or activity affecting commerce, for any labor organization to engage in any activity or conduct defined as an unfair labor practice in section 158(b)(4) of this title.

(b) Whoever shall be injured in his business or property by reason of any violation of subsection (a) of this section may sue therefor in any district court of the United States subject to the limitations and provisions of section 185 of this title without respect to the amount in controversy, or in any other court having jurisdiction of the parties, and shall recover the damages by him sustained and the cost of the suit.

Fair Labor Standards Act

U.S. Code, Title 29, Sections 201 to 219

FLSA IN A NUTSHELL

Enacted: 1938

Purpose: To establish a minimum hourly wage, premium pay for overtime work, equal pay for men and women, and rules for child labor

Coverage: Private and public sector employers and employees (with certain exclusions)

Responsible agency: U.S. Department of Labor Wage and Hour Division

Sec. 201. Short title

This chapter may be cited as the "Fair Labor Standards Act of 1938".

Sec. 202. Congressional finding and declaration of policy

(a) The Congress finds that the existence, in industries engaged in commerce or in the production of goods for commerce, of labor conditions detrimental to the maintenance of the minimum standard of living necessary for health, efficiency, and general well-being of workers (1) causes commerce and the channels and instrumentalities of commerce to be used to spread and perpetuate such labor conditions among the workers of the several States; (2) burdens commerce and the free flow of goods in commerce; (3) constitutes an unfair method of competition in commerce; (4) leads to labor disputes burdening and obstructing commerce and the free flow of goods in commerce; and (5) interferes with the orderly and fair marketing of goods in commerce. That Congress further finds that the employment of persons in domestic service in households affects commerce.

(b) It is declared to be the policy of this chapter, through the exercise by Congress of its power to regulate commerce among the several States and with foreign nations, to correct and as rapidly as practicable to eliminate the conditions above referred to in such industries without substantially curtailing employment or earning power.

Sec. 203. Definitions

As used in this chapter —

(a) "Person" means an individual, partnership, association, corporation, business trust, legal representative, or any organized group of persons.

(b) "Commerce" means trade, commerce, transportation, transmission, or communication among the several States or between any State and any place outside thereof.

(c) "State" means any State of the United States or the District of Columbia or any Territory or possession of the United States.

(d) "Employer" includes any person acting directly or indirectly in the interest of an employer in relation to an employee and includes a public agency, but does not include any labor organization (other than when acting as an employer) or anyone acting in the capacity of officer or agent of such labor organization.

(e)(1) Except as provided in paragraphs (2), (3), and (4), the term "employee" means any individual employed by an employer.

(2) In the case of an individual employed by a public agency, such term means —

(A) any individual employed by the Government of the United States —

(i) as a civilian in the military departments (as defined in section 102 of Title 5),

(ii) in any executive agency (as defined in section 105 of such title),

(iii) in any unit of the judicial branch of the Government which has positions in the competitive service,

(iv) in a nonappropriated fund instrumentality under the jurisdiction of the Armed Forces,

(v) in the Library of Congress, or

(vi) the Government Printing Office;

(B) any individual employed by the United States Postal Service or the Postal Rate Commission; and

(C) any individual employed by a State, political subdivision of a State, or an interstate governmental agency, other than such an individual —

(i) who is not subject to the civil service laws of the State, political subdivision, or agency which employs him; and

(ii) who —

(I) holds a public elective office of that State, political subdivision, or agency,

(II) is selected by the holder of such an office to be a member of his personal staff,

(III) is appointed by such an officeholder to serve on a policymaking level,

(IV) is an immediate adviser to such an officeholder with respect to the constitutional or legal powers of his office, or

(V) is an employee in the legislative branch or legislative body of that State, political subdivision, or agency and is not employed by the legislative library of such State, political subdivision, or agency.

(3) For purposes of subsection (u) of this section, such term does not include any individual employed by an employer engaged in agriculture if such individual is the parent, spouse, child, or other member of the employer's immediate family.

(4)(A) The term "employee" does not include any individual who volunteers to perform services for a public agency which is a State, a political subdivision of a State, or an interstate governmental agency, if —

    (i) the individual receives no compensation or is paid expenses, reasonable benefits, or a nominal fee to perform the services for which the individual volunteered; and

    (ii) such services are not the same type of services which the individual is employed to perform for such public agency.

(B) An employee of a public agency which is a State, political subdivision of a State, or an interstate governmental agency may volunteer to perform services for any other State, political subdivision, or interstate governmental agency, including a State, political subdivision or agency with which the employing State, political subdivision, or agency has a mutual aid agreement.

(5) The term "employee" does not include individuals who volunteer their services for humanitarian purposes to private non-profit food banks and who receive from the food banks groceries.

(f) "Agriculture" includes farming in all its branches and among other things includes the cultivation and tillage of the soil, dairying, the production, cultivation, growing, and harvesting of any agricultural or horticultural commodities (including commodities defined as agricultural commodities in section 1141j(g) of Title 12), the raising of livestock, bees, fur-bearing animals, or poultry, and any practices (including any forestry or lumbering operations) performed by a farmer or on a farm as an incident to or in conjunction with such farming operations, including preparation for market, delivery to storage or to market or to carriers for transportation to market.

(g) "Employ" includes to suffer or permit to work.

(h) "Industry" means a trade, business, industry, or other activity, or branch or group thereof, in which individuals are gainfully employed.

(i) "Goods" means goods (including ships and marine equipment), wares, products, commodities, merchandise, or articles or subjects of commerce of any character, or any part or ingredient thereof, but does not include goods after their delivery into the actual physical possession of the ultimate consumer thereof other than a producer, manufacturer, or processor thereof.

(j) "Produced" means produced, manufactured, mined, handled, or in any other manner worked on in any State; and for the purposes of this chapter an employee shall be deemed to have been engaged in the production of goods if such employee was employed in producing, manufacturing, mining, handling, transporting, or in any other manner working on such goods, or in any closely related process or occupation directly essential to the production thereof, in any State,

(k) "Sale" or "sell" includes any sale, exchange, contract to sell, consignment for sale, shipment for sale, or other disposition.

(*l*) "Oppressive child labor" means a condition of employment under which (1) any employee under the age of sixteen years is employed by an employer (other than a parent or a person standing in place of a parent employing his own child or a child in his custody under the age of sixteen years in an occupation other than manufacturing or mining or an occupation found by the Secretary of Labor to be particularly hazardous for the employment of children between the ages of sixteen and eighteen years or detrimental to their health or well-being) in any occupation, or (2) any employee between the ages of sixteen and eighteen years is employed by an employer in any occupation which the Secretary of Labor shall find and by order declare to be particularly hazardous for the employment of children between such ages or detrimental to their health or well-being; but oppressive child labor shall not be deemed to exist by virtue of the employment in any occupation of any person with respect to whom the employer shall have on file an unexpired certificate issued and held pursuant to regulations of the Secretary of Labor certifying that such person is above the oppressive child-labor age. The Secretary of Labor shall provide by regulation or by order that the employment of employees between the ages of fourteen and sixteen years in occupations other than manufacturing and mining shall not be deemed to constitute oppressive child labor if and to the extent that the Secretary of Labor determines that such employment is confined to periods which will not interfere with their schooling and to conditions which will not interfere with their health and well-being.

(m) "Wage" paid to any employee includes the reasonable cost, as determined by the Administrator, to the employer of furnishing such employee with board, lodging, or other facilities, if such board, lodging or other facilities are customarily furnished by such employer to his employees: *Provided*, That the cost of board, lodging, or other facilities shall not be included as a part of the wage paid to any employee to the extent it is excluded therefrom under the terms of a bona fide collective-bargaining agreement applicable to the particular employee: *Provided further*, That the Secretary is authorized to determine the fair value of such board, lodging, or other facilities for defined classes of employees and in defined areas, based on average cost to the employer or to groups of employers similarly situated, or average value to groups of employees, or other appropriate measures of fair value. Such evaluations, where applicable and pertinent, shall be used in lieu of actual measure of cost in determining the wage paid to any employee. In determining the wage an employer is required to pay a tipped employee, the amount paid such employee by the employee's employer shall be an amount equal to —

(1) the cash wage paid such employee which for purposes of such determination shall be not less than the cash wage required to be paid such an employee on August 20, 1996; and

(2) an additional amount on account of the tips received by such employee which amount is equal to the difference between the wage specified in paragraph (1) and the wage in effect under section 206(a)(1) of this title.

The additional amount on account of tips may not exceed the value of the tips actually received by an employee. The preceding 2 sentences shall not apply with respect to any tipped employee unless (1) such employee has been informed by the employer of the provisions of this subsection, and (2) all tips received by such employee have been retained by the employee, except that this subsection shall not be construed to prohibit the pooling of tips among employees who customarily and regularly receive tips.

(n) "Resale" shall not include the sale of goods to be used in residential or farm building construction, repair, or maintenance: *Provided*, That the sale is recognized as a bona fide retail sale in the industry.

(*o*) Hours Worked. - In determining for the purposes of sections 206 and 207 of this title the hours for which an employee is employed, there shall be excluded any time spent in changing clothes or washing at the beginning or end of each workday which was excluded from measured working time during the week involved by the express terms of or by custom or practice under a bona fide collective-bargaining agreement applicable to the particular employee.

(p) "American vessel" includes any vessel which is documented or numbered under the laws of the United States.

(q) "Secretary" means the Secretary of Labor.

(r)(1) "Enterprise" means the related activities performed (either through unified operation or common control) by any person or persons for a common business purpose, and includes all such activities whether performed in one or more establishments or by one or more corporate or other organizational units including departments of an establishment operated through leasing arrangements, but shall not include the related activities performed for such enterprise by an independent contractor. Within the meaning of this subsection, a retail or service establishment which is under independent ownership shall not be deemed to be so operated or controlled as to be other than a separate and distinct enterprise by reason of any arrangement, which includes, but is not necessarily limited to, and agreement, (A) that it will sell, or sell only, certain goods specified by a particular manufacturer, distributor, or advertiser, or (B) that it will join with other such establishments in the same industry for the purpose of collective purchasing, or (C) that it will have the exclusive right to sell the goods or use the brand name of a manufacturer, distributor, or advertiser within a specified area, or by reason of the fact that it occupies premises leased to it by a person who also leases premises to other retail or service establishments.

(2) For purposes of paragraph (1), the activities performed by any person or persons —

(A) in connection with the operation of a hospital, an institution primarily engaged in the care of the sick, the aged, the mentally ill or defective who reside on the premises of such institution, a school for mentally or physically handicapped or gifted children, a preschool, elementary or secondary school, or an institution of higher education (regardless of whether or not such hospital, institution, or school is operated for profit or not for profit), or

(B) in connection with the operation of a street, suburban or interurban electric railway, or local trolley or motorbus carrier, if the rates and services of such railway or carrier are subject to regulation by a State or local agency (regardless of whether or not such railway or carrier is public or private or operated for profit or not for profit), or

(C) in connection with the activities of a public agency, shall be deemed to be activities performed for a business purpose.

(s)(1) "Enterprise engaged in commerce or in the production of goods for commerce" means an enterprise that —

(A)(i) has employees engaged in commerce or in the production of goods for commerce, or that has employees handling, selling, or otherwise working on goods or materials that have been moved in or produced for commerce by any person; and

(ii) is an enterprise whose annual gross volume of sales made or business done is not less than $500,000 (exclusive of excise taxes at the retail level that are separately stated);

(B) is engaged in the operation of a hospital, an institution primarily engaged in the care of the sick, the aged, or the mentally ill or defective who reside on the premises of such institution, a school for mentally or physically handicapped or gifted children, a preschool, elementary or secondary school, or an institution of higher education (regardless of whether or not such hospital, institution, or school is public or private or operated for profit or not for profit); or

(C) is an activity of a public agency.

(2) Any establishment that has as its only regular employees the owner thereof or the parent, spouse, child, or other member of the immediate family of such owner shall not be considered to be an enterprise engaged in commerce or in the production of goods for commerce or a part of such an enterprise. The sales of such an establishment shall not be included for the purpose of determining the annual gross volume of sales of any enterprise for the purpose of this subsection.

(t) "Tipped employee" means any employee engaged in an occupation in which he customarily and regularly receives more than $30 a month in tips.

(u) "Man-day" means any day during which an employee performs any agricultural labor for not less than one hour.

(v) "Elementary school" means a day or residential school which provides elementary education, as determined under State law.

(w) "Secondary school" means a day or residential school which provides secondary education, as determined under State law.

(x) "Public agency" means the Government of the United States; the government of a State or political subdivision thereof; any agency of the United States (including the United States Postal Service and Postal Rate Commission), a State, or a political subdivision of a State; or any interstate governmental agency.

Sec. 204. Administration

(a) Creation of Wage and Hour Division in Department of Labor; Administrator

There is created in the Department of Labor a Wage and Hour Division which shall be under the direction of an Administrator, to be known as the Administrator of the Wage and Hour Division (in this chapter referred to as the "Administrator"). The Administrator shall be appointed by the President, by and with the advice and consent of the Senate.

(b) Appointment, selection, classification, and promotion of employees by Administrator

The Administrator may, subject to the civil-service laws, appoint such employees as he deems necessary to carry out his functions and duties under this chapter and shall fix their compensation in accordance with chapter 51 and subchapter III of chapter 53 of Title 5. The Administrator may establish and utilize such regional, local, or other agencies, and utilize such voluntary and uncompensated services, as may from time to time be needed. Attorneys appointed under this section may appear for and represent the Administrator in any litigation, but all such litigation shall be subject to the direction and control of the Attorney General. In the appointment, selection, classification, and promotion of officers and employees of the Administrator, no political test or qualification shall be permitted or given consideration, but all such appointments and promotions shall be given and made on the basis of merit and efficiency.

(c) Principal office of Administrator; jurisdiction

The principal office of the Administrator shall be in the District of Columbia, but he or his duly authorized representative may exercise any or all of his powers in any place.

(d) Biennial report to Congress; studies of exemptions to hour and wage provisions and means to prevent curtailment of employment opportunities

(1) The Secretary shall submit biennially in January a report to the Congress covering his activities for the preceding two years and including such information, data, and recommendations for further legislation in connection with the matters covered by this chapter as he may find advisable. Such report shall contain an evaluation and appraisal by the Secretary of the minimum wages and overtime coverage established by this chapter, together with his recommendations to the Congress. In making such evaluation and appraisal, the Secretary shall take into consideration any changes which may have occurred in the cost of living and in productivity and the level of wages in manufacturing, the ability of employers to absorb wage increases, and such other factors as he may deem pertinent. Such report shall also include a summary of the special certificates issued under section 214(b) of this title.

(2) The Secretary shall conduct studies on the justification or lack thereof for each of the special exemptions set forth in section 213 of this title, and the extent to which such exemptions apply to employees of establishments described in subsection (g) of such section and the economic effects of the application of such exemptions to such employees. The Secretary shall submit a report of his findings and recommendations to the Congress with respect to the studies conducted under this paragraph not later than January 1, 1976.

(3) The Secretary shall conduct a continuing study on means to prevent curtailment of employment opportunities for manpower groups which have had historically high incidences of unemployment (such as disadvantaged minorities, youth, elderly, and such other groups as the Secretary may designate). The first report of the results of such study shall be transmitted to the Congress not later than one year after the effective date of the Fair Labor Standards Amendments of 1974. Subsequent reports on such study shall be transmitted to the Congress at two-year intervals after such effective date. Each such report shall include suggestions respecting the Secretary's authority under section 214 of this title.

(e) Study of effects of foreign production on unemployment; report to President and Congress

Whenever the Secretary has reason to believe that in any industry under this chapter the competition of foreign producers in United States markets or in markets abroad, or both, has resulted, or is likely to result, in increased unemployment in the United States, he shall undertake an investigation to gain full information with respect to the matter. If he determines such increased unemployment has in fact resulted, or is in fact likely to result, from such competition, he shall make a full and complete report of his findings and determinations to the President and to the Congress: *Provided*, That he may also include in such report information on the increased employment resulting from additional exports in any industry under this chapter as he may determine to be pertinent to such report.

(f) Employees of Library of Congress; administration of provisions by Office of Personnel Management

The Secretary is authorized to enter into an agreement with the Librarian of Congress with respect to individuals employed in the Library of Congress to provide for the carrying out of the Secretary's functions under this chapter with respect to such individuals. Notwithstanding any other provision of this chapter, or any other law, the Director of the Office of Personnel Management is authorized to administer the provisions of this chapter with respect to any individual employed by the United States (other than an individual employed in the Library of Congress, United States Postal Service, Postal Rate Commission, or the Tennessee Valley Authority). Nothing in this subsection shall be construed to affect the right of an employee to bring an action for unpaid minimum wages, or unpaid overtime compensation, and liquidated damages under section 216(b) of this title.

Sec. 205. Special industry committees for American Samoa

(a) Establishment; residents as members of committees

The Administrator shall as soon as practicable appoint a special industry committee to recommend the minimum rate or rates of wages to be paid under section 206 of this title to employees in American Samoa engaged in commerce or in the production of goods for commerce or employed in any enterprise engaged in commerce or in the production of goods for commerce or the Administrator may appoint separate industry committees to recommend the minimum rate or rates of wages to be paid under said section to employees therein engaged in commerce or in the production of goods for commerce or employed in any enterprise engaged in commerce or in the production of goods for commerce in particular industries. An industry committee appointed under this subsection shall be composed of residents of American Samoa where the employees with respect to whom such committee was appointed are employed and residents of the United States outside of American Samoa. In determining the minimum rate or rates of wages to be paid, and in determining classifications, such industry committees shall be subject to the provisions of section 208 of this title.

(b) Appointment of committee without regard to other laws pertaining to the appointment and compensation of employees of the United States; composition of committees

An industry committee shall be appointed by the Administrator without regard to any other provisions of law regarding the appointment and compensation of employees of the United States. It shall include a number of disinterested persons representing the public, one of whom the Administrator shall designate as chairman, a like number of persons representing employees in the industry, and a like number representing employers in the industry. In the appointment of the persons representing each group, the Administrator shall give due regard to the geographical regions in which the industry is carried on.

(c) Quorum; compensation; employees

Two-thirds of the members of an industry committee shall constitute a quorum, and the decision of the committee shall require a vote of not less than a majority of all its members. Members of an industry committee shall receive as compensation for their services a reasonable per diem, which the Administrator shall by rules and regulations prescribe, for each day actually spent in the work of the committee, and shall in addition be reimbursed for their necessary traveling and other expenses. The Administrator shall furnish the committee with adequate legal, stenographic, clerical, and other assistance, and shall by rules and regulations prescribe the procedure to be followed by the committee.

(d) Submission of data to committees

The Administrator shall submit to an industry committee from time to time such data as he may have available on the matters referred to it, and shall cause to be brought before it in connection with such matters any witnesses whom he deems material. An industry committee may summon other witnesses or call upon the Administrator to furnish additional information to aid it in its deliberations.

Sec. 206. Minimum wage

(a) Employees engaged in commerce; home workers in Puerto Rico and Virgin Islands; employees in American Samoa; seamen on American vessels; agricultural employees

Every employer shall pay to each of his employees who in any workweek is engaged in commerce or in the production of goods for commerce, or is employed in an enterprise engaged in commerce or in the production of goods for commerce, wages at the following rates:

(1) except as otherwise provided in this section, not less than $4.25 an hour during the period ending September 30, 1996, not less than $4.75 an hour during the year beginning on October 1, 1996, and not less than $5.15 an hour beginning September 1, 1997;

(2) if such employee is a home worker in Puerto Rico or the Virgin Islands, not less than the minimum piece rate prescribed by regulation or order; or, if no such minimum piece rate is in effect, any piece rate adopted by such employer which shall yield, to the proportion or class of employees prescribed by regulation or order, not less than the applicable minimum hourly wage rate. Such minimum piece rates or employer piece rates shall be commensurate with, and shall be paid in lieu of, the minimum hourly wage rate applicable under the provisions of this section. The Administrator, or his authorized representative, shall have power to make such regulations or orders as are necessary or appropriate to carry out any of the provisions of this paragraph, including the power without limiting the generality of the foregoing, to define any operation or occupation which is performed by such home work employees in Puerto Rico or the Virgin Islands; to establish minimum piece rates for any operation or occupation so defined; to prescribe the method and procedure for ascertaining and promulgating minimum piece rates; to prescribe standards for employer piece rates, including the proportion or class of employees who shall receive not less than the minimum hourly wage rate; to define the term "home worker"; and to prescribe the conditions under which employers, agents, contractors, and subcontractors shall cause goods to be produced by home workers;

(3) if such employee is employed in American Samoa, in lieu of the rate or rates provided by this subsection or subsection (b) of this section, not less than the applicable rate established by the Secretary of Labor in accordance with recommendations of a special industry committee or committees which he shall appoint pursuant to sections 205 and 208 of this title. The minimum wage rate thus established shall not exceed the rate prescribed in paragraph (1) of this subsection;

(4) if such employee is employed as a seaman on an American vessel, not less than the rate which will provide to the employee, for the period covered by the wage payment, wages equal to compensation at the hourly rate prescribed by paragraph (1) of this subsection for all hours during such period when he was actually on duty (including periods aboard ship when the employee was on watch or was, at the direction of a superior officer, performing work or standing by, but not including off-duty periods which are provided pursuant to the employment agreement); or

(5) if such employee is employed in agriculture, not less than the minimum wage rate in effect under paragraph (1) after December 31, 1977.

(b) Additional applicability to employees pursuant to subsequent amendatory provisions

Every employer shall pay to each of his employees (other than an employee to whom subsection (a)(5) of this section applies) who in any workweek is engaged in commerce or in the production of goods for commerce, or is employed in an enterprise engaged in commerce or in the production of goods for commerce, and who in such workweek is brought within the purview of this section by the amendments made to this chapter by the Fair Labor Standards Amendments of 1966; title IX of the Education Amendments of 1972 (20 U.S.C. §1681 et seq.), or the Fair Labor Standards Amendments of 1974, wages at the following rate: Effective after December 31, 1977, not less than the minimum wage rate in effect under subsection (a)(1) of this section.

(c) Repealed

(d) Prohibition of sex discrimination

(1) No employer having employees subject to any provisions of this section shall discriminate, within any establishment in which such employees are employed, between employees on the basis of sex by paying wages to employees in such establishment at a rate less than the rate at which he pays wages to employees of the opposite sex in such establishment for equal work on jobs the performance of which requires equal skill, effort, and responsibility, and which are performed under similar working conditions, except where such payment is made pursuant to (i) a seniority system; (ii) a merit system; (iii) a system which measures earnings by quantity or quality of production; or (iv) a differential based on any other factor other than sex: *Provided*, That an employer who is paying a wage rate differential in violation of this subsection shall not, in order to comply with the provisions of this subsection, reduce the wage rate of any employee.

(2) No labor organization, or its agents, representing employees of an employer having employees subject to any provisions of this section shall cause or attempt to cause such an employer to discriminate against an employee in violation of paragraph (1) of this subsection.

(3) For purposes of administration and enforcement, any amounts owing to any employee which have been withheld in violation of this subsection shall be deemed to be unpaid minimum wages or unpaid overtime compensation under this chapter.

(4) As used in this subsection, the term "labor organization" means any organization of any kind, or any agency or employee representation committee or plan, in which employees participate and which exists for the purpose, in whole or in part, of dealing with employers concerning grievances, labor disputes, wages, rates of pay, hours of employment, or conditions of work.

(e) Employees of employers providing contract services to United States

(1) Notwithstanding the provisions of section 213 of this title (except subsections (a)(1) and (f) thereof), every employer providing any contract services (other than linen supply services) under a contract with the United States or any subcontract thereunder shall pay to each of his employees whose rate of pay is not governed by the Service Contract Act of 1965 (41 U.S.C. §351-357) or to whom subsection (a)(1) of this section is not applicable, wages at rates not less than the rates provided for in subsection (b) of this section.

(2) Notwithstanding the provisions of section 213 of this title (except subsections (a)(1) and (f) thereof) and the provisions of the Service Contract Act of 1965 (41 U.S.C. §351-357) every employer in an establishment providing linen supply services to the United States under a contract with the United States or any subcontract thereunder shall pay to each of his employees in

such establishment wages at rates not less than those prescribed in subsection (b) of this section, except that if more than 50 per centum of the gross annual dollar volume of sales made or business done by such establishment is derived from providing such linen supply services under any such contracts or subcontracts, such employer shall pay to each of his employees in such establishment wages at rates not less than those prescribed in subsection (a)(1) of this section.

(f) Employees in domestic service

Any employee —

(1) who in any workweek is employed in domestic service in a household shall be paid wages at a rate not less than the wage rate in effect under subsection (b) of this section unless such employee's compensation for such service would not because of section 209(a)(6) of the Social Security Act (42 U.S.C. §409(a)(6)) constitute wages for the purposes of title II of such Act (42 U.S.C. §401 et seq.), or

(2) who in any workweek —

(A) is employed in domestic service in one or more households, and

(B) is so employed for more than 8 hours in the aggregate,

shall be paid wages for such employment in such workweek at a rate not less than the wage rate in effect under subsection (b) of this section.

(g) Newly hired employees who are less than 20 years old

(1) In lieu of the rate prescribed by subsection (a)(1) of this section, any employer may pay any employee of such employer, during the first 90 consecutive calendar days after such employee is initially employed by such employer, a wage which is not less than $4.25 an hour.

(2) No employer may take any action to displace employees (including partial displacements such as reduction in hours, wages, or employment benefits) for purposes of hiring individuals at the wage authorized in paragraph (1).

(3) Any employer who violates this subsection shall be considered to have violated section 215(a)(3) of this title.

(4) This subsection shall only apply to an employee who has not attained the age of 20 years.

Sec. 207. Maximum hours

(a) Employees engaged in interstate commerce; additional applicability to employees pursuant to subsequent amendatory provisions

(1) Except as otherwise provided in this section, no employer shall employ any of his employees who in any workweek is engaged in commerce or in the production of goods for commerce, or is employed in an enterprise engaged in commerce or in the production of goods for commerce, for a workweek longer than forty hours unless such employee receives compensation for his employment in excess of the hours above specified at a rate not less than one and one-half times the regular rate at which he is employed.

(2) No employer shall employ any of his employees who in any workweek is engaged in commerce or in the production of goods for commerce, or is employed in an enterprise engaged in commerce or in the production of goods for commerce, and who in such workweek is brought within the purview of this subsection by the amendments made to this chapter by the Fair Labor Standards Amendments of 1966 —

(A) for a workweek longer than forty-four hours during the first year from the effective date of the Fair Labor Standards Amendments of 1966,

(B) for a workweek longer than forty-two hours during the second year from such date, or

(C) for a workweek longer than forty hours after the expiration of the second year from such date,

unless such employee receives compensation for his employment in excess of the hours above specified at a rate not less than one and one-half times the regular rate at which he is employed.

(b) Employment pursuant to collective bargaining agreement; employment by independently owned and controlled local enterprise engaged in distribution of petroleum products

No employer shall be deemed to have violated subsection (a) of this section by employing any employee for a workweek in excess of that specified in such subsection without paying the compensation for overtime employment prescribed therein if such employee is so employed —

(1) in pursuance of an agreement, made as a result of collective bargaining by representatives of employees certified as bona fide by the National Labor Relations Board, which provides that no employee shall be employed more than one thousand and forty hours during any period of twenty-six consecutive weeks; or

(2) in pursuance of an agreement, made as a result of collective bargaining by representatives of employees certified as bona fide by the National Labor Relations Board, which provides that during a specified period of fifty-two consecutive weeks the employee shall be employed not more than two thousand two hundred and forty hours and shall be guaranteed not less than one thousand eight hundred and forty-hours (or not less than forty-six weeks at the normal number of hours worked per week, but not less than thirty hours per week) and not more than two thousand and eighty hours of employment for which he shall receive compensation for all hours guaranteed or worked at rates not less than those applicable under the agreement to the work performed and for all hours in excess of the guaranty which are also in excess of the maximum workweek applicable to such employee under subsection (a) of this section or two thousand and eighty in such period at rates not less than one and one-half times the regular rate at which he is employed; or

(3) by an independently owned and controlled local enterprise (including an enterprise with more than one bulk storage establishment) engaged in the wholesale or bulk distribution of petroleum products if —

(A) the annual gross volume of sales of such enterprise is less than $1,000,000 exclusive of excise taxes,

(B) more than 75 per centum of such enterprise's annual dollar volume of sales is made within the State in which such enterprise is located, and

(C) not more than 25 per centum of the annual dollar volume of sales of such enterprise is to customers who are engaged in the bulk distribution of such products for resale, and such employee receives compensation for employment in excess of forty hours in any work-week at a rate not less than one and one-half times the minimum wage rate applicable to him under section 206 of this title,

and if such employee receives compensation for employment in excess of twelve hours in any work-day, or for employment in excess of fifty-six hours in any workweek, as the case may be, at a rate not less than one and one-half times the regular rate at which he is employed.

(c), (d) Repealed

(e) "Regular rate" defined

As used in this section the "regular rate" at which an employee is employed shall be deemed to include all remuneration for employment paid to, or on behalf of, the employee, but shall not be deemed to include —

(1) sums paid as gifts; payments in the nature of gifts made at Christmas time or on other special occasions, as a reward for service, the amounts of which are not measured by or dependent on hours worked, production, or efficiency;

(2) payments made for occasional periods when no work is performed due to vacation, holiday, illness, failure of the employer to provide sufficient work, or other similar cause; reasonable payments for traveling expenses, or other expenses, incurred by an employee in the furtherance of his employer's interests and properly reimbursable by the employer; and other similar payments to an employee which are not made as compensation for his hours of employment;

(3) Sums paid in recognition of services performed during a given period if either, (a) both the fact that payment is to be made and the amount of the payment are determined at the sole discretion of the employer at or near the end of the period and not pursuant to any prior contract, agreement, or promise causing the employee to expect such payments regularly; or (b) the payments are made pursuant to a bona fide profit-sharing plan or trust or bona fide thrift or savings plan, meeting the requirements of the Administrator set forth in appropriate regulations which he shall issue, having due regard among other relevant factors, to the extent to which the amounts paid to the employee are determined

without regard to hours of work, production, or efficiency; or (c) the payments are talent fees (as such talent fees are defined and delimited by regulations of the Administrator) paid to performers, including announcers, on radio and television programs;

(4) contributions irrevocably made by an employer to a trustee or third person pursuant to a bona fide plan for providing old-age, retirement, life, accident, or health insurance or similar benefits for employees;

(5) extra compensation provided by a premium rate paid for certain hours worked by the employee in any day of workweek because such hours are hours worked in excess of eight in a day or in excess of the maximum workweek applicable to such employee under subsection (a) of this section or in excess of the employee's normal working hours or regular working hours, as the case may be;

(6) extra compensation provided by a premium rate paid for work by the employee on Saturdays, Sundays, holidays, or regular days of rest, or on the sixth or seventh day of the workweek, where such premium rate is not less than one and one-half times the rate established in good faith for like work performed in nonovertime hours on other days; or

(7) extra compensation provided by a premium rate paid to the employee, in pursuance of an applicable employment contract or collective-bargaining agreement, for work outside of the hours established in good faith by the contract or agreement as the basic, normal, or regular work-day (not exceeding eight hours) or workweek (not exceeding the maximum workweek applicable to such employee under subsection (a) of this section, where such premium rate is not less than one and one-half times the rate established in good faith by the contract or agreement for like work performed during such workday or work-week.

(f) Employment necessitating irregular hours of work

No employer shall be deemed to have violated subsection (a) of this section by employing any employee for a workweek in excess of the maximum workweek applicable to such employee under subsection (a) of this section if such employee is employed pursuant to a bona fide individual contract, or pursuant to an agreement made as a result of collective bargaining by representatives of employees, if the duties of such employee necessitate irregular hours of work, and the contract or agreement (1) specifies a regular rate of pay of not less than the minimum hourly rate provided in subsection (a) or (b) of section 206 of this title (whichever may be applicable) and compensation at not less than one and one-half times such rate for all hours worked in excess of such maximum workweek, and (2) provides a weekly guaranty of pay for not more than sixty hours based on the rates so specified.

(g) Employment at piece rates

No employer shall be deemed to have violated subsection (a) of this section by employing any employee for a workweek in excess of the maximum workweek applicable to such employee under such subsection if, pursuant to an agreement or understanding arrived at between the employer and the employee before performance of the work, the amount paid to the employee for the number of hours worked by him in such workweek in excess of the maximum workweek applicable to such employee under such subsection —

(1) in the case of an employee employed at piece rates, is computed at piece rates not less than one and one-half times the bona fide piece rates applicable to the same work when performed during nonovertime hours; or

(2) in the case of an employee performing two or more kinds of work for which different hourly or piece rates have been established, is computed at rates not less than one and one-half times such bona fide rates applicable to the same work when performed during nonovertime hours; or

(3) is computed at a rate not less than one and one-half times the rate established by such agreement or understanding as the basic rate to be used in computing overtime compensation thereunder: *Provided*, That the rate so established shall be authorized by regulation by the Administrator as being substantially equivalent to the average hourly earnings of the employee, exclusive of overtime premiums, in the particular work over a representative period of time;

and if (i) the employee's average hourly earnings for the workweek exclusive of payments described in paragraphs (1) through (7) of subsection (e) of this section are not less than the minimum hourly rate required by applicable law, and (ii) extra overtime compensation is properly computed and paid on other forms of additional pay required to be included in computing the regular rate.

(h) Extra compensation creditable toward overtime compensation

Extra compensation paid as described in paragraphs (5), (6), and (7) of subsection (e) of this section shall be creditable toward overtime compensation payable pursuant to this section.

(i) Employment by retail or service establishment

No employer shall be deemed to have violated subsection (a) of this section by employing any employee of a retail or service establishment for a workweek in excess of the applicable workweek specified therein, if (1) the regular rate of pay of such employee is in excess of one and one-half times the minimum hourly rate applicable to him under section 206 of this title, and (2) more than half his compensation for a representative period (not less than one month) represents commissions on goods or services. In determining the proportion of compensation representing commissions, all earnings resulting from the application of a bona fide commission rate shall be deemed commissions on goods or services without regard to whether the computed commissions exceed the draw or guarantee.

(j) Employment in hospital or establishment engaged in care of sick, aged, or mentally ill

No employer engaged in the operation of a hospital or an establishment which is an institution primarily engaged in the care of the sick, the aged, or the mentally ill or defective who reside on the premises shall be deemed to have violated subsection (a) of this section if, pursuant to an agreement or understanding arrived at between the employer and the employee before performance of the work, a work period of fourteen consecutive days is accepted in lieu of the workweek of seven consecutive days for purposes of overtime computation and if, for his employment in excess of eight hours in any workday and in excess of eighty hours in such fourteen-day period, the employee receives compensation at a rate not less than one and one-half times the regular rate at which he is employed.

(k) Employment by public agency engaged in fire protection or law enforcement activities

No public agency shall be deemed to have violated subsection (a) of this section with respect to the employment of any employee in fire protection activities or any employee in law enforcement activities (including security personnel in correctional institutions) if —

(1) in a work period of 28 consecutive days the employee receives for tours of duty which in the aggregate exceed the lesser of (A) 216 hours, or (B) the average number of hours (as determined by the Secretary pursuant to section 6(c)(3) of the Fair Labor Standards Amendments of 1974) in tours of duty of employees engaged in such activities in work periods of 28 consecutive days in calendar year 1975; or

(2) in the case of such an employee to whom a work period of at least 7 but less than 28 days applies, in his work period the employee receives for tours of duty which in the aggregate exceed a number of hours which bears the same ratio to the number of consecutive days in his work period as 216 hours (or if lower, the number of hours referred to in clause (B) of paragraph (1)) bears to 28 days, compensation at a rate not less than one and one-half times the regular rate at which he is employed.

(l) Employment in domestic service in one or more households

No employer shall employ any employee in domestic service in one or more households for a workweek longer than forty hours unless such employee receives compensation for such employment in accordance with subsection (a) of this section.

(m) Employment in tobacco industry

For a period or periods of not more than fourteen workweeks in the aggregate in any calendar year, any employer may employ any employee for a workweek in excess of that specified in subsection (a) of this section without paying the compensation for overtime employment prescribed in such subsection, if such employee —

(1) is employed by such employer —

(A) to provide services (including stripping and grading) necessary and incidental to the sale at auction of green leaf tobacco of type 11, 12, 13, 14, 21, 22, 23, 24, 31, 35, 36, or 37 (as such types are defined by the Secretary of Agriculture), or in auction sale, buying, handling, stemming, redrying, packing, and storing of such tobacco,

(B) in auction sale, buying, handling, sorting, grading, packing, or storing green leaf tobacco of type 32 (as such type is defined by the Secretary of Agriculture), or

(C) in auction sale, buying, handling, stripping, sorting, grading, sizing, packing, or stemming prior to packing, of perishable cigar leaf tobacco of type 41, 42, 43, 44, 45, 46, 51, 52, 53, 54, 55, 61, or 62 (as such types are defined by the Secretary of Agriculture); and

(2) receives for —

(A) such employment by such employer which is in excess of ten hours in any workday, and

(B) such employment by such employer which is in excess of forty-eight hours in any workweek,

compensation at a rate not less than one and one-half times the regular rate at which he is employed.

An employer who receives an exemption under this subsection shall not be eligible for any other exemption under this section.

(n) Employment by street, suburban, or interurban electric railway, or local trolley or motorbus carrier

In the case of an employee of an employer engaged in the business of operating a street, suburban or interurban electric railway, or local trolley or motorbus carrier (regardless of whether or not such railway or carrier is public or private or operated for profit or not for profit), in determining the hours of employment of such an employee to which the rate prescribed by subsection (a) of this section applies there shall be excluded the hours such employee was employed in charter activities by such employer if (1) the employee's employment in such activities was pursuant to an

[43]

agreement or understanding with his employer arrived at before engaging in such employment, and (2) if employment in such activities is not part of such employee's regular employment.

(o) Compensatory time

(1) Employees of a public agency which is a State, a political subdivision of a State, or an interstate governmental agency may receive, in accordance with this subsection and in lieu of overtime compensation, compensatory time off at a rate not less than one and one-half hours for each hour of employment for which overtime compensation is required by this section.

(2) A public agency may provide compensatory time under paragraph (1) only —

(A) pursuant to —

(i) applicable provisions of a collective bargaining agreement, memorandum of understanding, or any other agreement between the public agency and representatives of such employees; or

(ii) in the case of employees not covered by subclause (i), an agreement or understanding arrived at between the employer and employee before the performance of the work; and

(B) if the employee has not accrued compensatory time in excess of the limit applicable to the employee prescribed by paragraph (3).

In the case of employees described in clause (A)(ii) hired prior to April 15, 1986, the regular practice in effect on April 15, 1986, with respect to compensatory time off for such employees in lieu of the receipt of overtime compensation, shall constitute an agreement or understanding under such clause (A)(ii). Except as provided in the previous sentence, the provision of compensatory time off to such employees for hours worked after April 14, 1986, shall be in accordance with this subsection.

(3)(A) If the work of an employee for which compensatory time may be provided included work in a public safety activity, an emergency response activity, or a seasonal activity, the employee engaged in such work may accrue not more than 480 hours of compensatory time for hours worked after April 15, 1986. If such work was any other work, the employee engaged in

such work may accrue not more than 240 hours of compensatory time for hours worked after April 15, 1986. Any such employee who, after April 15, 1986, has accrued 480 or 240 hours, as the case may be, of compensatory time off shall, for additional overtime hours of work, be paid overtime compensation.

(B) If compensation is paid to an employee for accrued compensatory time off, such compensation shall be paid at the regular rate earned by the employee at the time the employee receives such payment.

(4) An employee who has accrued compensatory time off authorized to be provided under paragraph (1) shall, upon termination of employment, be paid for the unused compensatory time at a rate of compensation not less than —

(A) the average regular rate received by such employee during the last 3 years of the employee's employment, or

(B) the final regular rate received by such employee, whichever is higher.

(5) An employee of a public agency which is a State, political subdivision of a State, or an interstate governmental agency —

(A) who has accrued compensatory time off authorized to be provided under paragraph (1), and

(B) who has requested the use of such compensatory time,

shall be permitted by the employee's employer to use such time within a reasonable period after making the request if the use of the compensatory time does not unduly disrupt the operations of the public agency.

(6) The hours an employee of a public agency performs court reporting transcript preparation duties shall not be considered as hours worked for the purposes of subsection (a) of this section if —

(A) such employee is paid at a per-page rate which is not less than —

(i) the maximum rate established by State law or local ordinance for the jurisdiction of such public agency,

(ii) the maximum rate otherwise established by a judicial or administrative officer and in effect on July 1, 1995, or

(iii) the rate freely negotiated between the employee and the party requesting the transcript, other than the judge who presided over the proceedings being transcribed, and

(B) the hours spent performing such duties are outside of the hours such employee performs other work (including hours for which the agency requires the employee's attendance) pursuant to the employment relationship with such public agency.

For purposes of this section, the amount paid such employee in accordance with subparagraph (A) for the performance of court reporting transcript preparation duties, shall not be considered in the calculation of the regular rate at which such employee is employed.

(7) For purposes of this subsection —

(A) the term "overtime compensation" means the compensation required by subsection (a), and

(B) the terms "compensatory time" and "compensatory time off" mean hours during which an employee is not working, which are not counted as hours worked during the applicable workweek or other work period for purposes of overtime compensation, and for which the employee is compensated at the employee's regular rate.

(p) Special detail work for fire protection and law enforcement employees; occasional or sporadic employment; substitution

(1) If an individual who is employed by a State, political subdivision of a State, or an interstate governmental agency in fire protection or law enforcement activities (including activities of security personnel in correctional institutions) and who, solely at such individual's option, agrees to be employed on a special detail by a separate or independent employer in fire protection, law enforcement, or related activities, the hours such individual was employed by such separate and independent employer shall be excluded by the public agency employing such individual in the calculation of the hours for which the employee is entitled to overtime compensation under this section if the public agency —

(A) requires that its employees engaged in fire protection, law enforcement, or security activi-

ties be hired by a separate and independent employer to perform the special detail,

(B) facilitates the employment of such employees by a separate and independent employer, or

(C) otherwise affects the condition of employment of such employees by a separate and independent employer.

(2) If an employee of a public agency which is a State, political subdivision of a State, or an interstate governmental agency undertakes, on an occasional or sporadic basis and solely at the employee's option, part-time employment for the public agency which is in a different capacity from any capacity in which the employee is regularly employed with the public agency, the hours such employee was employed in performing the different employment shall be excluded by the public agency in the calculation of the hours for which the employee is entitled to overtime compensation under this section.

(3) If an individual who is employed in any capacity by a public agency which is a State, political subdivision of a State, or an interstate governmental agency, agrees, with the approval of the public agency and solely at the option of such individual, to substitute during scheduled work hours for another individual who is employed by such agency in the same capacity, the hours such employee worked as a substitute shall be excluded by the public agency in the calculation of the hours for which the employee is entitled to overtime compensation under this section.

(q) Maximum hour exemption for employees receiving remedial education

Any employer may employ any employee for a period or periods of not more than 10 hours in the aggregate in any workweek in excess of the maximum workweek specified in subsection (a) of this section without paying the compensation for overtime employment prescribed in such subsection, if during such period or periods the employee is receiving remedial education that is —

(1) provided to employees who lack a high school diploma or educational attainment at the eighth grade level;

(2) designed to provide reading and other basic skills at an eighth grade level or below; and

(3) does not include job specific training.

Sec. 208. Wage orders in American Samoa

(a) Congressional policy; recommendation of wage rate by industry committee

The policy of this chapter with respect to industries or enterprises in American Samoa engaged in commerce or in the production of goods for commerce is to reach as rapidly as is economically feasible without substantially curtailing employment the objective of the minimum wage rate which would apply in each such industry under paragraph (1) or (5) of section 206(a) of this title but for section 206(c) of this title. The Administrator shall from time to time convene an industry committee or committees, appointed pursuant to section 205 of this title, and any such industry committee shall from time to time recommend the minimum rate or rates of wages to be paid under section 206 of this title by employers in American Samoa engaged in commerce or in the production of goods for commerce or in any enterprise engaged in commerce or in the production of goods for commerce in any such industry or classifications therein, and who but for section 206(a)(3) of this title would be subject to the minimum wage requirements of section 206(a)(1) of this title. Minimum rates of wages established in accordance with this section which are not equal to the otherwise applicable minimum wage rate in effect under paragraph (1) or (5) of section 206(a) of this title shall be reviewed by such a Committee once during each biennial period, beginning with the biennial period commencing July 1, 1958, except that the Secretary, in his discretion, may order an additional review during any such biennial period.

(b) Investigation of industry condition by industry committee; matters considered

Upon the convening of any such industry committee, the Administrator shall refer to it the question of the minimum wage rate or rates to be fixed for such industry. The industry committee shall investigate conditions in the industry and the committee, or any authorized subcommittee thereof, shall after due notice hear such witnesses and receive such evidence as may be necessary or appropriate to enable the committee to perform its duties and functions under this chapter. The committee shall recommend to the Administrator the highest minimum wage rates for the industry which it determines, having due regard to economic and competitive conditions, will not substantially curtail employment in the industry, and will not give any industry in American Samoa a competitive advantage over any industry in the United States outside of American Samoa; except that the committee shall recommend to the Secretary the minimum wage rate prescribed in section 206(a) or 206(b) of this title, which would be applicable but for section 206(a)(3) of this title, unless there is evidence in the record which establishes that the industry, or a predominant portion thereof, is unable to pay that wage due to such economic and competitive conditions.

(c) Classifications within industry; recommendation of wage rate

The industry committee shall recommend such reasonable classifications within any industry as it determines to be necessary for the purpose of fixing for each classification within such industry the highest minimum wage rate (not in excess of that in effect under paragraph (1) or (5) of section 206(a) of this title (as the case may be)) which (1) will not substantially curtail employment in such classification and (2) will not give a competitive advantage to any group in the industry, and shall recommend for each classification in the industry the highest minimum wage rate which the committee determines will not substantially curtail employment in such classification. In determining whether such classification should be made in any industry, in making such classifications, and in determining the minimum wage rates for such classifications, no classifications shall be made, and no minimum wage rate shall be fixed, solely on a regional basis, but the industry committee shall consider among other relevant factors the following:

(1) competitive conditions as affected by transportation, living, and production costs;

(2) the wages established for work of like or comparable character by collective labor agreements negotiated between employers and employees by representatives of their own choosing; and

(3) the wages paid for work of like or comparable character by employers who voluntarily maintain minimum wage standards in the industry.

No classification shall be made under this section on the basis of age or sex.

(d) Report by industry committee; publication in Federal Register

The industry committee shall file with the Secretary a report containing its findings of fact and recommendations with respect to the matters referred to it. Upon the filing of such report, the Secretary shall publish such recommendations in the Federal Register and shall provide by order that the recommendations contained in such report shall take effect upon the expiration of 15 days after the date of such publication.

(e) Orders

Orders issued under this section shall define the industries and classifications therein to which they are to apply, and shall contain such terms and conditions as the Administrator finds necessary to carry out the purposes of such orders, to prevent the circumvention or evasion thereof, and to safeguard the minimum wage rates established therein.

(f) Due notice of hearings by publication in Federal Register

Due notice of any hearing provided for in this section shall be given by publication in the Federal Register and by such other means as the Administrator deems reasonably calculated to give general notice to interested persons.

Sec. 209. Attendance of witnesses

For the purpose of any hearing or investigation provided for in this chapter, the provisions of sections 49 and 50 of Title 15 (relating to the attendance of witnesses and the production of books, papers, and documents), are made applicable to the jurisdiction, powers, and duties of the Administrator, the Secretary of Labor, and the industry committees.

Sec. 210. Court review of wage orders in Puerto Rico and the Virgin Islands

(a) Any person aggrieved by an order of the Secretary issued under section 208 of this title may obtain a review of such order in the United States Court of Appeals for any circuit wherein such person resides or has his principal place of business, or in the United States Court of Appeals for the

District of Columbia, by filing in such court, within 60 days after the entry of such order a written petition praying that the order of the Secretary be modified or set aside in whole or in part. A copy of such petition shall forthwith be transmitted by the clerk of the court to the Secretary, and thereupon the Secretary shall file in the court the record of the industry committee upon which the order complained of was entered, as provided in section 2112 of Title 28. Upon the filing of such petition such court shall have exclusive jurisdiction to affirm, modify (including provision for the payment of an appropriate minimum wage rate), or set aside such order in whole or in part, so far as it is applicable to the petitioner. The review by the court shall be limited to questions of law, and findings of fact by such industry committee when supported by substantial evidence shall be conclusive. No objection to the order of the Secretary shall be considered by the court unless such objection shall have been urged before such industry committee or unless there were reasonable grounds for failure so to do. If application is made to the court for leave to adduce additional evidence, and it is shown to the satisfaction of the court that such additional evidence may materially affect the result of the proceeding and that there were reasonable grounds for failure to adduce such evidence in the proceedings before such industry committee, the court may order such additional evidence to be taken before an industry committee and to be adduced upon the hearing in such manner and upon such terms and conditions as to the court may seem proper. Such industry committee may modify the initial findings by reason of the additional evidence so taken, and shall file with the court such modified or new findings which if supported by substantial evidence shall be conclusive, and shall also file its recommendation, if any, for the modification or setting aside of the original order. The judgment and decree of the court shall be final, subject to review by the Supreme Court of the United States upon certiorari or certification as provided in section 1254 of Title 28.

(b) The commencement of proceedings under subsection (a) of this section shall not, unless specifically ordered by the court, operate as a stay of the Administrator's order. The court shall not grant any stay of the order unless the person complaining of such order shall file in court an undertaking with a surety or sureties satisfactory to the court for the payment to the employees affected by the order, in the event such order is affirmed, of the amount by which the compensation such employees are entitled to receive under the order exceeds the compensation they actually receive while such stay is in effect.

Sec. 211. Collection of data

(a) Investigations and inspections

The Administrator or his designated representatives may investigate and gather data regarding the wages, hours, and other conditions and practices of employment in any industry subject to this chapter, and may enter and inspect such places and such records (and make such transcriptions thereof), question such employees, and investigate such facts, conditions, practices, or matters as he may deem necessary or appropriate to determine whether any person has violated any provision of this chapter, or which may aid in the enforcement of the provisions of this chapter. Except as provided in section 212 of this title and in subsection (b) of this section, the Administrator shall utilize the bureaus and divisions of the Department of Labor for all the investigations and inspections necessary under this section. Except as provided in section 212 of this title, the Administrator shall bring all actions under section 217 of this title to restrain violations of this chapter.

(b) State and local agencies and employees

With the consent and cooperation of State agencies charged with the administration of State labor laws, the Administrator and the Secretary of Labor may, for the purpose of carrying out their respective functions and duties under this chapter, utilize the services of State and local agencies and their employees and, notwithstanding any other provision of law, may reimburse such State and local agencies and their employees for services rendered for such purposes.

(c) Records

Every employer subject to any provision of this chapter or of any order issued under this chapter shall make, keep, and preserve such records of the persons employed by him and of the wages, hours, and other conditions and practices of employment maintained by him, and shall preserve such records for such periods of time, and shall make such

reports therefrom to the Administrator as he shall prescribe by regulation or order as necessary or appropriate for the enforcement of the provisions of this chapter or the regulations or orders thereunder. The employer of an employee who performs substitute work described in section 207(p)(3) of this title may not be required under this subsection to keep a record of the hours of the substitute work.

(d) Homework regulations

The Administrator is authorized to make such regulations and orders regulating, restricting, or prohibiting industrial homework as are necessary or appropriate to prevent the circumvention or evasion of and to safeguard the minimum wage rate prescribed in this chapter, and all existing regulations or orders of the Administrator relating to industrial homework are continued in full force and effect.

Sec. 212. Child labor provisions

(a) Restrictions on shipment of goods; prosecution; conviction

No producer, manufacturer, or dealer shall ship or deliver for shipment in commerce any goods produced in an establishment situated in the United States in or about which within thirty days prior to the removal of such goods therefrom any oppressive child labor has been employed: *Provided,* That any such shipment or delivery for shipment of such goods by a purchaser who acquired them in good faith in reliance on written assurance from the producer, manufacturer, or dealer that the goods were produced in compliance with the requirements of this section, and who acquired such goods for value without notice of any such violation, shall not be deemed prohibited by this subsection: *And provided further,* That a prosecution and conviction of a defendant for the shipment or delivery for shipment of any goods under the conditions herein prohibited shall be a bar to any further prosecution against the same defendant for shipments or deliveries for shipment of any such goods before the beginning of said prosecution.

(b) Investigations and inspections

The Secretary of Labor or any of his authorized representatives, shall make all investigations and inspections under section 211(a) of this title with respect to the employment of minors, and, subject to the direction and control of the Attorney General, shall bring all actions under section 217 of this title to enjoin any act or practice which is unlawful by reason of the existence of oppressive child labor, and shall administer all other provisions of this chapter relating to oppressive child labor.

(c) Oppressive child labor

No employer shall employ any oppressive child labor in commerce or in the production of goods for commerce or in any enterprise engaged in commerce or in the production of goods for commerce.

(d) Proof of age

In order to carry out the objectives of this section, the Secretary may by regulation require employers to obtain from any employee proof of age.

Sec. 213. Exemptions

(a) Minimum wage and maximum hour requirements

The provisions of sections 206 (except subsection (d) in the case of paragraph (1) of this subsection) and section 207 of this title shall not apply with respect to —

(1) any employee employed in a bona fide executive, administrative, or professional capacity (including any employee employed in the capacity of academic administrative personnel or teacher in elementary or secondary schools), or in the capacity of outside salesman (as such terms are defined and delimited from time to time by regulations of the Secretary, subject to the provisions of subchapter II of chapter 5 of Title 5, except that an employee of a retail or service establishment shall not be excluded from the definition of employee employed in a bona fide executive or administrative capacity because of the number of hours in his workweek which he devotes to activities not directly or closely related to the performance of executive or administrative activities, if less than 40 per centum of his hours worked in the workweek are devoted to such activities); or

(2) Repealed

(3) any employee employed by an establishment which is an amusement or recreational establishment organized camp, or religious or non-profit educational conference center, if (A) it does not operate for more than seven months in any calendar year, or (B) during the preceding calendar year, its average receipts for any six months of such year were not more than 33 1/3 per centum of its average receipts for the other six months of such year, except that the exemption from sections 206 and 207 of this title provided by this paragraph does not apply with respect to any employee of a private entity engaged in providing services or facilities (other than, in the case of the exemption from section 206 of this title, a private entity engaged in providing services and facilities directly related to skiing) in a national park or a national forest, or on land in the National Wildlife Refuge System, under a contract with the Secretary of the Interior or the Secretary of Agriculture; or

(4) Repealed

(5) any employee employed in the catching, taking, propagating, harvesting, cultivating, or farming of any kind of fish, shellfish, crustacea, sponges, seaweeds, or other aquatic forms of animal and vegetable life, or in the first processing, canning or packing such marine products at sea as an incident to, or in conjunction with, such fishing operations, including the going to and returning from work and loading and unloading when performed by any such employee; or

(6) any employee employed in agriculture (A) if such employee is employed by an employer who did not, during any calendar quarter during the preceding calendar year, use more than five hundred man-days of agricultural labor, (B) if such employee is the parent, spouse, child, or other member of his employer's immediate family, (C) if such employee (i) is employed as a hand harvest laborer and is paid on a piece rate basis in an operation which has been, and is customarily and generally recognized as having been, paid on a piece rate basis in the region of employment, (ii) commutes daily from his permanent residence to the farm on which he is so employed, and (iii) has been employed in agriculture less than thirteen weeks during the pre-

ceding calendar year, (D) if such employee (other than an employee described in clause (C) of this subsection) (i) is sixteen years of age or under and is employed as a hand harvest laborer, is paid on a piece rate basis in an operation which has been, and is customarily and generally recognized as having been, paid on a piece rate basis in the region of employment, (ii) is employed on the same farm as his parent or person standing in the place of his parent, and (iii) is paid at the same piece rate as employees over age sixteen are paid on the same farm, or (E) if such employee is principally engaged in the range production of livestock; or

(7) any employee to the extent that such employee is exempted by regulations, order, or certificate of the Secretary issued under section 214 of this title; or

(8) any employee employed in connection with the publication of any weekly, semiweekly, or daily newspaper with a circulation of less than four thousand the major part of which circulation is within the county where published or counties contiguous thereto; or

(9) Repealed

(10) any switchboard operator employed by an independently owned public telephone company which has not more than seven hundred and fifty stations; or

(11) Repealed

(12) any employee employed as a seaman on a vessel other than an American vessel; or

(13), (14) Repealed

(15) any employee employed on a casual basis in domestic service employment to provide babysitting services or any employee employed in domestic service employment to provide companionship services for individuals who (because of age or infirmity) are unable to care for themselves (as such terms are defined and delimited by regulations of the Secretary); or

(16) a criminal investigator who is paid availability pay under section 5545a of Title 5.

(17) any employee who is a computer systems analyst, computer programmer, software engineer, or other similarly skilled worker, whose primary duty is —

(A) the application of systems analysis techniques and procedures, including consulting with users, to determine hardware, software, or system functional specifications;

(B) the design, development, documentation, analysis, creation, testing, or modification of computer systems or programs, including prototypes, based on and related to user or system design specifications;

(C) the design, documentation, testing, creation, or modification of computer programs related to machine operating systems; or

(D) a combination of duties described in subparagraphs (A), (B), and (C) the performance of which requires the same level of skills, and

who, in the case of an employee who is compensated on an hourly basis, is compensated at a rate of not less than $27.63 an hour.

(b) Maximum hour requirements

The provisions of section 207 of this title shall not apply with respect to —

(1) any employee with respect to whom the Secretary of Transportation has power to establish qualifications and maximum hours of service pursuant to the provisions of section 31502 of Title 49; or

(2) any employee of an employer engaged in the operation of a rail carrier subject to part A of subtitle IV of Title 49; or

(3) any employee of a carrier by air subject to the provisions of title II of the Railway Labor Act (45 U.S.C. §181 et seq.); or

(4) Repealed

(5) any individual employed as an outside buyer of poultry, eggs, cream, or milk, in their raw or natural state; or

(6) any employee employed as a seaman; or

(7) Repealed

(8) Repealed

(9) any employee employed as an announcer, news editor, or chief engineer by a radio or television station the major studio of which is located (A) in a city or town of one hundred thousand population or less, according to the latest available

decennial census figures as compiled by the Bureau of the Census, except where such city or town is part of a standard metropolitan statistical area, as defined and designated by the Office of Management and Budget, which has a total population in excess of one hundred thousand, or (B) in a city or town of twenty-five thousand population or less, which is part of such an area but is at least 40 airline miles from the principal city in such area; or

(10)(A) any salesman, partsman, or mechanic primarily engaged in selling or servicing automobiles, trucks, or farm implements, if he is employed by a nonmanufacturing establishment primarily engaged in the business of selling such vehicles or implements to ultimate purchasers; or

(B) any salesman primarily engaged in selling trailers, boats, or aircraft, if he is employed by a nonmanufacturing establishment primarily engaged in the business of selling trailers, boats, or aircraft to ultimate purchasers; or

(11) any employee employed as a driver or driver's helper making local deliveries, who is compensated for such employment on the basis of trip rates, or other delivery payment plan, if the Secretary shall find that such plan has the general purpose and effect of reducing hours worked by such employees to, or below, the maximum workweek applicable to them under section 207(a) of this title; or

(12) any employee employed in agriculture or in connection with the operation or maintenance of ditches, canals, reservoirs, or waterways, not owned or operated for profit, or operated on a sharecrop basis, and which are used exclusively for supply and storing of water at least 90 percent of which was ultimately delivered for agricultural purposes during the preceding calendar year; or

(13) any employee with respect to his employment in agriculture by a farmer, notwithstanding other employment of such employee in connection with livestock auction operations in which such farmer is engaged as an adjunct to the raising of livestock, either on his own account or in conjunction with other farmers, if such employee (A) is primarily employed during his workweek in agriculture by such farmer, and (B) is paid for his employment in connection with such livestock

auction operations at a wage rate not less than that prescribed by section 206(a)(1) of this title; or

(14) any employee employed within the area of production (as defined by the Secretary) by an establishment commonly recognized as a country elevator, including such an establishment which sells products and services used in the operation of a farm, if no more than five employees are employed in the establishment in such operations; or

(15) any employee engaged in the processing of maple sap into sugar (other than refined sugar) or syrup; or

(16) any employee engaged (A) in the transportation and preparation for transportation of fruits or vegetables, whether or not performed by the farmer, from the farm to a place of first processing or first marketing within the same State, or (B) in transportation, whether or not performed by the farmer, between the farm and any point within the same State of persons employed or to be employed in the harvesting of fruits or vegetables; or

(17) any driver employed by an employer engaged in the business of operating taxicabs; or

(18), (19) Repealed

(20) any employee of a public agency who in any workweek is employed in fire protection activities or any employee of a public agency who in any workweek is employed in law enforcement activities (including security personnel in correctional institutions), if the public agency employs during the workweek less than 5 employees in fire protection or law enforcement activities, as the case may be; or

(21) any employee who is employed in domestic service in a household and who resides in such household; or

(22) Repealed

(23) Repealed

(24) any employee who is employed with his spouse by a nonprofit educational institution to serve as the parents of children —

(A) who are orphans or one of whose natural parents is deceased, or

(B) who are enrolled in such institution and reside in residential facilities of the institution, while such children are in residence at such institution, if such employee and his spouse reside in such facilities, receive, without cost, board and lodging from such institution, and are together compensated, on a cash basis, at an annual rate of not less than $10,000; or

(25), (26) Repealed

(27) any employee employed by an establishment which is a motion picture theater; or

(28) any employee employed in planting or tending trees, cruising, surveying, or felling timber, or in preparing or transporting logs or other forestry products to the mill, processing plant, railroad, or other transportation terminal, if the number of employees employed by his employer in such forestry or lumbering operations does not exceed eight;

(29) any employee of an amusement or recreational establishment located in a national park or national forest or on land in the National Wildlife Refuge System if such employee (A) is an employee of a private entity engaged in providing services or facilities in a national park or national forest, or on land in the National Wildlife Refuge System, under a contract with the Secretary of the Interior or the Secretary of Agriculture, and (B) receives compensation for employment in excess of fifty-six hours in any workweek at a rate not less than one and one-half times the regular rate at which he is employed; or

(30) a criminal investigator who is paid availability pay under section 5545a of Title 5.

(c) Child labor requirements

(1) Except as provided in paragraph (2) or (4), the provisions of section 212 of this title relating to child labor shall not apply to any employee employed in agriculture outside of school hours for the school district where such employee is living while he is so employed, if such employee —

(A) is less than twelve years of age and (i) is employed by his parent, or by a person standing in the place of his parent, on a farm owned or operated by such parent or person, or (ii) is employed, with the consent of his parent or

person standing in the place of his parent, on a farm, none of the employees of which are (because of subsection (a)(6)(A) of this section) required to be paid at the wage rate prescribed by section 206(a)(5) of this title,

(B) is twelve years or thirteen years of age and (i) such employment is with the consent of his parent or person standing in the place of his parent, or (ii) his parent or such person is employed on the same farm as such employee, or

(C) is fourteen years of age or older.

(2) The provisions of section 212 of this title relating to child labor shall apply to an employee below the age of sixteen employed in agriculture in an occupation that the Secretary of Labor finds and declares to be particularly hazardous for the employment of children below the age of sixteen, except where such employee is employed by his parent or by a person standing in the place of his parent on a farm owned or operated by such parent or person.

(3) The provisions of section 212 of this title relating to child labor shall not apply to any child employed as an actor or performer in motion pictures or theatrical productions, or in radio or television productions.

(4)(A) An employer or group of employers may apply to the Secretary for a waiver of the application of section 212 of this title to the employment for not more than eight weeks in any calendar year of individuals who are less than twelve years of age, but not less than ten years of age, as hand harvest laborers in an agricultural operation which has been, and is customarily and generally recognized as being, paid on a piece rate basis in the region in which such individuals would be employed. The Secretary may not grant such a waiver unless he finds, based on objective data submitted by the applicant, that —

(i) the crop to be harvested is one with a particularly short harvesting season and the application of section 212 of this title would cause severe economic disruption in the industry of the employer or group of employers applying for the waiver;

(ii) the employment of the individuals to whom the waiver would apply would not be deleterious to their health or well-being;

(iii) the level and type of pesticides and other chemicals used would not have an adverse effect on the health or well-being of the individuals to whom the waiver would apply;

(iv) individuals age twelve and above are not available for such employment; and

(v) the industry of such employer or group of employers has traditionally and substantially employed individuals under twelve years of age without displacing substantial job opportunities for individuals over sixteen years of age.

(B) Any waiver granted by the Secretary under subparagraph (A) shall require that —

(i) the individuals employed under such waiver be employed outside of school hours for the school district where they are living while so employed;

(ii) such individuals while so employed commute daily from their permanent residence to the farm on which they are so employed; and

(iii) such individuals be employed under such waiver (I) for not more than eight weeks between June 1 and October 15 of any calendar year, and (II) in accordance with such other terms and conditions as the Secretary shall prescribe for such individuals' protection.

(5)(A) In the administration and enforcement of the child labor provisions of this chapter, employees who are 16 and 17 years of age shall be permitted to load materials into, but not operate or unload materials from, scrap paper balers and paper box compactors —

(i) that are safe for 16- and 17-year-old employees loading the scrap paper balers or paper box compactors; and

(ii) that cannot be operated while being loaded.

(B) For purposes of subparagraph (A), scrap paper balers and paper box compactors shall be considered safe for 16- or 17-year-old employees to load only if —

(i)(I) the scrap paper balers and paper box compactors meet the American National

Standards Institute's Standard ANSI Z245.5-1990 for scrap paper balers and Standard ANSI Z245.2-1992 for paper box compactors; or

(II) the scrap paper balers and paper box compactors meet an applicable standard that is adopted by the American National Standards Institute after August 6, 1996, and that is certified by the Secretary to be at least as protective of the safety of minors as the standard described in subclause (I);

(ii) the scrap paper balers and paper box compactors include an on-off switch incorporating a key-lock or other system and the control of the system is maintained in the custody of employees who are 18 years of age or older;

(iii) the on-off switch of the scrap paper balers and paper box compactors is maintained in an off position when the scrap paper balers and paper box compactors are not in operation; and

(iv) the employer of 16- and 17-year-old employees provides notice, and posts a notice, on the scrap paper balers and paper box compactors stating that —

(I) the scrap paper balers and paper box compactors meet the applicable standard described in clause (i);

(II) 16- and 17-year-old employees may only load the scrap paper balers and paper box compactors; and

(III) any employee under the age of 18 may not operate or unload the scrap paper balers and paper box compactors.

The Secretary shall publish in the Federal Register a standard that is adopted by the American National Standards Institute for scrap paper balers or paper box compactors and certified by the Secretary to be protective of the safety of minors under clause (i)(II).

(C)(i) Employers shall prepare and submit to the Secretary reports —

(I) on any injury to an employee under the age of 18 that requires medical treatment (other than first aid) resulting from the employee's contact with a scrap paper baler or paper box compactor during the loading, operation, or unloading of the baler or compactor; and

(II) on any fatality of an employee under the age of 18 resulting from the employee's contact with a scrap paper baler or paper box compactor during the loading, operation, or unloading of the baler or compactor.

(ii) The reports described in clause (i) shall be used by the Secretary to determine whether or not the implementation of subparagraph (A) has had any effect on the safety of children.

(iii) The reports described in clause (i) shall provide —

(I) the name, telephone number, and address of the employer and the address of the place of employment where the incident occurred;

(II) the name, telephone number, and address of the employee who suffered an injury or death as a result of the incident;

(III) the date of the incident;

(IV) a description of the injury and a narrative describing how the incident occurred; and

(V) the name of the manufacturer and the model number of the scrap paper baler or paper box compactor involved in the incident.

(iv) The reports described in clause (i) shall be submitted to the Secretary promptly, but not later than 10 days after the date on which an incident relating to an injury or death occurred.

(v) The Secretary may not rely solely on the reports described in clause (i) as the basis for making a determination that any of the employers described in clause (i) has violated a provision of section 212 of this title relating to oppressive child labor or a regulation or order issued pursuant to section 212 of this title. The Secretary shall, prior to making such a determination, conduct an investigation and inspection in accordance with section 212(b) of this title.

(vi) The reporting requirements of this subparagraph shall expire 2 years after August 6, 1996.

(6) In the administration and enforcement of the child labor provisions of this Act, employees who are under 17 years of age may not drive automobiles or trucks on public roadways. Employees who are 17 years of age may drive automobiles or trucks on public roadways only if —

(A) such driving is restricted to daylight hours;

(B) the employee holds a State license valid for the type of driving involved in the job performed and has no records of any moving violation at the time of hire;

(C) the employee has successfully completed a State approved driver education course;

(D) the automobile or truck is equipped with a seat belt for the driver and any passengers and the employee's employer has instructed the employee that the seat belts must be used when driving the automobile or truck;

(E) the automobile or truck does not exceed 6,000 pounds of gross vehicle weight;

(F) such driving does not involve—

(i) the towing of vehicles;

(ii) route deliveries or route sales;

(iii) the transportation for hire of property, goods, or passengers;

(iv) urgent, time-sensitive deliveries;

(v) more than two trips away from the primary place of employment in any single day for the purpose of delivering goods of the employee's employer to a customer (other than urgent, time-sensitive deliveries);

(vi) more than two trips away from the primary place of employment in any single day for the purpose of transporting passengers (other than employees of the employer);

(vii) transporting more than three passengers (including employees of the employer); or

(viii) driving beyond a 30 mile radius from the employee's place of employment; and

(G) such driving is only occasional and incidental to the employee's employment.

For purposes of subparagraph (G), the term "occasional and incidental" is no more than one-third of an employee's worktime in any workday and no more than 20 percent of an employee's worktime in any workweek.

(d) Delivery of newspapers and wreathmaking

The provisions of sections 206, 207, and 212 of this title shall not apply with respect to any employee engaged in the delivery of newspapers to the consumer or to any homeworker engaged in the making of wreaths composed principally of natural holly, pine, cedar, or other evergreens (including the harvesting of the evergreens or other forest products used in making such wreaths).

(e) Maximum hour requirements and minimum wage employees

The provisions of section 207 of this title shall not apply with respect to employees for whom the Secretary of Labor is authorized to establish minimum wage rates as provided in section 206(a)(3) of this title, except with respect to employees for whom such rates are in effect; and with respect to such employees the Secretary may make rules and regulations providing reasonable limitations and allowing reasonable variations, tolerances, and exemptions to and from any or all of the provisions of section 207 of this title if he shall find, after a public hearing on the matter, and taking into account the factors set forth in section 206(a)(3) of this title, that economic conditions warrant such action.

(f) Employment in foreign countries and certain United States territories

The provisions of sections 206, 207, 211, and 212 of this title shall not apply with respect to any employee whose services during the workweek are performed in a workplace within a foreign country or within territory under the jurisdiction of the United States other than the following: a State of the United States; the District of Columbia; Puerto Rico; the Virgin Islands; outer Continental Shelf lands defined in the Outer Continental Shelf Lands Act (ch. 345, 67 Stat. 462) (43 U.S.C. §1331 et seq.); American Samoa; Guam; Wake Island; Eniwetok Atoll; Kwajalein Atoll; and Johnston Island.

(g) Certain employment in retail or service establishments, agriculture

The exemption from section 206 of this title provided by paragraph (6) of subsection (a) of this sec-

tion shall not apply with respect to any employee employed by an establishment (1) which controls, is controlled by, or is under common control with, another establishment the activities of which are not related for a common business purpose to, but materially support the activities of the establishment employing such employee; and (2) whose annual gross volume of sales made or business done, when combined with the annual gross volume of sales made or business done by each establishment which controls, is controlled by, or is under common control with, the establishment employing such employee, exceeds $10,000,000 (exclusive of excise taxes at the retail level which are separately stated).

(h) Maximum hour requirement: fourteen workweek limitation

The provisions of section 207 of this title shall not apply for a period or periods of not more than fourteen workweeks in the aggregate in any calendar year to any employee who —

(1) is employed by such employer —

(A) exclusively to provide services necessary and incidental to the ginning of cotton in an establishment primarily engaged in the ginning of cotton;

(B) exclusively to provide services necessary and incidental to the receiving, handling, and storing of raw cotton and the compressing of raw cotton when performed at a cotton warehouse or compress-warehouse facility, other than one operated in conjunction with a cotton mill, primarily engaged in storing and compressing;

(C) exclusively to provide services necessary and incidental to the receiving, handling, storing, and processing of cottonseed in an establishment primarily engaged in the receiving, handling, storing, and processing of cottonseed; or

(D) exclusively to provide services necessary and incidental to the processing of sugar cane or sugar beets in an establishment primarily engaged in the processing of sugar cane or sugar beets; and

(2) receives for —

(A) such employment by such employer which is in excess of ten hours in any workday, and

(B) such employment by such employer which is in excess of forty-eight hours in any workweek,

compensation at a rate not less than one and one-half times the regular rate at which he is employed.

Any employer who receives an exemption under this subsection shall not be eligible for any other exemption under this section or section 207 of this title.

(i) Cotton ginning

The provisions of section 207 of this title shall not apply for a period or periods of not more than fourteen workweeks in the aggregate in any period of fifty-two consecutive weeks to any employee who —

(1) is engaged in the ginning of cotton for market in any place of employment located in a county where cotton is grown in commercial quantities; and

(2) receives for any such employment during such workweeks —

(A) in excess of ten hours in any workday, and

(B) in excess of forty-eight hours in any workweek,

compensation at a rate not less than one and one-half times the regular rate at which he is employed. No week included in any fifty-two week period for purposes of the preceding sentence may be included for such purposes in any other fifty-two week period.

(j) Processing of sugar beets, sugar beet molasses, or sugar cane

The provisions of section 207 of this title shall not apply for a period or periods of not more than fourteen workweeks in the aggregate in any period of fifty-two consecutive weeks to any employee who —

(1) is engaged in the processing of sugar beets, sugar beet molasses, or sugar cane into sugar (other than refined sugar) or syrup; and

(2) receives for any such employment during such workweeks —

(A) in excess of ten hours in any workday, and

(B) in excess of forty-eight hours in any workweek,

compensation at a rate not less than one and one-half times the regular rate at which he is employed. No week included in any fifty-two week period for purposes of the preceding sentence may be included for such purposes in any other fifty-two week period.

Sec. 214. Employment under special certificates

(a) Learners, apprentices, messengers

The Secretary, to the extent necessary in order to prevent curtailment of opportunities for employment, shall by regulations or by orders provide for the employment of learners, of apprentices, and of messengers employed primarily in delivering letters and messages, under special certificates issued pursuant to regulations of the Secretary, at such wages lower than the minimum wage applicable under section 206 of this title and subject to such limitations as to time, number, proportion, and length of service as the Secretary shall prescribe.

(b) Students

(1)(A) The Secretary, to the extent necessary in order to prevent curtailment of opportunities for employment, shall by special certificate issued under a regulation or order provide, in accordance with subparagraph (B), for the employment, at a wage rate not less than 85 per centum of the otherwise applicable wage rate in effect under section 206 of this title or not less than $1.60 an hour, whichever is the higher, of full-time students (regardless of age but in compliance with applicable child labor laws) in retail or service establishments.

(B) Except as provided in paragraph (4)(B), during any month in which full-time students are to be employed in any retail or service establishment under certificates issued under this subsection the proportion of student hours of employment to the total hours of employment of all employees in such establishment may not exceed —

(i) in the case of a retail or service establishment whose employees (other than employees engaged in commerce or in the production of goods for commerce) were covered by this chapter before the effective date of the Fair Labor Standards Amendments of 1974 —

(I) the proportion of student hours of employment to the total hours of employment of all employees in such establishment for the corresponding month of the immediately preceding twelve-month period,

(II) the maximum proportion for any corresponding month of student hours of employment to the total hours of employment of all employees in such establishment applicable to the issuance of certificates under this section at any time before the effective date of the Fair Labor Standards Amendments of 1974 for the employment of students by such employer, or

(III) a proportion equal to one-tenth of the total hours of employment of all employees in such establishment,

whichever is greater;

(ii) in the case of retail or service establishment whose employees (other than employees engaged in commerce or in the production of goods for commerce) are covered for the first time on or after the effective date of the Fair Labor Standards Amendments of 1974 —

(I) the proportion of hours of employment of students in such establishment to the total hours of employment of all employees in such establishment for the corresponding month of the twelve-month period immediately prior to the effective date of such Amendments,

(II) the proportion of student hours of employment to the total hours of employment of all employees in such establishment for the corresponding month of the immediately preceding twelve-month period, or

(III) a proportion equal to one-tenth of the total hours of employment of all employees in such establishment,

whichever is greater; or

(iii) in the case of a retail or service establishment for which records of student hours worked are not available, the proportion of student hours of employment to the total hours of employment of all employees based

on the practice during the immediately preceding twelve-month period in (I) similar establishments of the same employer in the same general metropolitan area in which such establishment is located, (II) similar establishments of the same or nearby communities if such establishment is not in a metropolitan area, or (III) other establishments of the same general character operating in the community or the nearest comparable community.

For purpose of clauses (i), (ii), and (iii) of this subparagraph, the term "student hours of employment" means hours during which students are employed in a retail or service establishment under certificates issued under this subsection.

(2) The Secretary, to the extent necessary in order to prevent curtailment of opportunities for employment, shall by special certificate issued under a regulation or order provide for the employment, at a wage rate not less than 85 per centum of the wage rate in effect under section 206(a)(5) of this title or not less than $1.30 an hour, whichever is the higher, of full-time students (regardless of age but in compliance with applicable child labor laws) in any occupation in agriculture.

(3) The Secretary, to the extent necessary in order to prevent curtailment of opportunities for employment, shall by special certificate issued under a regulation or order provide for the employment by an institution of higher education, at a wage rate not less than 85 per centum of the otherwise applicable wage rate in effect under section 206 of this title or not less than $1.60 an hour, whichever is the higher, of full-time students (regardless of age but in compliance with applicable child labor laws) who are enrolled in such institution. The Secretary shall by regulation prescribe standards and requirements to insure that this paragraph will not create a substantial probability of reducing the full-time employment opportunities of persons other than those to whom the minimum wage rate authorized by this paragraph is applicable.

(4)(A) A special certificate issued under paragraph (1), (2), or (3) shall provide that the student or students for whom it is issued shall, except during vacation periods, be employed on a part-time basis and not in excess of twenty hours in any workweek.

(B) If the issuance of a special certificate under paragraph (1) or (2) for an employer will cause the number of students employed by such employer under special certificates issued under this subsection to exceed six, the Secretary may not issue such a special certificate for the employment of a student by such employer unless the Secretary finds employment of such student will not create a substantial probability of reducing the full-time employment opportunities of persons other than those employed under special certificates issued under this subsection. If the issuance of a special certificate under paragraph (1) or (2) for an employer will not cause the number of students employed by such employer under special certificates issued under this subsection to exceed six —

   (i) the Secretary may issue a special certificate under paragraph (1) or (2) for the employment of a student by such employer if such employer certifies to the Secretary that the employment of such student will not reduce the full-time employment opportunities of persons other than those employed under special certificates issued under this subsection, and

   (ii) in the case of an employer which is a retail or service establishment, subparagraph (B) of paragraph (1) shall not apply with respect to the issuance of special certificates for such employer under such paragraph.

The requirement of this subparagraph shall not apply in the case of the issuance of special certificates under paragraph (3) for the employment of full-time students by institutions of higher education; except that if the Secretary determines that an institution of higher education is employing students under certificates issued under paragraph (3) but in violation of the requirements of that paragraph or of regulations issued thereunder, the requirements of this subparagraph shall apply with respect to the issuance of special certificates under paragraph (3) for the employment of students by such institution.

(C) No special certificate may be issued under this subsection unless the employer for whom the certificate is to be issued provides evidence satisfactory to the Secretary of the student status of the employees to be employed under such special certificate.

(D) To minimize paperwork for, and to encourage, small businesses to employ students under special certificates issued under paragraphs (1) and (2), the Secretary shall, by regulation or order, prescribe a simplified application form to be used by employers in applying for such a certificate for the employment of not more than six full-time students. Such an application shall require only —

   (i) a listing of the name, address, and business of the applicant employer,

   (ii) a listing of the date the applicant began business, and

   (iii) the certification that the employment of such full-time students will not reduce the full-time employment opportunities of persons other than persons employed under special certificates.

(c) Handicapped workers

(1) The Secretary, to the extent necessary to prevent curtailment of opportunities for employment, shall by regulation or order provide for the employment, under special certificates, of individuals (including individuals employed in agriculture) whose earning or productive capacity is impaired by age, physical or mental deficiency, or injury, at wages which are —

   (A) lower than the minimum wage applicable under section 206 of this title,

   (B) commensurate with those paid to non-handicapped workers, employed in the vicinity in which the individuals under the certificates are employed, for essentially the same type, quality, and quantity of work, and

   (C) related to the individual's productivity.

(2) The Secretary shall not issue a certificate under paragraph (1) unless the employer provides written assurances to the Secretary that —

   (A) in the case of individuals paid on an hourly rate basis, wages paid in accordance with paragraph (1) will be reviewed by the employer at periodic intervals at least once every six months, and

(B) wages paid in accordance with paragraph (1) will be adjusted by the employer at periodic intervals, at least once each year, to reflect changes in the prevailing wage paid to experienced nonhandicapped individuals employed in the locality for essentially the same type of work.

(3) Notwithstanding paragraph (1), no employer shall be permitted to reduce the hourly wage rate prescribed by certificate under this subsection in effect on June 1, 1986, of any handicapped individual for a period of two years from such date without prior authorization of the Secretary.

(4) Nothing in this subsection shall be construed to prohibit an employer from maintaining or establishing work activities centers to provide therapeutic activities for handicapped clients.

(5)(A) Notwithstanding any other provision of this subsection, any employee receiving a special minimum wage at a rate specified pursuant to this subsection or the parent or guardian of such an employee may petition the Secretary to obtain a review of such special minimum wage rate. An employee or the employee's parent or guardian may file such a petition for and in behalf of the employee or in behalf of the employee and other employees similarly situated. No employee may be a party to any such action unless the employee or the employee's parent or guardian gives consent in writing to become such a party and such consent is filed with the Secretary.

(B) Upon receipt of a petition filed in accordance with subparagraph (A), the Secretary within ten days shall assign the petition to an administrative law judge appointed pursuant to section 3105 of Title 5. The administrative law judge shall conduct a hearing on the record in accordance with section 554 of Title 5 with respect to such petition within thirty days after assignment.

(C) In any such proceeding, the employer shall have the burden of demonstrating that the special minimum wage rate is justified as necessary in order to prevent curtailment of opportunities for employment.

(D) In determining whether any special minimum wage rate is justified pursuant to subparagraph (C), the administrative law judge shall consider —

(i) the productivity of the employee or employees identified in the petition and the conditions under which such productivity was measured; and

(ii) the productivity of other employees performing work of essentially the same type and quality for other employers in the same vicinity.

(E) The administrative law judge shall issue a decision within thirty days after the hearing provided for in subparagraph (B). Such action shall be deemed to be a final agency action unless within thirty days the Secretary grants a request to review the decision of the administrative law judge. Either the petitioner or the employer may request review by the Secretary within fifteen days of the date of issuance of the decision by the administrative law judge.

(F) The Secretary, within thirty days after receiving a request for review, shall review the record and either adopt the decision of the administrative law judge or issue exceptions. The decision of the administrative law judge, together with any exceptions, shall be deemed to be a final agency action.

(G) A final agency action shall be subject to judicial review pursuant to chapter 7 of Title 5. An action seeking such review shall be brought within thirty days of a final agency action described in subparagraph (F).

(d) Employment by schools

The Secretary may by regulation or order provide that sections 206 and 207 of this title shall not apply with respect to the employment by any elementary or secondary school of its students if such employment constitutes, as determined under regulations prescribed by the Secretary, an integral part of the regular education program provided by such school and such employment is in accordance with applicable child labor laws.

Sec. 215. Prohibited acts; prima facie evidence

(a) After the expiration of one hundred and twenty days from June 25, 1938, it shall be unlawful for any person —

(1) to transport, offer for transportation, ship, deliver, or sell in commerce, or to ship, deliver, or sell with knowledge that shipment or delivery or sale thereof in commerce is intended, any goods in the production of which any employee was employed in violation of section 206 or section 207 of this title, or in violation of any regulation or order of the Secretary issued under section 214 of this title; except that no provision of this chapter shall impose any liability upon any common carrier for the transportation in commerce in the regular course of its business of any goods not produced by such common carrier, and no provision of this chapter shall excuse any common carrier from its obligation to accept any goods for transportation; and except that any such transportation, offer, shipment, delivery, or sale of such goods by a purchaser who acquired them in good faith in reliance on written assurance from the producer that the goods were produced in compliance with the requirements of this chapter, and who acquired such goods for value without notice of any such violation, shall not be deemed unlawful;

(2) to violate any of the provisions of section 206 or section 207 of this title, or any of the provisions of any regulation or order of the Secretary issued under section 214 of this title;

(3) to discharge or in any other manner discriminate against any employee because such employee has filed any complaint or instituted or caused to be instituted any proceeding under or related to this chapter, or has testified or is about to testify in any such proceeding, or has served or is about to serve on an industry committee;

(4) to violate any of the provisions of section 212 of this title;

(5) to violate any of the provisions of section 211(c) of this title, or any regulation or order made or continued in effect under the provisions of section 211(d) of this title, or to make any statement, report, or record filed or kept pursuant to the provisions of such section or of any regulation or order thereunder, knowing such statement, report, or record to be false in a material respect.

(b) For the purposes of subsection (a)(1) of this section proof that any employee was employed in any place of employment where goods shipped or sold in commerce were produced, within ninety days prior to the removal of the goods from such place of employment, shall be prima facie evidence that such employee was engaged in the production of such goods.

Sec. 216. Penalties

(a) Fines and imprisonment

Any person who willfully violates any of the provisions of section 215 of this title shall upon conviction thereof be subject to a fine of not more than $10,000, or to imprisonment for not more than six months, or both. No person shall be imprisoned under this subsection except for an offense committed after the conviction of such person for a prior offense under this subsection.

(b) Damages; right of action; attorney's fees and costs; termination of right of action

Any employer who violates the provisions of section 206 or section 207 of this title shall be liable to the employee or employees affected in the amount of their unpaid minimum wages, or their unpaid overtime compensation, as the case may be, and in an additional equal amount as liquidated damages. Any employer who violates the provisions of section 215(a)(3) of this title shall be liable for such legal or equitable relief as may be appropriate to effectuate the purposes of section 215(a)(3) of this title, including without limitation employment, reinstatement, promotion, and the payment of wages lost and an additional equal amount as liquidated damages. An action to recover the liability prescribed in either of the preceding sentences may be maintained against any employer (including a public agency) in any Federal or State court of competent jurisdiction by any one or more employees for and in behalf of himself or themselves and other employees similarly situated. No employee shall be a party plaintiff to any such action unless he gives his consent in writing to become such a party and such consent is filed in the court in which such action is brought. The court in such action shall, in addition to any judgment awarded to the plaintiff or plaintiffs, allow a reasonable attorney's fee to be paid by the defendant, and costs of the action. The right provided by this subsection to bring an action by or on behalf of any employee, and the right of any employee to become a party plaintiff to any such action, shall terminate upon the filing of a complaint by the Secretary of Labor in an action under section 217 of this title in which (1) restraint is sought of any further delay in the payment of unpaid minimum wages, or the amount of unpaid overtime compensation, as the case may be, owing to such employee under section 206 or section 207 of this title by an employer liable therefor under the provisions of this subsection or (2) legal or equitable relief is sought as a result of alleged violations of section 215(a)(3) of this title.

(c) Payment of wages and compensation; waiver of claims; actions by the Secretary; limitation of actions

The Secretary is authorized to supervise the payment of the unpaid minimum wages or the unpaid overtime compensation owing to any employee or employees under section 206 or section 207 of this title, and the agreement of any employee to accept such payment shall upon payment in full constitute a waiver by such employee of any right he may have under subsection (b) of this section to such unpaid minimum wages or unpaid overtime compensation and an additional equal amount as liquidated damages. The Secretary may bring an action in any court of competent jurisdiction to recover the amount of unpaid minimum wages or overtime compensation and an equal amount as liquidated damages. The right provided by subsection (b) of this section to bring an action by or on behalf of any employee to recover the liability specified in the first sentence of such subsection and of any employee to become a party plaintiff to any such action shall terminate upon the filing of a complaint by the Secretary in an action under this subsection in which a recovery is sought of unpaid minimum wages or unpaid overtime compensation under sections 206 and 207 of this title or liquidated or other damages provided by this subsection owing to such employee by an employer liable under the provisions of subsection (b) of this section, unless such action is dismissed without prejudice on motion of the Secretary. Any sums thus recovered by the Secretary of Labor on behalf of an employee pursuant to this subsection shall be held in a special deposit account and shall be paid, on order of the Secretary of Labor,

directly to the employee or employees affected. Any such sums not paid to an employee because of inability to do so within a period of three years shall be covered into the Treasury of the United States as miscellaneous receipts. In determining when an action is commenced by the Secretary of Labor under this subsection for the purposes of the statutes of limitations provided in section 255(a) of this title, it shall be considered to be commenced in the case of any individual claimant on the date when the complaint is filed if he is specifically named as a party plaintiff in the complaint, or if his name did not so appear, on the subsequent date on which his name is added as a party plaintiff in such action.

(d) Savings provisions

In any action or proceeding commenced prior to, on, or after August 8, 1956, no employer shall be subject to any liability or punishment under this chapter or the Portal-to-Portal Act of 1947 (29 U.S.C. §251 et seq.) on account of his failure to comply with any provision or provisions of this chapter or such Act (1) with respect to work heretofore or hereafter performed in a workplace to which the exemption in section 213(f) of this title is applicable, (2) with respect to work performed in Guam, the Canal Zone or Wake Island before the effective date of this amendment of subsection (d), or (3) with respect to work performed in a possession named in section 206(a)(3) of this title at any time prior to the establishment by the Secretary, as provided therein, of a minimum wage rate applicable to such work.

(e) Civil penalties for child labor violations

Any person who violates the provisions of section 212 or section 213(c)(5) of this title, relating to child labor, or any regulation issued under section 212 or section 213(c)(5) of this title, shall be subject to a civil penalty of not to exceed $10,000 for each employee who was the subject of such a violation. Any person who repeatedly or willfully violates section 206 or 207 of this title shall be subject to a civil penalty of not to exceed $1,000 for each such violation. In determining the amount of any penalty under this subsection, the appropriateness of such penalty to the size of the business of the person charged and the gravity of the violation shall be considered. The amount of any penalty under this subsection, when finally determined, may be —

(1) deducted from any sums owing by the United States to the person charged;

(2) recovered in a civil action brought by the Secretary in any court of competent jurisdiction, in which litigation the Secretary shall be represented by the Solicitor of Labor; or

(3) ordered by the court, in an action brought for a violation of section 215(a)(4) of this title or a repeated or willful violation of section 215(a)(2) of this title, to be paid to the Secretary.

Any administrative determination by the Secretary of the amount of any penalty under this subsection shall be final, unless within fifteen days after receipt of notice thereof by certified mail the person charged with the violation takes exception to the determination that the violations for which the penalty is imposed occurred, in which event final determination of the penalty shall be made in an administrative proceeding after opportunity for hearing in accordance with section 554 of Title 5, and regulations to be promulgated by the Secretary. Except for civil penalties collected for violations of section 212 of this title, sums collected as penalties pursuant to this section shall be applied toward reimbursement of the costs of determining the violations and assessing and collecting such penalties, in accordance with the provisions of section 9a of this title. Civil penalties collected for violations of section 212 of this title shall be deposited in the general fund of the Treasury.

Sec. 216a. Repealed

Sec. 216b. Liability for overtime work performed prior to July 20, 1949

No employer shall be subject to any liability or punishment under this chapter (in any action or proceeding commenced prior to or on or after January 24, 1950), on account of the failure of said employer to pay an employee compensation for any period of overtime work performed prior to July 20, 1949, if the compensation paid prior to July 20, 1949, for such work was at least equal to the compensation which would have been payable for such work had subsections (d)(6), (7) and (g) of section 207 of this title been in effect at the time of such payment.

Sec. 217. Injunction proceedings

The district courts, together with the United States District Court for the District of the Canal Zone, the District Court of the Virgin Islands, and the District Court of Guam shall have jurisdiction, for cause shown, to restrain violations of section 215 of this title, including in the case of violations of section 215(a)(2) of this title the restraint of any withholding of payment of minimum wages or overtime compensation found by the court to be due to employees under this chapter (except sums which employees are barred from recovering, at the time of the commencement of the action to restrain the violations, by virtue of the provisions of section 255 of this title).

Sec. 218. Relation to other laws

(a) No provision of this chapter or of any order thereunder shall excuse noncompliance with any Federal or State law or municipal ordinance establishing a minimum wage higher than the minimum wage established under this chapter or a maximum work week lower than the maximum workweek established under this chapter, and no provision of this chapter relating to the employment of child labor shall justify noncompliance with any Federal or State law or municipal ordinance establishing a higher standard than the standard established under this chapter. No provision of this chapter shall justify any employer in reducing a wage paid by him which is in excess of the applicable minimum wage under this chapter, or justify any employer in increasing hours of employment maintained by him which are shorter than the maximum hours applicable under this chapter.

(b) Notwithstanding any other provision of this chapter (other than section 213(f) of this title) or any other law —

(1) any Federal employee in the Canal Zone engaged in employment of the kind described in section 5102(c)(7) of Title 5, or

(2) any employee employed in a nonappropriated fund instrumentality under the jurisdiction of the Armed Forces,

shall have his basic compensation fixed or adjusted at a wage rate that is not less than the appropriate wage rate provided for in section 206(a)(1) of this title (except that the wage rate provided for in section 206(b) of this title shall apply to any employee who performed services during the workweek in a work place within the Canal Zone), and shall have his overtime compensation set at an hourly rate not less than the overtime rate provided for in section 207(a)(1) of this title.

Sec. 219. Separability

If any provision of this chapter or the application of such provision to any person or circumstance is held invalid, the remainder of this chapter and the application of such provision to other persons or circumstances shall not be affected thereby.

Labor-Management Reporting and Disclosure Act (Landrum-Griffin Act)

U.S. Code, Title 29, Sections 401 to 531

SUBCHAPTER I - GENERAL PROVISIONS

Sec.

401. Congressional declaration of findings, purposes, and policy.

402. Definitions.

SUBCHAPTER II - BILL OF RIGHTS OF MEMBERS OF LABOR ORGANIZATIONS

411. Bill of rights; constitution and bylaws of labor organizations.

412. Civil action for infringement of rights; jurisdiction.

413. Retention of existing rights of members.

414. Right to copies of collective bargaining agreements.

415. Information to members of provisions of chapter.

SUBCHAPTER III - REPORTING BY LABOR ORGANIZATIONS, OFFICERS AND EMPLOYEES OF LABOR ORGANIZATIONS, AND EMPLOYERS

431. Report of labor organizations.

432. Report of officers and employees of labor organizations.

433. Report of employers.

434. Exemption of attorney-client communications.

435. Reports and documents as public information.

436. Retention of records.

437. Time for making reports.

438. Rules and regulations; simplified reports.

439. Violations and penalties.

440. Civil action for enforcement by Secretary; jurisdiction.

441. Surety company reports; contents; waiver or modification of requirements respecting contents of reports.

SUBCHAPTER IV - TRUSTEESHIPS

461. Reports.

462. Purposes for establishment of trusteeship.

463. Unlawful acts relating to labor organization under trusteeship.

464. Civil action for enforcement.

465. Report to Congress.

466. Additional rights and remedies; exclusive jurisdiction of district court; res judicata.

SUBCHAPTER V - ELECTIONS

SUBCHAPTER VI - SAFEGUARDS FOR LABOR ORGANIZATIONS

SUBCHAPTER VII - MISCELLANEOUS PROVISIONS

LMRDA IN A NUTSHELL

Enacted: 1959

Purpose: To prohibit union corruption, regulate union election procedures, and protect individual rights within unions

Coverage: Unions which have membership from the private sector

Responsible agency: U.S. Department of Labor Office of Labor-Management Standards

SUBCHAPTER 1: GENERAL PROVISIONS

Sec. 401. Congressional declaration of findings, purposes, and policy

(a) Standards for labor-management relations

The Congress finds that, in the public interest, it continues to be the responsibility of the Federal Government to protect employees' rights to organize, choose their own representatives, bargain collectively, and otherwise engage in concerted activities for their mutual aid or protection; that the relations between employers and labor organizations and the millions of workers they represent have a substantial impact on the commerce of the Nation; and that in order to accomplish the objective of a free flow of commerce it is essential that labor organizations, employers, and their officials adhere to the highest standards of responsibility and ethical conduct in administering the affairs of their organizations, particularly as they affect labor-management relations.

(b) Protection of rights of employees and the public

The Congress further finds, from recent investigations in the labor and management fields, that there have been a number of instances of breach of trust, corruption, disregard of the rights of individual employees, and other failures to observe high standards of responsibility and ethical conduct which require further and supplementary legislation that will afford necessary protection of the rights and interests of employees and the public generally as they relate to the activities of labor organizations, employers, labor relations consultants, and their officers and representatives.

(c) Necessity to eliminate or prevent improper practices

The Congress, therefore, further finds and declares that the enactment of this chapter is necessary to eliminate or prevent improper practices on the part of labor organizations, employers, labor relations consultants, and their officers and representatives which distort and defeat the policies of the Labor Management Relations Act, 1947, as amended (29 U.S.C. §141 et seq.), and the Railway Labor Act, as amended (45 U.S.C. §151 et seq.), and have the tendency or necessary effect of burdening or obstructing commerce by (1) impairing the efficiency, safety, or operation of the instrumentalities of commerce; (2) occurring in the current of commerce; (3) materially affecting, restraining, or controlling the flow of raw materials or manufactured or processed goods into or from the channels of commerce, or the prices of such materials or goods in commerce; or (4) causing diminution of employment and wages in such volume as substantially to impair or disrupt the market for goods flowing into or from the channels of commerce.

Sec. 402. Definitions

For the purposes of this chapter —

(a) "Commerce" means trade, traffic, commerce,

transportation, transmission, or communication among the several States or between any State and any place outside thereof.

(b) "State" includes any State of the United States, the District of Columbia, Puerto Rico, the Virgin Islands, American Samoa, Guam, Wake Island, the Canal Zone, and Outer Continental Shelf lands defined in the Outer Continental Shelf Lands Act (43 U.S.C. §1331 et seq.).

(c) "Industry affecting commerce" means any activity, business, or industry in commerce or in which a labor dispute would hinder or obstruct commerce or the free flow of commerce and includes any activity or industry "affecting commerce" within the meaning of the Labor Management Relations Act, 1947, as amended (29 U.S.C. §141 et seq.), or the Railway Labor Act, as amended (45 U.S.C. §151 et seq.).

(d) "Person" includes one or more individuals, labor organizations, partnerships, associations, corporations, legal representatives, mutual companies, joint-stock companies, trusts, unincorporated organizations, trustees, trustees in cases under Title 11, or receivers.

(e) "Employer" means any employer or any group or association of employers engaged in an industry affecting commerce (1) which is, with respect to employees engaged in an industry affecting commerce, an employer within the meaning of any law of the United States relating to the employment of any employees or (2) which may deal with any labor organization concerning grievances, labor disputes, wages, rates of pay, hours of employment, or conditions of work, and includes any person acting directly or indirectly as an employer or as an agent of an employer in relation to an employee but does not include the United States or any corporation wholly owned by the Government of the United States or any State or political subdivision thereof.

(f) "Employee" means any individual employed by an employer, and includes any individual whose work has ceased as a consequence of, or in connection with, any current labor dispute or because of any unfair labor practice or because of exclusion or expulsion from a labor organization in any manner or for any reason inconsistent with the requirements of this chapter.

(g) "Labor dispute" includes any controversy concerning terms, tenure, or conditions of employment, or concerning the association or representation of persons in negotiating, fixing, maintaining, changing, or seeking to arrange terms or conditions of employment, regardless of whether the disputants stand in the proximate relation of employer and employee.

(h) "Trusteeship" means any receivership, trusteeship, or other method of supervision or control whereby a labor organization suspends the autonomy otherwise available to a subordinate body under its constitution or bylaws.

(i) "Labor organization" means a labor organization engaged in an industry affecting commerce and includes any organization of any kind, any agency, or employee representation committee, group, association, or plan so engaged in which employees participate and which exists for the purpose, in whole or in part, of dealing with employers concerning grievances, labor disputes, wages, rates of pay, hours, or other terms or conditions of employment, and any conference, general committee, joint or system board, or joint council so engaged which is subordinate to a national or international labor organization, other than a State or local central body.

(j) A labor organization shall be deemed to be engaged in an industry affecting commerce if it —

(1) is the certified representative of employees under the provisions of the National Labor Relations Act, as amended (29 U.S.C. §151 et seq.), or the Railway Labor Act, as amended (45 U.S.C. §151 et seq.); or

(2) although not certified, is a national or international labor organization or a local labor organization recognized or acting as the representative of employees of an employer or employers engaged in an industry affecting commerce; or

(3) has chartered a local labor organization or subsidiary body which is representing or actively seeking to represent employees of employers within the meaning of paragraph (1) or (2); or

(4) has been chartered by a labor organization representing or actively seeking to represent employees within the meaning of paragraph (1) or (2) as the local or subordinate body through which such employees may enjoy membership or become affiliated with such labor organization; or

(5) is a conference, general committee, joint or system board, or joint council, subordinate to a national or international labor organization, which includes a labor organization engaged in an industry affecting commerce within the meaning of any of the preceding paragraphs of this subsection, other than a State or local central body.

(k) "Secret ballot" means the expression by ballot, voting machine, or otherwise, but in no event by proxy, of a choice with respect to any election or vote taken upon any matter, which is cast in such a manner that the person expressing such choice cannot be identified with the choice expressed.

(l) "Trust in which a labor organization is interested" means a trust or other fund or organization (1) which was created or established by a labor organization, or one or more of the trustees or one or more members of the governing body of which is selected or appointed by a labor organization, and (2) a primary purpose of which is to provide benefits for the members of such labor organization or their beneficiaries.

(m) "Labor relations consultant" means any person who, for compensation, advises or represents an employer, employer organization, or labor organization concerning employee organizing, concerted activities, or collective bargaining activities.

(n) "Officer" means any constitutional officer, any person authorized to perform the functions of president, vice president, secretary, treasurer, or other executive functions of a labor organization, and any member of its executive board or similar governing body.

(o) "Member" or "member in good standing", when used in reference to a labor organization, includes any person who has fulfilled the requirements for membership in such organization, and who neither has voluntarily withdrawn from membership nor has been expelled or suspended from membership after appropriate proceedings consistent with lawful provisions of the constitution and bylaws of such organization.

(p) "Secretary" means the Secretary of Labor.

(q) "Officer, agent, shop steward, or other representative," when used with respect to a labor organization, includes elected officials and key administrative personnel, whether elected or appointed (such as business agents, heads of departments or major units, and organizers who exercise substantial independent authority), but does not include salaried nonsupervisory professional staff, stenographic, and service personnel.

(r) "District court of the United States" means a United States district court and a United States court of any place subject to the jurisdiction of the United States.

SUBCHAPTER II: BILL OF RIGHTS OF MEMBERS OF LABOR ORGANIZATIONS

Sec. 411. Bill of rights; constitution and bylaws of labor organizations

(a)(1) Equal rights

Every member of a labor organization shall have equal rights and privileges within such organization to nominate candidates, to vote in elections or referendums of the labor organization, to attend membership meetings, and to participate in the deliberations and voting upon the business of such meetings, subject to reasonable rules and regulations in such organization's constitution and bylaws.

(2) Freedom of speech and assembly

Every member of any labor organization shall have the right to meet and assemble freely with other members; and to express any views, arguments, or opinions; and to express at meetings of the labor organization his views, upon candidates in an election of the labor organization or upon any business properly before the meeting, subject to the organization's established and reasonable rules pertaining to the conduct of meetings: *Provided*, That nothing herein shall be construed to impair the right of a labor organization to adopt and enforce reasonable rules as to the responsibility of every member toward the organization as an institution and to his refraining from conduct that would interfere with its performance of its legal or contractual obligations.

(3) Dues, initiation fees, and assessments

Except in the case of a federation of national or international labor organizations, the rates of dues and initiation fees payable by members of any labor organization in effect on September 14, 1959 shall not be increased, and no general or special assessment shall be levied upon such members, except —

(A) in the case of a local labor organization, (i) by majority vote by secret ballot of the members in good standing voting at a general or special membership meeting, after reasonable notice of the intention to vote upon such question, or (ii) by majority vote of the members in good standing voting in a membership referendum conducted by secret ballot; or

(B) in the case of a labor organization, other than a local labor organization or a federation of national or international labor organizations, (i) by majority vote of the delegates voting at a regular convention, or at a special convention of such labor organization held upon not less than thirty days' written notice to the principal office of each local or constituent labor organization entitled to such notice, or (ii) by majority vote of the members in good standing of such labor organization voting in a membership referendum conducted by secret ballot, or (iii) by majority vote of the members of the executive board or similar governing body of such labor organization, pursuant to express authority contained in the constitution and bylaws of such labor organization: *Provided*, That such action on the part of the executive board or similar governing body shall be effective only until the next regular convention of such labor organization.

(4) Protection of the right to sue

No labor organization shall limit the right of any member thereof to institute an action in any court, or in a proceeding before any administrative agency, irrespective of whether or not the labor organization or its officers are named as defendants or respondents in such action or proceeding, or the right of any member of a labor organization to appear as a witness in any judicial, administrative, or legislative proceeding, or to petition any legislature or to communicate with any legislator: *Provided*, That any such member may be required to exhaust reasonable hearing procedures (but not to exceed a four-month lapse of time) within such organization, before instituting legal or administrative proceedings against such organizations or any officer thereof: *And provided further*, That no interested employer or employer association shall directly or indirectly finance, encourage, or participate in, except as a party, any such action, proceeding, appearance, or petition.

(5) Safeguards against improper disciplinary action

No member of any labor organization may be fined, suspended, expelled, or otherwise disciplined except for nonpayment of dues by such organization or by any officer thereof unless such member has been (A) served with written specific charges; (B) given a reasonable time to prepare his defense; (C) afforded a full and fair hearing.

(b) Invalidity of constitution and bylaws

Any provision of the constitution and bylaws of any labor organization which is inconsistent with the provisions of this section shall be of no force or effect.

Sec. 412. Civil action for infringement of rights; jurisdiction

Any person whose rights secured by the provisions of this subchapter have been infringed by any violation of this subchapter may bring a civil action in a district court of the United States for such relief (including injunctions) as may be appropriate. Any such action against a labor organization shall be brought in the district court of the United States for the district where the alleged violation occurred, or where the principal office of such labor organization is located.

Sec. 413. Retention of existing rights of members

Nothing contained in this subchapter shall limit the rights and remedies of any member of a labor organization under any State or Federal law or before any court or other tribunal, or under the constitution and bylaws of any labor organization.

Sec. 414. Right to copies of collective bargaining agreements

It shall be the duty of the secretary or corresponding principal officer of each labor organization, in the case of a local labor organization, to forward a copy of each collective bargaining agreement made by such labor organization with any employer to any employee who requests such a copy and whose rights as such employee are directly affected by such agreement, and in the case of a labor organization other than a local labor organization, to forward a copy of any such agreement to each constituent unit which has members directly affected by such agreement; and such officer shall maintain at the principal office of the labor organization of which he is an officer copies of any such agreement made or received by such labor organization, which copies shall be available for inspection by any member or by any employee whose rights are affected by such agreement. The provisions of section 440 of this

title shall be applicable in the enforcement of this section.

Sec. 415. Information to members of provisions of chapter

Every labor organization shall inform its members concerning the provisions of this chapter.

SUBCHAPTER III: REPORTING BY LABOR ORGANIZATIONS, OFFICERS AND EMPLOYEES OF LABOR ORGANIZATIONS, AND EMPLOYERS

Sec. 431. Report of labor organizations

(a) Adoption and filing of constitution and bylaws; contents of report

Every labor organization shall adopt a constitution and bylaws and shall file a copy thereof with the Secretary, together with a report, signed by its president and secretary or corresponding principal officers, containing the following information —

(1) the name of the labor organization, its mailing address, and any other address at which it maintains its principal office or at which it keeps the records referred to in this subchapter;

(2) the name and title of each of its officers;

(3) the initiation fee or fees required from a new or transferred member and fees for work permits required by the reporting labor organization;

(4) the regular dues or fees or other periodic payments required to remain a member of the reporting labor organization; and

(5) detailed statements, or references to specific provisions of documents filed under this subsection which contain such statements, showing the provision made and procedures followed with respect to each of the following: (A) qualifications for or restrictions on membership, (B) levying of assessments, (C) participation in insurance or other benefit plans, (D) authorization for disbursement of funds of the labor organization, (E) audit of financial transactions of the labor organization, (F) the calling of regular and special meetings, (G) the selection of officers and stewards and of any representatives to other bodies composed of labor organizations' representatives, with a specific statement of the manner in which each officer was elected, appointed, or otherwise selected, (H) discipline or removal of officers or agents for breaches of their trust, (I) imposition of fines, suspensions, and expulsions of members, including the grounds for such action and any provision made for notice, hearing, judgment on the evidence, and appeal procedures, (J) authorization for bargaining demands, (K) ratification of contract terms, (L) authorization for strikes, and (M) issuance of work permits. Any change in the information required by this subsection shall be reported to the Secretary at the time the reporting labor organization files with the Secretary the annual financial report required by subsection (b) of this section.

(b) Annual financial report; filing; contents

Every labor organization shall file annually with the Secretary a financial report signed by its president and treasurer or corresponding principal officers containing the following information in such detail as may be necessary accurately to disclose its financial condition and operations for its preceding fiscal year —

(1) assets and liabilities at the beginning and end of the fiscal year;

(2) receipts of any kind and the sources thereof;

(3) salary, allowances, and other direct or indirect disbursements (including reimbursed expenses) to each officer and also to each employee who, during such fiscal year, received more than $10,000 in the aggregate from such labor organization and any other labor organization affiliated with it or with which it is affiliated, or which is affiliated with the same national or international labor organization;

(4) direct and indirect loans made to any officer, employee, or member, which aggregated more than $250 during the fiscal year, together with a statement of the purpose, security, if any, and arrangements for repayment;

(5) direct and indirect loans to any business enterprise, together with a statement of the purpose, security, if any, and arrangements for repayment; and

(6) other disbursements made by it including the purposes thereof;

all in such categories as the Secretary may prescribe.

(c) Availability of information to members; examination of books, records, and accounts

Every labor organization required to submit a report under this subchapter shall make available the information required to be contained in such report to all of its members, and every such labor organization and its officers shall be under a duty enforceable at the suit of any member of such organization in any State court of competent jurisdiction or in the district court of the United States for the district in which such labor organization maintains its principal office, to permit such member for just cause to examine any books, records, and accounts necessary to verify such report. The court in such action may, in its discretion, in addition to any judgment awarded to the plaintiff or plaintiffs, allow a reasonable attorney's fee to be paid by the defendant, and costs of the action.

Sec. 432. Report of officers and employees of labor organizations

(a) Filing; contents of report

Every officer of a labor organization and every employee of a labor organization (other than an employee performing exclusively clerical or custodial services) shall file with the Secretary a signed report listing and describing for his preceding fiscal year —

(1) any stock, bond, security, or other interest, legal or equitable, which he or his spouse or minor child directly or indirectly held in, and any income or any other benefit with monetary value (including reimbursed expenses) which he or his spouse or minor child derived directly or indirectly from, an employer whose employees such labor organization represents or is actively seeking to represent, except payments and other benefits received as a bona fide employee of such employer;

(2) any transaction in which he or his spouse or minor child engaged, directly or indirectly, involving any stock, bond, security, or loan to or from, or other legal or equitable interest in the business of an employer whose employees such labor organization represents or is actively seeking to represent;

(3) any stock, bond, security, or other interest, legal or equitable, which he or his spouse or minor child directly or indirectly held in, and any income or any other benefit with monetary value (including reimbursed expenses) which he or his spouse or minor child directly or indirectly derived from, any business a substantial part of

which consists of buying from, selling or leasing to, or otherwise dealing with, the business of an employer whose employees such labor organization represents or is actively seeking to represent;

(4) any stock, bond, security, or other interest, legal or equitable, which he or his spouse or minor child directly or indirectly held in, and any income or any other benefit with monetary value (including reimbursed expenses) which he or his spouse or minor child directly or indirectly derived from, a business any part of which consists of buying from, or selling or leasing directly or indirectly to, or otherwise dealing with such labor organization;

(5) any direct or indirect business transaction or arrangement between him or his spouse or minor child and any employer whose employees his organization represents or is actively seeking to represent, except work performed and payments and benefits received as a bona fide employee of such employer and except purchases and sales of goods or services in the regular course of business at prices generally available to any employee of such employer; and

(6) any payment of money or other thing of value (including reimbursed expenses) which he or his spouse or minor child received directly or indirectly from any employer or any person who acts as a labor relations consultant to an employer, except payments of the kinds referred to in section 186(c) of this title.

(b) Report of certain bona fide investments

The provisions of paragraphs (1), (2), (3), (4), and (5) of subsection (a) of this section shall not be construed to require any such officer or employee to report his bona fide investments in securities traded on a securities exchange registered as a national securities exchange under the Securities Exchange Act of 1934 (15 U.S.C. §78a et seq.), in shares in an investment company registered under the Investment Company Act of 1940 (15 U.S.C. §80a-1 et seq.), or in securities of a public utility holding company registered under the Public Utility Holding Company Act of 1935 (15 U.S.C. §79 et seq.), or to report any income derived therefrom.

(c) Exemption from filing requirement

Nothing contained in this section shall be construed to require any officer or employee of a labor organization to file a report under subsection (a) of this section unless he or his spouse or minor child

holds or has held an interest, has received income or any other benefit with monetary value or a loan, or has engaged in a transaction described therein.

Sec. 433. Report of employers

(a) Filing and contents of report of payments, loans, promises, agreements, or arrangements

Every employer who in any fiscal year made —

(1) any payment or loan, direct or indirect, of money or other thing of value (including reimbursed expenses), or any promise or agreement therefor, to any labor organization or officer, agent, shop steward, or other representative of a labor organization, or employee of any labor organization, except (A) payments or loans made by any national or State bank, credit union, insurance company, savings and loan association or other credit institution and (B) payments of the kind referred to in section 186(c) of this title;

(2) any payment (including reimbursed expenses) to any of his employees, or any group or committee of such employees, for the purpose of causing such employee or group or committee of employees to persuade other employees to exercise or not to exercise, or as the manner of exercising, the right to organize and bargain collectively through representatives of their own choosing unless such payments were contemporaneously or previously disclosed to such other employees;

(3) any expenditure, during the fiscal year, where an object thereof, directly or indirectly, is to interfere with, restrain, or coerce employees in the exercise of the right to organize and bargain collectively through representatives of their own choosing, or is to obtain information concerning the activities of employees or a labor organization in connection with a labor dispute involving such employer, except for use solely in conjunction with an administrative or arbitral proceeding or a criminal or civil judicial proceeding;

(4) any agreement or arrangement with a labor relations consultant or other independent contractor or organization pursuant to which such person undertakes activities where an object thereof, directly or indirectly, is to persuade employees to exercise or not to exercise, or persuade employees as to the manner of exercising, the right to organize and bargain collectively through representatives of their own choosing, or undertakes to supply such employer with information concerning the activities of employees or a labor organization in connection with a labor dispute involving such employer, except information for use solely in conjunction with an administrative or arbitral proceeding or a criminal or civil judicial proceeding; or

(5) any payment (including reimbursed expenses) pursuant to an agreement or arrangement described in subdivision (4);

shall file with the Secretary a report, in a form prescribed by him, signed by its president and treasurer or corresponding principal officers showing in detail the date and amount of each such payment, loan, promise, agreement, or arrangement and the name, address, and position, if any, in any firm or labor organization of the person to whom it was made and a full explanation of the circumstances of all such payments, including the terms of any agreement or understanding pursuant to which they were made.

(b) Persuasive activities relating to the right to organize and bargain collectively; supplying information of activities in connection with labor disputes; filing and contents of report of agreement or arrangement

Every person who pursuant to any agreement or arrangement with an employer undertakes activities where an object thereof is, directly or indirectly —

(1) to persuade employees to exercise or not to exercise, or persuade employees as to the manner of exercising, the right to organize and bargain collectively through representatives of their own choosing; or

(2) to supply an employer with information concerning the activities of employees or a labor organization in connection with a labor dispute involving such employer, except information for use solely in conjunction with an administrative or arbitral proceeding or a criminal or civil judicial proceeding;

shall file within thirty days after entering into such agreement or arrangement a report with the Secretary, signed by its president and treasurer or corresponding principal officers, containing the name under which such person is engaged in doing business and the address of its principal office, and a detailed statement of the terms and conditions of such agreement or arrangement. Every such person shall file annually, with respect to each fiscal year during which payments were made as a result of such an agreement or arrangement, a report with the Secretary, signed by its president and treasurer or corresponding principal officers, containing a statement (A) of its receipts of any kind from employers on account of labor relations advice or services, designating the sources thereof, and (B) of its disbursements of any kind, in connection with such services and the purposes thereof. In each such case such information shall be set forth in such categories as the Secretary may prescribe.

(c) Advisory or representative services exempt from filing requirements

Nothing in this section shall be construed to require any employer or other person to file a report covering the services of such person by reason of his giving or agreeing to give advice to such employer or representing or agreeing to represent such employer before any court, administrative agency, or tribunal of arbitration or engaging or agreeing to engage in collective bargaining on behalf of such employer with respect to wages, hours, or other terms or conditions of employment or the negotiation of an agreement or any question arising thereunder.

(d) Exemption from filing requirements generally

Nothing contained in this section shall be construed to require an employer to file a report under subsection (a) of this section unless he has made an expenditure, payment, loan, agreement, or arrangement of the kind described therein. Nothing contained in this section shall be construed to require any other person to file a report under subsection (b) of this section unless he was a party to an agreement or arrangement of the kind described therein.

(e) Services by and payments to regular officers, supervisors, and employees of employer

Nothing contained in this section shall be construed to require any regular officer, supervisor, or employee of an employer to file a report in connection with services rendered to such employer nor shall any employer be required to file a report covering expenditures made to any regular officer, supervisor, or employee of an employer as compensation for service as a regular officer, supervisor, or employee of such employer.

(f) Rights protected by section 158(c) of this title

Nothing contained in this section shall be construed as an amendment to, or modification of the rights protected by, section 158(c) of this title.

(g) "Interfere with, restrain, or coerce" defined

The term "interfere with, restrain, or coerce" as used in this section means interference, restraint, and coercion which, if done with respect to the exercise of rights guaranteed in section 157 of this title, would, under section 158(a) of this title, constitute an unfair labor practice.

Sec. 434. Exemption of attorney-client communications

Nothing contained in this chapter shall be construed to require an attorney who is a member in good standing of the bar of any State, to include in any report required to be filed pursuant to the provisions of this chapter any information which was lawfully communicated to such attorney by any of his clients in the course of a legitimate attorney-client relationship.

Sec. 435. Reports and documents as public information

(a) Publication; statistical and research purposes

The contents of the reports and documents filed with the Secretary pursuant to sections 431, 432, 433, and 441 of this title shall be public information, and the Secretary may publish any information and data which he obtains pursuant to the provisions of this subchapter. The Secretary may use the information and data for statistical and research purposes, and compile and publish such studies, analyses, reports, and surveys based thereon as he may deem appropriate.

(b) Inspection and examination of information and data

The Secretary shall by regulation make reasonable provision for the inspection and examination, on the request of any person, of the information and data contained in any report or other document filed with him pursuant to section 431, 432, 433, or 441 of this title.

(c) Copies of reports or documents; availability to State agencies

The Secretary shall by regulation provide for the furnishing by the Department of Labor of copies of reports or other documents filed with the Secretary pursuant to this subchapter, upon payment of a charge based upon the cost of the service. The Secretary shall make available without payment of a charge, or require any person to furnish, to such State agency as is designated by law or by the Governor of the State in which such person has his principal place of business or headquarters, upon request of the Governor of such State, copies of any reports and documents filed by such person with the Secretary pursuant to section 431, 432, 433, or 441 of this title, or of information and data contained therein. No person shall be required by reason of any law of any State to furnish to any officer or agency of such State any information included in a report filed by such person with the Secretary pursuant to the provisions of this subchapter, if a copy of such report, or of the portion thereof containing such information, is furnished to such officer or agency. All moneys received in payment of such charges fixed by the Secretary pursuant to this subsection shall be deposited in the general fund of the Treasury.

Sec. 436. Retention of records

Every person required to file any report under this subchapter shall maintain records on the matters required to be reported which will provide in sufficient detail the necessary basic information and data from which the documents filed with the Secretary may be verified, explained, or clarified, and checked for accuracy and completeness, and shall include vouchers, worksheets, receipts, and applicable resolutions, and shall keep such records available for examination for a period of not less than five years after the filing of the documents based on the information which they contain.

Sec. 437. Time for making reports

(a) Each labor organization shall file the initial report required under section 431(a) of this title within ninety days after the date on which it first becomes subject to this chapter.

(b) Each person required to file a report under section 431(b), 432, 433(a), the second sentence of 433(b), or section 441 of this title shall file such report within ninety days after the end of each of its fiscal years; except that where such person is subject to section 431(b), 432, 433(a), the second sentence of 433(b), or section 441 of this title, as the case may be, for only a portion of such a fiscal year (because September 14, 1959, occurs during such person's fiscal year or such person becomes subject to this chapter during its fiscal year or such person may consider that portion as the entire fiscal year in making such report.

Sec. 438. Rules and regulations; simplified reports

The Secretary shall have authority to issue, amend, and rescind rules and regulations prescribing the form and publication of reports required to be filed under this subchapter and such other reasonable rules and regulations (including rules prescribing reports concerning trusts in which a labor organization is interested) as he may find necessary to prevent the circumvention or evasion of such reporting requirements. In exercising his power under this section the Secretary shall prescribe by general rule simplified reports for labor organizations or employers for whom he finds that by virtue of their size a detailed report would be unduly burdensome, but the Secretary may revoke such provision for simplified forms of any labor organization or employer if he determines, after such investigation as he deems proper and due notice and opportunity for a hearing, that the purposes of this section would be served thereby.

Sec. 439. Violations and penalties

(a) Willful violations of provisions of subchapter

Any person who willfully violates this subchapter shall be fined not more than $10,000 or imprisoned for not more than one year, or both.

(b) False statements or representations of fact with knowledge of falsehood

Any person who makes a false statement or representation of a material fact, knowing it to be false, or who knowingly fails to disclose a material fact, in any document, report, or other information required under the provisions of this subchapter shall be fined not more than $10,000 or imprisoned for not more than one year, or both.

(c) False entry in or willful concealment, etc., of books and records

Any person who willfully makes a false entry in or willfully conceals, withholds, or destroys any books, records, reports, or statements required to be kept by any provision of this subchapter shall be fined not more than $10,000 or imprisoned for not more than one year, or both.

(d) Personal responsibility of individuals required to sign reports

Each individual required to sign reports under sections 431 and 433 of this title shall be personally responsible for the filing of such reports and for any statement contained therein which he knows to be false.

Sec. 440. Civil action for enforcement by Secretary; jurisdiction

Whenever it shall appear that any person has violated or is about to violate any of the provisions of this subchapter, the Secretary may bring a civil action for such relief (including injunctions) as may be appropriate. Any such action may be brought in the district court of the United States where the violation occurred or, at the option of the parties, in the United States District Court for the District of Columbia.

Sec. 441. Surety company reports; contents; waiver or modification of requirements respecting contents of reports

Each surety company which issues any bond required by this chapter or the Employee Retirement Income Security Act of 1974 (29 U.S.C. §1001 et seq.) shall file annually with the Secretary, with respect to each fiscal year during which any such bond was in force, a report, in such form and detail as he may prescribe by regulation, filed by the president and treasurer or corresponding principal officers of the surety company, describing its bond experience under each such chapter or Act, including information as to the premiums received, total claims paid, amounts recovered by way of subrogation, administrative and legal expenses and such related data and information as the Secretary shall determine to be necessary in the public interest and to carry out the policy of the chapter. Notwithstanding the foregoing, if the Secretary finds that any such specific information cannot be practicably ascertained or would be uninformative, the Secretary may modify or waive the requirement for such information.

SUBCHAPTER IV: TRUSTEESHIPS

Sec. 461. Reports

(a) Filing and contents; annual financial report

Every labor organization which has or assumes trusteeship over any subordinate labor organization shall file with the Secretary within thirty days after September 14, 1959 or the imposition of any such trusteeship, and semiannually thereafter, a report, signed by its president and treasurer or corresponding principal officers, as well as by the trustees of such subordinate labor organization, containing the following information: (1) the name and address of the subordinate organization; (2) the date of establishing the trusteeship; (3) a detailed statement of the reason or reasons for establishing or continuing the trusteeship; and (4) the nature and extent of participation by the membership of the subordinate organization in the selection of delegates to represent such organization in regular or special conventions or other policy-determining bodies and in the election of officers of the labor organization which has assumed trusteeship over such subordinate organization. The initial report shall also include a full and complete account of the financial condition of such subordinate organization as of the time trusteeship was assumed over it. During the continuance of a trusteeship the labor organization which has assumed trusteeship over a subordinate labor organization shall file on behalf of the subordinate labor organization the annual financial report required by section 431(b) of this title signed by the president and treasurer or corresponding principal officers of the labor organization which has assumed such trusteeship and the trustees of the subordinate labor organization.

(b) Applicability of other laws

The provisions of sections 431(c), 435, 436, 438, and 440 of this title shall be applicable to reports filed under this subchapter.

(c) Penalty for violations

Any person who willfully violates this section shall be fined not more than $10,000 or imprisoned for not more than one year, or both.

(d) False statements and entries; failure to disclose material facts; withholding, concealing or destroying documents, books, records, reports, or statements; penalty

Any person who makes a false statement or representation of a material fact, knowing it to be false, or who knowingly fails to disclose a material fact, in any report required under the provisions of this section or willfully makes any false entry in or willfully withholds, conceals, or destroys any documents, books, records, reports, or statements upon which such report is based, shall be fined not more than $10,000 or imprisoned for not more than one year, or both.

(e) Personal liability

Each individual required to sign a report under this section shall be personally responsible for the filing of such report and for any statement contained therein which he knows to be false.

Sec. 462. Purposes for establishment of trusteeship

Trusteeships shall be established and administered by a labor organization over a subordinate body only in accordance with the constitution and bylaws of the organization which has assumed trusteeship over the subordinate body and for the purpose of correcting corruption or financial malpractice, assuring the performance of collective bargaining agreements or other duties of a bargaining representative, restoring democratic procedures, or otherwise carrying out the legitimate objects of such labor organization.

Sec. 463. Unlawful acts relating to labor organization under trusteeship

(a) During any period when a subordinate body of a labor organization is in trusteeship, it shall be unlawful (1) to count the vote of delegates from such body in any convention or election of officers of the labor organization unless the delegates have been chosen by secret ballot in an election in which all the members in good standing of such subordinate body were eligible to participate, or (2) to transfer to such organization any current receipts or other funds of the subordinate body except the normal per capital tax and assessments payable by subordinate bodies not in trusteeship: *Provided,* That nothing herein contained shall prevent the distribution of the assets of a labor organization in accordance with its constitution and bylaws upon the bona fide dissolution thereof.

(b) Any person who willfully violates this section shall be fined not more than $10,000 or imprisoned for not more than one year, or both.

Sec. 464. Civil action for enforcement

(a) Complaint; investigation; commencement of action by Secretary, member or subordinate body of labor organization; jurisdiction

Upon the written complaint of any member or subordinate body of a labor organization alleging that such organization has violated the provisions of this subchapter (except section 461 of this title) the Secretary shall investigate the complaint and if the

Secretary finds probable cause to believe that such violation has occurred and has not been remedied he shall, without disclosing the identity of the complainant, bring a civil action in any district court of the United States having jurisdiction of the labor organization for such relief (including injunctions) as may be appropriate. Any member or subordinate body of a labor organization affected by any violation of this subchapter (except section 461 of this title) may bring a civil action in any district court of the United States having jurisdiction of the labor organization for such relief (including injunctions) as may be appropriate.

(b) Venue

For the purpose of actions under this section, district courts of the United States shall be deemed to have jurisdiction of a labor organization (1) in the district in which the principal office of such labor organization is located, or (2) in any district in which its duly authorized officers or agents are engaged in conducting the affairs of the trusteeship.

(c) Presumptions of validity or invalidity of trusteeship

In any proceeding pursuant to this section a trusteeship established by a labor organization in conformity with the procedural requirements of its constitution and bylaws and authorized or ratified after a fair hearing either before the executive board or before such other body as may be provided in accordance with its constitution or bylaws shall be presumed valid for a period of eighteen months from the date of its establishment and shall not be subject to attack during such period except upon clear and convincing proof that the trusteeship was not established or maintained in good faith for a purpose allowable under section 462 of this title. After the expiration of eighteen months the trusteeship shall be presumed invalid in any such proceeding and its discontinuance shall be decreed unless the labor organization shall show by clear and convincing proof that the continuation of the trusteeship is necessary for a purpose allowable under section 462 of this title. In the latter event the court may dismiss the complaint or retain jurisdiction of the cause on such conditions and for such period as it deems appropriate.

Sec. 465. Report to Congress

The Secretary shall submit to the Congress at the expiration of three years from September 14, 1959, a report upon the operation of this subchapter.

Sec. 466. Additional rights and remedies; exclusive jurisdiction of district court; res judicata

The rights and remedies provided by this subchapter shall be in addition to any and all other rights and remedies at law or in equity: *Provided,* That upon the filing of a complaint by the Secretary the jurisdiction of the district court over such trusteeship shall be exclusive and the final judgment shall be res judicata.

SUBCHAPTER V: ELECTIONS

Sec. 481. Terms of office and election procedures

(a) Officers of national or international labor organizations; manner of election

Every national or international labor organization, except a federation of national or international labor organizations, shall elect its officers not less often than once every five years either by secret ballot among the members in good standing or at a convention of delegates chosen by secret ballot.

(b) Officers of local labor organizations; manner of election

Every local labor organization shall elect its officers not less often than once every three years by secret ballot among the members in good standing.

(c) Requests for distribution of campaign literature; civil action for enforcement; jurisdiction; inspection of membership lists; adequate safeguards to insure fair election

Every national or international labor organization, except a federation of national or international labor organizations, and every local labor organization, and its officers, shall be under a duty, enforceable at the suit of any bona fide candidate for office in such labor organization in the district court of the United States in which such labor organization maintains its principal office, to comply with all reasonable requests of any candidate to distribute by mail or otherwise at the candidate's expense campaign literature in aid of such person's candidacy to all members in good standing of such labor organization and to refrain from discrimination in favor of or against any candidate with respect to the use of lists of members, and whenever such labor organizations or its officers authorize the distribution by mail or otherwise to members of campaign literature on behalf of any candidate or of the labor organization itself with reference to such election, similar distribution at the request of any other bona fide candidate shall be made by such labor organization and its officers, with equal treatment as to the expense of such distribution. Every bona fide candidate shall have the right, once within 30 days prior to an election of a labor organization in which he is a candidate, to inspect a list containing the names and last known addresses of all members of the labor organization who are subject to a collective bargaining agreement requiring membership therein as a condition of employment, which list shall be maintained and kept at the principal office of such labor organization by a designated official thereof. Adequate safeguards to insure a fair election shall be provided, including the right of any candidate to have an observer at the polls and at the counting of the ballots.

(d) Officers of intermediate bodies; manner of election

Officers of intermediate bodies, such as general committees, system boards, joint boards, or joint councils, shall be elected not less often than once every four years by secret ballot among the members in good standing or by labor organization officers representative of such members who have been elected by secret ballot.

(e) Nomination of candidates; eligibility; notice of election; voting rights; counting and publication of results; preservation of ballots and records

In any election required by this section which is to be held by secret ballot a reasonable opportunity shall be given for the nomination of candidates and every member in good standing shall be eligible to be a candidate and to hold office (subject to section 504 of this title and to reasonable qualifications uniformly imposed) and shall have the right to vote for or otherwise support the candidate or candidates of his choice, without being subject to penalty, discipline, or improper interference or reprisal of any kind by such organization or any member thereof. Not less than fifteen days prior to the election notice thereof shall be mailed to each member at his last known home address. Each member in good standing shall be entitled to one vote. No member whose dues have been withheld by his employer for pay-

ment to such organization pursuant to his voluntary authorization provided for in a collective bargaining agreement shall be declared ineligible to vote or be a candidate for office in such organization by reason of alleged delay or default in the payment of dues. The votes cast by members of each local labor organization shall be counted, and the results published, separately. The election officials designated in the constitution and bylaws or the secretary, if no other official is designated, shall preserve for one year the ballots and all other records pertaining to the election. The election shall be conducted in accordance with the constitution and bylaws of such organization insofar as they are not inconsistent with the provisions of this subchapter.

(f) Election of officers by convention of delegates; manner of conducting convention; preservation of records

When officers are chosen by a convention of delegates elected by secret ballot, the convention shall be conducted in accordance with the constitution and bylaws of the labor organization insofar as they are not inconsistent with the provisions of this subchapter. The officials designated in the constitution and bylaws or the secretary, if no other is designated, shall preserve for one year the credentials of the delegates and all minutes and other records of the convention pertaining to the election of officers.

(g) Use of dues, assessments or similar levies, and funds of employer for promotion of candidacy of person

No moneys received by any labor organization by way of dues, assessment, or similar levy, and no moneys of an employer shall be contributed or applied to promote the candidacy of any person in any election subject to the provisions of this subchapter. Such moneys of a labor organization may be utilized for notices, factual statements of issues not involving candidates, and other expenses necessary for the holding of an election.

(h) Removal of officers guilty of serious misconduct

If the Secretary, upon application of any member of a local labor organization, finds after hearing in accordance with subchapter II of chapter 5 of Title 5 that the constitution and bylaws of such labor organization do not provide an adequate procedure for the removal of an elected officer guilty of serious misconduct, such officer may be removed, for cause shown and after notice and hearing, by the members in good standing voting in a secret ballot, conducted by the officers of such labor organization in accordance with its constitution and bylaws insofar as they are not inconsistent with the provisions of this subchapter.

(i) Rules and regulations for determining adequacy of removal procedures

The Secretary shall promulgate rules and regulations prescribing minimum standards and procedures for determining the adequacy of the removal procedures to which reference is made in subsection (h) of this section.

Sec. 482. Enforcement

(a) Filing of complaint; presumption of validity of challenged election

A member of a labor organization —

(1) who has exhausted the remedies available under the constitution and bylaws of such organization and of any parent body, or

(2) who has invoked such available remedies without obtaining a final decision within three calendar months after their invocation,

may file a complaint with the Secretary within one calendar month thereafter alleging the violation of any provision of section 481 of this title (including violation of the constitution and bylaws of the labor organization pertaining to the election and removal of officers). The challenged election shall be presumed valid pending a final decision thereon (as hereinafter provided) and in the interim the affairs of the organization shall be conducted by the officers elected or in such other manner as its constitution and bylaws may provide.

(b) Investigation of complaint; commencement of civil action by Secretary; jurisdiction; preservation of assets

The Secretary shall investigate such complaint and, if he finds probable cause to believe that a violation of this subchapter has occurred and has not been remedied, he shall, within sixty days after the filing of such complaint, bring a civil action against the labor organization as an entity in the district court of the United States in which such labor organization maintains its principal office to set aside the invalid election, if any, and to direct the conduct of an election or hearing

and vote upon the removal of officers under the supervision of the Secretary and in accordance with the provisions of this subchapter and such rules and regulations as the Secretary may prescribe. The court shall have power to take such action as it deems proper to preserve the assets of the labor organization.

(c) Declaration of void election; order for new election; certification of election to court; decree; certification of result of vote for removal of officers

If, upon a preponderance of the evidence after a trial upon the merits, the court finds —

(1) that an election has not been held within the time prescribed by section 481 of this title, or

(2) that the violation of section 481 of this title may have affected the outcome of an election,

the court shall declare the election, if any, to be void and direct the conduct of a new election under supervision of the Secretary and, so far as lawful and practicable, in conformity with the constitution and bylaws of the labor organization. The Secretary shall promptly certify to the court the names of the persons elected, and the court shall thereupon enter a decree declaring such persons to be the officers of the labor organization. If the proceeding is for the removal of officers pursuant to subsection (h) of section 481 of this title, the Secretary shall certify the results of the vote and the court shall enter a decree declaring whether such persons have been removed as officers of the labor organization.

(d) Review of orders; stay of order directing election

An order directing an election, dismissing a complaint, or designating elected officers of a labor organization shall be appealable in the same manner as the final judgment in a civil action, but an order directing an election shall not be stayed pending appeal.

Sec. 483. Application of other laws; existing rights and remedies; exclusiveness of remedy for challenging election

No labor organization shall be required by law to conduct elections of officers with greater frequency or in a different form or manner than is required by its own constitution or bylaws, except as otherwise provided by this subchapter. Existing rights and remedies to enforce the constitution and bylaws of a labor organization with respect to elections prior to the conduct thereof shall not be affected by the provisions of this subchapter. The remedy provided by this subchapter for challenging an election already conducted shall be exclusive.

SUBCHAPTER VI: SAFEGUARDS FOR LABOR ORGANIZATIONS

Sec. 501. Fiduciary responsibility of officers of labor organizations

(a) Duties of officers; exculpatory provisions and resolutions void

The officers, agents, shop stewards, and other representatives of a labor organization occupy positions of trust in relation to such organization and its members as a group. It is, therefore, the duty of each such person, taking into account the special problems and functions of a labor organization, to hold its money and property solely for the benefit of the organization and its members and to manage, invest, and expend the same in accordance with its constitution and bylaws and any resolutions of the governing bodies adopted thereunder, to refrain from dealing with such organization as an adverse party or in behalf of an adverse party in any matter connected with his duties and from holding or acquiring any pecuniary or personal interest which conflicts with the interests of such organization, and to account to the organization for any profit received by him in whatever capacity in connection with transactions conducted by him or under his direction on behalf of the organization. A general exculpatory provision in the constitution and bylaws of such a labor organization or a general exculpatory resolution of a governing body purporting to relieve any such person of liability for breach of the duties declared by this section shall be void as against public policy.

(b) Violation of duties; action by member after refusal or failure by labor organization to commence proceedings; jurisdiction; leave of court; counsel fees and expenses

When any officer, agent, shop steward, or representative of any labor organization is alleged to have violated the duties declared in subsection (a) of this section and the labor organization or its governing board or officers refuse or fail to sue or recover damages or secure an accounting or other appropriate

relief within a reasonable time after being requested to do so by any member of the labor organization, such member may sue such officer, agent, shop steward, or representative in any district court of the United States or in any State court of competent jurisdiction to recover damages or secure an accounting or other appropriate relief for the benefit of the labor organization. No such proceeding shall be brought except upon leave of the court obtained upon verified application and for good cause shown, which application may be made ex parte. The trial judge may allot a reasonable part of the recovery in any action under this subsection to pay the fees of counsel prosecuting the suit at the instance of the member of the labor organization and to compensate such member for any expenses necessarily paid or incurred by him in connection with the litigation.

(c) Embezzlement of assets; penalty

Any person who embezzles, steals, or unlawfully and willfully abstracts or converts to his own use, or the use of another, any of the moneys, funds, securities, property, or other assets of a labor organization of which he is an officer, or by which he is employed, directly or indirectly, shall be fined not more than $10,000 or imprisoned for not more than five years, or both.

Sec. 502. Bonding of officers and employees of labor organizations; amount, form, and placement of bonds; penalty for violation

(a) Every officer, agent, shop steward, or other representative or employee of any labor organization (other than a labor organization whose property and annual financial receipts do not exceed $5,000 in value), or of a trust in which a labor organization is interested, who handles funds or other property thereof shall be bonded to provide protection against loss by reason of acts of fraud or dishonesty on his part directly or through connivance with others. The bond of each such person shall be fixed at the beginning of the organization's fiscal year and shall be in an amount not less than 10 per centum of the funds handled by him and his predecessor or predecessors, if any, during the preceding fiscal year, but in no case more than $500,000. If the labor organization or the trust in which a labor organization is interested does not have a preceding fiscal year, the amount of the bond shall be, in the case of a local labor organization, not less than $1,000, and in the case of any other labor organization or of a trust in which a labor organization is interested, not less than $10,000. Such bonds shall be individual or schedule in form, and shall have a corporate surety company as surety thereon. Any person who is not covered by such bonds shall not be permitted to receive, handle, disburse, or otherwise exercise custody or control of the funds or other property of a labor organization or of a trust in which a labor organization is interested. No such bond shall be placed through an agent or broker or with a surety company in which any labor organization or any officer, agent, shop steward, or other representative of a labor organization has any direct or indirect interest. Such surety company shall be a corporate surety which holds a grant of authority from the Secretary of the Treasury under sections 9304-9308 of Title 31, as an acceptable surety on Federal bonds: *Provided*, That when in the opinion of the Secretary a labor organization has made other bonding arrangements which would provide the protection required by this section at comparable cost or less, he may exempt such labor organization from placing a bond through a surety company holding such grant of authority.

(b) Any person who willfully violates this section shall be fined not more than $10,000 or imprisoned for not more than one year, or both.

Sec. 503. Financial transactions between labor organization and officers and employees

(a) Direct and indirect loans

No labor organization shall make directly or indirectly any loan or loans to any officer or employee of such organization which results in a total indebtedness on the part of such officer or employee to the labor organization in excess of $2,000.

(b) Direct or indirect payment of fines

No labor organization or employer shall directly or indirectly pay the fine of any officer or employee convicted of any willful violation of this chapter.

(c) Penalty for violations

Any person who willfully violates this section shall be fined not more than $5,000 or imprisoned for not more than one year, or both.

Sec. 504. Prohibition against certain persons holding office

(a) Membership in Communist Party; persons convicted of robbery, bribery, etc.

No person who is or has been a member of the Communist Party or who has been convicted of, or served any part of a prison term resulting from his conviction of, robbery, bribery, extortion, embezzlement, grand larceny, burglary, arson, violation of narcotics laws, murder, rape, assault with intent to kill, assault which inflicts grievous bodily injury, or a violation of subchapter III or IV of this chapter any felony involving abuse or misuse of such person's position or employment in a labor organization or employee benefit plan to seek or obtain an illegal gain at the expense of the members of the labor organization or the beneficiaries of the employee benefit plan, or conspiracy to commit any such crimes or attempt to commit any such crimes, or a crime in which any of the foregoing crimes is an element, shall serve or be permitted to serve —

(1) as a consultant or adviser to any labor organization,

(2) as an officer, director, trustee, member of any executive board or similar governing body, business agent, manager, organizer, employee, or representative in any capacity of any labor organization,

(3) as a labor relations consultant or adviser to a person engaged in an industry or activity affecting commerce, or as an officer, director, agent, or employee of any group or association of employers dealing with any labor organization, or in a position having specific collective bargaining authority or direct responsibility in the area of labor-management relations in any corporation or association engaged in an industry or activity affecting commerce, or

(4) in a position which entitles its occupant to a share of the proceeds of, or as an officer or executive or administrative employee of, any entity whose activities are in whole or substantial part devoted to providing goods or services to any labor organization, or

(5) in any capacity, other than in his capacity as a member of such labor organization, that involves decisionmaking authority concerning, or decisionmaking authority over, or custody of, or control of the moneys, funds, assets, or property of any labor organization, during or for the period of thirteen years after such conviction or after the end of such imprisonment, whichever is later, unless the sentencing court on the motion of the person convicted sets a lesser period of at least three years after such conviction or after the end of such imprisonment, whichever is later, or unless prior to the end of such period, in the case of a person so convicted or imprisoned, (A) his citizenship rights, having been revoked as a result of such conviction, have been fully restored, or (B) if the offense is a Federal offense, the sentencing judge or, if the offense is a State or local offense, the United States district court for the district in which the offense was committed, pursuant to sentencing guidelines and policy statements under section 994(a) of Title 28, determines that such person's service in any capacity referred to in clauses (1) through (5) would not be contrary to the purposes of this chapter. Prior to making any such determination the court shall hold a hearing and shall give notice of such proceeding by certified mail to the Secretary of Labor and to State, county, and Federal prosecuting officials in the jurisdiction or jurisdictions in which such person was convicted. The court's determination in any such proceeding shall be final. No person shall knowingly hire, retain, employ, or otherwise place any other person to serve in any capacity in violation of this subsection.

(b) Penalty for violations

Any person who willfully violates this section shall be fined not more than $10,000 or imprisoned for not more than five years, or both.

(c) Definitions

For the purpose of this section —

(1) A person shall be deemed to have been "convicted" and under the disability of "conviction" from the date of the judgment of the trial court, regardless of whether that judgment remains under appeal.

(2) A period of parole shall not be considered as part of a period of imprisonment.

(d) Salary of person barred from labor organization office during appeal of conviction

Whenever any person —

(1) by operation of this section, has been barred from office or other position in a labor organization as a result of a conviction, and

(2) has filed an appeal of that conviction,

any salary which would be otherwise due such person by virtue of such office or position, shall be placed in escrow by the individual employer or organization responsible for payment of such salary. Payment of such salary into escrow shall continue for the duration of the appeal or for the period of time during which such salary would be otherwise due, whichever period is shorter. Upon the final reversal of such person's conviction on appeal, the amounts in escrow shall be paid to such person. Upon the final sustaining of such person's conviction on appeal, the amounts in escrow shall be returned to the individual employer or organization responsible for payments of those amounts. Upon final reversal of such person's conviction, such person shall no longer be barred by this statute from assuming any position from which such person was previously barred.

SUBCHAPTER VII: MISCELLANEOUS PROVISIONS

Sec. 521. Investigations by Secretary; applicability of other laws

(a) The Secretary shall have power when he believes it necessary in order to determine whether any person has violated or is about to violate any provision of this chapter (except subchapter II of this chapter) to make an investigation and in connection therewith he may enter such places and inspect such records and accounts and question such persons as he may deem necessary to enable him to determine the facts relative thereto. The Secretary may report to interested persons or officials concerning the facts required to be shown in any report required by this chapter and concerning the reasons for failure or refusal to file such a report or any other matter which he deems to be appropriate as a result of such an investigation.

(b) For the purpose of any investigation provided for in this chapter, the provisions of sections 49 and 50 of Title 15 (relating to the attendance of witnesses and the production of books, papers, and documents), are made applicable to the jurisdiction, powers, and duties of the Secretary or any officers designated by him.

Sec. 522. Extortionate picketing; penalty for violation

(a) It shall be unlawful to carry on picketing on or about the premises of any employer for the purpose of, or as part of any conspiracy or in furtherance of any plan or purpose for, the personal profit or enrichment of any individual (except a bona fide increase in wages or other employee benefits) by taking or obtaining any money or other thing of value from such employer against his will or with his consent.

(b) Any person who willfully violates this section shall be fined not more than $10,000 or imprisoned not more than twenty years, or both.

Sec. 523. Retention of rights under other Federal and State laws

(a) Except as explicitly provided to the contrary, nothing in this chapter shall reduce or limit the responsibilities of any labor organization or any officer, agent, shop steward, or other representative of a labor organization, or of any trust in which a labor organization is interested, under any other Federal law or under the laws of any State, and, except as explicitly provided to the contrary, nothing in this chapter shall take away any right or bar any remedy to which members of a labor organization are entitled under such other Federal law or law of any State.

(b) Nothing contained in this chapter and section 186(a)-(c) of this title shall be construed to supersede or impair or otherwise affect the provisions of the Railway Labor Act, as amended (45 U.S.C. §151 et seq.), or any of the obligations, rights, benefits, privileges, or immunities of any carrier, employee, organization, representative, or person subject thereto; nor shall anything contained in this chapter be construed to confer any rights, privileges, immunities, or defenses upon employers, or to impair or otherwise affect the rights of any person under the National Labor Relations Act, as amended (29 U.S.C. §151 et seq.).

Sec. 524. Effect on State laws

Nothing in this chapter shall be construed to impair or diminish the authority of any State to enact and enforce general criminal laws with respect to robbery, bribery, extortion, embezzlement, grand larceny, burglary, arson, violation of narcotics laws, murder, rape, assault with intent to kill, or assault which inflicts grievous bodily injury, or conspiracy to commit any of such crimes.

Sec. 524a. Elimination of racketeering activities threat; State legislation governing collective bargaining representative

Notwithstanding this or any other Act regulating labor-management relations, each State shall have

the authority to enact and enforce, as part of a comprehensive statutory system to eliminate the threat of pervasive racketeering activity in an industry that is, or over time has been, affected by such activity, a provision of law that applies equally to employers, employees, and collective bargaining representatives, which provision of law governs service in any position in a local labor organization which acts or seeks to act in that State as a collective bargaining representative pursuant to the National Labor Relations Act (29 U.S.C. §151 et seq.), in the industry that is subject to that program.

Sec. 525. Service of process

For the purposes of this chapter, service of summons, subpena, or other legal process of a court of the United States upon an officer or agent of a labor organization in his capacity as such shall constitute service upon the labor organization.

Sec. 526. Applicability of administrative procedure provisions

The provisions of subchapter II of chapter 5, and chapter 7, of Title 5 shall be applicable to the issuance, amendment, or rescission of any rules or regulations, or any adjudication authorized or required pursuant to the provisions of this chapter.

Sec. 527. Cooperation with other agencies and departments

In order to avoid unnecessary expense and duplication of functions among Government agencies, the Secretary may make such arrangements or agreements for cooperation or mutual assistance in the performance of his functions under this chapter and the functions of any such agency as he may find to be practicable and consistent with law. The Secretary may utilize the facilities or services of any department, agency, or establishment of the United States or of any State or political subdivision of a State, including the services of any of its employees, with the lawful consent of such department, agency, or establishment; and each department, agency, or establishment of the United States is authorized and directed to cooperate with the Secretary and, to the extent permitted by law, to provide such information and facilities as he may request for his assistance in the performance of his functions under this chapter. The Attorney General or his representative shall receive from the Secretary for appropriate action such evidence developed in the performance of his functions under this chapter as may be found to warrant consideration for criminal prosecution under the provisions of this chapter or other Federal law.

Sec. 528. Criminal contempt

No person shall be punished for any criminal contempt allegedly committed outside the immediate presence of the court in connection with any civil action prosecuted by the Secretary or any other person in any court of the United States under the provisions of this chapter unless the facts constituting such criminal contempt are established by the verdict of the jury in a proceeding in the district court of the United States, which jury shall be chosen and empaneled in the manner prescribed by the law governing trial juries in criminal prosecutions in the district courts of the United States.

Sec. 529. Prohibition on certain discipline by labor organization

It shall be unlawful for any labor organization, or any officer, agent, shop steward, or other representative of a labor organization, or any employee thereof to fine, suspend, expel, or otherwise discipline any of its members for exercising any right to which he is entitled under the provisions of this chapter. The provisions of section 412 of this title shall be applicable in the enforcement of this section.

Sec. 530. Deprivation of rights by violence; penalty

It shall be unlawful for any person through the use of force or violence, or threat of the use of force or violence, to restrain, coerce, or intimidate, or attempt to restrain, coerce, or intimidate any member of a labor organization for the purpose of interfering with or preventing the exercise of any right to which he is entitled under the provisions of this chapter. Any person who willfully violates this section shall be fined not more than $1,000 or imprisoned for not more than one year, or both.

Sec. 531. Separability

If any provision of this chapter, or the application of such provision to any person or circumstances, shall be held invalid, the remainder of this chapter or the application of such provision to persons or circumstances other than those as to which it is held invalid, shall not be affected thereby.

Age Discrimination in Employment Act

U.S. Code, Title 29, Sections 621 to 634

Sec.

ADEA IN A NUTSHELL

Enacted: 1967

Purpose: To prevent discrimination against workers 40 years of age and older

Coverage: Private sector employers with 20 or more employees, public agencies, employment agencies, unions

Responsible agency: Equal Employment Opportunity Commission

Sec. 621. Congressional statement of findings and purpose

(a) The Congress hereby finds and declares that —

(1) in the face of rising productivity and affluence, older workers find themselves disadvantaged in their efforts to retain employment, and especially to regain employment when displaced from jobs;

(2) the setting of arbitrary age limits regardless of potential for job performance has become a common practice, and certain otherwise desirable practices may work to the disadvantage of older persons;

(3) the incidence of unemployment, especially long-term unemployment with resultant deterioration of skill, morale, and employer acceptability is, relative to the younger ages, high among older workers; their numbers are great and growing; and their employment problems grave;

(4) the existence in industries affecting commerce, of arbitrary discrimination in employment because of age, burdens commerce and the free flow of goods in commerce.

[84]

(b) It is therefore the purpose of this chapter to promote employment of older persons based on their ability rather than age; to prohibit arbitrary age discrimination in employment; to help employers and workers find ways of meeting problems arising from the impact of age on employment.

Sec. 622. Education and research program; recommendation to Congress

(a) The Secretary of Labor shall undertake studies and provide information to labor unions, management, and the general public concerning the needs and abilities of older workers, and their potentials for continued employment and contribution to the economy. In order to achieve the purposes of this chapter, the Secretary of Labor shall carry on a continuing program of education and information, under which he may, among other measures —

(1) undertake research, and promote research, with a view to reducing barriers to the employment of older persons, and the promotion of measures for utilizing their skills;

(2) publish and otherwise make available to employers, professional societies, the various media of communication, and other interested persons the findings of studies and other materials for the promotion of employment;

(3) foster through the public employment service system and through cooperative effort the development of facilities of public and private agencies for expanding the opportunities and potentials of older persons;

(4) sponsor and assist State and community informational and educational programs.

(b) Not later than six months after the effective date of this chapter, the Secretary shall recommend to the Congress any measures he may deem desirable to change the lower or upper age limits set forth in section 631 of this title.

Sec. 623. Prohibition of age discrimination

(a) Employer practices

It shall be unlawful for an employer —

(1) to fail or refuse to hire or to discharge any individual or otherwise discriminate against any individual with respect to his compensation, terms, conditions, or privileges of employment, because of such individual's age;

(2) to limit, segregate, or classify his employees in any way which would deprive or tend to deprive any individual of employment opportunities or otherwise adversely affect his status as an employee, because of such individual's age; or

(3) to reduce the wage rate of any employee in order to comply with this chapter.

(b) Employment agency practices

It shall be unlawful for an employment agency to fail or refuse to refer for employment, or otherwise to discriminate against, any individual because of such individual's age, or to classify or refer for employment any individual on the basis of such individual's age.

(c) Labor organization practices

It shall be unlawful for a labor organization —

(1) to exclude or to expel from its membership, or otherwise to discriminate against, any individual because of his age;

(2) to limit, segregate, or classify its membership, or to classify or fail or refuse to refer for employment any individual, in any way which would deprive or tend to deprive any individual of employment opportunities, or would limit such employment opportunities or otherwise adversely affect his status as an employee or as an applicant for employment, because of such individual's age;

(3) to cause or attempt to cause an employer to discriminate against an individual in violation of this section.

(d) Opposition to unlawful practices; participation in investigations, proceedings, or litigation

It shall be unlawful for an employer to discriminate against any of his employees or applicants for employment, for an employment agency to discriminate against any individual, or for a labor organization to discriminate against any member thereof or applicant for membership, because such individual, member or applicant for membership has opposed any practice made unlawful by this section, or because such individual, member or applicant for membership has made a charge, testified, assisted, or participated in any manner in an investigation, proceeding, or litigation under this chapter.

(e) Printing or publication of notice or advertisement indicating preference, limitation, etc.

It shall be unlawful for an employer, labor organization, or employment agency to print or publish, or cause to be printed or published, any notice or advertisement relating to employment by such an employer or membership in or any classification or referral for employment by such a labor organization, or relating to any classification or referral for employment by such an employment agency, indicating any preference, limitation, specification, or discrimination, based on age.

(f) Lawful practices; age an occupational qualification; other reasonable factors; laws of foreign workplace; seniority system; employee benefit plans; discharge or discipline for good cause

It shall not be unlawful for an employer, employment agency, or labor organization —

(1) to take any action otherwise prohibited under subsections (a), (b), (c), or (e) of this section where age is a bona fide occupational qualification reasonably necessary to the normal operation of the particular business, or where the differentiation is based on reasonable factors other than age, or where such practices involve an employee in a workplace in a foreign country, and compliance with such subsections would cause such employer, or a corporation controlled by such employer, to violate the laws of the country in which such workplace is located;

(2) to take any action otherwise prohibited under subsection (a), (b), (c), or (e) of this section —

(A) to observe the terms of a bona fide seniority system that is not intended to evade the purposes of this chapter, except that no such seniority system shall require or permit the involuntary retirement of any individual specified by section 631(a) of this title because of the age of such individual; or

(B) to observe the terms of a bona fide employee benefit plan —

(i) where, for each benefit or benefit package, the actual amount of payment made or cost incurred on behalf of an older worker is no less than that made or incurred on behalf of a younger worker, as permissible under section 1625.10, Title 29, Code of Federal Regulations (as in effect on June 22, 1989); or

(ii) that is a voluntary early retirement incentive plan consistent with the relevant purpose or purposes of this chapter.

Notwithstanding clause (i) or (ii) of subparagraph (B), no such employee benefit plan or voluntary early retirement incentive plan shall excuse the failure to hire any individual, and no such employee benefit plan shall require or permit the involuntary retirement of any individual specified by section 631(a) of this title, because of the age of such individual. An employer, employment agency, or labor organization acting under subparagraph (A), or under clause (i) or (ii) of subparagraph (B), shall have the burden of proving that such actions are lawful in any civil enforcement proceeding brought under this chapter; or

(3) to discharge or otherwise discipline an individual for good cause.

(g) Repealed

(h) Practices of foreign corporations controlled by American employers; foreign employers not controlled by American employers; factors determining control

(1) If an employer controls a corporation whose place of incorporation is in a foreign country, any practice by such corporation prohibited under this section shall be presumed to be such practice by such employer.

(2) The prohibitions of this section shall not apply where the employer is a foreign person not controlled by an American employer.

(3) For the purpose of this subsection the determination of whether an employer controls a corporation shall be based upon the —

(A) interrelation of operations,

(B) common management,

(C) centralized control of labor relations, and

(D) common ownership or financial control, of the employer and the corporation.

(i) Employee pension benefit plans; cessation or reduction of benefit accrual or of allocation to employee account; distribution of benefits after attainment of normal retirement age; compliance; highly compensated employees

(1) Except as otherwise provided in this subsection, it shall be unlawful for an employer, an employment agency, a labor organization, or any combination thereof to establish or maintain an employee pension benefit plan which requires or permits —

(A) in the case of a defined benefit plan, the cessation of an employee's benefit accrual, or the reduction of the rate of an employee's benefit accrual, because of age, or

(B) in the case of a defined contribution plan, the cessation of allocations to an employee's account, or the reduction of the rate at which amounts are allocated to an employee's account, because of age.

(2) Nothing in this section shall be construed to prohibit an employer, employment agency, or labor organization from observing any provision of an employee pension benefit plan to the extent that such provision imposes (without regard to age) a limitation on the amount of benefits that the plan provides or a limitation on the number of years of service or years of participation which are taken into account for purposes of determining benefit accrual under the plan.

(3) In the case of any employee who, as of the end of any plan year under a defined benefit plan, has attained normal retirement age under such plan —

(A) if distribution of benefits under such plan with respect to such employee has commenced as of the end of such plan year, then any requirement of this subsection for continued accrual of benefits under such plan with respect to such employee during such plan year shall be treated as satisfied to the extent of the actuarial equivalent of in-service distribution of benefits, and

(B) if distribution of benefits under such plan with respect to such employee has not commenced as of the end of such year in accordance with section 1056(a)(3) of this title and section 401(a)(14)(C) of Title 26, and the payment of benefits under such plan with respect to such employee is not suspended during such plan year pursuant to section 1053(a)(3)(B) of this title or section 411(a)(3)(B) of Title 26, then any requirement of this subsection for continued accrual of benefits under such plan with respect to such employee during such plan year shall be treated as satisfied to the extent of any adjustment in the benefit payable under the plan during such plan year attributable to the delay in the distribution of benefits after the attainment of normal retirement age.

The provisions of this paragraph shall apply in accordance with regulations of the Secretary of the Treasury. Such regulations shall provide for the application of the preceding provisions of this paragraph to all employee pension benefit plans subject to this subsection and may provide for the application of such provisions, in the case of any such employee, with respect to any period of time within a plan year.

(4) Compliance with the requirements of this subsection with respect to an employee pension benefit plan shall constitute compliance with the requirements of this section relating to benefit accrual under such plan.

(5) Paragraph (1) shall not apply with respect to any employee who is a highly compensated employee (within the meaning of section 414(q) of Title 26) to the extent provided in regulations prescribed by the Secretary of the Treasury for purposes of precluding discrimination in favor of highly compensated employees within the meaning of subchapter D of chapter 1 of Title 26.

(6) A plan shall not be treated as failing to meet the requirements of paragraph (1) solely because the subsidized portion of any early retirement benefit is disregarded in determining benefit accruals or it is a plan permitted by subsection (m).

(7) Any regulations prescribed by the Secretary of the Treasury pursuant to clause (v) of section 411(b)(1)(H) of Title 26 and subparagraphs (C) and (D) of section 411(b)(2) of Title 26 shall apply with respect to the requirements of this subsection in the same manner and to the same extent as such regulations apply with respect to the requirements of such sections 411(b)(1)(H) and 411(b)(2).

(8) A plan shall not be treated as failing to meet the requirements of this section solely because such plan provides a normal retirement age described in section 1002(24)(B) of this title and section 411(a)(8)(B) of Title 26.

(9) For purposes of this subsection —

(A) The terms "employee pension benefit plan", "defined benefit plan", "defined contribution plan", and "normal retirement age" have the meanings provided such terms in section 1002 of this title.

(B) The term "compensation" has the meaning provided by section 414(s) of Title 26.

(j) Employment as firefighter or law enforcement officer

It shall not be unlawful for an employer which is a State, a political subdivision of a State, an agency or instrumentality of a State or a political subdivision of a State, or an interstate agency to fail or refuse to hire or to discharge any individual because of such individual's age if such action is taken —

(1) with respect to the employment of an individual as a firefighter or as a law enforcement officer, the employer has complied with section 3(d)(2) of the Age Discrimination in Employment Amendments of 1996 if the individual was discharged after the date described in such section, and the individual has attained —

(A) the age of hiring or retirement, respectively, in effect under applicable State or local law on March 3, 1983; or

(B)(i) if the individual was not hired, the age of hiring in effect on the date of such failure or refusal to hire under applicable State or local law enacted after September 30, 1996; or

(ii) if applicable State or local law was enacted after September 30, 1996, and the individual was discharged, the higher of —

(I) the age of retirement in effect on the date of such discharge under such law; and

(II) age 55; and

(2) pursuant to a bona fide hiring or retirement plan that is not a subterfuge to evade the purposes of this chapter.

(k) Seniority system or employee benefit plan; compliance

A seniority system or employee benefit plan shall comply with this chapter regardless of the date of adoption of such system or plan.

(l) Lawful practices; minimum age as condition of eligibility for retirement benefits; deductions from severance pay; reduction of long-term disability benefits

Notwithstanding clause (i) or (ii) of subsection (f)(2)(B) of this section —

(1) It shall not be a violation of subsection (a), (b), (c), or (e) of this section solely because —

(A) an employee pension benefit plan (as defined in section 1002(2) of this title) provides for the attainment of a minimum age as a condition of eligibility for normal or early retirement benefits; or

(B) a defined benefit plan (as defined in section 1002(35) of this title) provides for —

(i) payments that constitute the subsidized portion of an early retirement benefit; or

(ii) social security supplements for plan participants that commence before the age and terminate at the age (specified by the plan) when participants are eligible to receive reduced or unreduced old-age insurance benefits under title II of the Social Security Act (42 U.S.C. §401 et seq.), and that do not exceed such old-age insurance benefits.

(2)(A) It shall not be a violation of subsection (a), (b), (c), or (e) of this section solely because following a contingent event unrelated to age —

(i) the value of any retiree health benefits received by an individual eligible for an immediate pension;

(ii) the value of any additional pension benefits that are made available solely as a result of the contingent event unrelated to age and following which the individual is eligible for not less than an immediate and unreduced pension; or

(iii) the values described in both clauses (i) and (ii);

are deducted from severance pay made available as a result of the contingent event unrelated to age.

(B) For an individual who receives immediate pension benefits that are actuarially reduced under subparagraph (A)(i), the amount of the deduction available pursuant to subparagraph (A)(i) shall be reduced by the same percentage as the reduction in the pension benefits.

(C) For purposes of this paragraph, severance pay shall include that portion of supplemental unemployment compensation benefits (as described in section 501(c)(17) of Title 26) that —

(i) constitutes additional benefits of up to 52 weeks;

(ii) has the primary purpose and effect of continuing benefits until an individual becomes eligible for an immediate and unreduced pension; and

(iii) is discontinued once the individual becomes eligible for an immediate and unreduced pension.

(D) For purposes of this paragraph and solely in order to make the deduction authorized under this paragraph, the term "retiree health benefits" means benefits provided pursuant to a group health plan covering retirees, for which (determined as of the contingent event unrelated to age) —

(i) the package of benefits provided by the employer for the retirees who are below age 65 is at least comparable to benefits provided under title XVIII of the Social Security Act (42 U.S.C. §1395 et seq.);

(ii) the package of benefits provided by the employer for the retirees who are age 65 and above is at least comparable to that offered under a plan that provides a benefit package with one-fourth the value of benefits provided under title XVIII of such Act; or

(iii) the package of benefits provided by the employer is as described in clauses (i) and (ii).

(E)(i) If the obligation of the employer to provide retiree health benefits is of limited duration, the value for each individual shall be calculated at a rate of $3,000 per year for benefit years before age 65, and $750 per year for benefit years beginning at age 65 and above.

(ii) If the obligation of the employer to provide retiree health benefits is of unlimited

duration, the value for each individual shall be calculated at a rate of $48,000 for individuals below age 65, and $24,000 for individuals age 65 and above.

(iii) The values described in clauses (i) and (ii) shall be calculated based on the age of the individual as of the date of the contingent event unrelated to age. The values are effective on October 16, 1990, and shall be adjusted on an annual basis, with respect to a contingent event that occurs subsequent to the first year after October 16, 1990, based on the medical component of the Consumer Price Index for all-urban consumers published by the Department of Labor.

(iv) If an individual is required to pay a premium for retiree health benefits, the value calculated pursuant to this subparagraph shall be reduced by whatever percentage of the overall premium the individual is required to pay.

(F) If an employer that has implemented a deduction pursuant to subparagraph (A) fails to fulfill the obligation described in subparagraph (E), any aggrieved individual may bring an action for specific performance of the obligation described in subparagraph (E). The relief shall be in addition to any other remedies provided under Federal or State law.

(3) It shall not be a violation of subsection (a), (b), (c), or (e) of this section solely because an employer provides a bona fide employee benefit plan or plans under which long-term disability benefits received by an individual are reduced by any pension benefits (other than those attributable to employee contributions) —

(A) paid to the individual that the individual voluntarily elects to receive; or

(B) for which an individual who has attained the later of age 62 or normal retirement age is eligible.

(m) Voluntary retirement incentive plans

Notwithstanding subsection (f)(2)(B), it shall not be a violation of subsection (a), (b), (c), or (e) solely because a plan of an institution of higher education (as defined in section 101 of the Higher Education Act of 1965) offers employees who are serving under a contract of unlimited tenure (or similar arrangement providing for unlimited tenure) supplemental benefits upon voluntary retirement that are reduced or eliminated on the basis of age, if—

(1) such institution does not implement with respect to such employees any age-based reduction or cessation of benefits that are not supplemental benefits except as permitted by other provisions of this Act;

(2) such supplemental benefits are in addition to any retirement or severance benefits which have been offered generally to employees serving under a contract of unlimited tenure (or similar arrangement providing for unlimited tenure), independent of any early retirement or exit-incentive plan, within the preceding 365 days; and

(3) any employee who attains the minimum age and satisfies all non-age-based conditions for receiving a benefit under the plan has an opportunity lasting not less than 180 days to elect to retire and to receive the maximum benefit that could then be elected by a younger but otherwise similarly situated employee, and the plan does not require retirement to occur sooner than 180 days after such election.

Sec. 624. Study by Secretary of Labor; reports to President and Congress; scope of study; implementation of study; transmittal date of reports

(a)(1) The Secretary of Labor is directed to undertake an appropriate study of institutional and other arrangements giving rise to involuntary retirement, and report his findings and any appropriate legislative recommendations to the President and to the Congress. Such study shall include —

(A) an examination of the effect of the amendment made by section 3(a) of the Age Discrimination in Employment Act Amendments of 1978 in raising the upper age limitation established by section 631(a) of this title to 70 years of age;

(B) a determination of the feasibility of eliminating such limitation;

(C) a determination of the feasibility of raising such limitation above 70 years of age; and

(D) an examination of the effect of the exemption contained in section 631(c) of this title, relating to certain executive employees, and the exemption contained in section 631(d) of this title, relating to tenured teaching personnel.

(2) The Secretary may undertake the study required by paragraph (1) of this subsection directly or by contract or other arrangement.

(b) The report required by subsection (a) of this section shall be transmitted to the President and to the Congress as an interim report not later than January 1, 1981, and in final form not later than January 1, 1982.

Sec. 625. Administration

The Secretary shall have the power —

(a) Delegation of functions; appointment of personnel; technical assistance

to make delegations, to appoint such agents and employees, and to pay for technical assistance on a fee for service basis, as he deems necessary to assist him in the performance of his functions under this chapter;

(b) Cooperation with other agencies, employers, labor organizations, and employment agencies

to cooperate with regional, State, local, and other agencies, and to cooperate with and furnish technical assistance to employers, labor organizations, and employment agencies to aid in effectuating the purposes of this chapter.

Sec. 626. Recordkeeping, investigation, and enforcement

(a) Attendance of witnesses; investigations, inspections, records, and homework regulations

The Equal Employment Opportunity Commission shall have the power to make investigations and require the keeping of records necessary or appropriate for the administration of this chapter in accordance with the powers and procedures provided in sections 209 and 211 of this title.

(b) Enforcement; prohibition of age discrimination under fair labor standards; unpaid minimum wages and unpaid overtime compensation; liquidated damages; judicial relief; conciliation, conference, and persuasion

The provisions of this chapter shall be enforced in accordance with the powers, remedies, and procedures provided in sections 211(b), 216 (except for subsection

(a) thereof), and 217 of this title, and subsection (c) of this section. Any act prohibited under section 623 of this title shall be deemed to be a prohibited act under section 215 of this title. Amounts owing to a person as a result of a violation of this chapter shall be deemed to be unpaid minimum wages or unpaid overtime compensation for purposes of sections 216 and 217 of this title: *Provided*, That liquidated damages shall be payable only in cases of willful violations of this chapter. In any action brought to enforce this chapter the court shall have jurisdiction to grant such legal or equitable relief as may be appropriate to effectuate the purposes of this chapter, including without limitation judgments compelling employment, reinstatement or promotion, or enforcing the liability for amounts deemed to be unpaid minimum wages or unpaid overtime compensation under this section. Before instituting any action under this section, the Equal Employment Opportunity Commission shall attempt to eliminate the discriminatory practice or practices alleged, and to effect voluntary compliance with the requirements of this chapter through informal methods of conciliation, conference, and persuasion.

(c) Civil actions; persons aggrieved; jurisdiction; judicial relief; termination of individual action upon commencement of action by Commission; jury trial

(1) Any person aggrieved may bring a civil action in any court of competent jurisdiction for such legal or equitable relief as will effectuate the purposes of this chapter: *Provided*, That the right of any person to bring such action shall terminate upon the commencement of an action by the Equal Employment Opportunity Commission to enforce the right of such employee under this chapter.

(2) In an action brought under paragraph (1), a person shall be entitled to a trial by jury of any issue of fact in any such action for recovery of amounts owing as a result of a violation of this chapter, regardless of whether equitable relief is sought by any party in such action.

(d) Filing of charge with Commission; timeliness; conciliation, conference, and persuasion

No civil action may be commenced by an individual under this section until 60 days after a charge alleging unlawful discrimination has been filed with the Equal Employment Opportunity Commission. Such a charge shall be filed —

(1) within 180 days after the alleged unlawful practice occurred; or

(2) in a case to which section 633(b) of this title applies, within 300 days after the alleged unlawful practice occurred, or within 30 days after receipt by the individual of notice of termination of proceedings under State law, whichever is earlier.

Upon receiving such a charge, the Commission shall promptly notify all persons named in such charge as prospective defendants in the action and shall promptly seek to eliminate any alleged unlawful practice by informal methods of conciliation, conference, and persuasion.

(e) Reliance on administrative rulings; notice of dismissal or termination; civil action after receipt of notice

Section 259 of this title shall apply to actions under this chapter. If a charge filed with the Commission under this chapter is dismissed or the proceedings of the Commission are otherwise terminated by the Commission, the Commission shall notify the person aggrieved. A civil action may be brought under this section by a person defined in section 630(a) of this title against the respondent named in the charge within 90 days after the date of the receipt of such notice.

(f) Waiver

(1) An individual may not waive any right or claim under this chapter unless the waiver is knowing and voluntary. Except as provided in paragraph (2), a waiver may not be considered knowing and voluntary unless at a minimum —

(A) the waiver is part of an agreement between the individual and the employer that is written in a manner calculated to be understood by such individual, or by the average individual eligible to participate;

(B) the waiver specifically refers to rights or claims arising under this chapter;

(C) the individual does not waive rights or claims that may arise after the date the waiver is executed;

(D) the individual waives rights or claims only in exchange for consideration in addition to anything of value to which the individual already is entitled;

(E) the individual is advised in writing to consult with an attorney prior to executing the agreement;

(F)(i) the individual is given a period of at least 21 days within which to consider the agreement; or

(ii) if a waiver is requested in connection with an exit incentive or other employment termination program offered to a group or class of employees, the individual is given a period of at least 45 days within which to consider the agreement;

(G) the agreement provides that for a period of at least 7 days following the execution of such agreement, the individual may revoke the agreement, and the agreement shall not become effective or enforceable until the revocation period has expired;

(H) if a waiver is requested in connection with an exit incentive or other employment termination program offered to a group or class of employees, the employer (at the commencement of the period specified in subparagraph (F)) informs the individual in writing in a manner calculated to be understood by the average individual eligible to participate, as to —

(i) any class, unit, or group of individuals covered by such program, any eligibility factors for such program, and any time limits applicable to such program; and

(ii) the job titles and ages of all individuals eligible or selected for the program, and the ages of all individuals in the same job classification or organizational unit who are not eligible or selected for the program.

(2) A waiver in settlement of a charge filed with the Equal Employment Opportunity Commission, or an action filed in court by the individual or the individual's representative, alleging age discrimination of a kind prohibited under section 623 or 633a of this title may not be considered knowing and voluntary unless at a minimum —

(A) subparagraphs (A) through (E) of paragraph (1) have been met; and

(B) the individual is given a reasonable period of time within which to consider the settlement agreement.

(3) In any dispute that may arise over whether any of the requirements, conditions, and circumstances set forth in subparagraph (A), (B), (C), (D), (E), (F), (G), or (H) of paragraph (1), or subparagraph (A) or (B) of paragraph (2), have been met, the party asserting the validity of a waiver shall have the burden of proving in a court of competent jurisdiction that a waiver was knowing and voluntary pursuant to paragraph (1) or (2).

(4) No waiver agreement may affect the Commission's rights and responsibilities to enforce this chapter. No waiver may be used to justify interfering with the protected right of an employee to file a charge or participate in an investigation or proceeding conducted by the Commission.

Sec. 627. Notices to be posted

Every employer, employment agency, and labor organization shall post and keep posted in conspicuous places upon its premises a notice to be prepared or approved by the Equal Employment Opportunity Commission setting forth information as the Commission deems appropriate to effectuate the purposes of this chapter.

Sec. 628. Rules and regulations; exemptions

In accordance with the provisions of subchapter II of chapter 5 of Title 5, the Equal Employment Opportunity Commission may issue such rules and regulations as it may consider necessary or appropriate for carrying out this chapter, and may establish such reasonable exemptions to and from any or all provisions of this chapter as it may find necessary and proper in the public interest.

Sec. 629. Criminal penalties

Whoever shall forcibly resist, oppose, impede, intimidate or interfere with a duly authorized representative of the Equal Employment Opportunity Commission while it is engaged in the performance of duties under this chapter shall be punished by a fine of not more than $500 or by imprisonment for not more than one year, or by both: *Provided, however,* That no person shall be imprisoned under this section except when there has been a prior conviction hereunder.

Sec. 630. Definitions

For the purposes of this chapter —

(a) The term "person" means one or more individuals, partnerships, associations, labor organizations, corporations, business trust, legal representatives, or any organized groups of persons.

(b) The term "employer" means a person engaged in an industry affecting commerce who has twenty or more employees for each working day in each of twenty or more calendar weeks in the current or preceding calendar year: *Provided,* That prior to June 30, 1968, employers having fewer than fifty employees shall not be considered employers. The term also means (1) any agent of such a person, and (2) a State or political subdivision of a State and any agency or instrumentality of a State or a political subdivision of a State, and any interstate agency, but such term does not include the United States, or a corporation wholly owned by the Government of the United States.

(c) The term "employment agency" means any person regularly undertaking with or without compensation to procure employees for an employer and includes an agent of such a person; but shall not include an agency of the United States.

(d) The term "labor organization" means a labor organization engaged in an industry affecting commerce, and any agent of such an organization, and includes any organization of any kind, any agency, or employee representation committee, group, association, or plan so engaged in which employees participate and which exists for the purpose, in whole or in part, of dealing with employers concerning grievances, labor disputes, wages, rates of pay, hours, or other terms or conditions of employment, and any conference, general committee, joint or system board, or joint council so engaged which is subordinate to a national or international labor organization.

(e) A labor organization shall be deemed to be engaged in an industry affecting commerce if (1) it maintains or operates a hiring hall or hiring office which procures employees for an employer or procures for employees opportunities to work for an employer, or (2) the number of its members (or, where it is a labor organization composed of other labor organizations or their representatives, if the aggregate number of the members of such other labor organization) is fifty or more prior to July 1, 1968, or twenty-five or more on or after July 1, 1968, and such labor organization —

(1) is the certified representative of employees under the provisions of the National Labor Relations Act, as amended (29 U.S.C. §151 et seq.), or the Railway Labor Act, as amended (45 U.S.C. §151 et seq.); or

(2) although not certified, is a national or international labor organization or a local labor organization recognized or acting as the representative of employees of an employer or employers engaged in an industry affecting commerce; or

(3) has chartered a local labor organization or subsidiary body which is representing or actively seeking to represent employees of employers within the meaning of paragraph (1) or (2); or

(4) has been chartered by a labor organization representing or actively seeking to represent employees within the meaning of paragraph (1) or (2) as the local or subordinate body through which such employees may enjoy membership or become affiliated with such labor organization; or

(5) is a conference, general committee, joint or system board, or joint council subordinate to a national or international labor organization, which includes a labor organization engaged in an industry affecting commerce within the meaning of any of the preceding paragraphs of this subsection.

(f) The term "employee" means an individual employed by any employer except that the term "employee" shall not include any person elected to public office in any State or political subdivision of any State by the qualified voters thereof, or any person chosen by such officer to be on such officer's personal staff, or an appointee on the policymaking level or an immediate adviser with respect to the exercise of the constitutional or legal powers of the office. The exemption set forth in the preceding sentence shall not include employees subject to the civil service laws of a State government, governmental agency, or political subdivision. The term "employee" includes any individual who is a citizen of the United States employed by an employer in a workplace in a foreign country.

(g) The term "commerce" means trade, traffic, commerce, transportation, transmission, or communication among the several States; or between a State and any place outside thereof; or within the District of Columbia, or a possession of the United States; or between points in the same State but through a point outside thereof.

(h) The term "industry affecting commerce" means any activity, business, or industry in commerce or in which a labor dispute would hinder or obstruct commerce or the free flow of commerce and includes any activity or industry "affecting commerce" within the meaning of the Labor-Management Reporting and Disclosure Act of 1959 (29 U.S.C. §401 et seq.).

(i) The term "State" includes a State of the United States, the District of Columbia, Puerto Rico, the Virgin Islands, American Samoa, Guam, Wake Island, the Canal Zone, and Outer Continental Shelf lands defined in the Outer Continental Shelf Lands Act (43 U.S.C. §1331 et seq.).

(j) The term "firefighter" means an employee, the duties of whose position are primarily to perform work directly connected with the control and extinguishment of fires or the maintenance and use of firefighting apparatus and equipment, including an employee engaged in this activity who is transferred to a supervisory or administrative position.

(k) The term "law enforcement officer" means an employee, the duties of whose position are primarily the investigation, apprehension, or detention of individuals suspected or convicted of offenses against the criminal laws of a State, including an employee engaged in this activity who is transferred to a supervisory or administrative position. For the purpose of this subsection, "detention" includes the duties of employees assigned to guard individuals incarcerated in any penal institution.

(*l*) The term "compensation, terms, conditions, or privileges of employment" encompasses all employee benefits, including such benefits provided pursuant to a bona fide employee benefit plan.

Sec. 631. Age limits

(a) Individuals at least 40 years of age

The prohibitions in this chapter shall be limited to individuals who are at least 40 years of age.

(b) Employees or applicants for employment in Federal Government

In the case of any personnel action affecting employees or applicants for employment which is subject to the provisions of section 633a of this title, the prohibitions established in section 633a of this title shall be limited to individuals who are at least 40 years of age.

(c) Bona fide executives or high policymakers

(1) Nothing in this chapter shall be construed to prohibit compulsory retirement of any employee who has attained 65 years of age and who, for the 2-year period immediately before retirement, is employed in a bona fide executive or a high policymaking position, if such employee is entitled to an immediate nonforfeitable annual retirement benefit from a pension, profit-sharing, savings, or deferred compensation plan, or any combination of such plans, of the employer of such employee, which equals, in the aggregate, at least $44,000.

(2) In applying the retirement benefit test of paragraph (1) of this subsection, if any such retirement benefit is in a form other than a straight life annuity (with no ancillary benefits), or if employees contribute to any such plan or make rollover contributions, such benefit shall be adjusted in accordance with regulations prescribed by the Equal Employment Opportunity Commission, after consultation with the Secretary of the Treasury, so that the benefit is the equivalent of a straight life annuity (with no ancillary benefits) under a plan to which employees do not contribute and under which no rollover contributions are made.

Sec. 632. Annual report to Congress

The Equal Employment Opportunity Commission shall submit annually in January a report to the Congress covering its activities for the preceding year and including such information, data and recommendations for further legislation in connection with the matters covered by this chapter as it may find advisable. Such report shall contain an evaluation and appraisal by the Commission of the effect of the minimum and maximum ages established by this chapter, together with its recommendations to the Congress. In making such evaluation and appraisal, the Commission shall take into consideration any changes which may have occurred in the general age level of the population, the effect of the chapter upon workers not covered by its provisions, and such other factors as it may deem pertinent.

Sec. 633. Federal-State relationship

(a) Federal action superseding State action

Nothing in this chapter shall affect the jurisdiction of any agency of any State performing like functions with regard to discriminatory employment practices on account of age except that upon commencement of action under this chapter such action shall supersede any State action.

(b) Limitation of Federal action upon commencement of State proceedings

In the case of an alleged unlawful practice occurring in a State which has a law prohibiting discrimination in employment because of age and establishing or authorizing a State authority to grant or seek relief from such discriminatory practice, no suit may be brought under section 626 of this title before the expiration of sixty days after proceedings have been commenced under the State law, unless such proceedings have been earlier terminated: *Provided*, That such sixty-day period shall be extended to one hundred and twenty days during the first year after the effective date of such State law. If any requirement for the commencement of such proceedings is imposed by a State authority other than a requirement of the filing of a written and signed statement of the facts upon which the proceeding is based, the proceeding shall be deemed to have been commenced for the purposes of this subsection at the time such statement is sent by registered mail to the appropriate State authority.

Sec. 633a. Nondiscrimination on account of age in Federal Government employment

(a) Federal agencies affected

All personnel actions affecting employees or applicants for employment who are at least 40 years of age (except personnel actions with regard to aliens employed outside the limits of the United States) in military departments as defined in section 102 of Title 5, in executive agencies as defined in section 105 of Title 5 (including employees and applicants for employment who are paid from non-appropriated funds), in the United States Postal Service and the Postal Rate Commission, in those units in the government of the District of Columbia having positions in the competitive service, and in those units of the judicial branch of the Federal Government having positions in the competitive service in the Smithsonian Institution, and in the Government Printing Office, the General Accounting Office, and the Library of Congress shall be made free from any discrimination based on age.

(b) Enforcement by Equal Employment Opportunity Commission and by Librarian of Congress in the Library of Congress; remedies; rules, regulations, orders, and instructions of Commission: compliance by Federal agencies; powers and duties of Commission; notification of final action on complaint of discrimination; exemptions: bona fide occupational qualification

Except as otherwise provided in this subsection, the Equal Employment Opportunity Commission is authorized to enforce the provisions of subsection (a) of this section through appropriate remedies, including reinstatement or hiring of employees with or without backpay, as will effectuate the policies of this section. The Equal Employment Opportunity Commission shall issue such rules, regulations, orders, and instructions as it deems necessary and appropriate to carry out its responsibilities under this section. The Equal Employment Opportunity Commission shall —

(1) be responsible for the review and evaluation of the operation of all agency programs designed to carry out the policy of this section, periodically obtaining and publishing (on at least a semiannual basis) progress reports from each department, agency, or unit referred to in subsection (a) of this section;

(2) consult with and solicit the recommendations of interested individuals, groups, and organizations relating to nondiscrimination in employment on account of age; and

(3) provide for the acceptance and processing of complaints of discrimination in Federal employment on account of age.

The head of each such department, agency, or unit shall comply with such rules, regulations, orders, and instructions of the Equal Employment Opportunity Commission which shall include a provision that an employee or applicant for employment shall be notified of any final action taken on any complaint of discrimination filed by him thereunder. Reasonable exemptions to the provisions of this section may be established by the Commission but only when the Commission has established a maximum age requirement on the basis of a determination that age is a bona fide occupational qualification necessary to the performance of the duties of the position. With respect to employment in the Library of Congress, authorities granted in this subsection to the Equal Employment Opportunity Commission shall be exercised by the Librarian of Congress.

(c) Civil actions; jurisdiction; relief

Any person aggrieved may bring a civil action in any Federal district court of competent jurisdiction for such legal or equitable relief as will effectuate the purposes of this chapter.

(d) Notice to Commission; time of notice; Commission notification of prospective defendants; Commission elimination of unlawful practices

When the individual has not filed a complaint concerning age discrimination with the Commission, no civil action may be commenced by any individual under this section until the individual has given the Commission not less than thirty days' notice of an intent to file such action. Such notice shall be filed within one hundred and eighty days after the alleged unlawful practice occurred. Upon receiving a notice of intent to sue, the Commission shall promptly notify all persons named therein as prospective defendants in the action and take any appropriate action to assure the elimination of any unlawful practice.

(e) Duty of Government agency or official

Nothing contained in this section shall relieve any Government agency or official of the responsibility to assure nondiscrimination on account of age in employment as required under any provision of Federal law.

(f) Applicability of statutory provisions to personnel action of Federal departments, etc.

Any personnel action of any department, agency, or other entity referred to in subsection (a) of this section shall not be subject to, or affected by, any provision of this chapter, other than the provisions of section 631(b) of this title and the provisions of this section.

(g) Study and report to President and Congress by Equal Employment Opportunity Commission; scope

(1) The Equal Employment Opportunity Commission shall undertake a study relating to the effects of the amendments made to this section by the Age Discrimination in Employment Act Amendments of 1978, and the effects of section 631(b) of this title.

(2) The Equal Employment Opportunity Commission shall transmit a report to the President and to the Congress containing the findings of the Commission resulting from the study of the Commission under paragraph (1) of this subsection. Such report shall be transmitted no later than January 1, 1980.

Sec. 634. Authorization of appropriations

There are hereby authorized to be appropriated such sums as may be necessary to carry out this chapter.

Occupational Safety and Health Act

U.S. Code, Title 29, Sections 651 to 678

Sec.

OSH ACT IN A NUTSHELL

Enacted: 1970

Purpose: To ensure safe and healthful working conditions

Coverage: Private sector employers except for industries regulated by other federal agencies such as mining and seafaring

Responsible agency: Occupational Safety and Health Administration

Sec. 651. Congressional statement of findings and declaration of purpose and policy

(a) The Congress finds that personal injuries and illnesses arising out of work situations impose a substantial burden upon, and are a hindrance to, interstate commerce in terms of lost production, wage loss, medical expenses, and disability compensation payments.

(b) The Congress declares it to be its purpose and policy, through the exercise of its powers to regulate commerce among the several States and with foreign nations and to provide for the general welfare, to assure so far as possible every working man and woman in the Nation safe and healthful working conditions and to preserve our human resources —

(1) by encouraging employers and employees in their efforts to reduce the number of occupational safety and health hazards at their places of employment, and to stimulate employers and employees to institute new and to perfect existing programs for providing safe and healthful working conditions;

(2) by providing that employers and employees have separate but dependent responsibilities and rights with respect to achieving safe and healthful working conditions;

(3) by authorizing the Secretary of Labor to set mandatory occupational safety and health standards applicable to businesses affecting interstate commerce, and by creating an Occupational Safety and Health Review Commission for carrying out adjudicatory functions under this chapter;

(4) by building upon advances already made through employer and employee initiative for providing safe and healthful working conditions;

(5) by providing for research in the field of occupational safety and health, including the psychological factors involved, and by developing innovative methods, techniques, and approaches for dealing with occupational safety and health problems;

(6) by exploring ways to discover latent diseases, establishing causal connections between diseases and work in environmental conditions, and conducting other research relating to health problems, in recognition of the fact that occupational health standards present problems often different from those involved in occupational safety;

(7) by providing medical criteria which will assure insofar as practicable that no employee will suffer diminished health, functional capacity, or life expectancy as a result of his work experience;

(8) by providing for training programs to increase the number and competence of personnel engaged in the field of occupational safety and health;

(9) by providing for the development and promulgation of occupational safety and health standards;

(10) by providing an effective enforcement program which shall include a prohibition against giving advance notice of any inspection and sanctions for any individual violating this prohibition;

(11) by encouraging the States to assume the fullest responsibility for the administration and enforcement of their occupational safety and health laws by providing grants to the States to assist in identifying their needs and responsibilities in the area of occupational safety and health, to develop plans in accordance with the provisions of this chapter, to improve the administration and enforcement of State occupational safety and health laws, and to conduct experimental and demonstration projects in connection therewith;

(12) by providing for appropriate reporting procedures with respect to occupational safety and health which procedures will help achieve the objectives of this chapter and accurately describe the nature of the occupational safety and health problem;

(13) by encouraging joint labor-management efforts to reduce injuries and disease arising out of employment.

Sec. 652. Definitions

For the purposes of this chapter —

(1) The term "Secretary" means the Secretary of Labor.

(2) The term "Commission" means the Occupational Safety and Health Review Commission established under this chapter.

(3) The term "commerce" means trade, traffic, commerce, transportation, or communication among the several States, or between a State and any place outside thereof, or within the District of Columbia, or a possession of the United States (other than the Trust Territory of the Pacific Islands), or between points in the same State but through a point outside thereof.

(4) The term "person" means one or more individuals, partnerships, associations, corporations, business trusts, legal representatives, or any organized group of persons.

(5) The term "employer" means a person engaged in a business affecting commerce who has employees, but does not include the United States (not including the United States Postal Service) or any State or political subdivision of a State.

(6) The term "employee" means an employee of an employer who is employed in a business of his employer which affects commerce.

(7) The term "State" includes a State of the United States, the District of Columbia, Puerto Rico, the Virgin Islands, American Samoa, Guam, and the Trust Territory of the Pacific Islands.

(8) The term "occupational safety and health standard" means a standard which requires conditions, or the adoption or use of one or more practices, means, methods, operations, or processes, reasonably necessary or appropriate to provide safe or healthful employment and places of employment.

(9) The term "national consensus standard" means any occupational safety and health standard or modification thereof which (1), has been adopted and promulgated by a nationally recognized standards-producing organization under procedures whereby it can be determined by the Secretary that persons interested and affected by the scope or provisions of the standard have reached substantial agreement on its adoption, (2) was formulated in a manner which afforded an opportunity for diverse views to be considered and (3) has been designated as such a standard by the Secretary, after consultation with other appropriate Federal agencies.

(10) The term "established Federal standard" means any operative occupational safety and health standard established by any agency of the United States and presently in effect, or contained in any Act of Congress in force on December 29, 1970.

(11) The term "Committee" means the National Advisory Committee on Occupational Safety and Health established under this chapter.

(12) The term "Director" means the Director of the National Institute for Occupational Safety and Health.

(13) The term "Institute" means the National Institute for Occupational Safety and Health established under this chapter.

(14) The term "Workmen's Compensation Commission" means the National Commission on State Workmen's Compensation Laws established under this chapter.

Sec. 653. Geographic applicability; judicial enforcement; applicability to existing standards; report to Congress on duplication and coordination of Federal laws; workmen's compensation law or common law or statutory rights, duties, or liabilities of employers and employees unaffected

(a) This chapter shall apply with respect to employment performed in a workplace in a State, the District of Columbia, the Commonwealth of Puerto Rico, the Virgin Islands, American Samoa, Guam, the Trust Territory of the Pacific Islands, Lake Island, Outer Continental Shelf lands defined in the Outer Continental Shelf Lands Act (43 U.S.C. §1331 et seq.), Johnston Island, and the Canal Zone. The Secretary of the Interior shall, by regulation, provide for judicial enforcement of this chapter by the courts established for areas in which there are no United States district courts having jurisdiction.

(b)(1) Nothing in this chapter shall apply to working conditions of employees with respect to which other Federal agencies, and State agencies acting under section 2021 of Title 42, exercise statutory authority to prescribe or enforce standards or regulations affecting occupational safety or health.

(2) The safety and health standards promulgated under the Act of June 30, 1936, commonly known as the Walsh-Healey Act (41 U.S.C. §35 et seq.), the Service Contract Act of 1965 (41 U.S.C. §351 et seq.), Public Law 91-54, Act of August 9, 1969, Public Law 85-742, Act of August 23, 1958, and the National Foundation on Arts and Humanities Act (20 U.S.C. §951 et seq.) are superseded on the effective date of corresponding standards, promulgated under this chapter, which are determined by the Secretary to be more effective. Standards issued under the laws listed in this paragraph and in effect on or after the effective date of this chapter shall be deemed to be occupational safety and health standards issued under this chapter, as well as under such other Acts.

(3) The Secretary shall, within three years after the effective date of this chapter, report to the Congress his recommendations for legislation to avoid unnecessary duplication and to achieve coordination between this chapter and other Federal laws.

(4) Nothing in this chapter shall be construed to supersede or in any manner affect any workmen's compensation law or to enlarge or diminish or affect in any other manner the common law or statutory rights, duties, or liabilities of employers and employees under any law with respect to injuries, diseases, or death of employees arising out of, or in the course of, employment.

Sec. 654. Duties of employers and employees

(a) Each employer —

(1) shall furnish to each of his employees employment and a place of employment which are free from recognized hazards that are causing or are likely to cause death or serious physical harm to his employees;

(2) shall comply with occupational safety and health standards promulgated under this chapter.

(b) Each employee shall comply with occupational safety and health standards and all rules, regulations, and orders issued pursuant to this chapter which are applicable to his own actions and conduct.

Sec. 655. Standards

(a) Promulgation by Secretary of national consensus standards and established Federal standards; time for promulgation; conflicting standards

Without regard to chapter 5 of Title 5 or to the other subsections of this section, the Secretary shall, as soon as practicable during the period beginning with the effective date of this chapter and ending two years after such date, by rule promulgate as an occupational safety or health standard any national consensus standard, and any established Federal standard, unless he determines that the promulgation of such a standard would not result in improved safety or health for specifically designated employees. In the event of conflict among any such standards, the Secretary shall promulgate the standard which assures the greatest protection of the safety or health of the affected employees.

(b) Procedure for promulgation, modification, or revocation of standards

The Secretary may by rule promulgate, modify, or revoke any occupational safety or health standard in the following manner:

(1) Whenever the Secretary, upon the basis of information submitted to him in writing by an interested person, a representative of any organization of employers or employees, a nationally recognized standards-producing organization, the Secretary of Health and Human Services, the National Institute for Occupational Safety and Health, or a State or political subdivision, or on the basis of information developed by the Secretary or otherwise available to him, determines that a rule should be promulgated in order to serve the objectives of this chapter, the Secretary may request the recommendations of an advisory committee appointed under section 656 of this title. The Secretary shall provide such an advisory committee with any proposals of his own or of the Secretary of Health and Human Services, together with all pertinent factual information developed by the Secretary or the Secretary of Health and Human Services, or otherwise available, including the results of research, demonstrations, and experiments. An advisory committee shall submit to the Secretary its recommendations regarding the rule to be promulgated within ninety days from the date of its appointment or within such longer or shorter period as may be prescribed by the Secretary, but in no event for a period which is longer than two hundred and seventy days.

(2) The Secretary shall publish a proposed rule promulgating, modifying, or revoking an occupational safety or health standard in the Federal Register and shall afford interested persons a period of thirty days after publication to submit written data or comments. Where an advisory committee is appointed and the Secretary determines that a rule should be issued, he shall publish the proposed rule within sixty days after the submission of the advisory committee's recommendations or the expiration of the period prescribed by the Secretary for such submission.

(3) On or before the last day of the period provided for the submission of written data or comments under paragraph (2), any interested person may file with the Secretary written objections to the proposed rule, stating the grounds therefor and requesting a public hearing on such objections. Within thirty days after the last day for filing such objections, the Secretary shall publish in the Federal Register a notice specifying the occupational safety or health standard to which objections have been filed and a hearing requested, and specifying a time and place for such hearing.

(4) Within sixty days after the expiration of the period provided for the submission of written data or comments under paragraph (2), or within sixty days after the completion of any hearing held under paragraph (3), the Secretary shall issue a rule promulgating, modifying, or revoking an occupational safety or health standard or make a determination that a rule should not be issued. Such a rule may contain a provision delaying its effective date for such period (not in excess of ninety days) as the Secretary determines may be

necessary to insure that affected employers and employees will be informed of the existence of the standard and of its terms and that employers affected are given an opportunity to familiarize themselves and their employees with the existence of the requirements of the standard.

(5) The Secretary, in promulgating standards dealing with toxic materials or harmful physical agents under this subsection, shall set the standard which most adequately assures, to the extent feasible, on the basis of the best available evidence, that no employee will suffer material impairment of health or functional capacity even if such employee has regular exposure to the hazard dealt with by such standard for the period of his working life. Development of standards under this subsection shall be based upon research, demonstrations, experiments, and such other information as may be appropriate. In addition to the attainment of the highest degree of health and safety protection for the employee, other considerations shall be the latest available scientific data in the field, the feasibility of the standards, and experience gained under this and other health and safety laws. Whenever practicable, the standard promulgated shall be expressed in terms of objective criteria and of the performance desired.

(6)(A) Any employer may apply to the Secretary for a temporary order granting a variance from a standard or any provision thereof promulgated under this section. Such temporary order shall be granted only if the employer files an application which meets the requirements of clause (B) and establishes that (i) he is unable to comply with a standard by its effective date because of unavailability of professional or technical personnel or of materials and equipment needed to come into compliance with the standard or because necessary construction or alteration of facilities cannot be completed by the effective date, (ii) he is taking all available steps to safeguard his employees against the hazards covered by the standard, and (iii) he has an effective program for coming into compliance with the standard as quickly as practicable. Any temporary order issued under this paragraph shall prescribe the practices, means, methods, operations, and processes which the employer must adopt and use while the order is in effect and state in detail his program for coming into compliance with the standard. Such a temporary order may be granted only after notice to employees and an opportunity for a hearing: *Provided,* That the Secretary may issue one interim order to be effective until a decision is made on the basis of the hearing. No temporary order may be in effect for longer than the period needed by the employer to achieve compliance with the standard or one year, whichever is shorter, except that such an order may be renewed not more than twice (I) so long as the requirements of this paragraph are met and (II) if an application for renewal is filed at least 90 days prior to the expiration date of the order. No interim renewal of an order may remain in effect for longer than 180 days.

(B) An application for a temporary order under this paragraph (6) shall contain:

(i) a specification of the standard or portion thereof from which the employer seeks a variance,

(ii) a representation by the employer, supported by representations from qualified persons having firsthand knowledge of the facts represented, that he is unable to comply with the standard or portion thereof and a detailed statement of the reasons therefor,

(iii) a statement of the steps he has taken and will take (with specific dates) to protect employees against the hazard covered by the standard,

(iv) a statement of when he expects to be able to comply with the standard and what steps he has taken and what steps he will take (with dates specified) to come into compliance with the standard, and

(v) a certification that he has informed his employees of the application by giving a copy thereof to their authorized representative, posting a statement giving a summary of the application and specifying where a copy may be examined at the place or places where notices to employees are normally posted, and by other appropriate means.

A description of how employees have been informed shall be contained in the certification. The information to employees shall also inform them of their right to petition the Secretary for a hearing.

(C) The Secretary is authorized to grant a variance from any standard or portion thereof

whenever he determines, or the Secretary of Health and Human Services certifies, that such variance is necessary to permit an employer to participate in an experiment approved by him or the Secretary of Health and Human Services designed to demonstrate or validate new and improved techniques to safeguard the health or safety of workers.

(7) Any standard promulgated under this subsection shall prescribe the use of labels or other appropriate forms of warning as are necessary to insure that employees are apprised of all hazards to which they are exposed, relevant symptoms and appropriate emergency treatment, and proper conditions and precautions of safe use or exposure. Where appropriate, such standard shall also prescribe suitable protective equipment and control or technological procedures to be used in connection with such hazards and shall provide for monitoring or measuring employee exposure at such locations and intervals, and in such manner as may be necessary for the protection of employees. In addition, where appropriate, any such standard shall prescribe the type and frequency of medical examinations or other tests which shall be made available, by the employer or at his cost, to employees exposed to such hazards in order to most effectively determine whether the health of such employees is adversely affected by such exposure. In the event such medical examinations are in the nature of research, as determined by the Secretary of Health and Human Services, such examinations may be furnished at the expense of the Secretary of Health and Human Services. The results of such examinations or tests shall be furnished only to the Secretary or the Secretary of Health and Human Services, and, at the request of the employee, to his physician. The Secretary, in consultation with the Secretary of Health and Human Services, may by rule promulgated pursuant to section 553 of Title 5, make appropriate modifications in the foregoing requirements relating to the use of labels or other forms of warning, monitoring or measuring, and medical examinations, as may be warranted by experience, information, or medical or technological developments acquired subsequent to the promulgation of the relevant standard.

(8) Whenever a rule promulgated by the Secretary differs substantially from an existing national consensus standard, the Secretary shall, at the same time, publish in the Federal Register a statement of the reasons why the rule as adopted will better effectuate the purposes of this chapter than the national consensus standard.

(c) Emergency temporary standards

(1) The Secretary shall provide, without regard to the requirements of chapter 5 of Title 5, for an emergency temporary standard to take immediate effect upon publication in the Federal Register if he determines (A) that employees are exposed to grave danger from exposure to substances or agents determined to be toxic or physically harmful or from new hazards, and (B) that such emergency standard is necessary to protect employees from such danger.

(2) Such standard shall be effective until superseded by a standard promulgated in accordance with the procedures prescribed in paragraph (3) of this subsection.

(3) Upon publication of such standard in the Federal Register the Secretary shall commence a proceeding in accordance with subsection (b) of this section, and the standard as published shall also serve as a proposed rule for the proceeding. The Secretary shall promulgate a standard under this paragraph no later than six months after publication of the emergency standard as provided in paragraph (2) of this subsection.

(d) Variances from standards; procedure

Any affected employer may apply to the Secretary for a rule or order for a variance from a standard promulgated under this section. Affected employees shall be given notice of each such application and an opportunity to participate in a hearing. The Secretary shall issue such rule or order if he determines on the record, after opportunity for an inspection where appropriate and a hearing, that the proponent of the variance has demonstrated by a preponderance of the evidence that the conditions, practices, means, methods, operations, or processes used or proposed to be used by an employer will provide employment and places of employment to his employees which are as safe and healthful as those which would prevail if he complied with the standard. The rule or order so issued shall prescribe the conditions the employer must maintain, and the practices, means, methods, operations, and processes which he must adopt and utilize to the extent they differ from the standard in question. Such a rule or order may be modified or revoked upon application by an employer, employees,

or by the Secretary on his own motion, in the manner prescribed for its issuance under this subsection at any time after six months from its issuance.

(e) Statement of reasons for Secretary's determinations; publication in Federal Register

Whenever the Secretary promulgates any standard, makes any rule, order, or decision, grants any exemption or extension of time, or compromises, mitigates, or settles any penalty assessed under this chapter, he shall include a statement of the reasons for such action, which shall be published in the Federal Register.

(f) Judicial review

Any person who may be adversely affected by a standard issued under this section may at any time prior to the sixtieth day after such standard is promulgated file a petition challenging the validity of such standard with the United States court of appeals for the circuit wherein such person resides or has his principal place of business, for a judicial review of such standard. A copy of the petition shall be forthwith transmitted by the clerk of the court to the Secretary. The filing of such petition shall not, unless otherwise ordered by the court, operate as a stay of the standard. The determinations of the Secretary shall be conclusive if supported by substantial evidence in the record considered as a whole.

(g) Priority for establishment of standards

In determining the priority for establishing standards under this section, the Secretary shall give due regard to the urgency of the need for mandatory safety and health standards for particular industries, trades, crafts, occupations, businesses, workplaces or work environments. The Secretary shall also give due regard to the recommendations of the Secretary of Health and Human Services regarding the need for mandatory standards in determining the priority for establishing such standards.

Sec. 656. Administration

(a) National Advisory Committee on Occupational Safety and Health; establishment; membership; appointment; Chairman; functions; meetings; compensation; secretarial and clerical personnel

(1) There is hereby established a National Advisory Committee on Occupational Safety and

Health consisting of twelve members appointed by the Secretary, four of whom are to be designated by the Secretary of Health and Human Services, without regard to the provisions of Title 5 governing appointments in the competitive service, and composed of representatives of management, labor, occupational safety and occupational health professions, and of the public. The Secretary shall designate one of the public members as Chairman. The members shall be selected upon the basis of their experience and competence in the field of occupational safety and health.

(2) The Committee shall advise, consult with, and make recommendations to the Secretary and the Secretary of Health and Human Services on matters relating to the administration of this chapter. The Committee shall hold no fewer than two meetings during each calendar year. All meetings of the Committee shall be open to the public and a transcript shall be kept and made available for public inspection.

(3) The members of the Committee shall be compensated in accordance with the provisions of section 3109 of Title 5.

(4) The Secretary shall furnish to the Committee an executive secretary and such secretarial, clerical, and other services as are deemed necessary to the conduct of its business.

(b) **Advisory committees; appointment; duties; membership; compensation; reimbursement to member's employer; meetings; availability of records; conflict of interest**

An advisory committee may be appointed by the Secretary to assist him in his standard-setting functions under section 655 of this title. Each such committee shall consist of not more than fifteen members and shall include as a member one or more designees of the Secretary of Health and Human Services, and shall include among its members an equal number of persons qualified by experience and affiliation to present the viewpoint of the employers involved, and of persons similarly qualified to present the viewpoint of the workers involved, as well as one or more representatives of health and safety agencies of the States. An advisory committee may also include such other persons as the Secretary may appoint who are qualified by knowledge and experience to make a useful contribution to the work of such committee, including

one or more representatives of professional organizations of technicians or professionals specializing in occupational safety or health, and one or more representatives of nationally recognized standards-producing organizations, but the number of persons so appointed to any such advisory committee shall not exceed the number appointed to such committee as representatives of Federal and State agencies. Persons appointed to advisory committees from private life shall be compensated in the same manner as consultants or experts under section 3109 of Title 5. The Secretary shall pay to any State which is the employer of a member of such a committee who is a representative of the health or safety agency of that State, reimbursement sufficient to cover the actual cost to the State resulting from such representative's membership on such committee. Any meeting of such committee shall be open to the public and an accurate record shall be kept and made available to the public. No member of such committee (other than representatives of employers and employees) shall have an economic interest in any proposed rule.

(c) **Use of services, facilities, and personnel of Federal, State, and local agencies; reimbursement; employment of experts and consultants or organizations; renewal of contracts; compensation; travel expenses**

In carrying out his responsibilities under this chapter, the Secretary is authorized to —

(1) use, with the consent of any Federal agency, the services, facilities, and personnel of such agency, with or without reimbursement, and with the consent of any State or political subdivision thereof, accept and use the services, facilities, and personnel of any agency of such State or subdivision with reimbursement; and

(2) employ experts and consultants or organizations thereof as authorized by section 3109 of Title 5, except that contracts for such employment may be renewed annually; compensate individuals so employed at rates not in excess of the rate specified at the time of service for grade GS-18 under section 5332 of Title 5, including travel time, and allow them while away from their homes or regular places of business, travel expenses (including per diem in lieu of subsistence) as authorized by section 5703 of Title 5 for persons in the Government service employed intermittently, while so employed.

Sec. 657. Inspections, investigations, and record keeping

(a) Authority of Secretary to enter, inspect, and investigate places of employment; time and manner

In order to carry out the purposes of this chapter, the Secretary, upon presenting appropriate credentials to the owner, operator, or agent in charge, is authorized —

(1) to enter without delay and at reasonable times any factory, plant, establishment, construction site, or other area, workplace or environment where work is performed by an employee of an employer; and

(2) to inspect and investigate during regular working hours and at other reasonable times, and within reasonable limits and in a reasonable manner, any such place of employment and all pertinent conditions, structures, machines, apparatus, devices, equipment, and materials therein, and to question privately any such employer, owner, operator, agent, or employee.

(b) Attendance and testimony of witnesses and production of evidence; enforcement of subpoena

In making his inspections and investigations under this chapter the Secretary may require the attendance and testimony of witnesses and the production of evidence under oath. Witnesses shall be paid the same fees and mileage that are paid witnesses in the courts of the United States. In case of a contumacy, failure, or refusal of any person to obey such an order, any district court of the United States or the United States courts of any territory or possession, within the jurisdiction of which such person is found, or resides or transacts business, upon the application by the Secretary, shall have jurisdiction to issue to such person an order requiring such person to appear to produce evidence if, as, and when so ordered, and to give testimony relating to the matter under investigation or in question, and any failure to obey such order of the court may be punished by said court as a contempt thereof.

(c) Maintenance, preservation, and availability of records; issuance of regulations; scope of records; periodic inspections by employer; posting of notices by employer; notification of employee of corrective action

(1) Each employer shall make, keep and preserve, and make available to the Secretary or the Secretary of Health and Human Services, such records regarding his activities relating to this chapter as the Secretary, in cooperation with the Secretary of Health and Human Services, may prescribe by regulation as necessary or appropriate for the enforcement of this chapter or for developing information regarding the causes and prevention of occupational accidents and illnesses. In order to carry out the provisions of this paragraph such regulations may include provisions requiring employers to conduct periodic inspections. The Secretary shall also issue regulations requiring that employers, through posting of notices or other appropriate means, keep their employees informed of their protections and obligations under this chapter, including the provisions of applicable standards.

(2) The Secretary, in cooperation with the Secretary of Health and Human Services, shall prescribe regulations requiring employers to maintain accurate records of, and to make periodic reports on, work-related deaths, injuries and illnesses other than minor injuries requiring only first aid treatment and which do not involve medical treatment, loss of consciousness, restriction of work or motion, or transfer to another job.

(3) The Secretary, in cooperation with the Secretary of Health and Human Services, shall issue regulations requiring employers to maintain accurate records of employee exposures to potentially toxic materials or harmful physical agents which are required to be monitored or measured under section 655 of this title. Such regulations shall provide employees or their representatives with an opportunity to observe such monitoring or measuring, and to have access to the records thereof. Such regulations shall also make appropriate provision for each employee or former employee to have access to such records as will indicate his own exposure to toxic materials or harmful physical agents. Each employer shall promptly notify any employee who has been or is being exposed to toxic materials or harmful physical agents in concentrations or at levels which exceed those prescribed by an applicable occupational safety and health standard promulgated under section 655 of this title, and shall inform any employee who is being thus exposed of the corrective action being taken.

(d) Obtaining of information

Any information obtained by the Secretary, the Secretary of Health and Human Services, or a State agency under this chapter shall be obtained with a minimum burden upon employers, especially those operating small businesses. Unnecessary duplication of efforts in obtaining information shall be reduced to the maximum extent feasible.

(e) Employer and authorized employee representatives to accompany Secretary or his authorized representative on inspection of workplace; consultation with employees where no authorized employee representative is present

Subject to regulations issued by the Secretary, a representative of the employer and a representative authorized by his employees shall be given an opportunity to accompany the Secretary or his authorized representative during the physical inspection of any workplace under subsection (a) of this section for the purpose of aiding such inspection. Where there is no authorized employee representative, the Secretary or his authorized representative shall consult with a reasonable number of employees concerning matters of health and safety in the workplace.

(f) Request for inspection by employees or representative of employees; grounds; procedure; determination of request; notification of Secretary or representative prior to or during any inspection of violations; procedure for review of refusal by representative of Secretary to issue citation for alleged violations

(1) Any employees or representative of employees who believe that a violation of a safety or health standard exists that threatens physical harm, or that an imminent danger exists, may request an inspection by giving notice to the Secretary or his authorized representative of such violation or danger. Any such notice shall be reduced to writing, shall set forth with reasonable particularity the grounds for the notice, and shall be signed by the employees or representative of employees, and a copy shall be provided the employer or his agent no later than at the time of inspection, except that, upon the request of the person giving such notice, his name and the names of individual employees referred to therein

shall not appear in such copy or on any record published, released, or made available pursuant to subsection (g) of this section. If upon receipt of such notification the Secretary determines there are reasonable grounds to believe that such violation or danger exists, he shall make a special inspection in accordance with the provisions of this section as soon as practicable, to determine if such violation or danger exists. If the Secretary determines there are no reasonable grounds to believe that a violation or danger exists he shall notify the employees or representative of the employees in writing of such determination.

(2) Prior to or during any inspection of a workplace, any employees or representative of employees employed in such workplace may notify the Secretary or any representative of the Secretary responsible for conducting the inspection, in writing, of any violation of this chapter which they have reason to believe exists in such workplace. The Secretary shall, by regulation, establish procedures for informal review of any refusal by a representative of the Secretary to issue a citation with respect to any such alleged violation and shall furnish the employees or representative of employees requesting such review a written statement of the reasons for the Secretary's final disposition of the case.

(g) Compilation, analysis, and publication of reports and information; rules and regulations

(1) The Secretary and Secretary of Health and Human Services are authorized to compile, analyze, and publish, either in summary or detailed form, all reports or information obtained under this section.

(2) The Secretary and the Secretary of Health and Human Services shall each prescribe such rules and regulations as he may deem necessary to carry out their responsibilities under this chapter, including rules and regulations dealing with the inspection of an employer's establishment.

(h) Results of enforcement activities; not to be used to evaluate employees

The Secretary shall not use the results of enforcement activities, such as the number of citations issued or penalties assessed, to evaluate employees directly involved in enforcement activities under this chapter or to impose quotas or goals with regard to the results of such activities.

Sec. 658. Citations

(a) Authority to issue; grounds; contents; notice in lieu of citation for de minimis violations

If, upon inspection or investigation, the Secretary or his authorized representative believes that an employer has violated a requirement of section 654 of this title, of any standard, rule or order promulgated pursuant to section 655 of this title, or of any regulations prescribed pursuant to this chapter, he shall with reasonable promptness issue a citation to the employer. Each citation shall be in writing and shall describe with particularity the nature of the violation, including a reference to the provision of the chapter, standard, rule, regulation, or order alleged to have been violated. In addition, the citation shall fix a reasonable time for the abatement of the violation. The Secretary may prescribe procedures for the issuance of a notice in lieu of a citation with respect to de minimis violations which have no direct or immediate relationship to safety or health.

(b) Posting

Each citation issued under this section, or a copy or copies thereof, shall be prominently posted, as prescribed in regulations issued by the Secretary, at or near each place a violation referred to in the citation occurred.

(c) Time for issuance

No citation may be issued under this section after the expiration of six months following the occurrence of any violation.

Sec. 659. Enforcement procedures

(a) Notification of employer of proposed assessment of penalty subsequent to issuance of citation; time for notification of Secretary by employer of contest by employer of citation or proposed assessment; citation and proposed assessment as final order upon failure of employer to notify of contest and failure of employees to file notice

If, after an inspection or investigation, the Secretary issues a citation under section 658(a) of this title, he shall, within a reasonable time after the termination of such inspection or investigation, notify the employer by certified mail of the penalty, if any, proposed to be assessed under section 666 of this title and that the employer has fifteen working days within which to notify the Secretary that he wishes to contest the citation or proposed assessment of penalty. If, within fifteen working days from the receipt of the notice issued by the Secretary the employer fails to notify the Secretary that he intends to contest the citation or proposed assessment of penalty, and no notice is filed by any employee or representative of employees under subsection (c) of this section within such time, the citation and the assessment, as proposed, shall be deemed a final order of the Commission and not subject to review by any court or agency.

(b) Notification of employer of failure to correct in allotted time period violation for which citation was issued and proposed assessment of penalty for failure to correct; time for notification of Secretary by employer of contest by employer of notification of failure to correct or proposed assessment; notification or proposed assessment as final order upon failure of employer to notify of contest

If the Secretary has reason to believe that an employer has failed to correct a violation for which a citation has been issued within the period permitted for its correction (which period shall not begin to run until the entry of a final order by the Commission in the case of any review proceedings under this section initiated by the employer in good faith and not solely for delay or avoidance of penalties), the Secretary shall notify the employer by certified mail of such failure and of the penalty proposed to be assessed under section 666 of this title by reason of such failure, and that the employer has fifteen working days within which to notify the Secretary that he wishes to contest the Secretary's notification or the proposed assessment of penalty. If, within fifteen working days from the receipt of notification issued by the Secretary, the employer fails to notify the Secretary that he intends to contest the notification or proposed assessment of penalty, the notification or proposed assessment of penalty, the notification and assessment, as proposed, shall be deemed a final order of the Commission and not subject to review by any court or agency.

(c) Advisement of Commission by Secretary of notification of contest by employer of citation or notification or of filing of notice by any employee or representative of employees; hearing by Commission; orders of Commission and Secretary; rules of procedure

If an employer notifies the Secretary that he intends to contest a citation issued under section 658(a) of this title or notification issued under subsection (a) or (b) of this section, or if, within fifteen working days of the issuance of a citation under section 658(a) of this title, any employee or representative of employees files a notice with the Secretary alleging that the period of time fixed in the citation for the abatement of the violation is unreasonable, the Secretary shall immediately advise the Commission of such notification, and the Commission shall afford an opportunity for a hearing (in accordance with section 554 of Title 5 but without regard to subsection (a)(3) of such section). The Commission shall thereafter issue an order, based on findings of fact, affirming, modifying, or vacating the Secretary's citation or proposed penalty, or directing other appropriate relief, and such order shall become final thirty days after its issuance. Upon a showing by an employer of a good faith effort to comply with the abatement requirements of a citation, and that abatement has not been completed because of factors beyond his reasonable control, the Secretary, after an opportunity for a hearing as provided in this subsection, shall issue an order affirming or modifying the abatement requirements in such citation. The rules of procedure prescribed by the Commission shall provide affected employees or representatives of affected employees an opportunity to participate as parties to hearings under this subsection.

Sec. 660. Judicial review

(a) Filing of petition by persons adversely affected or aggrieved; orders subject to review; jurisdiction; venue; procedure; conclusiveness of record and findings of Commission; appropriate relief; finality of judgment

Any person adversely affected or aggrieved by an order of the Commission issued under subsection (c) of section 659 of this title may obtain a review of such order in any United States court of appeals for the circuit in which the violation is alleged to have occurred or where the employer has its principal office, or in the Court of Appeals for the District of Columbia Circuit, by filing in such court within sixty days following the issuance of such order a written petition praying that the order be modified or set aside. A copy of such petition shall be forthwith transmitted by the clerk of the court to the Commission and to the other parties, and thereupon the Commission shall file in the court the record in the proceeding as provided in section 2112 of Title 28. Upon such filing, the court shall have jurisdiction of the proceeding and of the question determined therein, and shall have power to grant such temporary relief or restraining order as it deems just and proper, and to make and enter upon the pleadings, testimony, and proceedings set forth in such record a decree affirming, modifying, or setting aside in whole or in part, the order of the Commission and enforcing the same to the extent that such order is affirmed or modified. The commencement of proceedings under this subsection shall not, unless ordered by the court, operate as a stay of the order of the Commission. No objection that has not been urged before the Commission shall be considered by the court, unless the failure or neglect to urge such objection shall be excused because of extraordinary circumstances. The findings of the Commission with respect to questions of fact, if supported by substantial evidence on the record considered as a whole, shall be conclusive. If any party shall apply to the court for leave to adduce additional evidence and shall show to the satisfaction of the court that such additional evidence is material and that there were reasonable grounds for the failure to adduce such evidence in the hearing before the Commission, the court may order such additional evidence to be taken before the Commission and to be made a part of the record. The Commission may modify its findings as to the facts, or make new findings, by reason of additional evidence so taken and filed, and it shall file such modified or new findings, which findings with respect to questions of fact, if supported by substantial evidence on the record considered as a whole, shall be conclusive, and its recommendations, if any, for the modification or setting aside of its original order. Upon the filing of the record with it, the jurisdiction of the court shall be exclusive and its judgment and decree shall be final, except that the same shall be subject to review by the Supreme Court of the United States, as provided in section 1254 of Title 28.

(b) Filing of petition by Secretary; orders subject to review; jurisdiction; venue; procedure; conclusiveness of record and findings of Commission; enforcement of orders; contempt proceedings

The Secretary may also obtain review or enforcement of any final order of the Commission by filing a petition for such relief in the United States court of appeals for the circuit in which the alleged violation occurred or in which the employer has its principal office, and the provisions of subsection (a) of this section shall govern such proceedings to the extent applicable. If no petition for review, as provided in subsection (a) of this section, is filed within sixty days after service of the Commission's order, the Commission's findings of fact and order shall be conclusive in connection with any petition for enforcement which is filed by the Secretary after the expiration of such sixty-day period. In any such case, as well as in the case of a noncontested citation or notification by the Secretary which has become a final order of the Commission under subsection (a) or (b) of section 659 of this title, the clerk of the court, unless otherwise ordered by the court, shall forthwith enter a decree enforcing the order and shall transmit a copy of such decree to the Secretary and the employer named in the petition. In any contempt proceeding brought to enforce a decree of a court of appeals entered pursuant to this subsection or subsection (a) of this section, the court of appeals may assess the penalties provided in section 666 of this title, in addition to invoking any other available remedies.

(c) Discharge or discrimination against employee for exercise of rights under this chapter; prohibition; procedure for relief

(1) No person shall discharge or in any manner discriminate against any employee because such employee has filed any complaint or instituted or caused to be instituted any proceeding under or related to this chapter or has testified or is about to testify in any such proceeding or because of the exercise by such employee on behalf of himself or others of any right afforded by this chapter.

(2) Any employee who believes that he has been discharged or otherwise discriminated against by any person in violation of this subsection may, within thirty days after such violation occurs, file a complaint with the Secretary alleging such discrimination. Upon receipt of such complaint, the Secretary shall cause such investigation to be made as he deems appropriate. If upon such investigation, the Secretary determines that the provisions of this subsection have been violated, he shall bring an action in any appropriate United States district court against such person. In any such action the United States district courts shall have jurisdiction, for cause shown to restrain violations of paragraph (1) of this subsection and order all appropriate relief including rehiring or reinstatement of the employee to his former position with back pay.

(3) Within 90 days of the receipt of a complaint filed under this subsection the Secretary shall notify the complainant of his determination under paragraph (2) of this subsection.

Sec. 661. Occupational Safety and Health Review Commission

(a) Establishment; membership; appointment; Chairman

The Occupational Safety and Health Review Commission is hereby established. The Commission shall be composed of three members who shall be appointed by the President, by and with the advice and consent of the Senate, from among persons who by reason of training, education, or experience are qualified to carry out the functions of the Commission under this chapter. The President shall designate one of the members of the Commission to serve as Chairman.

(b) Terms of office; removal by President

The terms of members of the Commission shall be six years except that (1) the members of the Commission first taking office shall serve, as designated by the President at the time of appointment, one for a term of two years, one for a term of four years, and one for a term of six years, and (2) a vacancy caused by the death, resignation, or removal of a member prior to the expiration of the term for which he was appointed shall be filled only for the remainder of such unexpired term. A member of the Commission may be removed by the President for inefficiency, neglect of duty, or malfeasance in office.

(c) Omitted

(d) Principal office; hearings or other proceedings at other places

The principal office of the Commission shall be in the District of Columbia. Whenever the Commission deems that the convenience of the public or of the parties may be promoted, or delay or expense may be minimized, it may hold hearings or conduct other proceedings at any other place.

(e) Functions and duties of Chairman; appointment and compensation of administrative law judges and other employees

The Chairman shall be responsible on behalf of the Commission for the administrative operations of the Commission and shall appoint such administrative law judges and other employees as he deems necessary to assist in the performance of the Commission's functions and to fix their compensation in accordance with the provisions of chapter 51 and subchapter III of chapter 53 of Title 5 relating to classification and General Schedule pay rates: *Provided*, That assignment, removal and compensation of administrative law judges shall be in accordance with sections 3105, 3344, 5372, and 7521 of Title 5.

(f) Quorum; official action

For the purpose of carrying out its functions under this chapter, two members of the Commission shall constitute a quorum and official action can be taken only on the affirmative vote of at least two members.

(g) Hearings and records open to public; promulgation of rules; applicability of Federal Rules of Civil Procedure

Every official act of the Commission shall be entered of record, and its hearings and records shall be open to the public. The Commission is authorized to make such rules as are necessary for the orderly transaction of its proceedings. Unless the Commission has adopted a different rule, its proceedings shall be in accordance with the Federal Rules of Civil Procedure.

(h) Depositions and production of documentary evidence; fees

The Commission may order testimony to be taken by deposition in any proceeding pending before it at any state of such proceeding. Any person may be compelled to appear and depose, and to produce books, papers, or documents, in the same manner as witnesses may be compelled to appear and testify and produce like documentary evidence before the Commission. Witnesses whose depositions are taken under this subsection, and the persons taking such depositions, shall be entitled to the same fees as are paid for like services in the courts of the United States.

(i) Investigatory powers

For the purpose of any proceeding before the Commission, the provisions of section 161 of this title are hereby made applicable to the jurisdiction and powers of the Commission.

(j) Administrative law judges; determinations; report as final order of Commission

A administrative law judge appointed by the Commission shall hear, and make a determination upon, any proceeding instituted before the Commission and any motion in connection therewith, assigned to such administrative law judge by the Chairman of the Commission, and shall make a report of any such determination which constitutes his final disposition of the proceedings. The report of the administrative law judge shall become the final order of the Commission within thirty days after such report by the administrative law judge, unless within such period any Commission member has directed that such report shall be reviewed by the Commission.

(k) Appointment and compensation of administrative law judges

Except as otherwise provided in this chapter, the administrative law judges shall be subject to the laws governing employees in the classified civil service, except that appointments shall be made without regard to section 5108 of Title 5. Each administrative law judge shall receive compensation at a rate not less than that prescribed for GS-16 under section 5332 of Title 5.

Sec. 662. Injunction proceedings

(a) Petition by Secretary to restrain imminent dangers; scope of order

The United States district courts shall have jurisdiction, upon petition of the Secretary, to restrain any conditions or practices in any place of employment which are such that a danger exists which could reasonably be expected to cause death or serious physical harm immediately or before the imminence of such danger can be eliminated through the enforcement procedures otherwise provided by this chapter. Any order issued under this section may require such steps to be taken as may be necessary to avoid, correct, or remove such imminent danger and prohibit the employment or presence of any individual in locations or under conditions where such imminent danger exists, except individuals whose presence is necessary to avoid, correct, or remove such imminent danger or to maintain the capacity of a continuous process operation to resume normal operations without a complete cessation of operations, or where a cessation of operations is necessary, to permit such to be accomplished in a safe and orderly manner.

(b) Appropriate injunctive relief or temporary restraining order pending outcome of enforcement proceeding; applicability of Rule 65 of Federal Rules of Civil Procedure

Upon the filing of any such petition the district court shall have jurisdiction to grant such injunctive relief or temporary restraining order pending the outcome of an enforcement proceeding pursuant to this chapter. The proceeding shall be as provided by Rule 65 of the Federal Rules, Civil Procedure, except that no temporary restraining order issued without notice shall be effective for a period longer than five days.

(c) Notification of affected employees and employers by inspector of danger and of recommendation to Secretary to seek relief

Whenever and as soon as an inspector concludes that conditions or practices described in subsection (a) of this section exist in any place of employment, he shall inform the affected employees and employers of the danger and that he is recommending to the Secretary that relief be sought.

(d) Failure of Secretary to seek relief; writ of mandamus

If the Secretary arbitrarily or capriciously fails to seek relief under this section, any employee who may be injured by reason of such failure, or the representative of such employees, might bring an action against the Secretary in the United States district court for the district in which the imminent danger is alleged to exist or the employer has its principal office, or for the District of Columbia, for a writ of mandamus to compel the Secretary to seek such an order and for such further relief as may be appropriate.

Sec. 663. Representation in civil litigation

Except as provided in section 518(a) of Title 28 relating to litigation before the Supreme Court, the Solicitor of Labor may appear for and represent the Secretary in any civil litigation brought under this chapter but all such litigations shall be subject to the direction and control of the Attorney General.

Sec. 664. Disclosure of trade secrets; protective orders

All information reported to or otherwise obtained by the Secretary or his representative in connection with any inspection or proceeding under this chapter which contains or which might reveal a trade secret referred to in section 1905 of Title 18 shall be considered confidential for the purpose of that section, except that such information may be disclosed to other officers or employees concerned with carrying out this chapter or when relevant in any proceeding under this chapter. In any such proceeding the Secretary, the Commission, or the court shall issue such orders as may be appropriate to protect the confidentiality of trade secrets.

Sec. 665. Variations, tolerances, and exemptions from required provisions; procedure; duration

The Secretary, on the record, after notice and opportunity for a hearing may provide such reasonable limitations and may make such rules and regulations allowing reasonable variations, tolerances, and exemptions to and from any or all provisions of this chapter as he may find necessary and proper to avoid serious impairment of the national defense. Such action shall not be in effect for more than six months without notification to affected employees and an opportunity being afforded for a hearing.

Sec. 666. Civil and criminal penalties

(a) Willful or repeated violation

Any employer who willfully or repeatedly violates the requirements of section 654 of this title, any standard, rule, or order promulgated pursuant to section 655 of this title, or regulations prescribed pursuant to this chapter may be assessed a civil penalty of not more than $70,000 for each violation, but not less than $5,000 for each willful violation.

(b) Citation for serious violation

Any employer who has received a citation for a serious violation of the requirements of section 654 of this title, of any standard, rule, or order promulgated pursuant to section 655 of this title, or of any regulations prescribed pursuant to this chapter, shall be assessed a civil penalty of up to $7,000 for each such violation.

(c) Citation for violation determined not serious

Any employer who has received a citation for a violation of the requirements of section 654 of this title, of any standard, rule, or order promulgated pursuant to section 655 of this title, or of regulations prescribed pursuant to this chapter, and such violation is specifically determined not to be of a serious nature, may be assessed a civil penalty of up to $7,000 for each such violation.

(d) Failure to correct violation

Any employer who fails to correct a violation for which a citation has been issued under section 658(a) of this title within the period permitted for its correction (which period shall not begin to run until the date of the final order of the Commission in the case of any review proceeding under section 659 of this title initiated by the employer in good faith and not solely for delay or avoidance of penalties), may be assessed a civil penalty of not more than $7,000 for each day during which such failure or violation continues.

(e) Willful violation causing death to employee

Any employer who willfully violates any standard, rule, or order promulgated pursuant to section 655 of this title, or of any regulations prescribed pursuant to this chapter, and that violation caused death to any employee, shall, upon conviction, be punished by a fine of not more than $10,000 or by imprisonment for not more than six months, or by both; except that if the conviction is for a violation committed after a first conviction of such person, punishment shall be by a fine of not more than $20,000 or by imprisonment for not more than one year, or by both.

(f) Giving advance notice of inspection

Any person who gives advance notice of any inspection to be conducted under this chapter, without authority from the Secretary or his designees, shall, upon conviction, be punished by a fine of not more than $1,000 or by imprisonment for not more than six months, or by both.

(g) False statements, representations or certification

Whoever knowingly makes any false statement, representation, or certification in any application, record, report, plan, or other document filed or required to be maintained pursuant to this chapter shall, upon conviction, be punished by a fine of not more than $10,000, or by imprisonment for not more than six months, or by both.

(h) Omitted

(i) Violation of posting requirements

Any employer who violates any of the posting requirements, as prescribed under the provisions of this chapter, shall be assessed a civil penalty of up to $7,000 for each violation.

(j) Authority of Commission to assess civil penalties

The Commission shall have authority to assess all civil penalties provided in this section, giving due consideration to the appropriateness of the penalty with respect to the size of the business of the employer being charged, the gravity of the violation, the good faith of the employer, and the history of previous violations.

(k) Determination of serious violation

For purposes of this section, a serious violation shall be deemed to exist in a place of employment if there is a substantial probability that death or serious physical harm could result from a condition which exists, or from one or more practices, means, methods, operations, or processes which have been adopted or are in use, in such place of employment unless the employer did not, and could not with the exercise of reasonable diligence, know of the presence of the violation.

(l) Procedure for payment of civil penalties

Civil penalties owned under this chapter shall be paid to the Secretary for deposit into the Treasury of the United States and shall accrue to the United States and may be recovered in a civil action in the name of the United States brought in the United States district court for the district where the violation is alleged to have occurred or where the employer has its principal office.

Sec. 667. State jurisdiction and plans

(a) Assertion of State standards in absence of applicable Federal standards

Nothing in this chapter shall prevent any State agency or court from asserting jurisdiction under State law over any occupational safety or health issue with respect to which no standard is in effect under section 655 of this title.

(b) Submission of State plan for development and enforcement of State standards to preempt applicable Federal standards

Any State which, at any time, desires to assume responsibility for development and enforcement therein of occupational safety and health standards relating to any occupational safety or health issue with respect to which a Federal standard has been promulgated under section 655 of this title shall submit a State plan for the development of such standards and their enforcement.

(c) Conditions for approval of plan

The Secretary shall approve the plan submitted by a State under subsection (b) of this section, or any modification thereof, if such plan in his judgment —

(1) designates a State agency or agencies as the agency or agencies responsible for administering the plan throughout the State,

(2) provides for the development and enforcement of safety and health standards relating to one or more safety or health issues, which standards (and the enforcement of which standards) are or will be at least as effective in providing safe and healthful employment and places of employment as the standards promulgated under section 655 of this title which relate to the same issues, and which standards, when applicable to products which are distributed or used in interstate commerce, are required by compelling local conditions and do not unduly burden interstate commerce,

(3) provides for a right of entry and inspection of all workplaces subject to this chapter which is

at least as effective as that provided in section 657 of this title, and includes a prohibition on advance notice of inspections,

(4) contains satisfactory assurances that such agency or agencies have or will have the legal authority and qualified personnel necessary for the enforcement of such standards,

(5) gives satisfactory assurances that such State will devote adequate funds to the administration and enforcement of such standards,

(6) contains satisfactory assurances that such State will, to the extent permitted by its law, establish and maintain an effective and comprehensive occupational safety and health program applicable to all employees of public agencies of the State and its political subdivisions, which program is as effective as the standards contained in an approved plan,

(7) requires employers in the State to make reports to the Secretary in the same manner and to the same extent as if the plan were not in effect, and

(8) provides that the State agency will make such reports to the Secretary in such form and containing such information, as the Secretary shall from time to time require.

(d) Rejection of plan; notice and opportunity for hearing

If the Secretary rejects a plan submitted under subsection (b) of this section, he shall afford the State submitting the plan due notice and opportunity for a hearing before so doing.

(e) Discretion of Secretary to exercise authority over comparable standards subsequent to approval of State plan; duration; retention of jurisdiction by Secretary upon determination of enforcement of plan by State

After the Secretary approves a State plan submitted under subsection (b) of this section, he may, but shall not be required to, exercise his authority under sections 657, 658, 659, 662, and 666 of this title with respect to comparable standards promulgated under section 655 of this title, for the period specified in the next sentence. The Secretary may exercise the authority referred to above until he determines, on the basis of actual operations under the State plan, that the criteria set forth in subsection (c) of this section are being applied, but he shall not make such determination for at least three years after the plan's approval under subsection (c) of this section. Upon making the determination referred to in the preceding sentence, the provisions of sections 654(a)(2), 657 (except for the purpose of carrying out subsection (f) of this section), 658, 659, 662, and 666 of this title, and standards promulgated under section 655 of this title, shall not apply with respect to any occupational safety or health issues covered under the plan, but the Secretary may retain jurisdiction under the above provisions in any proceeding commenced under section 658 or 659 of this title before the date of determination.

(f) Continuing evaluation by Secretary of State enforcement of approved plan; withdrawal of approval of plan by Secretary; grounds; procedure; conditions for retention of jurisdiction by State

The Secretary shall, on the basis of reports submitted by the State agency and his own inspections make a continuing evaluation of the manner in which each State having a plan approved under this section is carrying out such plan. Whenever the Secretary finds, after affording due notice and opportunity for a hearing, that in the administration of the State plan there is a failure to comply substantially with any provision of the State plan (or any assurance contained therein), he shall notify the State agency of his withdrawal of approval of such plan and upon receipt of such notice such plan shall cease to be in effect, but the State may retain jurisdiction in any case commenced before the withdrawal of the plan in order to enforce standards under the plan whenever the issues involved do not relate to the reasons for the withdrawal of the plan.

(g) Judicial review of Secretary's withdrawal of approval or rejection of plan; jurisdiction; venue; procedure; appropriate relief; finality of judgment

The State may obtain a review of a decision of the Secretary withdrawing approval of or rejecting its plan by the United States court of appeals for the circuit in which the State is located by filing in such court within thirty days following receipt of notice of such decision a petition to modify or set aside in whole or in part the action of the Secretary. A copy of such petition shall forthwith be served upon the Secretary, and thereupon the Secretary shall certify and file in the court the record upon which the decision complained of was issued as provided in section 2112 of Title 28. Unless the court finds that the Secretary's decision in rejecting a proposed State plan or withdrawing his approval of such a plan is not supported by substantial evidence the court shall affirm the Secretary's decision. The judgment of the court shall be subject to review by the Supreme Court of the United States upon certiorari or certification as provided in section 1254 of Title 28.

(h) Temporary enforcement of State standards

The Secretary may enter into an agreement with a State under which the State will be permitted to continue to enforce one or more occupational health and safety standards in effect in such State until final action is taken by the Secretary with respect to a plan submitted by a State under subsection (b) of this section, or two years from December 29, 1970, whichever is earlier.

Sec. 668. Programs of Federal agencies

(a) Establishment, development, and maintenance by head of each Federal agency

It shall be the responsibility of the head of each Federal agency (not including the United States Postal Service) to establish and maintain an effective and comprehensive occupational safety and health program which is consistent with the standards promulgated under section 655 of this title. The head of each agency shall (after consultation with representatives of the employees thereof) —

(1) provide safe and healthful places and conditions of employment, consistent with the standards set under section 655 of this title;

(2) acquire, maintain, and require the use of safety equipment, personal protective equipment, and devices reasonably necessary to protect employees;

(3) keep adequate records of all occupational accidents and illnesses for proper evaluation and necessary corrective action;

(4) consult with the Secretary with regard to the adequacy as to form and content of records kept pursuant to subsection (a)(3) of this section; and

(5) make an annual report to the Secretary with respect to occupational accidents and injuries and the agency's program under this section. Such report shall include any report submitted under section 7902(e)(2) of Title 5.

(b) Report by Secretary to President

The Secretary shall report to the President a summary or digest of reports submitted to him under subsection (a)(5) of this section, together with his evaluations of and recommendations derived from such reports.

(c) Omitted

(d) Access by Secretary to records and reports required of agencies

The Secretary shall have access to records and reports kept and filed by Federal agencies pursuant to subsections (a)(3) and (5) of this section unless those records and reports are specifically required by Executive order to be kept secret in the interest of the national defense or foreign policy, in which case the Secretary shall have access to such information as will not jeopardize national defense or foreign policy.

Sec. 669. Research and related activities

(a) Authority of Secretary of Health and Human Services to conduct research, experiments, and demonstrations, develop plans, establish criteria, promulgate regulations, authorize programs, and publish results and industry-wide studies; consultations

(1) The Secretary of Health and Human Services, after consultation with the Secretary and with other appropriate Federal departments or agencies, shall conduct (directly or by grants or contracts) research, experiments, and demonstrations relating to occupational safety and health, including studies of psychological factors involved, and relating to innovative methods, techniques, and approaches for dealing with occupational safety and health problems.

(2) The Secretary of Health and Human Services shall from time to time consult with the Secretary in order to develop specific plans for such research, demonstrations, and experiments as are necessary to produce criteria, including criteria identifying toxic substances, enabling the

Secretary to meet his responsibility for the formulation of safety and health standards under this chapter; and the Secretary of Health and Human Services, on the basis of such research, demonstrations, and experiments and any other information available to him, shall develop and publish at least annually such criteria as will effectuate the purposes of this chapter.

(3) The Secretary of Health and Human Services, on the basis of such research, demonstrations, and experiments, and any other information available to him, shall develop criteria dealing with toxic materials and harmful physical agents and substances which will describe exposure levels that are safe for various periods of employment, including but not limited to the exposure levels at which no employee will suffer impaired health or functional capacities or diminished life expectancy as a result of his work experience.

(4) The Secretary of Health and Human Services shall also conduct special research, experiments, and demonstrations relating to occupational safety and health as are necessary to explore new problems, including those created by new technology in occupational safety and health, which may require ameliorative action beyond that which is otherwise provided for in the operating provisions of this chapter. The Secretary of Health and Human Services shall also conduct research into the motivational and behavioral factors relating to the field of occupational safety and health.

(5) The Secretary of Health and Human Services, in order to comply with his responsibilities under paragraph (2), and in order to develop needed information regarding potentially toxic substances or harmful physical agents, may prescribe regulations requiring employers to measure, record, and make reports on the exposure of employees to substances or physical agents which the Secretary of Health and Human Services reasonably believes may endanger the health or safety of employees. The Secretary of Health and Human Services also is authorized to establish such programs of medical examinations and tests as may be necessary for determining the incidence of occupational illnesses and the susceptibility of employees to such illnesses. Nothing in this or any other provision of this chapter shall be deemed to authorize or require medical examination, immunization, or treatment for those who object thereto on religious grounds, except where such is necessary for the protection of the health or safety of others. Upon the request of any employer who is required to measure and record exposure of employees to substances or physical agents as provided under this subsection, the Secretary of Health and Human Services shall furnish full financial or other assistance to such employer for the purpose of defraying any additional expense incurred by him in carrying out the measuring and recording as provided in this subsection.

(6) The Secretary of Health and Human Services shall publish within six months of December 29, 1970, and thereafter as needed but at least annually a list of all known toxic substances by generic family or other useful grouping, and the concentrations at which such toxicity is known to occur. He shall determine following a written request by any employer or authorized representative of employees, specifying with reasonable particularity the grounds on which the request is made, whether any substance normally found in the place of employment has potentially toxic effects in such concentrations as used or found; and shall submit such determination both to employers and affected employees as soon as possible. If the Secretary of Health and Human Services determines that any substance is potentially toxic at the concentrations in which it is used or found in a place of employment, and such substance is not covered by an occupational safety or health standard promulgated under section 655 of this title, the Secretary of Health and Human Services shall immediately submit such determination to the Secretary, together with all pertinent criteria.

(7) Within two years of December 29, 1970, and annually thereafter the Secretary of Health and Human Services shall conduct and publish industrywide studies of the effect of chronic or low-level exposure to industrial materials, processes, and stresses on the potential for illness, disease, or loss of functional capacity in aging adults.

(b) Authority of Secretary of Health and Human Services to make inspections and question employers and employees

The Secretary of Health and Human Services is authorized to make inspections and question employers and employees as provided in section 657 of this title in order to carry out his functions and responsibilities under this section.

(c) Contracting authority of Secretary of Labor; cooperation between Secretary of Labor and Secretary of Health and Human Services

The Secretary is authorized to enter into contracts, agreements, or other arrangements with appropriate public agencies or private organizations for the purpose of conducting studies relating to his responsibilities under this chapter. In carrying out his responsibilities under this subsection, the Secretary shall cooperate with the Secretary of Health and Human Services in order to avoid any duplication of efforts under this section.

(d) Dissemination of information to interested parties

Information obtained by the Secretary and the Secretary of Health and Human Services under this section shall be disseminated by the Secretary to employers and employees and organizations thereof.

(e) Delegation of functions of Secretary of Health and Human Services to Director of the National Institute for Occupational Safety and Health

The functions of the Secretary of Health and Human Services under this chapter shall, to the extent feasible, be delegated to the Director of the National Institute for Occupational Safety and Health established by section 671 of this title.

Sec. 670. Training and employee education

(a) Authority of Secretary of Health and Human Services to conduct education and informational programs; consultations

The Secretary of Health and Human Services, after consultation with the Secretary and with other appropriate Federal departments and agencies, shall conduct, directly or by grants or contracts (1) education programs to provide an adequate supply of qualified personnel to carry out the purposes of this chapter, and (2) informational programs on the importance of and proper use of adequate safety and health equipment.

(b) Authority of Secretary of Labor to conduct short-term training of personnel

The Secretary is also authorized to conduct, directly or by grants or contracts, short-term training of personnel engaged in work related to his responsibilities under this chapter.

(c) Authority of Secretary of Labor to establish and supervise education and training programs and consult and advise interested parties

The Secretary, in consultation with the Secretary of Health and Human Services, shall (1) provide for the establishment and supervision of programs for the education and training of employers and employees in the recognition, avoidance, and prevention of unsafe or unhealthful working conditions in employments covered by this chapter, and (2) consult with and advise employers and employees, and organizations representing employers and employees as to effective means of preventing occupational injuries and illnesses.

(d) Authority of Secretary to establish and support cooperative agreements with States: compliance assistance program

(1) The Secretary shall establish and support cooperative agreements with the States under which employers subject to this chapter may consult with State personnel with respect to —

(A) the application of occupational safety and health requirements under this chapter or under State plans approved under section 667 of this title; and

(B) voluntary efforts that employers may undertake to establish and maintain safe and healthful employment and places of employment.

Such agreements may provide, as a condition of receiving funds under such agreements, for contributions by States towards meeting the costs of such agreements.

(2) Pursuant to such agreements the State shall provide on-site consultation at the employer's worksite to employers who request such assistance. The State may also provide other education and training programs for employers and employees in the State. The State shall ensure that on-site consultations conducted pursuant to such agreements include provision for the participation by employees.

(3) Activities under this subsection shall be conducted independently of any enforcement activity. If an employer fails to take immediate action to eliminate employee exposure to an imminent danger identified in a consultation or fails to correct a serious hazard so identified within a reasonable time, a report shall be made to the appropriate enforcement authority for such action as is appropriate.

(4) The Secretary shall, by regulation after notice and opportunity for comment, establish rules under which an employer—

(A) which requests and undergoes an on-site consultative visit provided under this subsection;

(B) which corrects the hazards that have been identified during the visit within the time frames established by the State and agrees to request a subsequent consultative visit if major changes in working conditions or work processes occur which introduce new hazards in the workplace; and

(C) which is implementing procedures for regularly identifying and preventing hazards regulated under this chapter and maintains appropriate involvement of, and training for, management and non-management employees in achieving safe and healthful working conditions,

may be exempt from an inspection (except an inspection requested under section 657(f) of this title or an inspection to determine the cause of a workplace accident which resulted in the death of one or more employees or hospitalization for three or more employees) for a period of 1 year from the closing of the consultative visit.

(5) A State shall provide worksite consultations under paragraph (2) at the request of an employer. Priority in scheduling such consultations shall be assigned to requests from small businesses which are in higher hazard industries or have the most hazardous conditions at issue in the request.

Sec. 671. National Institute for Occupational Safety and Health

(a) Statement of purpose

It is the purpose of this section to establish a National Institute for Occupational Safety and Health in the Department of Health and Human Services in order to carry out the policy set forth in section 651 of this title and to perform the functions of the Secretary of Health and Human Services under sections 669 and 670 of this title.

(b) Establishment; Director; appointment; term

There is hereby established in the Department of Health and Human Services a National Institute for Occupational Safety and Health. The Institute shall be headed by a Director who shall be appointed by the Secretary of Health and Human Services, and who shall serve for a term of six years unless previously removed by the Secretary of Health and Human Services.

(c) Development and establishment of standards; performance of functions of Secretary of Health and Human Services

The Institute is authorized to —

(1) develop and establish recommended occupational safety and health standards; and

(2) perform all functions of the Secretary of Health and Human Services under sections 669 and 670 of this title.

(d) Authority of Director

Upon his own initiative, or upon the request of the Secretary or the Secretary of Health and Human Services, the Director is authorized (1) to conduct such research and experimental programs as he determines are necessary for the development of criteria for new and improved occupational safety and health standards, and (2) after consideration of the results of such research and experimental programs make recommendations concerning new or improved occupational safety and health standards. Any occupational safety and health standard recommended pursuant to this section shall immediately be forwarded to the Secretary of Labor, and to the Secretary of Health and Human Services.

(e) Additional authority of Director

In addition to any authority vested in the Institute by other provisions of this section, the Director, in carrying out the functions of the Institute, is authorized to —

(1) prescribe such regulations as he deems necessary governing the manner in which its functions shall be carried out;

(2) receive money and other property donated, bequeathed, or devised, without condition or restriction other than that it be used for the purposes of the Institute and to use, sell, or otherwise dispose of such property for the purpose of carrying out its functions;

(3) receive (and use, sell, or otherwise dispose of, in accordance with paragraph (2)), money and

other property donated, bequeathed or devised to the Institute with a condition or restriction, including a condition that the Institute use other funds of the Institute for the purposes of the gift;

(4) in accordance with the civil service laws, appoint and fix the compensation of such personnel as may be necessary to carry out the provisions of this section;

(5) obtain the services of experts and consultants in accordance with the provisions of section 3109 of Title 5;

(6) accept and utilize the services of voluntary and noncompensated personnel and reimburse them for travel expenses, including per diem, as authorized by section 5703 of Title 5;

(7) enter into contracts, grants or other arrangements, or modifications thereof to carry out the provisions of this section, and such contracts or modifications thereof may be entered into without performance or other bonds, and without regard to section 5 of Title 41, or any other provision of law relating to competitive bidding;

(8) make advance, progress, and other payments which the Director deems necessary under this title without regard to the provisions of section 3324(a) and (b) of Title 31; and

(9) make other necessary expenditures.

(f) Annual reports

The Director shall submit to the Secretary of Health and Human Services, to the President, and to the Congress an annual report of the operations of the Institute under this chapter, which shall include a detailed statement of all private and public funds received and expended by it, and such recommendations as he deems appropriate.

(g) Lead-based paint activities

(1) Training grant program

(A) The Institute, in conjunction with the Administrator of the Environmental Protection Agency, may make grants for the training and education of workers and supervisors who are or may be directly engaged in lead-based paint activities.

(B) Grants referred to in subparagraph (A) shall be awarded to nonprofit organizations (including colleges and universities, joint labor-management trust funds, States, and nonprofit government employee organizations) —

(i) which are engaged in the training and education of workers and supervisors who are or who may be directly engaged in lead-based paint activities (as defined in title IV of the Toxic Substances Control Act [15 U.S.C. §2681 et seq.]),

(ii) which have demonstrated experience in implementing and operating health and safety training and education programs, and

(iii) with a demonstrated ability to reach, and involve in lead-based paint training programs, target populations of individuals who are or will be engaged in lead-based paint activities.

Grants under this subsection shall be awarded only to those organizations that fund at least 30 percent of their lead-based paint activities training programs from non-Federal sources, excluding in-kind contributions. Grants may also be made to local governments to carry out such training and education for their employees.

(C) There are authorized to be appropriated, at a minimum, $10,000,000 to the Institute for each of the fiscal years 1994 through 1997 to make grants under this paragraph.

(2) Evaluation of programs

The Institute shall conduct periodic and comprehensive assessments of the efficacy of the worker and supervisor training programs developed and offered by those receiving grants under this section. The Director shall prepare reports on the results of these assessments addressed to the Administrator of the Environmental Protection Agency to include recommendations as may be appropriate for the revision of these programs. The sum of $500,000 is authorized to be appropriated to the Institute for each of the fiscal years 1994 through 1997 to carry out this paragraph.

Sec. 671a. Workers' family protection

(a) Short title

This section may be cited as the "Workers' Family Protection Act".

(b) Findings and purpose

(1) Findings

Congress finds that —

(A) hazardous chemicals and substances that can threaten the health and safety of workers are being transported out of industries on workers' clothing and persons;

(B) these chemicals and substances have the potential to pose an additional threat to the health and welfare of workers and their families;

(C) additional information is needed concerning issues related to employee transported contaminant releases; and

(D) additional regulations may be needed to prevent future releases of this type.

(2) Purpose

It is the purpose of this section to —

(A) increase understanding and awareness concerning the extent and possible health impacts of the problems and incidents described in paragraph (1);

(B) prevent or mitigate future incidents of home contamination that could adversely affect the health and safety of workers and their families;

(C) clarify regulatory authority for preventing and responding to such incidents; and

(D) assist workers in redressing and responding to such incidents when they occur.

(c) Evaluation of employee transported contaminant releases

(1) Study

(A) In general

Not later than 18 months after October 26, 1992, the Director of the National Institute for Occupational Safety and Health thereafter in this section referred to as the "Director"), in cooperation with the Secretary of Labor, the Administrator of the Environmental Protection Agency, the Administrator of the Agency for Toxic Substances and Disease Registry, and the heads of other Federal Government agencies as determined to be appropriate by the Director, shall conduct a study to evaluate the potential for, the prevalence of, and the issues related to the contamination of workers' homes with hazardous chemicals and substances, including infectious agents, transported from the workplaces of such workers.

(B) Matters to be evaluated

In conducting the study and evaluation under subparagraph (A), the Director shall —

(i) conduct a review of past incidents of home contamination through the utilization of literature and of records concerning past investigations and enforcement actions undertaken by —

(I) the National Institute for Occupational Safety and Health;

(II) the Secretary of Labor to enforce the Occupational Safety and Health Act of 1970 (29 U.S.C. §651 et seq.);

(III) States to enforce occupational safety and health standards in accordance with section 18 of such Act (29 U.S.C. §667); and

(IV) other government agencies (including the Department of Energy and the Environmental Protection Agency), as the Director may determine to be appropriate;

(ii) evaluate current statutory, regulatory, and voluntary industrial hygiene or other measures used by small, medium and large employers to prevent or remediate home contamination;

(iii) compile a summary of the existing research and case histories conducted on incidents of employee transported contaminant releases, including —

(I) the effectiveness of workplace housekeeping practices and personal protective equipment in preventing such incidents;

(II) the health effects, if any, of the resulting exposure on workers and their families;

(III) the effectiveness of normal house cleaning and laundry procedures for removing hazardous materials and agents from workers' homes and personal clothing;

(IV) indoor air quality, as the research concerning such pertains to the fate of chemicals transported from a workplace into the home environment; and

(V) methods for differentiating exposure health effects and relative risks associated with specific agents from other sources of exposure inside and outside the home;

(iv) identify the role of Federal and State agencies in responding to incidents of home contamination;

(v) prepare and submit to the Task Force established under paragraph (2) and to the appropriate committees of Congress, a report concerning the results of the matters studied or evaluated under clauses (i) through (iv); and

(vi) study home contamination incidents and issues and worker and family protection policies and practices related to the special circumstances of firefighters and prepare and submit to the appropriate committees of Congress a report concerning the findings with respect to such study.

(2) Development of investigative strategy

(A) Task force

Not later than 12 months after October 26, 1992, the Director shall establish a working group, to be known as the "Workers' Family Protection Task Force". The Task Force shall —

(i) be composed of not more than 15 individuals to be appointed by the Director from among individuals who are representative of workers, industry, scientists, industrial hygienists, the National Research Council, and government agencies, except that not more than one such individual shall be from each appropriate government agency and the number of individuals appointed to represent industry and workers shall be equal in number;

(ii) review the report submitted under paragraph (1)(B)(v);

(iii) determine, with respect to such report, the additional data needs, if any, and the need for additional evaluation of the scientific issues related to and the feasibility of developing such additional data; and

(iv) if additional data are determined by the Task Force to be needed, develop a recommended investigative strategy for use in obtaining such information.

(B) Investigative strategy

(i) Content

The investigative strategy developed under subparagraph (A)(iv) shall identify data gaps that can and cannot be filled, assumptions and uncertainties associated with various components of such strategy, a timetable for the implementation of such strategy, and methodologies used to gather any required data.

(ii) Peer review

The Director shall publish the proposed investigative strategy under subparagraph (A)(iv) for public comment and utilize other methods, including technical conferences or seminars, for the purpose of obtaining comments concerning the proposed strategy.

(iii) Final strategy

After the peer review and public comment is conducted under clause (ii), the Director, in consultation with the heads of other government agencies, shall propose a final strategy for investigating issues related to home contamination that shall be implemented by the National Institute for Occupational Safety and Health and other Federal agencies for the period of time necessary to enable such agencies to obtain the information identified under subparagraph (A)(iii).

(C) Construction

Nothing in this section shall be construed as precluding any government agency from investigating issues related to home contamination using existing procedures until such time as a final strategy is developed or from taking actions in addition to those proposed in the strategy after its completion.

(3) Implementation of investigative strategy

Upon completion of the investigative strategy under subparagraph (B)(iii), each Federal agency or department shall fulfill the role assigned to it by the strategy.

(d) Regulations

(1) In general

Not later than 4 years after October 26, 1992, and periodically thereafter, the Secretary of Labor, based on the information developed under subsection (c) of this section and on other information available to the Secretary, shall —

(A) determine if additional education about, emphasis on, or enforcement of existing regulations or standards is needed and will be sufficient, or if additional regulations or standards are needed with regard to employee transported releases of hazardous materials; and

(B) prepare and submit to the appropriate committees of Congress a report concerning the result of such determination.

(2) Additional regulations or standards

If the Secretary of Labor determines that additional regulations or standards are needed under paragraph (1), the Secretary shall promulgate, pursuant to the Secretary's authority under the Occupational Safety and Health Act of 1970 (29 U.S.C. §651 et seq.), such regulations or standards as determined to be appropriate not later than 3 years after such determination.

(e) Authorization of appropriations

There are authorized to be appropriated from sums otherwise authorized to be appropriated, for each fiscal year such sums as may be necessary to carry out this section.

Sec. 672. Grants to States

(a) Designation of State agency to assist State in identifying State needs and responsibilities and in developing State plans

The Secretary is authorized, during the fiscal year ending June 30, 1971, and the two succeeding fiscal years, to make grants to the States which have designated a State agency under section 667 of this title to assist them —

(1) in identifying their needs and responsibilities in the area of occupational safety and health,

(2) in developing State plans under section 667 of this title, or

(3) in developing plans for —

(A) establishing systems for the collection of information concerning the nature and frequency of occupational injuries and diseases;

(B) increasing the expertise and enforcement capabilities of their personnel engaged in occupational safety and health programs; or

(C) otherwise improving the administration and enforcement of State occupational safety and health laws, including standards thereunder, consistent with the objectives of this chapter.

(b) Experimental and demonstration projects

The Secretary is authorized, during the fiscal year ending June 30, 1971, and the two succeeding fiscal years, to make grants to the States for experimental and demonstration projects consistent with the objectives set forth in subsection (a) of this section.

(c) Designation by Governor of appropriate State agency for receipt of grant

The Governor of the State shall designate the appropriate State agency for receipt of any grant made by the Secretary under this section.

(d) Submission of application

Any State agency designated by the Governor of the State desiring a grant under this section shall submit an application therefor to the Secretary.

(e) Approval or rejection of application

The Secretary shall review the application, and shall, after consultation with the Secretary of Health and Human Services, approve or reject such application.

(f) Federal share

The Federal share for each State grant under subsection (a) or (b) of this section may not exceed 90 per centum of the total cost of the application. In the event the Federal share for all States under either such subsection is not the same, the differences among the States shall be established on the basis of objective criteria.

(g) Administration and enforcement of programs contained in approved State plans; Federal share

The Secretary is authorized to make grants to the States to assist them in administering and enforcing programs for occupational safety and health contained in State plans approved by the Secretary pursuant to section 667 of this title. The Federal share for each State grant under this subsection may not exceed 50 per centum of the total cost to the State of such a program. The last sentence of subsection (f) of this section shall be applicable in determining the Federal share under this subsection.

(h) Report to President and Congress

Prior to June 30, 1973, the Secretary shall, after consultation with the Secretary of Health and Human Services, transmit a report to the President and to the Congress, describing the experience under the grant programs authorized by this section and making any recommendations he may deem appropriate.

Sec. 673. Statistics

(a) Development and maintenance of program of collection, compilation, and analysis; employments subject to coverage; scope

In order to further the purposes of this chapter, the Secretary, in consultation with the Secretary of Health and Human Services, shall develop and maintain an effective program of collection, compilation, and analysis of occupational safety and health statistics. Such program may cover all employments whether or not subject to any other provisions of this chapter but shall not cover employments excluded by section 653 of this title. The Secretary shall compile accurate statistics on work injuries and illnesses which shall include all disabling, serious, or significant injuries and illnesses, whether or not involving loss of time from work, other than minor injuries requiring only first aid treatment and which do not involve medical treatment, loss of consciousness, restriction of work or motion, or transfer to another job.

(b) Authority of Secretary to promote, encourage, or engage in programs, make grants, and grant or contract for research and investigations

To carry out his duties under subsection (a) of this section, the Secretary may —

(1) promote, encourage, or directly engage in programs of studies, information and communication concerning occupational safety and health statistics;

(2) make grants to States or political subdivisions thereof in order to assist them in developing and administering programs dealing with occupational safety and health statistics; and

(3) arrange, through grants or contracts, for the conduct of such research and investigations as give promise of furthering the objectives of this section. —

(c) Federal share for grants

The Federal share for each grant under subsection (b) of this section may be up to 50 per centum of the State's total cost.

(d) Utilization by Secretary of State or local services, facilities, and employees; consent; reimbursement

The Secretary may, with the consent of any State or political subdivision thereof, accept and use the services, facilities, and employees of the agencies of such State or political subdivision, with or without reimbursement, in order to assist him in carrying out his functions under this section.

(e) Reports by employers

On the basis of the records made and kept pursuant to section 657(c) of this title, employers shall file such reports with the Secretary as he shall prescribe by regulation, as necessary to carry out his functions under this chapter.

(f) Supersedure of agreements between Department of Labor and States for collection of statistics

Agreements between the Department of Labor and States pertaining to the collection of occupational safety and health statistics already in effect on the effective date of this chapter shall remain in effect until superseded by grants or contracts made under this chapter.

Sec. 674. Audit of grant recipient; maintenance of records; contents of records; access to books, etc.

(a) Each recipient of a grant under this chapter shall keep such records as the Secretary or the Secretary of Health and Human Services shall prescribe, including records which fully disclose the amount and disposition by such recipient of the proceeds of such grant, the total cost of the project or undertaking in connection with which such grant is made or used, and the amount of that portion of the cost of the project or undertaking supplied by other sources, and such other records as will facilitate an effective audit.

(b) The Secretary or the Secretary of Health and Human Services, and the Comptroller General of the United States, or any of their duly authorized representatives, shall have access for the purpose of audit and examination to any books, documents, papers, and records of the recipients of any grant under this chapter that are pertinent to any such grant.

Sec. 675. Annual reports by Secretary of Labor and Secretary of Health and Human Services; contents

Within one hundred and twenty days following the convening of each regular session of each Congress, the Secretary and the Secretary of Health and Human Services shall each prepare and submit to the President for transmittal to the Congress a report upon the subject matter of this chapter, the progress toward achievement of the purpose of this chapter, the needs and requirements in the field of occupational safety and health, and any other relevant information. Such reports shall include information regarding occupational safety and health standards, and criteria for such standards, developed during the preceding year; evaluation of standards and criteria previously developed under this chapter, defining areas of emphasis for new criteria and standards; an evaluation of the degree of observance of applicable occupational safety and health standards, and a summary of inspection and enforcement activity undertaken; analysis and evaluation of research activities for which results have been obtained under governmental and nongovernmental sponsorship; an analysis of major occupational diseases; evaluation of available control and measurement technology for hazards for which standards or criteria have been developed during the preceding year; description of cooperative efforts undertaken between Government agencies and other interested parties in the implementation of this chapter during the preceding year; a progress report on the development of an adequate supply of trained manpower in the field of occupational safety and health, including estimates of future needs and the efforts being made by Government and others to meet those needs; listing of all toxic substances in industrial usage for which labeling requirements, criteria, or standards have not yet been established; and such recommendations for additional legislation as are deemed necessary to protect the safety and health of the worker and improve the administration of this chapter.

Sec. 676. Omitted

Sec. 677. Separability

If any provision of this chapter, or the application of such provision to any person or circumstance, shall be held invalid, the remainder of this chapter, or the application of such provision to persons or circumstances other than those as to which it is held invalid, shall not be affected thereby.

Consolidated Omnibus Budget Reconciliation Act

U.S. Code, Title 29, Sections 1161 to 1168

Sec.

COBRA IN A NUTSHELL

Enacted: 1986

Purpose: To allow employees and their family members to continue participation in group health plans on a self-paying basis after layoff, discharge, divorce, death, or other qualifying event

Coverage: Private sector employers with 20 or more employees

Responsible agency: U.S. Department of Labor Pension and Welfare Benefits Administration

---

Sec. 1161. Plans must provide continuation coverage to certain individuals

(a) In general

The plan sponsor of each group health plan shall provide, in accordance with this part, that each qualified beneficiary who would lose coverage under the plan as a result of a qualifying event is entitled, under the plan, to elect, within the election period, continuation coverage under the plan.

(b) Exception for certain plans

Subsection (a) of this section shall not apply to any group health plan for any calendar year if all employers maintaining such plan normally employed fewer than 20 employees on a typical business day during the preceding calendar year.

Sec. 1162. Continuation coverage

For purposes of section 1161 of this title, the term "continuation coverage" means coverage under the plan which meets the following requirements:

(1) Type of benefit coverage

The coverage must consist of coverage which, as of the time the coverage is being provided, is identical to the coverage provided under the plan to similarly situated beneficiaries under the plan with respect to whom a qualifying event has not occurred. If coverage is modified under the plan for any group of similarly situated beneficiaries, such coverage shall also be modified in the same manner for all individuals who are qualified beneficiaries under the plan pursuant to this part in connection with such group.

(2) Period of coverage

The coverage must extend for at least the period beginning on the date of the qualifying event and ending not earlier than the earliest of the following:

(A) Maximum required period

(i) General rule for terminations and reduced hours

In the case of a qualifying event described in section 1163(2) of this title, except as provided in clause (ii), the date which is 18 months after the date of the qualifying event.

(ii) Special rule for multiple qualifying events

If a qualifying event (other than a qualifying event described in section 1163(6) of this title) occurs during the 18 months after the date of a qualifying event described in section 1163(2) of this title, the date which is 36 months after the date of the qualifying event described in section 1163(2) of this title.

(iii) Special rule for certain bankruptcy proceedings

In the case of a qualifying event described in section 1163(6) of this title (relating to bankruptcy proceedings), the date of the death of the covered employee or qualified beneficiary (described in section 1167(3)(C)(iii) of this title), or in the case of the surviving spouse or dependent children of the covered employee, 36 months after the date of the death of the covered employee.

(iv) General rule for other qualifying events

In the case of a qualifying event not described in section 1163(2) or 1163(6) of this title, the date which is 36 months after the date of the qualifying event.

(v) Medicare entitlement followed by qualifying event

In the case of a qualifying event described in section 1163(2) of this title that occurs less than 18 months after the date the covered employee becomes entitled to benefits under Title XVIII of the Social Security Act (42 U.S.C. §1395 et seq.), the period of coverage for qualified beneficiaries other than the covered employee shall not terminate under this subparagraph before the close of the 36-month period beginning on the date the covered employee became so entitled.

In the case of an individual who is determined, under Title II or XVI of the Social Security Act (42 U.S.C. §401 et seq. or 1381 et seq.), to have been disabled at any time during the first 60 days of continuation coverage under this part, any reference in clause (i) or (ii) to 18 months is deemed a reference to 29 months (with respect to all qualified beneficiaries), but only if the qualified beneficiary has provided notice of such determination under section 1166(3) of this title before the end of such 18 months.

(B) End of plan

The date on which the employer ceases to provide any group health plan to any employee.

(C) Failure to pay premium

The date on which coverage ceases under the plan by reason of a failure to make timely payment of any premium required under the plan with respect to the qualified beneficiary. The payment of any premium (other than any payment referred to in the last sentence of paragraph (3)) shall be considered to be timely if made within 30 days after the date due or within such longer period as applies to or under the plan.

(D) Group health plan coverage or medicare entitlement

The date on which the qualified beneficiary first becomes, after the date of the election —

(i) covered under any other group health plan (as an employee or otherwise) which does not contain any exclusion or limitation with respect to any preexisting condition of such beneficiary, (other than such an exclusion or limitation which does not apply to (or is satisfied by) such beneficiary by reason of chapter 100 of Title 26, part 7 of this subtitle, or Title XXVII of the Public Health Service Act (42 U.S.C. §300gg et seq.); or

(ii) in the case of a qualified beneficiary other than a qualified beneficiary described in section 1167(3)(C) of this title, entitled to benefits under Title XVIII of the Social Security Act (42 U.S.C. §1395 et seq.).

(E) Termination of extended coverage for disability

In the case of a qualified beneficiary who is disabled at any time during the first 60 days of continuation coverage under this part, the month that begins more than 30 days after the date of the final determination under Title II or XVI of the Social Security Act (42 U.S.C. §401 et seq. or 1381 et seq.) that the qualified beneficiary is no longer disabled.

(3) Premium requirements

The plan may require payment of a premium for any period of continuation coverage, except that such premium -

(A) shall not exceed 102 percent of the applicable premium for such period, and

(B) may, at the election of the payor, be made in monthly installments.

In no event may the plan require the payment of any premium before the day which is 45 days after the day on which the qualified beneficiary made the initial election for continuation coverage. In the case of an individual described in the last sentence of paragraph (2)(A), any reference in subparagraph (A) of this paragraph to "102 percent" is deemed a reference to "150 percent" for any month after the 18th month of continuation coverage described in clause (i) or (ii) of paragraph (2)(A).

(4) No requirement of insurability

The coverage may not be conditioned upon, or discriminate on the basis of lack of, evidence of insurability.

(5) Conversion option

In the case of a qualified beneficiary whose period of continuation coverage expires under paragraph (2)(A), the plan must, during the 180-day period ending on such expiration date, provide to the qualified beneficiary the option of enrollment under a conversion health plan otherwise generally available under the plan.

Sec. 1163. Qualifying event

For purposes of this part, the term "qualifying event" means, with respect to any covered employee, any of the following events which, but for the continuation coverage required under this part, would result in the loss of coverage of a qualified beneficiary:

(1) The death of the covered employee.

(2) The termination (other than by reason of such employee's gross misconduct), or reduction of hours, of the covered employee's employment.

(3) The divorce or legal separation of the covered employee from the employee's spouse.

(4) The covered employee becoming entitled to benefits under Title XVIII of the Social Security Act (42 U.S.C. §1395 et seq.).

(5) A dependent child ceasing to be a dependent child under the generally applicable requirements of the plan.

(6) A proceeding in a case under Title 11, commencing on or after July 1, 1986, with respect to the employer from whose employment the covered employee retired at any time.

In the case of an event described in paragraph (6), a loss of coverage includes a substantial elimination of coverage with respect to a qualified beneficiary described in section 1167(3)(C) of this title within one year before or after the date of commencement of the proceeding.

Sec. 1164. Applicable premium

For purposes of this part —

(1) In general

The term "applicable premium" means, with respect to any period of continuation coverage of qualified beneficiaries, the cost to the plan for such period of the coverage for similarly situated beneficiaries with respect to whom a qualifying event has not occurred (without regard to whether such cost is paid by the employer or employee).

(2) Special rule for self-insured plans

To the extent that a plan is a self-insured plan —

(A) In general

Except as provided in subparagraph (B), the applicable premium for any period of continuation coverage of qualified beneficiaries shall be equal to a reasonable estimate of the cost of providing coverage for such period for similarly situated beneficiaries which —

(i) is determined on an actuarial basis, and

(ii) takes into account such factors as the Secretary may prescribe in regulations.

(B) Determination on basis of past cost

If an administrator elects to have this subparagraph apply, the applicable premium for any period of continuation coverage of qualified beneficiaries shall be equal to —

(i) the cost to the plan for similarly situated beneficiaries for the same period occurring during the preceding determination period under paragraph (3), adjusted by

(ii) the percentage increase or decrease in the implicit price deflator of the gross national product (calculated by the Department of Commerce and published in the Survey of Current Business) for the 12-month period ending on the last day of the sixth month of such preceding determination period.

(C) Subparagraph (B) not to apply where significant change

An administrator may not elect to have subparagraph (B) apply in any case in which there is any significant difference, between the determination period and the preceding determination period, in coverage under, or in employees covered by, the plan. The determination under the preceding sentence for any determination period shall be made at the same time as the determination under paragraph (3).

(3) Determination period

The determination of any applicable premium shall be made for a period of 12 months and shall be made before the beginning of such period.

Sec. 1165. Election

For purposes of this part —

(1) Election period

The term "election period" means the period which —

(A) begins not later than the date on which coverage terminates under the plan by reason of a qualifying event,

(B) is of at least 60 days' duration, and

(C) ends not earlier than 60 days after the later of —

(i) the date described in subparagraph (A), or

(ii) in the case of any qualified beneficiary who receives notice under section 1166(4) of this title, the date of such notice.

(2) Effect of election on other beneficiaries

Except as otherwise specified in an election, any election of continuation coverage by a qualified beneficiary described in subparagraph (A)(i) or (B) of section 1167(3) of this title shall be deemed to include an election of continuation coverage on behalf of any other qualified beneficiary who would lose coverage under the plan by reason of the qualifying event. If there is a choice among types of coverage under the plan, each qualified beneficiary is entitled to make a separate selection among such types of coverage.

Sec. 1166. Notice requirements

(a) In general

In accordance with regulations prescribed by the Secretary —

(1) the group health plan shall provide, at the time of commencement of coverage under the plan, written notice to each covered employee and spouse of the employee (if any) of the rights provided under this subsection,

(2) the employer of an employee under a plan must notify the administrator of a qualifying event described in paragraph (1), (2), (4), or (6) of section 1163 of this title within 30 days (or, in the case of a group health plan which is a multiemployer plan, such longer period of time as may be provided in the terms of the plan) of the date of the qualifying event,

(3) each covered employee or qualified beneficiary is responsible for notifying the administrator of the occurrence of any qualifying event described in paragraph (3) or (5) of section 1163 of this title within 60 days after the date of the qualifying event and each qualified beneficiary who is determined, under Title II or XVI of the Social Security Act (42 U.S.C. §§401 et seq. or 1381 et seq.), to have been disabled at any time during the first 60 days of continuation coverage under this part is responsible for notifying the plan administrator of such determination within 60 days after the date of the determination and for notifying the plan administrator within 30 days after the date of any final determination under such title or titles that the qualified beneficiary is no longer disabled, and

(4) the administrator shall notify —

(A) in the case of a qualifying event described in paragraph (1), (2), (4), or (6) of section 1163 of this title, any qualified beneficiary with respect to such event, and

(B) in the case of a qualifying event described in paragraph (3) or (5) of section 1163 of this title where the covered employee notifies the administrator under paragraph (3), any qualified beneficiary with respect to such event,

of such beneficiary's rights under this subsection.

(b) Alternative means of compliance with requirements for notification of multiemployer plans by employers

The requirements of subsection (a)(2) of this section shall be considered satisfied in the case of a multiemployer plan in connection with a qualifying event described in paragraph (2) of section 1163 of this title if the plan provides that the determination of the occurrence of such qualifying event will be made by the plan administrator.

(c) Rules relating to notification of qualified beneficiaries by plan administrator

For purposes of subsection (a)(4) of this section, any notification shall be made within 14 days (or, in the case of a group health plan which is a multiemployer plan, such longer period of time as may be provided in the terms of the plan) of the date on which the administrator is notified under paragraph (2) or (3), whichever is applicable, and any such notification to an individual who is a qualified beneficiary as the spouse of the covered employee shall be treated as notification to all other qualified beneficiaries residing with such spouse at the time such notification is made.

Sec. 1167. Definitions and special rules

For purposes of this part —

(1) Group health plan

The term "group health plan" means an employee welfare benefit plan providing medical care (as defined in section 213(d) of Title 26) to participants or beneficiaries directly or through insurance, reimbursement, or otherwise. Such term shall not include any plan substantially all of the coverage under which is for qualified long-term care services (as defined in section 7702B(c) of Title 26. Such term shall include a child who is born to or placed for adoption with the covered employee during the period as continuation coverage under this part.

(2) Covered employee

The term "covered employee" means an individual who is (or was) provided coverage under a group health plan by virtue of the performance of services by the individual for 1 or more persons maintaining the plan (including as an employee defined in section 401(c)(1) of Title 26).

(3) Qualified beneficiary

(A) In general

The term "qualified beneficiary" means, with respect to a covered employee under a group health plan, any other individual who, on the day before the qualifying event for that employee, is a beneficiary under the plan —

(i) as the spouse of the covered employee, or

(ii) as the dependent child of the employee.

Such term shall also include a child who is born to or placed for adoption with the covered employee during the period of continuation coverage under this part.

(B) Special rule for terminations and reduced employment

In the case of a qualifying event described in section 1163(2) of this title, the term "qualified beneficiary" includes the covered employee.

(C) Special rule for retirees and widows

In the case of a qualifying event described in section 1163(6) of this title, the term "qualified beneficiary" includes a covered employee who had retired on or before the date of substantial elimination of coverage and any other individual who, on the day before such qualifying event, is a beneficiary under the plan —

(i) as the spouse of the covered employee,

(ii) as the dependent child of the employee, or

(iii) as the surviving spouse of the covered employee.

(4) Employer

Subsection (n) (relating to leased employees) and subsection (t) (relating to application of controlled group rules to certain employee benefits) of section 414 of Title 26 shall apply for purposes of this part in the same manner and to the same extent as such subsections apply for purposes of section 106 of Title 26. Any regulations pre-scribed by the Secretary pursuant to the preced-ing sentence shall be consistent and coextensive with any regulations prescribed for similar pur-poses by the Secretary of the Treasury (or such Secretary's delegate) under such subsections.

(5) Optional extension of required periods

A group health plan shall not be treated as fail-ing to meet the requirements of this part solely because the plan provides both —

(A) that the period of extended coverage referred to in section 1162(2) of this title com-mences with the date of the loss of coverage, and

(B) that the applicable notice period provided under section 1166(a)(2) of this title commences with the date of the loss of coverage.

Sec. 1168. Regulations

The Secretary may prescribe regulations to carry out the provisions of this part.

Employee Polygraph Protection Act

U.S. Code, Title 29, Sections 2001 to 2009

EPPA IN A NUTSHELL

Enacted: 1988

Purpose: To restrict use of lie detector tests

Coverage: Private sector employers

Responsible agency: U.S. Department of Labor Wage and Hour Division

Sec. 2001. Definitions

As used in this chapter:

(1) Commerce

The term "commerce" has the meaning provided by section 203(b) of this title.

(2) Employer

The term "employer" includes any person acting directly or indirectly in the interest of an employer in relation to an employee or prospective employee.

(3) Lie detector

The term "lie detector" includes a polygraph, deceptograph, voice stress analyzer, psychological stress evaluator, or any other similar device (whether mechanical or electrical) that is used, or the results of which are used, for the purpose of rendering a diagnostic opinion regarding the honesty or dishonesty of an individual.

(4) Polygraph

The term "polygraph" means an instrument that —

(A) records continuously, visually, permanently, and simultaneously changes in cardiovascular, respiratory, and electrodermal patterns as minimum instrumentation standards; and

(B) is used, or the results of which are used, for the purpose of rendering a diagnostic opinion regarding the honesty or dishonesty of an individual.

(5) Secretary

The term "Secretary" means the Secretary of Labor.

Sec. 2002. Prohibitions on lie detector use

Except as provided in sections 2006 and 2007 of this title, it shall be unlawful for any employer engaged in or affecting commerce or in the production of goods for commerce —

(1) directly or indirectly, to require, request, suggest, or cause any employee or prospective employee to take or submit to any lie detector test;

(2) to use, accept, refer to, or inquire concerning the results of any lie detector test of any employee or prospective employee;

(3) to discharge, discipline, discriminate against in any manner, or deny employment or promotion to, or threaten to take any such action against —

(A) any employee or prospective employee who refuses, declines, or fails to take or submit to any lie detector test, or

(B) any employee or prospective employee on the basis of the results of any lie detector test; or

(4) to discharge, discipline, discriminate against in any manner, or deny employment or promotion to, or threaten to take any such action against, any employee or prospective employee because —

(A) such employee or prospective employee has filed any complaint or instituted or caused to be instituted any proceeding under or related to this chapter,

(B) such employee or prospective employee has testified or is about to testify in any such proceeding, or

(C) of the exercise by such employee or prospective employee, on behalf of such employee or another person, of any right afforded by this chapter.

Sec. 2003. Notice of protection

The Secretary shall prepare, have printed, and distribute a notice setting forth excerpts from, or summaries of, the pertinent provisions of this chapter. Each employer shall post and maintain such notice in conspicuous places on its premises where notices to employees and applicants to employment are customarily posted.

Sec. 2004. Authority of Secretary

(a) In general

The Secretary shall —

(1) issue such rules and regulations as may be necessary or appropriate to carry out this chapter;

(2) cooperate with regional, State, local, and other agencies, and cooperate with and furnish technical assistance to employers, labor organizations, and employment agencies to aid in effectuating the purposes of this chapter; and

(3) make investigations and inspections and require the keeping of records necessary or appropriate for the administration of this chapter.

(b) Subpoena authority

For the purpose of any hearing or investigation under this chapter, the Secretary shall have the authority contained in sections 49 and 50 of Title 15.

Sec. 2005. Enforcement provisions

(a) Civil penalties

(1) In general

Subject to paragraph (2), any employer who violates any provision of this chapter may be assessed a civil penalty of not more than $10,000.

(2) Determination of amount

In determining the amount of any penalty under paragraph (1), the Secretary shall take into account the previous record of the person in terms of compliance with this chapter and the gravity of the violation.

(3) Collection

Any civil penalty assessed under this subsection shall be collected in the same manner as is required by subsections (b) through (e) of section 1853 of this title with respect to civil penalties assessed under subsection (a) of such section.

(b) Injunctive actions by Secretary

The Secretary may bring an action under this section to restrain violations of this chapter. The Solicitor of Labor may appear for and represent the Secretary in any litigation brought under this chapter. In any action brought under this section, the district courts of the United States shall have jurisdiction, for cause shown, to issue temporary or permanent restraining orders and injunctions to require compliance with this chapter, including such legal or equitable relief incident thereto as may be appropriate, including, but not limited to, employment, reinstatement, promotion, and the payment of lost wages and benefits.

(c) Private civil actions

(1) Liability

An employer who violates this chapter shall be liable to the employee or prospective employee affected by such violation. Such employer shall be liable for such legal or equitable relief as may be appropriate, including, but not limited to, employment, reinstatement, promotion, and the payment of lost wages and benefits.

(2) Court

An action to recover the liability prescribed in paragraph (1) may be maintained against the employer in any Federal or State court of competent jurisdiction by an employee or prospective employee for or on behalf of such employee, prospective employee, and other employees or prospective employees similarly situated. No such action may be commenced more than 3 years after the date of the alleged violation.

(3) Costs

The court, in its discretion, may allow the prevailing party other than the United States) reasonable costs, including attorney's fees.

(d) Waiver of rights prohibited

The rights and procedures provided by this chapter may not be waived by contract or otherwise, unless such waiver is part of a written settlement agreed to and signed by the parties to the pending action or complaint under this chapter.

Sec. 2006. Exemptions

(a) No application to governmental employers

This chapter shall not apply with respect to the United States Government, any State or local government, or any political subdivision of a State or local government.

(b) National defense and security exemption

(1) National defense

Nothing in this chapter shall be construed to prohibit the administration, by the Federal Government, in the performance of any counterintelligence function, of any lie detector test to —

(A) any expert or consultant under contract to the Department of Defense or any employee of any contractor of such Department; or

(B) any expert or consultant under contract with the Department of Energy in connection with the atomic energy defense activities of such Department or any employee of any contractor of such Department in connection with such activities.

(2) Security

Nothing in this chapter shall be construed to prohibit the administration, by the Federal Government, in the performance of any intelligence or counterintelligence function, of any lie detector test to —

(A)(i) any individual employed by, assigned to, or detailed to, the National Security Agency, the Defense Intelligence Agency, the National Imagery and Mapping Agency, or the Central Intelligence Agency,

(ii) any expert or consultant under contract to any such agency,

(iii) any employee of a contractor to any such agency,

(iv) any individual applying for a position in any such agency, or

(v) any individual assigned to a space where sensitive cryptologic information is produced, processed, or stored for any such agency; or

(B) any expert, or consultant (or employee of such expert or consultant) under contract with any Federal Government department, agency, or program whose duties involve access to information that has been classified at the level of top secret or designated as being within a special access program under section 4.2(a) of Executive Order 12356 (or a successor Executive order).

(c) FBI contractors exemption

Nothing in this chapter shall be construed to prohibit the administration, by the Federal Government, in the performance of any counterintelligence function, of any lie detector test to an employee of a contractor of the Federal Bureau of Investigation of the Department of Justice who is engaged in the performance of any work under the contract with such Bureau.

(d) Limited exemption for ongoing investigations

Subject to sections 2007 and 2009 of this title, this chapter shall not prohibit an employer from requesting an employee to submit to a polygraph test if —

(1) the test is administered in connection with an ongoing investigation involving economic loss

or injury to the employer's business, such as theft, embezzlement, misappropriation, or an act of unlawful industrial espionage or sabotage;

(2) the employee had access to the property that is the subject of the investigation;

(3) the employer has a reasonable suspicion that the employee was involved in the incident or activity under investigation; and

(4) the employer executes a statement, provided to the examinee before the test, that —

(A) sets forth with particularity the specific incident or activity being investigated and the basis for testing particular employees,

(B) is signed by a person (other than a polygraph examiner) authorized to legally bind the employer,

(C) is retained by the employer for at least 3 years, and

(D) contains at a minimum —

(i) an identification of the specific economic loss or injury to the business of the employer,

(ii) a statement indicating that the employee had access to the property that is the subject of the investigation, and

(iii) a statement describing the basis of the employer's reasonable suspicion that the employee was involved in the incident or activity under investigation.

(e) Exemption for security services

(1) In general

Subject to paragraph (2) and sections 2007 and 2009 of this title, this chapter shall not prohibit the use of polygraph tests on prospective employees by any private employer whose primary business purpose consists of providing armored car personnel, personnel engaged in the design, installation, and maintenance of security alarm systems, or other uniformed or plainclothes security personnel and whose function includes protection of —

(A) facilities, materials, or operations having a significant impact on the health or safety of any State or political subdivision thereof, or the national security of the United States, as deter-

mined under rules and regulations issued by the Secretary within 90 days after June 27, 1988, including —

(i) facilities engaged in the production, transmission, or distribution of electric or nuclear power,

(ii) public water supply facilities,

(iii) shipments or storage of radioactive or other toxic waste materials, and

(iv) public transportation, or

(B) currency, negotiable securities, precious commodities or instruments, or proprietary information.

(2) Access

The exemption provided under this subsection shall not apply if the test is administered to a prospective employee who would not be employed to protect facilities, materials, operations, or assets referred to in paragraph (1).

(f) Exemption for drug security, drug theft, or drug diversion investigations

(1) In general

Subject to paragraph (2) and sections 2007 and 2009 of this title, this chapter shall not prohibit the use of a polygraph test by any employer authorized to manufacture, distribute, or dispense a controlled substance listed in schedule I, II, III, or IV of section 812 of Title 21.

(2) Access

The exemption provided under this subsection shall apply —

(A) if the test is administered to a prospective employee who would have direct access to the manufacture, storage, distribution, or sale of any such controlled substance; or

(B) in the case of a test administered to a current employee, if —

(i) the test is administered in connection with an ongoing investigation of criminal or other misconduct involving, or potentially involving, loss or injury to the manufacture, distribution, or dispensing of any such controlled substance by such employer, and

(ii) the employee had access to the person or property that is the subject of the investigation.

Sec. 2007. Restrictions on use of exemptions

(a) Test as basis for adverse employment action

(1) Under ongoing investigations exemption

Except as provided in paragraph (2), the exemption under subsection (d) of section 2006 of this title shall not apply if an employee is discharged, disciplined, denied employment or promotion, or otherwise discriminated against in any manner on the basis of the analysis of a polygraph test chart or the refusal to take a polygraph test, without additional supporting evidence. The evidence required by such subsection may serve as additional supporting evidence.

(2) Under other exemptions

In the case of an exemption described in subsection (e) or (f) of such section, the exemption shall not apply if the results of an analysis of a polygraph test chart are used, or the refusal to take a polygraph test is used, as the sole basis upon which an adverse employment action described in paragraph (1) is taken against an employee or prospective employee.

(b) Rights of examinee

The exemptions provided under subsections (d), (e), and (f) of section 2006 of this title shall not apply unless the requirements described in the following paragraphs are met:

(1) All phases

Throughout all phases of the test —

(A) the examinee shall be permitted to terminate the test at any time;

(B) the examinee is not asked questions in a manner designed to degrade, or needlessly intrude on, such examinee;

(C) the examinee is not asked any question concerning —

(i) religious beliefs or affiliations,

(ii) beliefs or opinions regarding racial matters,

(iii) political beliefs or affiliations,

(iv) any matter relating to sexual behavior; and

(v) beliefs, affiliations, opinions, or lawful activities regarding unions or labor organizations; and

(D) the examiner does not conduct the test if there is sufficient written evidence by a physician that the examinee is suffering from a medical or psychological condition or undergoing treatment that might cause abnormal responses during the actual testing phase.

(2) Pretest phase

During the pretest phase, the prospective examinee —

(A) is provided with reasonable written notice of the date, time, and location of the test, and of such examinee's right to obtain and consult with legal counsel or an employee representative before each phase of the test;

(B) is informed in writing of the nature and characteristics of the tests and of the instruments involved;

(C) is informed, in writing —

(i) whether the testing area contains a two-way mirror, a camera, or any other device through which the test can be observed,

(ii) whether any other device, including any device for recording or monitoring the test, will be used, or

(iii) that the employer or the examinee may (with mutual knowledge) make a recording of the test;

(D) is read and signs a written notice informing such examinee —

(i) that the examinee cannot be required to take the test as a condition of employment,

(ii) that any statement made during the test may constitute additional supporting evidence for the purposes of an adverse employment action described in subsection (a) of this section,

(iii) of the limitations imposed under this section,

(iv) of the legal rights and remedies available to the examinee if the polygraph test is not conducted in accordance with this chapter, and

(v) of the legal rights and remedies of the employer under this chapter (including the rights of the employer under section 2008(c)(2) of this title); and

(E) is provided an opportunity to review all questions to be asked during the test and is informed of the right to terminate the test at any time.

(3) Actual testing phase

During the actual testing phase, the examiner does not ask such examinee any question relevant during the test that was not presented in writing for review to such examinee before the test.

(4) Post-test phase

Before any adverse employment action, the employer shall —

(A) further interview the examinee on the basis of the results of the test; and

(B) provide the examinee with —

(i) a written copy of any opinion or conclusion rendered as a result of the test, and

(ii) a copy of the questions asked during the test along with the corresponding charted responses.

(5) Maximum number and minimum duration of tests

The examiner shall not conduct and complete more than five polygraph tests on a calendar day on which the test is given, and shall not conduct any such test for less than a 90-minute duration.

(c) Qualifications and requirements of examiners

The exemptions provided under subsections (d), (e), and (f) of section 2006 of this title shall not apply unless the individual who conducts the polygraph test satisfies the requirements under the following paragraphs:

(1) Qualifications

The examiner —

(A) has a valid and current license granted by licensing and regulatory authorities in the State in which the test is to be conducted, if so required by the State; and

(B) maintains a minimum of a $50,000 bond or an equivalent amount of professional liability coverage.

(2) Requirements

The examiner —

(A) renders any opinion or conclusion regarding the test —

(i) in writing and solely on the basis of an analysis of polygraph test charts,

(ii) that does not contain information other than admissions, information, case facts, and interpretation of the charts relevant to the purpose and stated objectives of the test, and

(iii) that does not include any recommendation concerning the employment of the examinee; and

(B) maintains all opinions, reports, charts, written questions, lists, and other records relating to the test for a minimum period of 3 years after administration of the test.

Sec. 2008. Disclosure of information

(a) In general

A person, other than the examinee, may not disclose information obtained during a polygraph test, except as provided in this section.

(b) Permitted disclosures

A polygraph examiner may disclose information acquired from a polygraph test only to —

(1) the examinee or any other person specifically designated in writing by the examinee;

(2) the employer that requested the test; or

(3) any court, governmental agency, arbitrator, or mediator, in accordance with due process of law, pursuant to an order from a court of competent jurisdiction.

(c) Disclosure by employer

An employer (other than an employer described in subsection (a), (b), or (c) of section 2006 of this title) for whom a polygraph test is conducted may disclose information from the test only to -

(1) a person in accordance with subsection (b) of this section; or

(2) a governmental agency, but only insofar as the disclosed information is an admission of criminal conduct.

Sec. 2009. Effect on other law and agreements

Except as provided in subsections (a), (b), and (c) of section 2006 of this title, this chapter shall not preempt any provision of any State or local law or of any negotiated collective bargaining agreement that prohibits lie detector tests or is more restrictive with respect to lie detector tests than any provision of this chapter.

Worker Adjustment and Retraining Notification Act

U.S. Code, Title 29, Sections 2101 to 2109

Sec.

WARN IN A NUTSHELL

Enacted: 1988

Purpose: To require employers to provide 60 days notice to employees prior to closings and mass layoffs

Coverage: Private sector employers with more than 100 or more employees

Responsible agency: U.S. Department of Labor Employment and Training Administration

---

Sec. 2101. Definitions; exclusions from definition of loss of employment

(a) Definitions

As used in this chapter —

(1) the term "employer" means any business enterprise that employs —

  (A) 100 or more employees, excluding part-time employees; or

  (B) 100 or more employees who in the aggregate work at least 4,000 hours per week (exclusive of hours of overtime);

(2) the term "plant closing" means the permanent or temporary shutdown of a single site of employment, or one or more facilities or operating units within a single site of employment, if the shutdown results in an employment loss at the single site of employment during any 30-day period for 50 or more employees excluding any part-time employees;

(3) the term "mass layoff" means a reduction in force which —

  (A) is not the result of a plant closing; and

  (B) results in an employment loss at the single site of employment during any 30-day period for —

    (i)(I) at least 33 percent of the employees (excluding any part-time employees); and

      (II) at least 50 employees (excluding any part-time employees); or

    (ii) at least 500 employees (excluding any part-time employees);

(4) the term "representative" means an exclusive representative of employees within the meaning of section 159(a) or 158(f) of this title or section 152 of Title 45;

(5) the term "affected employees" means employees who may reasonably be expected to experience an employment loss as a consequence of a proposed plant closing or mass layoff by their employer;

(6) subject to subsection (b) of this section, the term "employment loss" means (A) an employment termination, other than a discharge for cause, voluntary departure, or retirement, (B) a layoff exceeding 6 months, or (C) a reduction in hours of work of more than 50 percent during each month of any 6-month period;

(7) the term "unit of local government" means any general purpose political subdivision of a State which has the power to levy taxes and spend funds, as well as general corporate and police powers; and

(8) the term "part-time employee" means an employee who is employed for an average of fewer than 20 hours per week or who has been employed for fewer than 6 of the 12 months preceding the date on which notice is required.

(b) Exclusions from definition of employment loss

(1) In the case of a sale of part or all of an employer's business, the seller shall be responsible for providing notice for any plant closing or mass layoff in accordance with section 2102 of this title, up to and including the effective date of the sale. After the effective date of the sale of part or all of an employer's business, the purchaser shall be responsible for providing notice for any plant closing or mass layoff in accordance with section 2102 of this title. Notwithstanding any other provision of this chapter, any person who is an employee of the seller (other than a part-time employee) as of the effective date of the sale shall be considered an employee of the purchaser immediately after the effective date of the sale.

(2) Notwithstanding subsection (a)(6) of this section, an employee may not be considered to have experienced an employment loss if the closing or layoff is the result of the relocation or consolidation of part or all of the employer's business and, prior to the closing or layoff —

(A) the employer offers to transfer the employee to a different site of employment within a reasonable commuting distance with no more than a 6-month break in employment; or

(B) the employer offers to transfer the employee to any other site of employment regardless of distance with no more than a 6-month break in employment, and the employee accepts within 30 days of the offer or of the closing or layoff, whichever is later.

Sec. 2102. Notice required before plant closings and mass layoffs

(a) Notice to employees, State dislocated worker units, and local governments

An employer shall not order a plant closing or mass layoff until the end of a 60-day period after the employer serves written notice of such an order —

(1) to each representative of the affected employees as of the time of the notice or, if there is no such representative at that time, to each affected employee; and

(2) to the State dislocated worker unit or office (referred to in section 1661(b)(2) of this title), or the state or entity designated by the state to carry out rapid response activities under section 2864(a)(2)(A) of this title, and the chief elected official of the unit of local government within which such closing or layoff is to occur.

If there is more than one such unit, the unit of local government which the employer shall notify is the unit of local government to which the employer pays the highest taxes for the year preceding the year for which the determination is made.

(b) Reduction of notification period

(1) An employer may order the shutdown of a single site of employment before the conclusion of the 60-day period if as of the time that notice would have been required the employer was actively seeking capital or business which, if obtained, would have enabled the employer to avoid or postpone the shutdown and the employer reasonably and in good faith believed that giving the notice required would have precluded the employer from obtaining the needed capital or business.

(2)(A) An employer may order a plant closing or mass layoff before the conclusion of the 60-day period if the closing or mass layoff is caused by business circumstances that were not reasonably foreseeable as of the time that notice would have been required.

(B) No notice under this chapter shall be required if the plant closing or mass layoff is due to any form of natural disaster, such as a flood, earthquake, or the drought currently ravaging the farmlands of the United States.

(3) An employer relying on this subsection shall give as much notice as is practicable and at that time shall give a brief statement of the basis for reducing the notification period.

(c) Extension of layoff period

A layoff of more than 6 months which, at its outset, was announced to be a layoff of 6 months or less, shall be treated as an employment loss under this chapter unless —

(1) the extension beyond 6 months is caused by business circumstances (including unforeseeable changes in price or cost) not reasonably foreseeable at the time of the initial layoff; and

(2) notice is given at the time it becomes reasonably foreseeable that the extension beyond 6 months will be required.

(d) Determinations with respect to employment loss

For purposes of this section, in determining whether a plant closing or mass layoff has occurred or will occur, employment losses for 2 or more groups at a single site of employment, each of which is less than the minimum number of employees specified in section 2101(a)(2) or (3) of this title but which in the aggregate exceed that minimum number, and which occur within any 90-day period shall be considered to be a plant closing or mass layoff unless the employer demonstrates that the employment losses are the result of separate and distinct actions and causes and are not an attempt by the employer to evade the requirements of this chapter.

Sec. 2103. Exemptions

This chapter shall not apply to a plant closing or mass layoff if—

(1) the closing is of a temporary facility or the closing or layoff is the result of the completion of a particular project or undertaking, and the affected employees were hired with the understanding that their employment was limited to the duration of the facility or the project or undertaking; or

(2) the closing or layoff constitutes a strike or constitutes a lockout not intended to evade the requirements of this chapter. Nothing in this chapter shall require an employer to serve written notice pursuant to section 2102(a) of this title when permanently replacing a person who is deemed to be an economic striker under the National Labor Relations Act (29 U.S.C. §151 et seq.): *Provided,* That nothing in this chapter shall be deemed to validate or invalidate any judicial or administrative ruling relating to the hiring of permanent replacements for economic strikers under the National Labor Relations Act.

Sec. 2104. Administration and enforcement of requirements

(a) Civil actions against employers

(1) Any employer who orders a plant closing or mass layoff in violation of section 2102 of this title shall be liable to each aggrieved employee who suffers an employment loss as a result of such closing or layoff for —

(A) back pay for each day of violation at a rate of compensation not less than the higher of —

(i) the average regular rate received by such employee during the last 3 years of the employee's employment; or

(ii) the final regular rate received by such employee; and

(B) benefits under an employee benefit plan described in section 1002(3) of this title, including the cost of medical expenses incurred during the employment loss which would have been covered under an employee benefit plan if the employment loss had not occurred.

Such liability shall be calculated for the period of the violation, up to a maximum of 60 days, but in no event for more than one-half the number of days the employee was employed by the employer.

(2) The amount for which an employer is liable under paragraph (1) shall be reduced by —

(A) any wages paid by the employer to the employee for the period of the violation;

(B) any voluntary and unconditional payment by the employer to the employee that is not required by any legal obligation; and

(C) any payment by the employer to a third party or trustee (such as premiums for health benefits or payments to a defined contribution pension plan) on behalf of and attributable to the employee for the period of the violation.

In addition, any liability incurred under paragraph (1) with respect to a defined benefit pension plan may be reduced by crediting the employee with service for all purposes under such a plan for the period of the violation.

(3) Any employer who violates the provisions of section 2102 of this title with respect to a unit of local government shall be subject to a civil penalty of not more than $500 for each day of such violation, except that such penalty shall not apply if the employer pays to each aggrieved employee the amount for which the employer is liable to that employee within 3 weeks from the date the employer orders the shutdown or layoff.

(4) If an employer which has violated this chapter proves to the satisfaction of the court that the act or omission that violated this chapter was in good faith and that the employer had reasonable grounds for believing that the act or omission was not a violation of this chapter the court may, in its discretion, reduce the amount of the liability or penalty provided for in this section.

(5) A person seeking to enforce such liability, including a representative of employees or a unit of local government aggrieved under paragraph (1) or (3), may sue either for such person or for other persons similarly situated, or both, in any district court of the United States for any district in which the violation is alleged to have occurred, or in which the employer transacts business.

(6) In any such suit, the court, in its discretion, may allow the prevailing party a reasonable attorney's fee as part of the costs.

(7) For purposes of this subsection, the term, aggrieved employee" means an employee who has worked for the employer ordering the plant closing or mass layoff and who, as a result of the failure by the employer to comply with section 2102 of this title, did not receive timely notice either directly or through his or her representative as required by section 2102 of this title.

(b) Exclusivity of remedies

The remedies provided for in this section shall be the exclusive remedies for any violation of this chapter. Under this chapter, a Federal court shall not have authority to enjoin a plant closing or mass layoff.

Sec. 2105. Procedures in addition to other rights of employees

The rights and remedies provided to employees by this chapter are in addition to, and not in lieu of, any other contractual or statutory rights and remedies of the employees, and are not intended to alter or affect such rights and remedies, except that the period of notification required by this chapter shall run concurrently with any period of notification required by contractor by any other statute.

Sec. 2106. Procedures encouraged where not required

It is the sense of Congress that an employer who is not required to comply with the notice requirements of section 2102 of this title should, to the extent possible, provide notice to its employees about a proposal to close a plant or permanently reduce its workforce.

Sec. 2107. Authority to prescribe regulations

(a) The Secretary of Labor shall prescribe such regulations as may be necessary to carry out this chapter. Such regulations shall, at a minimum, include interpretative regulations describing the methods by which employers may provide for appropriate service of notice as required by this chapter.

(b) The mailing of notice to an employee's last known address or inclusion of notice in the employee's paycheck will be considered acceptable methods for fulfillment of the employer's obligation to give notice to each affected employee under this chapter.

Sec. 2108. Effect on other laws

The giving of notice pursuant to this chapter, if done in good faith compliance with this chapter, shall not constitute a violation of the National Labor Relations Act (29 U.S.C. §151 et seq.) or the Railway Labor Act (45 U.S.C. §151 et seq.).

Sec. 2109. Report on employment and international competitiveness

Two years after August 4, 1988, the Comptroller General shall submit to the Committee on Small Business of both the House and Senate, the Committee on Labor and Human Resources, and the Committee on Education and Labor a report containing a detailed and objective analysis of the effect of this chapter on employers (especially small- and medium-sized businesses), the economy (international competitiveness), and employees (in terms of levels and conditions of employment). The Comptroller General shall assess both costs and benefits, including the effect on productivity, competitiveness, unemployment rates and compensation, and worker retraining and readjustment.

Family and Medical Leave Act

U.S. Code, Title 29, Sections 2601 to 2654

FMLA IN A NUTSHELL

Enacted: 1993

Purpose: To allow employees to be absent from work or to take leaves in the event of serious health conditions, childbirth, or other qualifying events

Coverage: Private sector employers with more than 50 employees, public agencies

Responsible agency: U.S. Department of Labor Wage and Hour Division

Sec. 2601. Findings and purposes

(a) Findings

Congress finds that —

(1) the number of single-parent households and two-parent households in which the single parent or both parents work is increasing significantly;

(2) it is important for the development of children and the family unit that fathers and mothers be able to participate in early childrearing and the care of family members who have serious health conditions;

(3) the lack of employment policies to accommodate working parents can force individuals to choose between job security and parenting;

(4) there is inadequate job security for employees who have serious health conditions that prevent them from working for temporary periods;

(5) due to the nature of the roles of men and women in our society, the primary responsibility for family caretaking often falls on women, and such responsibility affects the working lives of women more than it affects the working lives of men; and

(6) employment standards that apply to one gender only have serious potential for encouraging employers to discriminate against employees and applicants for employment who are of that gender.

(b) Purposes

It is the purpose of this Act —

(1) to balance the demands of the workplace with the needs of families, to promote the stability and economic security of families, and to promote national interests in preserving family integrity;

(2) to entitle employees to take reasonable leave for medical reasons, for the birth or adoption of a child, and for the care of a child, spouse, or parent who has a serious health condition;

(3) to accomplish the purposes described in paragraphs (1) and (2) in a manner that accommodates the legitimate interests of employers;

(4) to accomplish the purposes described in paragraphs (1) and (2) in a manner that, consistent with the Equal Protection Clause of the Fourteenth Amendment, minimizes the potential for employment discrimination on the basis of sex by ensuring generally that leave is available for eligible medical reasons (including maternity-related disability) and for compelling family reasons, on a gender-neutral basis; and

(5) to promote the goal of equal employment opportunity for women and men, pursuant to such clause.

Sec. 2611. Definitions

As used in this subchapter:

(1) Commerce

The terms "commerce" and "industry or activity affecting commerce" mean any activity, business, or industry in commerce or in which a labor dispute would hinder or obstruct commerce or the free flow of commerce, and include "commerce" and any "industry affecting commerce", as defined in paragraphs (1) and (3) of section 142 of this title.

(2) Eligible employee

(A) In general

The term "eligible employee" means an employee who has been employed —

(i) for at least 12 months by the employer with respect to whom leave is requested under section 2612 of this title; and

(ii) for at least 1,250 hours of service with such employer during the previous 12-month period.

(B) Exclusions

The term "eligible employee" does not include —

(i) any Federal officer or employee covered under subchapter V of chapter 63 of Title 5; or

(ii) any employee of an employer who is employed at a worksite at which such employer employs less than 50 employees if the total number of employees employed by that employer within 75 miles of that worksite is less than 50.

(C) Determination

For purposes of determining whether an employee meets the hours of service requirement specified in subparagraph (A)(ii), the legal standards established under section 207 of this title shall apply.

(3) Employ; employee; State

The terms "employ", "employee", and "State" have the same meanings given such terms in subsections (c), (e), and (g) of section 203 of this title.

(4) Employer

(A) In general

The term "employer" —

(i) means any person engaged in commerce or in any industry or activity affecting commerce who employs 50 or more employees for each working day during each of 20 or more calendar workweeks in the current or preceding calendar year;

(ii) includes —

(I) any person who acts, directly or indirectly, in the interest of an employer to any of the employees of such employer; and

(II) any successor in interest of an employer;

(iii) includes any "public agency", as defined in section 203(x) of this title; and

(iv) includes the General Accounting Office and the Library of Congress.

(B) Public agency

For purposes of subparagraph (A)(iii), a public agency shall be considered to be a person engaged in commerce or in an industry or activity affecting commerce.

(5) Employment benefits

The term "employment benefits" means all benefits provided or made available to employees by an employer, including group life insurance, health insurance, disability insurance, sick leave, annual leave, educational benefits, and pensions, regardless of whether such benefits are provided by a practice or written policy of an employer or through an "employee benefit plan", as defined in section 1002(3) of this title.

(6) Health care provider

The term "health care provider" means —

(A) a doctor of medicine or osteopathy who is authorized to practice medicine or surgery (as appropriate) by the State in which the doctor practices; or

(B) any other person determined by the Secretary to be capable of providing health care services.

(7) Parent

The term "parent" means the biological parent of an employee or an individual who stood in loco parentis to an employee when the employee was a son or daughter.

(8) Person

The term "person" has the same meaning given such term in section 203(a) of this title.

(9) Reduced leave schedule

The term "reduced leave schedule" means a leave schedule that reduces the usual number of hours per workweek, or hours per workday, of an employee.

(10) Secretary

The term "Secretary" means the Secretary of Labor.

(11) Serious health condition

The term "serious health condition" means an illness, injury, impairment, or physical or mental condition that involves —

(A) inpatient care in a hospital, hospice, or residential medical care facility; or

(B) continuing treatment by a health care provider.

(12) Son or daughter

The term "son or daughter" means a biological, adopted, or foster child, a stepchild, a legal ward, or a child of a person standing in loco parentis, who is —

(A) under 18 years of age; or

(B) 18 years of age or older and incapable of self-care because of a mental or physical disability.

(13) Spouse

The term "spouse" means a husband or wife, as the case may be.

Sec. 2612. Leave requirement

(a) In general

(1) Entitlement to leave

Subject to section 2613 of this title, an eligible employee shall be entitled to a total of 12 workweeks of leave during any 12-month period for one or more of the following:

(A) Because of the birth of a son or daughter of the employee and in order to care for such son or daughter.

(B) Because of the placement of a son or daughter with the employee for adoption or foster care.

(C) In order to care for the spouse, or a son, daughter, or parent, of the employee, if such spouse, son, daughter, or parent has a serious health condition.

(D) Because of a serious health condition that makes the employee unable to perform the functions of the position of such employee.

(2) Expiration of entitlement

The entitlement to leave under subparagraphs (A) and (B) of paragraph (1) for a birth or placement of a son or daughter shall expire at the end of the 12-month period beginning on the date of such birth or placement.

(b) Leave taken intermittently or on reduced leave schedule

(1) In general

Leave under subparagraph (A) or (B) of subsection (a)(1) of this section shall not be taken by an employee intermittently or on a reduced leave schedule unless the employee and the employer of the employee agree otherwise. Subject to paragraph (2), subsection (e)(2) of this section, and section 2613(b)(5) of this title, leave under subparagraph (C) or (D) of subsection (a)(1) of this section may be taken intermittently or on a reduced leave schedule when medically necessary. The taking of leave intermittently or on a reduced leave schedule pursuant to this paragraph shall not result in a reduction in the total amount of leave to which the employee is entitled under subsection (a) of this section beyond the amount of leave actually taken.

(2) Alternative position

If an employee requests intermittent leave, or leave on a reduced leave schedule, under subparagraph (C) or (D) of subsection (a)(1) of this section, that is foreseeable based on planned medical treatment, the employer may require such employee to transfer temporarily to an available alternative position offered by the employer for which the employee is qualified and that —

(A) has equivalent pay and benefits; and

(B) better accommodates recurring periods of leave than the regular employment position of the employee.

(c) Unpaid leave permitted

Except as provided in subsection (d) of this section, leave granted under subsection (a) may consist of unpaid leave. Where an employee is otherwise exempt under regulations issued by the Secretary pursuant to section 213(a)(1) of this title, the compliance of an employer with this subchapter by providing unpaid leave shall not affect the exempt status of the employee under such section.

(d) Relationship to paid leave

(1) Unpaid leave

If an employer provides paid leave for fewer than 12 workweeks, the additional weeks of leave necessary to attain the 12 workweeks of leave required under this subchapter may be provided without compensation.

(2) Substitution of paid leave

(A) In general

An eligible employee may elect, or an employer may require the employee, to substitute any of the accrued paid vacation leave, personal leave, or family leave of the employee for leave provided under subparagraph (A), (B), or (C) of subsection (a)(1) of this section for any part of the 12-week period of such leave under such subsection.

(B) Serious health condition

An eligible employee may elect, or an employer may require the employee, to substitute any of the accrued paid vacation leave, personal leave, or medical or sick leave of the employee for leave provided under subparagraph (C) or (D) of subsection (a)(1) of this section for any part of the 12-week period of such leave under such subsection, except that nothing in this subchapter shall require an employer to provide paid sick leave or paid medical leave in any situation in which such employer would not normally provide any such paid leave.

(e) Foreseeable leave

(1) Requirement of notice

In any case in which the necessity for leave under subparagraph (A) or (B) of subsection (a)(1) of this section is foreseeable based on an expected birth or placement, the employee shall provide the employer with not less than 30 days' notice, before the date the leave is to begin, of the employee's intention to take leave under such subparagraph, except that if the date of the birth or placement requires leave to begin in less than 30 days, the employee shall provide such notice as is practicable.

(2) Duties of employee

In any case in which the necessity for leave under subparagraph (C) or (D) of subsection (a)(1) of this section is foreseeable based on planned medical treatment, the employee —

(A) shall make a reasonable effort to schedule the treatment so as not to disrupt unduly the operations of the employer, subject to the approval of the health care provider of the employee or the health care provider of the son, daughter, spouse, or parent of the employee, as appropriate; and

(B) shall provide the employer with not less than 30 days' notice, before the date the leave is to begin, of the employee's intention to take leave under such subparagraph, except that if the date of the treatment requires leave to begin in less than 30 days, the employee shall provide such notice as is practicable.

(f) Spouses employed by the same employer

In any case in which a husband and wife entitled to leave under subsection (a) of this section are employed by the same employer, the aggregate number of workweeks of leave to which both may be entitled may be limited to 12 workweeks during any 12-month period, if such leave is taken —

(1) under subparagraph (A) or (B) of subsection (a)(1) of this section; or

(2) to care for a sick parent under subparagraph (C) of such subsection.

Sec. 2613. Certification

(a) In general

An employer may require that a request for leave under subparagraph (C) or (D) of section 2612(a)(1) of this title be supported by a certification issued by the health care provider of the eligible employee or of the son, daughter, spouse, or parent of the employee, as appropriate. The employee shall provide, in a timely manner, a copy of such certification to the employer.

(b) Sufficient certification

Certification provided under subsection (a) of this section shall be sufficient if it states —

(1) the date on which the serious health condition commenced;

(2) the probable duration of the condition;

(3) the appropriate medical facts within the knowledge of the health care provider regarding the condition;

(4)(A) for purposes of leave under section 2612(a)(1)(C) of this title, a statement that the eligible employee is needed to care for the son, daughter, spouse, or parent and an estimate of the amount of time that such employee is needed to care for the son, daughter, spouse, or parent; and

(B) for purposes of leave under section 2612(a)(1)(D) of this title, a statement that the employee is unable to perform the functions of the position of the employee;

(5) in the case of certification for intermittent leave, or leave on a reduced leave schedule, for planned medical treatment, the dates on which

such treatment is expected to be given and the duration of such treatment;

(6) in the case of certification for intermittent leave, or leave on a reduced leave schedule, under section 2612(a)(1)(D) of this title, a statement of the medical necessity for the intermittent leave or leave on a reduced leave schedule, and the expected duration of the intermittent leave or reduced leave schedule; and

(7) in the case of certification for intermittent leave, or leave on a reduced leave schedule, under section 2612(a)(1)(C) of this title, a statement that the employee's intermittent leave or leave on a reduced leave schedule is necessary for the care of the son, daughter, parent, or spouse who has a serious health condition, or will assist in their recovery, and the expected duration and schedule of the intermittent leave or reduced leave schedule.

(c) Second opinion

(1) In general

In any case in which the employer has reason to doubt the validity of the certification provided under subsection (a) of this section for leave under subparagraph (C) or (D) of section 2612(a)(1) of this title, the employer may require, at the expense of the employer, that the eligible employee obtain the opinion of a second health care provider designated or approved by the employer concerning any information certified under subsection (b) of this section for such leave.

(2) Limitation

A health care provider designated or approved under paragraph (1) shall not be employed on a regular basis by the employer.

(d) Resolution of conflicting opinions

(1) In general

In any case in which the second opinion described in subsection (c) of this section differs from the opinion in the original certification provided under subsection (a) of this section, the employer may require, at the expense of the employer, that the employee obtain the opinion of a third health care provider designated or approved jointly by the employer and the employee concerning the information certified under subsection (b) of this section.

(2) Finality

The opinion of the third health care provider concerning the information certified under subsection (b) of this section shall be considered to be final and shall be binding on the employer and the employee.

(e) Subsequent recertification

The employer may require that the eligible employee obtain subsequent recertifications on a reasonable basis.

Sec. 2614. Employment and benefits protection

(a) Restoration to position

(1) In general

Except as provided in subsection (b) of this section, any eligible employee who takes leave under section 2612 of this title for the intended purpose of the leave shall be entitled, on return from such leave —

(A) to be restored by the employer to the position of employment held by the employee when the leave commenced; or

(B) to be restored to an equivalent position with equivalent employment benefits, pay, and other terms and conditions of employment.

(2) Loss of benefits

The taking of leave under section 2612 of this title shall not result in the loss of any employment benefit accrued prior to the date on which the leave commenced.

(3) Limitations

Nothing in this section shall be construed to entitle any restored employee to —

(A) the accrual of any seniority or employment benefits during any period of leave; or

(B) any right, benefit, or position of employment other than any right, benefit, or position to which the employee would have been entitled had the employee not taken the leave.

(4) Certification

As a condition of restoration under paragraph (1) for an employee who has taken leave under section 2612(a)(1)(D) of this title, the employer may have a uniformly applied practice or policy that requires each such employee to receive certification from the health care provider of the employee that the employee is able to resume work, except that nothing in this paragraph shall supersede a valid State or local law or a collective bargaining agreement that governs the return to work of such employees.

(5) Construction

Nothing in this subsection shall be construed to prohibit an employer from requiring an employee on leave under section 2612 of this title to report periodically to the employer on the status and intention of the employee to return to work.

(b) Exemption concerning certain highly compensated employees

(1) Denial of restoration

An employer may deny restoration under subsection (a) of this section to any eligible employee described in paragraph (2) if —

(A) such denial is necessary to prevent substantial and grievous economic injury to the operations of the employer;

(B) the employer notifies the employee of the intent of the employer to deny restoration on such basis at the time the employer determines that such injury would occur; and

(C) in any case in which the leave has commenced, the employee elects not to return to employment after receiving such notice.

(2) Affected employees

An eligible employee described in paragraph (1) is a salaried eligible employee who is among the highest paid 10 percent of the employees employed by the employer within 75 miles of the facility at which the employee is employed.

(c) Maintenance of health benefits

(1) Coverage

Except as provided in paragraph (2), during any period that an eligible employee takes leave under section 2612 of this title, the employer shall maintain coverage under any "group health plan" (as defined in section 5000(b)(1) of Title 26) for the duration of such leave at the level and under the conditions coverage would have been provided if the employee had continued in employment continuously for the duration of such leave.

(2) Failure to return from leave

The employer may recover the premium that the employer paid for maintaining coverage for the employee under such group health plan during any period of unpaid leave under section 2612 of this title if —

(A) the employee fails to return from leave under section 2612 of this title after the period of leave to which the employee is entitled has expired; and

(B) the employee fails to return to work for a reason other than —

(i) the continuation, recurrence, or onset of a serious health condition that entitles the employee to leave under subparagraph (C) or (D) of section 2612(a)(1) of this title; or

(ii) other circumstances beyond the control of the employee.

(3) Certification

(A) Issuance

An employer may require that a claim that an employee is unable to return to work because of the continuation, recurrence, or onset of the serious health condition described in paragraph (2)(B)(i) be supported by —

(i) a certification issued by the health care provider of the son, daughter, spouse, or parent of the employee, as appropriate, in the case of an employee unable to return to work because of a condition specified in section 2612(a)(1)(C) of this title; or

(ii) a certification issued by the health care provider of the eligible employee, in the case of an employee unable to return to work because of a condition specified in section 2612(a)(1)(D) of this title.

(B) Copy

The employee shall provide, in a timely manner, a copy of such certification to the employer.

(C) Sufficiency of certification

(i) Leave due to serious health condition of employee

The certification described in subparagraph (A)(ii) shall be sufficient if the certification states that a serious health condition prevented the employee from being able to perform the functions of the position of the employee on the date that the leave of the employee expired.

(ii) Leave due to serious health condition of family member

The certification described in subparagraph (A)(i) shall be sufficient if the certification states that the employee is needed to care for the son, daughter, spouse, or parent who has a serious health condition on the date that the leave of the employee expired.

Sec. 2615. Prohibited acts

(a) Interference with rights

(1) Exercise of rights

It shall be unlawful for any employer to interfere with, restrain, or deny the exercise of or the attempt to exercise, any right provided under this subchapter.

(2) Discrimination

It shall be unlawful for any employer to discharge or in any other manner discriminate against any individual for opposing any practice made unlawful by this subchapter.

(b) Interference with proceedings or inquiries

It shall be unlawful for any person to discharge or in any other manner discriminate against any individual because such individual —

(1) has filed any charge, or has instituted or caused to be instituted any proceeding, under or related to this subchapter;

(2) has given, or is about to give, any information in connection with any inquiry or proceeding relating to any right provided under this subchapter; or

(3) has testified, or is about to testify, in any inquiry or proceeding relating to any right provided under this subchapter.

Sec. 2616. Investigative authority

(a) In general

To ensure compliance with the provisions of this subchapter, or any regulation or order issued under

this subchapter, the Secretary shall have, subject to subsection (c) of this section, the investigative authority provided under section 211(a) of this title.

(b) Obligation to keep and preserve records

Any employer shall make, keep, and preserve records pertaining to compliance with this subchapter in accordance with section 211(c) of this title and in accordance with regulations issued by the Secretary.

(c) Required submissions generally limited to annual basis

The Secretary shall not under the authority of this section require any employer or any plan, fund, or program to submit to the Secretary any books or records more than once during any 12-month period, unless the Secretary has reasonable cause to believe there may exist a violation of this subchapter or any regulation or order issued pursuant to this subchapter, or is investigating a charge pursuant to section 2617(b) of this title.

(d) Subpoena powers

For the purposes of any investigation provided for in this section, the Secretary shall have the subpoena authority provided for under section 209 of this title.

Sec. 2617. Enforcement

(a) Civil action by employees

(1) Liability

Any employer who violates section 2615 of this title shall be liable to any eligible employee affected —

(A) for damages equal to —

(i) the amount of —

(I) any wages, salary, employment benefits, or other compensation denied or lost to such employee by reason of the violation; or

(II) in a case in which wages, salary, employment benefits, or other compensation have not been denied or lost to the employee, any actual monetary losses sustained by the employee as a direct result of the violation, such as the cost of providing care, up to a sum equal to 12 weeks of wages or salary for the employee;

(ii) the interest on the amount described in clause (i) calculated at the prevailing rate; and

(iii) an additional amount as liquidated damages equal to the sum of the amount described in clause (i) and the interest described in clause (ii), except that if an employer who has violated section 2615 of this title proves to the satisfaction of the court that the act or omission which violated section 2615 of this title was in good faith and that the employer had reasonable grounds for believing that the act or omission was not a violation of section 2615 of this title, such court may, in the discretion of the court, reduce the amount of the liability to the amount and interest determined under clauses (i) and (ii), respectively; and

(B) for such equitable relief as may be appropriate, including employment, reinstatement, and promotion.

(2) Right of action

An action to recover the damages or equitable relief prescribed in paragraph (1) may be maintained against any employer (including a public agency) in any Federal or State court of competent jurisdiction by any one or more employees for and in behalf of —

(A) the employees; or

(B) the employees and other employees similarly situated.

(3) Fees and costs

The court in such an action shall, in addition to any judgment awarded to the plaintiff, allow a reasonable attorney's fee, reasonable expert witness fees, and other costs of the action to be paid by the defendant.

(4) Limitations

The right provided by paragraph (2) to bring an action by or on behalf of any employee shall terminate —

(A) on the filing of a complaint by the Secretary in an action under subsection (d) of this section in which restraint is sought of any further delay in the payment of the amount described in paragraph (1)(A) to such employee by an employer responsible under paragraph (1) for the payment; or

(B) on the filing of a complaint by the Secretary in an action under subsection (b) of this section in which a recovery is sought of the damages described in paragraph (1)(A) owing to an eligible employee by an employer liable under paragraph (1),

unless the action described in subparagraph (A) or (B) is dismissed without prejudice on motion of the Secretary.

(b) Action by Secretary

(1) Administrative action

The Secretary shall receive, investigate, and attempt to resolve complaints of violations of section 2615 of this title in the same manner that the Secretary receives, investigates, and attempts to resolve complaints of violations of sections 206 and 207 of this title.

(2) Civil action

The Secretary may bring an action in any court of competent jurisdiction to recover the damages described in subsection (a)(1)(A) of this section.

(3) Sums recovered

Any sums recovered by the Secretary pursuant to paragraph (2) shall be held in a special deposit account and shall be paid, on order of the Secretary, directly to each employee affected. Any such sums not paid to an employee because of inability to do so within a period of 3 years shall be deposited into the Treasury of the United States as miscellaneous receipts.

(c) Limitation

(1) In general

Except as provided in paragraph (2), an action may be brought under this section not later than 2 years after the date of the last event constituting the alleged violation for which the action is brought.

(2) Willful violation

In the case of such action brought for a willful violation of section 2615 of this title, such action may be brought within 3 years of the date of the last event constituting the alleged violation for which such action is brought.

(3) Commencement

In determining when an action is commenced by the Secretary under this section for the purposes of this subsection, it shall be considered to be commenced on the date when the complaint is filed.

(d) Action for injunction by Secretary

The district courts of the United States shall have jurisdiction, for cause shown, in an action brought by the Secretary —

(1) to restrain violations of section 2615 of this title, including the restraint of any withholding of payment of wages, salary, employment benefits, or other compensation, plus interest, found by the court to be due to eligible employees; or

(2) to award such other equitable relief as may be appropriate, including employment, reinstatement, and promotion.

(e) Solicitor of Labor

The Solicitor of Labor may appear for and represent the Secretary on any litigation brought under this section.

(f) General Accounting Office and Library of Congress

In the case of the General Accounting Office and the Library of Congress, the authority of the Secretary of Labor under this title shall be exercised respectively by the Comptroller General of the United States and the Librarian of Congress.

Sec. 2618. Special rules concerning employees of local educational agencies

(a) Application

(1) In general

Except as otherwise provided in this section, the rights (including the rights under section 2614 of this title, which shall extend throughout the period of leave of any employee under this section), remedies, and procedures under this subchapter shall apply to —

(A) any "local educational agency" (as defined in section 8801 of Title 20) and an eligible employee of the agency; and

(B) any private elementary or secondary school and an eligible employee of the school.

(2) Definitions

For purposes of the application described in paragraph (1):

(A) Eligible employee

The term "eligible employee" means an eligible employee of an agency or school described in paragraph (1).

(B) Employer

The term "employer" means an agency or school described in paragraph (1).

(b) Leave does not violate certain other Federal laws

A local educational agency and a private elementary or secondary school shall not be in violation of the Individuals with Disabilities Education Act (20 U.S.C. §1400 et seq.), section 794 of this title), or title VI of the Civil Rights Act of 1964 (42 U.S.C. §2000d et seq.), solely as a result of an eligible employee of such agency or school exercising the rights of such employee under this subchapter.

(c) Intermittent leave or leave on reduced schedule for instructional employees

(1) In general

Subject to paragraph (2), in any case in which an eligible employee employed principally in an instructional capacity by any such educational agency or school requests leave under subparagraph (C) or (D) of section 2612(a)(1) of this title that is foreseeable based on planned medical treatment and the employee would be on leave for greater than 20 percent of the total number of working days in the period during which the leave would extend, the agency or school may require that such employee elect either —

(A) to take leave for periods of a particular duration, not to exceed the duration of the planned medical treatment; or

(B) to transfer temporarily to an available alternative position offered by the employer for which the employee is qualified, and that —

(i) has equivalent pay and benefits; and

(ii) better accommodates recurring periods of leave than the regular employment position of the employee.

(2) Application

The elections described in subparagraphs (A) and (B) of paragraph (1) shall apply only with respect to an eligible employee who complies with section 2612(e)(2) of this title.

(d) Rules applicable to periods near conclusion of academic term

The following rules shall apply with respect to periods of leave near the conclusion of an academic term in the case of any eligible employee employed principally in an instructional capacity by any such educational agency or school:

(1) Leave more than 5 weeks prior to end of term

If the eligible employee begins leave under section 2612 of this title more than 5 weeks prior to the end of the academic term, the agency or school may require the employee to continue taking leave until the end of such term, if —

(A) the leave is of at least 3 weeks duration; and

(B) the return to employment would occur during the 3-week period before the end of such term.

(2) Leave less than 5 weeks prior to end of term

If the eligible employee begins leave under subparagraph (A), (B), or (C) of section 2612(a)(1) of this title during the period that commences 5 weeks prior to the end of the academic term, the agency or school may require the employee to continue taking leave until the end of such term, if —

(A) the leave is of greater than 2 weeks duration; and

(B) the return to employment would occur during the 2-week period before the end of such term.

(3) Leave less than 3 weeks prior to end of term

If the eligible employee begins leave under subparagraph (A), (B), or (C) of section 2612(a)(1) of this title during the period that commences 3 weeks prior to the end of the academic term and the duration of the leave is greater than 5 working days, the agency or school may require the employee to continue to take leave until the end of such term.

(e) Restoration to equivalent employment position

For purposes of determinations under section 2614(a)(1)(B) of this title (relating to the restoration of an eligible employee to an equivalent position), in the case of a local educational agency or a private elementary or secondary school, such determination shall be made on the basis of established school board policies and practices, private school policies and practices, and collective bargaining agreements.

(f) Reduction of amount of liability

If a local educational agency or a private elementary or secondary school that has violated this subchapter proves to the satisfaction of the court that the agency, school, or department had reasonable grounds for believing that the underlying act or omission was not a violation of this subchapter, such court may, in the discretion of the court, reduce the amount of the liability provided for under section 2617(a)(1)(A) of this title to the amount and interest determined under clauses (i) and (ii), respectively, of such section.

Sec. 2619. Notice

(a) In general

Each employer shall post and keep posted, in conspicuous places on the premises of the employer where notices to employees and applicants for employment are customarily posted, a notice, to be prepared or approved by the Secretary, setting forth excerpts from, or summaries of, the pertinent provisions of this subchapter and information pertaining to the filing of a charge.

(b) Penalty

Any employer that willfully violates this section may be assessed a civil money penalty not to exceed $100 for each separate offense.

Sec. 2631. Establishment

There is established a commission to be known as the Commission on Leave (referred to in this subchapter as the "Commission").

Sec. 2632. Duties

The Commission shall —

(1) conduct a comprehensive study of —

(A) existing and proposed mandatory and voluntary policies relating to family and temporary medical leave, including policies provided by employers not covered under this Act;

(B) the potential costs, benefits, and impact on productivity, job creation and business growth of such policies on employers and employees;

(C) possible differences in costs, benefits, and impact on productivity, job creation and business growth of such policies on employers based on business type and size;

(D) the impact of family and medical leave policies on the availability of employee benefits provided by employers, including employers not covered under this Act;

(E) alternate and equivalent State enforcement of subchapter I of this chapter with respect to employees described in section 2618(a) of this title;

(F) methods used by employers to reduce administrative costs of implementing family and medical leave policies;

(G) the ability of the employers to recover, under section 2614(c)(2) of this title, the premiums described in such section; and

(H) the impact on employers and employees of policies that provide temporary wage replacement during periods of family and medical leave.

(2) not later than 2 years after the date on which the Commission first meets, prepare and submit, to the appropriate Committees of Congress, a report concerning the subjects listed in paragraph (1).

Sec. 2633. Membership

(a) Composition

(1) Appointments

The Commission shall be composed of 12 voting members and 4 ex officio members to be appointed not later than 60 days after February 5, 1993, as follows:

(A) Senators

One Senator shall be appointed by the Majority Leader of the Senate, and one Senator shall be appointed by the Minority Leader of the Senate.

(B) Members of House of Representatives

One Member of the House of Representatives shall be appointed by the Speaker of the House of Representatives, and one Member of the House of Representatives shall be appointed by the Minority Leader of the House of Representatives.

(C) Additional members

(i) Appointment

Two members each shall be appointed by —

(I) the Speaker of the House of Representatives;

(II) the Majority Leader of the Senate;

(III) the Minority Leader of the House of Representatives; and

(IV) the Minority Leader of the Senate.

(ii) Expertise

Such members shall be appointed by virtue of demonstrated expertise in relevant family, temporary disability, and labor management issues. Such members shall include representatives of employers, including employers from large businesses and from small businesses.

(2) Ex officio members

The Secretary of Health and Human Services, the Secretary of Labor, the Secretary of Commerce, and the Administrator of the Small Business Administration shall serve on the Commission as nonvoting ex officio members.

(b) Vacancies

Any vacancy on the Commission shall be filled in the manner in which the original appointment was made. The vacancy shall not affect the power of the remaining members to execute the duties of the Commission.

(c) Chairperson and vice chairperson

The Commission shall elect a chairperson and a vice chairperson from among the members of the Commission.

(d) Quorum

Eight members of the Commission shall constitute a quorum for all purposes, except that a lesser number may constitute a quorum for the purpose of holding hearings.

Sec. 2634. Compensation

(a) Pay

Members of the Commission shall serve without compensation.

(b) Travel expenses

Members of the Commission shall be allowed reasonable travel expenses, including a per diem allowance, in accordance with section 5703 of Title 5 when performing duties of the Commission.

Sec. 2635. Powers

(a) Meetings

The Commission shall first meet not later than 30 days after the date on which all members are appointed, and the Commission shall meet thereafter on the call of the chairperson or a majority of the members.

(b) Hearings and sessions

The Commission may hold such hearings, sit and act at such times and places, take such testimony, and receive such evidence as the Commission considers appropriate. The Commission may administer oaths or affirmations to witnesses appearing before it.

(c) Access to information

The Commission may secure directly from any Federal agency information necessary to enable it to carry out this subchapter, if the information may be disclosed under section 552 of Title 5. Subject to the previous sentence, on the request of the chairperson or vice chairperson of the Commission, the head of such agency shall furnish such information to the Commission.

(d) Use of facilities and services

Upon the request of the Commission, the head of any Federal agency may make available to the Commission any of the facilities and services of such agency.

(e) Personnel from other agencies

On the request of the Commission, the head of any Federal agency may detail any of the personnel of such agency to serve as an Executive Director of the Commission or assist the Commission in carrying out the duties of the Commission. Any detail shall not interrupt or otherwise affect the civil service status or privileges of the Federal employee.

(f) Voluntary service

Notwithstanding section 1342 of Title 31, the chairperson of the Commission may accept for the Commission voluntary services provided by a member of the Commission.

Sec. 2636. Termination

The Commission shall terminate 30 days after the date of the submission of the report of the Commission to Congress.

Sec. 2651. Effect on other laws

(a) Federal and State antidiscrimination laws

Nothing in this Act or any amendment made by this Act shall be construed to modify or affect any Federal or State law prohibiting discrimination on the basis of race, religion, color, national origin, sex, age, or disability.

(b) State and local laws

Nothing in this Act or any amendment made by this Act shall be construed to supersede any provision of any State or local law that provides greater family or medical leave rights than the rights established under this Act or any amendment made by this Act.

Sec. 2652. Effect on existing employment benefits

a) More protective

Nothing in this Act or any amendment made by this Act shall be construed to diminish the obligation of an employer to comply with any collective bargaining agreement or any employment benefit program or plan that provides greater family or medical leave rights to employees than the rights established under this Act or any amendment made by this Act.

(b) Less protective

The rights established for employees under this Act or any amendment made by this Act shall not be diminished by any collective bargaining agreement or any employment benefit program or plan.

Sec. 2653. Encouragement of more generous leave policies

Nothing in this Act or any amendment made by this Act shall be construed to discourage employers from adopting or retaining leave policies more generous than any policies that comply with the requirements under this Act or any amendment made by this Act.

Sec. 2654. Regulations

The Secretary of Labor shall prescribe such regulations as are necessary to carry out subchapter I of this chapter and this subchapter not later than 120 days after February 5, 1993.

Federal Service Labor-Management Relations Act

U.S. Code, Title 5, Sections 7101 to 7135

SUBCHAPTER I - GENERAL PROVISIONS

Sec. 7101. Findings and purpose

(a) The Congress finds that —

(1) experience in both private and public employment indicates that the statutory protection of the right of employees to organize, bargain collectively, and participate through labor organizations of their own choosing in decisions which affect them —

(A) safeguards the public interest,

(B) contributes to the effective conduct of public business, and

(C) facilitates and encourages the amicable settlements of disputes between employees and their employers involving conditions of employment; and

(2) the public interest demands the highest standards of employee performance and the continued development and implementation of modern and progressive work practices to facilitate and improve employee performance and the efficient accomplishment of the operations of the Government.

Therefore, labor organizations and collective bargaining in the civil service are in the public interest.

(b) It is the purpose of this chapter to prescribe certain rights and obligations of the employees of the Federal Government and to establish procedures which are designed to meet the special requirements and needs of the Government. The provisions of this chapter should be interpreted in a manner consistent with the requirement of an effective and efficient Government.

Sec. 7102. Employees' rights

Each employee shall have the right to form, join, or assist any labor organization, or to refrain from any such activity, freely and without fear of penalty or reprisal, and each employee shall be protected in the exercise of such right. Except as otherwise provided under this chapter, such right includes the right —

(1) to act for a labor organization in the capacity of a representative and the right, in that capacity, to present the views of the labor organization to heads of agencies and other officials of the executive branch of the Government, the Congress, or other appropriate authorities, and

(2) to engage in collective bargaining with respect to conditions of employment through representatives chosen by employees under this chapter.

Sec. 7103. Definitions; application

(a) For the purpose of this chapter —

(1) "person" means an individual, labor organization, or agency;

(2) "employee" means an individual —

(A) employed in an agency; or

(B) whose employment in an agency has ceased because of any unfair labor practice under section 7116 of this title and who has not obtained any other regular and substantially equivalent employment, as determined under regulations prescribed by the Federal Labor Relations Authority;

but does not include —

(i) an alien or noncitizen of the United States who occupies a position outside the United States;

(ii) a member of the uniformed services;

(iii) a supervisor or a management official;

(iv) an officer or employee in the Foreign Service of the United States employed in the Department of State, the International Communication Agency, the Agency for

International Development, the Department of Agriculture, or the Department of Commerce; or

(v) any person who participates in a strike in violation of section 7311 of this Title;

(3) "agency" means an Executive agency (including a nonappropriated fund instrumentality described in section 2105(c) of this title and the Veterans' Canteen Service, Department of Veterans Affairs), the Library of Congress, the Government Printing Office, and the Smithsonian Institution, but does not include —

(A) the General Accounting Office;

(B) the Federal Bureau of Investigation;

(C) the Central Intelligence Agency;

(D) the National Security Agency;

(E) the Tennessee Valley Authority;

(F) the Federal Labor Relations Authority; or

(G) the Federal Service Impasses Panel.

(4) "labor organization" means an organization composed in whole or in part of employees, in which employees participate and pay dues, and which has as a purpose the dealing with an agency concerning grievances and conditions of employment, but does not include —

(A) an organization which, by its constitution, bylaws, tacit agreement among its members, or otherwise, denies membership because of race, color, creed, national origin, sex, age, preferential or nonpreferential civil service status, political affiliation, marital status, or handicapping condition;

(B) an organization which advocates the overthrow of the constitutional form of government of the United States;

(C) an organization sponsored by an agency; or

(D) an organization which participates in the conduct of a strike against the Government or any agency thereof or imposes a duty or obligation to conduct, assist, or participate in such a strike;

(5) "dues" means dues, fees, and assessments;

(6) "Authority" means the Federal Labor Relations Authority described in section 7104(a) of this title;

(7) "Panel" means the Federal Service Impasses Panel described in section 7119(c) of this title;

(8) "collective bargaining agreement" means an agreement entered into as a result of collective bargaining pursuant to the provisions of this chapter;

(9) "grievance" means any complaint —

(A) by any employee concerning any matter relating to the employment of the employee;

(B) by any labor organization concerning any matter relating to the employment of any employee; or

(C) by any employee labor organization, or agency concerning —

(i) the effect or interpretation, or a claim of breach, of a collective bargaining agreement; or

(ii) any claimed violation, misinterpretation, or misapplication of any law, rule, or regulation affecting conditions of employment;

(10) "supervisor" means an individual employed by an agency having authority in the interest of the agency to hire, direct, assign, promote, reward, transfer, furlough, layoff, recall, suspend, discipline, or remove employees, to adjust their grievances, or to effectively recommend such action, if the exercise of the authority is not merely routine or clerical in nature but requires the consistent exercise of independent judgment, except that, with respect to any unit which includes firefighters or nurses, the term "supervisor" includes only those individuals who devote a preponderance of their employment time to exercising such authority;

(11) "management official" means an individual employed by an agency in a position the duties and responsibilities of which require or authorize the individual to formulate, determine, or influence the policies of the agency;

(12) "collective bargaining" means the performance of the mutual obligation of the representative of an agency and the exclusive representative of employees in an appropriate unit in the agency to meet at reasonable times and to consult and bargain in a good-faith effort to reach agreement with respect to the conditions of employment affecting such employees and to execute, if requested by either party, a written document

incorporating any collective bargaining agreement reached, but the obligation referred to in this paragraph does not compel either party to agree to a proposal or to make a concession;

(13) "confidential employee" means an employee who acts in a confidential capacity with respect to an individual who formulates or effectuates management policies in the field of labor-management relations;

(14) "conditions of employment" means personnel policies, practices, and matters, whether established by rule, regulation, or otherwise, affecting working conditions, except that such term does not include policies, practices, and matters —

(A) relating to political activities prohibited under subchapter III of chapter 73 of this title;

(B) relating to the classification of any position; or

(C) to the extent such matters are specifically provided for by Federal statute;

(15) "professional employee" means —

(A) an employee engaged in the performance of work —

(i) requiring knowledge of an advanced type in a field of science or learning customarily acquired by a prolonged course of specialized intellectual instruction and study in an institution of higher learning or a hospital (as distinguished from knowledge acquired by a general academic education, or from an apprenticeship, or from training in the performance of routine mental, manual, mechanical, or physical activities);

(ii) requiring the consistent exercise of discretion and judgment in its performance;

(iii) which is predominantly intellectual and varied in character (as distinguished from routine mental, manual, mechanical, or physical work); and

(iv) which is of such character that the output produced or the result accomplished by such work cannot be standardized in relation to a given period of time; or

(B) an employee who has completed the courses of specialized intellectual instruction and study described in subparagraph (A)(i) of this paragraph and is performing related work under appropriate direction or guidance to qualify the employee as a professional employee described in subparagraph (A) of this paragraph;

(16) "exclusive representative" means any labor organization which —

(A) is certified as the exclusive representative of employees in an appropriate unit pursuant to section 7111 of this title; or

(B) was recognized by an agency immediately before the effective date of this chapter as the exclusive representative of employees in an appropriate unit —

(i) on the basis of an election, or

(ii) on any basis other than an election,

and continues to be so recognized in accordance with the provisions of this chapter;

(17) "firefighter" means any employee engaged in the performance of work directly connected with the control and extinguishment of fires or the maintenance and use of firefighting apparatus and equipment; and

(18) "United States" means the 50 States, the District of Columbia, the Commonwealth of Puerto Rico, Guam, the Virgin Islands, the Trust Territory of the Pacific Islands, and any territory or possession of the United States.

(b)(1) The President may issue an order excluding any agency or subdivision thereof from coverage under this chapter if the President determines that —

(A) the agency or subdivision has as a primary function intelligence, counterintelligence, investigative, or national security work, and

(B) the provisions of this chapter cannot be applied to that agency or subdivision in a manner consistent with national security requirements and considerations.

(2) The President may issue an order suspending any provision of this chapter with respect to any agency, installation, or activity located outside the 50 States and the District of Columbia, if the President determines that the suspension is necessary in the interest of national security.

Sec. 7104. Federal Labor Relations Authority

(a) The Federal Labor Relations Authority is composed of three members, not more than 2 of whom may be adherents of the same political party. No member shall engage in any other business or employment or hold another office or position in the Government of the United States except as otherwise provided by law.

(b) Members of the Authority shall be appointed by the President by and with the advice and consent of the Senate, and may be removed by the President only upon notice and hearing and only for inefficiency, neglect of duty, or malfeasance in office. The President shall designate one member to serve as Chairman of the Authority. The Chairman is the chief executive and administrative officer of the Authority.

(c) A member of the Authority shall be appointed for a term of 5 years. An individual chosen to fill a vacancy shall be appointed for the unexpired term of the member replaced. The term of any member shall not expire before the earlier of —

(1) the date on which the member's successor takes office, or

(2) the last day of the Congress beginning after the date on which the member's term of office would (but for this paragraph) expire.

(d) A vacancy in the Authority shall not impair the right of the remaining members to exercise all of the powers of the Authority.

(e) The Authority shall make an annual report to the President for transmittal to the Congress which shall include information as to the cases it has heard and the decisions it has rendered.

(f)(1) The General Counsel of the Authority shall be appointed by the President, by and with the advice and consent of the Senate, for a term of 5 years. The General Counsel may be removed at any time by the President. The General Counsel shall hold no other office or position in the Government of the United States except as provided by law.

(2) The General Counsel may —

(A) investigate alleged unfair labor practices under this chapter,

(B) file and prosecute complaints under this chapter, and

(C) exercise such other powers of the Authority as the Authority may prescribe.

(3) The General Counsel shall have direct authority over, and responsibility for, all employees in the office of General Counsel, including employees of the General Counsel in the regional offices of the Authority.

Sec. 7105. Powers and duties of the Authority

(a)(1) The Authority shall provide leadership in establishing policies and guidance relating to matters under this chapter, and, except as otherwise provided, shall be responsible for carrying out the purpose of this chapter.

(2) The Authority shall, to the extent provided in this chapter and in accordance with regulations prescribed by the Authority -

(A) determine the appropriateness of units for labor organization representation under section 7112 of this title;

(B) supervise or conduct elections to determine whether a labor organization has been selected as an exclusive representative by a majority of the employees in an appropriate unit and otherwise administer the provisions of section 7111 of this title relating to the according of exclusive recognition to labor organizations;

(C) prescribe criteria and resolve issues relating to the granting of national consultation rights under section 7113 of this title;

(D) prescribe criteria and resolve issues relating to determining compelling need for agency rules or regulations under section 7117(b) of this title;

(E) resolves issues relating to the duty to bargain in good faith under section 7117(c) of this title;

(F) prescribe criteria relating to the granting of consultation rights with respect to conditions of employment under section 7117(d) of this title;

(G) conduct hearings and resolve complaints of unfair labor practices under section 7118 of this title;

(H) resolve exceptions to arbitrator's awards under section 7122 of this title; and

(I) take such other actions as are necessary and appropriate to effectively administer the provisions of this chapter.

(b) The Authority shall adopt an official seal which shall be judicially noticed.

(c) The principal office of the Authority shall be in or about the District of Columbia, but the Authority may meet and exercise any or all of its powers at any time or place. Except as otherwise expressly provided by law, the Authority may, by one or more of its members or by such agents as it may designate, make any appropriate inquiry necessary to carry out its duties wherever persons subject to this chapter are located. Any member who participates in the inquiry shall not be disqualified from later participating in a decision of the Authority in any case relating to the inquiry.

(d) The Authority shall appoint an Executive Director and such regional directors, administrative law judges under section 3105 of this title, and other individuals as it may from time to time find necessary for the proper performance of its functions. The Authority may delegate to officers and employees appointed under this subsection authority to perform such duties and make such expenditures as may be necessary.

(e)(1) The Authority may delegate to any regional director its authority under this chapter —

(A) to determine whether a group of employees is an appropriate unit;

(B) to conduct investigations and to provide for hearings;

(C) to determine whether a question of representation exists and to direct an election; and

(D) to supervise or conduct secret ballot elections and certify the results thereof.

(2) The Authority may delegate to any administrative law judge appointed under subsection (d) of this section its authority under section 7118 of this title to determine whether any person has engaged in or is engaging in an unfair labor practice.

(f) If the Authority delegates any authority to any regional director or administrative law judge to take any action pursuant to subsection (e) of this section, the Authority may, upon application by any interested person filed within 60 days after the date of the action, review such action, but the review shall not, unless specifically ordered by the Authority, operate as a stay of action. The Authority may affirm, modify, or reverse any action reviewed under this subsection. If the Authority does not undertake to grant review of the action under this subsection within 60 days after the later of —

(1) the date of the action; or

(2) the date of the filing of any application under this subsection for review of the action;

the action shall become the action of the Authority at the end of such 60-day period.

(g) In order to carry out its functions under this chapter, the Authority may —

(1) hold hearings;

(2) administer oaths, take the testimony or deposition of any person under oath, and issue subpenas as provided in section 7132 of this title; and

(3) may require an agency or a labor organization to cease and desist from violations of this chapter and require it to take any remedial action it considers appropriate to carry out the policies of this chapter.

(h) Except as provided in section 518 of Title 28, relating to litigation before the Supreme Court, attorneys designated by the Authority may appear for the Authority and represent the Authority in any civil action brought in connection with any function carried out by the Authority pursuant to this title or as otherwise authorized by law.

(i) In the exercise of the functions of the Authority under this title, the Authority may request from the Director of the Office of Personnel Management an advisory opinion concerning the proper interpretation of rules, regulations, or policy directives issued by the Office of Personnel Management in connection with any matter before the Authority.

Sec. 7106. Management rights

(a) Subject to subsection (b) of this section, nothing in this chapter shall affect the authority of any management official of any agency —

(1) to determine the mission, budget, organization, number of employees, and internal security practices of the agency; and

(2) in accordance with applicable laws —

(A) to hire, assign, direct, layoff, and retain employees in the agency, or to suspend, remove, reduce in grade or pay, or take other disciplinary action against such employees;

(B) to assign work, to make determinations with respect to contracting out, and to determine the personnel by which agency operations shall be conducted;

(C) with respect to filling positions, to make selections for appointments from —

(i) among properly ranked and certified candidates for promotion; or

(ii) any other appropriate source; and

(D) to take whatever actions may be necessary to carry out the agency mission during emergencies.

(b) Nothing in this section shall preclude any agency and any labor organization from negotiating —

(1) at the election of the agency, on the numbers, types, and grades of employees or positions assigned to any organizational subdivision, work project, or tour of duty, or on the technology, methods, and means of performing work;

(2) procedures which management officials of the agency will observe in exercising any authority under this section; or

(3) appropriate arrangements for employees adversely affected by the exercise of any authority under this section by such management officials.

SUBCHAPTER II - RIGHTS AND DUTIES OF AGENCIES AND LABOR ORGANIZATIONS

Sec. 7111. Exclusive recognition of labor organizations

(a) An agency shall accord exclusive recognition to a labor organization if the organization has been selected as the representative, in a secret ballot election, by a majority of the employees in an appropriate unit who cast valid ballots in the election.

(b) If a petition is filed with the Authority —

(1) by any person alleging —

(A) in the case of an appropriate unit for which there is no exclusive representative, that 30 percent of the employees in the appropriate unit wish to be represented for the purpose of collective bargaining by an exclusive representative, or

(B) in the case of an appropriate unit for which there is an exclusive representative, that 30 percent of the employees in the unit allege that the exclusive representative is no longer the representative of the majority of the employees in the unit; or

(2) by any person seeking clarification of, or an amendment to, a certification then in effect or a matter relating to representation;

the Authority shall investigate the petition, and if it has reasonable cause to believe that a question of representation exists, it shall provide an opportunity for a hearing (for which a transcript shall be kept) after a reasonable notice. If the Authority finds on the record of the hearing that a question of representation exists, the Authority shall supervise or conduct an election on the question by secret ballot and shall certify the results thereof. An election under this subsection shall not be conducted in any appropriate unit or in any subdivision thereof within which, in the preceding 12 calendar months, a valid election under this subsection has been held.

(c) A labor organization which —

(1) has been designated by at least 10 percent of the employees in the unit specified in any petition filed pursuant to subsection (b) of this section;

(2) has submitted a valid copy of a current or recently expired collective bargaining agreement for the unit; or

(3) has submitted other evidence that it is the exclusive representative of the employees involved;

may intervene with respect to a petition filed pursuant to subsection (b) of this section and shall be placed on the ballot of any election under such subsection (b) with respect to the petition.

(d) The Authority shall determine who is eligible to vote in any election under this section and shall establish rules governing any such election, which shall include rules allowing employees eligible to vote the opportunity to choose —

(1) from labor organizations on the ballot, that labor organization which the employees wish to have represent them; or

(2) not to be represented by a labor organization.

In any election in which no choice on the ballot receives a majority of the votes cast, a runoff election shall be conducted between the two choices receiving the highest number of votes. A labor organization which receives the majority of the votes cast in an election shall be certified by the Authority as the exclusive representative.

(e) A labor organization seeking exclusive recognition shall submit to the Authority and the agency involved a roster of its officers and representatives, a copy of its constitution and bylaws, and a statement of its objectives.

(f) Exclusive recognition shall not be accorded to a labor organization —

(1) if the Authority determines that the labor organization is subject to corrupt influences or influences opposed to democratic principles;

(2) in the case of a petition filed pursuant to subsection (b)(1)(A) of this section, if there is not credible evidence that at least 30 percent of the employees in the unit specified in the petition wish to be represented for the purpose of collective bargaining by the labor organization seeking exclusive recognition;

(3) if there is then in effect a lawful written collective bargaining agreement between the agency involved and an exclusive representative (other than the labor organization seeking exclusive recognition) covering any employees included in the unit specified in the petition, unless —

(A) the collective bargaining agreement has been in effect for more than 3 years, or

(B) the petition for exclusive recognition is filed not more than 105 days and not less than 60 days before the expiration date of the collective bargaining agreement; or

(4) if the Authority has, within the previous 12 calendar months, conducted a secret ballot election for the unit described in any petition under this section and in such election a majority of the employees voting chose a labor organization for certification as the unit's exclusive representative.

(g) Nothing in this section shall be construed to prohibit the waiving of hearings by stipulation for the purpose of a consent election in conformity with regulations and rules or decisions of the Authority.

Sec. 7112. Determination of appropriate units for labor organization representation

(a) The Authority shall determine the appropriateness of any unit. The Authority shall determine in each case whether, in order to ensure employees the fullest freedom in exercising the rights guaranteed under this chapter, the appropriate unit should be established on an agency, plant, installation, functional, or other basis and shall determine any unit to be an appropriate unit only if the determination will ensure a clear and identifiable community of interest among the employees in the unit and will promote effective dealings with, and efficiency of the operations of the agency involved.

(b) A unit shall not be determined to be appropriate under this section solely on the basis of the extent to which employees in the proposed unit have organized, nor shall a unit be determined to be appropriate if it includes —

(1) except as provided under section 7135(a)(2) of this title, any management official or supervisor;

(2) a confidential employee;

(3) an employee engaged in personnel work in other than a purely clerical capacity;

(4) an employee engaged in administering the provisions of this chapter;

(5) both professional employees and other employees, unless a majority of the professional employees vote for inclusion in the unit;

(6) any employee engaged in intelligence, counterintelligence, investigative, or security work which directly affects national security; or

(7) any employee primarily engaged in investigation or audit functions relating to the work of individuals employed by an agency whose duties directly affect the internal security of the agency, but only if the functions are undertaken to ensure that the duties are discharged honestly and with integrity.

(c) Any employee who is engaged in administering any provision of law relating to labor-management relations may not be represented by a labor organization —

(1) which represents other individuals to whom such provision applies; or

(2) which is affiliated directly or indirectly with an organization which represents other individuals to whom such provision applies.

(d) Two or more units which are in an agency and for which a labor organization is the exclusive representative may, upon petition by the agency or labor organization, be consolidated with or without an election into a single larger unit if the Authority considers the larger unit to be appropriate. The Authority shall certify the labor organization as the exclusive representative of the new larger unit.

Sec. 7113. National consultation rights

(a) If, in connection with any agency, no labor organization has been accorded exclusive recognition on an agency basis, a labor organization which is the exclusive representative of a substantial number of the employees of the agency, as determined in accordance with criteria prescribed by the Authority, shall be granted national consultation rights by the agency. National consultation rights shall terminate when the labor organization no longer meets the criteria prescribed by the Authority. Any issue relating to any labor organization's eligibility for, or continuation of, national consultation rights shall be subject to determination by the Authority.

(b)(1) Any labor organization having national consultation rights in connection with any agency under subsection (a) of this section shall —

(A) be informed of any substantive change in conditions of employment proposed by the agency, and

(B) be permitted reasonable time to present its views and recommendations regarding the changes.

(2) If any views or recommendations are presented under paragraph (1) of this subsection to an agency by any labor organization -

(A) the agency shall consider the views or recommendations before taking final action on any matter with respect to which the views or recommendations are presented; and

(B) the agency shall provide the labor organization a written statement of the reasons for taking the final action.

(c) Nothing in this section shall be construed to limit the right of any agency or exclusive representative to engage in collective bargaining.

Sec. 7114. Representation rights and duties

(a)(1) A labor organization which has been accorded exclusive recognition is the exclusive representative of the employees in the unit it represents and is entitled to act for, and negotiate collective bargaining agreements covering, all employees in the unit. An exclusive representative is responsible for representing the interests of all employees in the unit it represents without discrimination and without regard to labor organization membership.

(2) An exclusive representative of an appropriate unit in an agency shall be given the opportunity to be represented at -

(A) any formal discussion between one or more representatives of the agency and one or more employees in the unit or their representatives concerning any grievance or any personnel policy or practices or other general condition of employment; or

(B) any examination of an employee in the unit by a representative of the agency in connection with an investigation if —

(i) the employee reasonably believes that the examination may result in disciplinary action against the employee; and

(ii) the employee requests representation.

(3) Each agency shall annually inform its employees of their rights under paragraph (2)(B) of this subsection.

(4) Any agency and any exclusive representative in any appropriate unit in the agency, through appropriate representatives, shall meet and negotiate in good faith for the purposes of arriving at a collective bargaining agreement. In addition, the agency and the exclusive representative may determine appropriate techniques, consistent with the provisions of section 7119 of this title, to assist in any negotiation.

(5) The rights of an exclusive representative under the provisions of this subsection shall not be construed to preclude an employee from —

(A) being represented by an attorney or other representative, other than the exclusive representative, of the employee's own choosing in any grievance or appeal action; or

(B) exercising grievance or appellate rights established by law, rule, or regulation;

except in the case of grievance or appeal procedures negotiated under this chapter.

(b) The duty of an agency and an exclusive representative to negotiate in good faith under subsection (a) of this section shall include the obligation —

(1) to approach the negotiations with a sincere resolve to reach a collective bargaining agreement;

(2) to be represented at the negotiations by duly authorized representatives prepared to discuss and negotiate on any condition of employment;

(3) to meet at reasonable times and convenient places as frequently as may be necessary, and to avoid unnecessary delays;

(4) in the case of an agency, to furnish to the exclusive representative involved, or its authorized representative, upon request and, to the extent not prohibited by law, data -

(A) which is normally maintained by the agency in the regular course of business;

(B) which is reasonably available and necessary for full and proper discussion, understanding, and negotiation of subjects within the scope of collective bargaining; and

(C) which does not constitute guidance, advice, counsel, or training provided for management officials or supervisors, relating to collective bargaining; and

(5) if agreement is reached, to execute on the request of any party to the negotiation a written document embodying the agreed terms, and to take such steps as are necessary to implement such agreement.

(c)(1) An agreement between any agency and an exclusive representative shall be subject to approval by the head of the agency.

(2) The head of the agency shall approve the agreement within 30 days from the date the agreement is executed if the agreement is in accordance with the provisions of this chapter and any other applicable law, rule, or regulation (unless the agency has granted an exception to the provision).

(3) If the head of the agency does not approve or disapprove the agreement within the 30-day period, the agreement shall take effect and shall be binding on the agency and the exclusive representative subject to the provisions of this chapter and any other applicable law, rule, or regulation.

(4) A local agreement subject to a national or other controlling agreement at a higher level shall be approved under the procedures of the controlling agreement or, if none, under regulations prescribed by the agency.

Sec. 7115. Allotments to representatives

(a) If an agency has received from an employee in an appropriate unit a written assignment which authorizes the agency to deduct from the pay of the employee amounts for the payment of regular and periodic dues of the exclusive representative of the unit, the agency shall honor the assignment and make an appropriate allotment pursuant to the assignment. Any such allotment shall be made at no cost to the exclusive representative or the employee. Except as provided under subsection (b) of this section, any such assignment may not be revoked for a period of 1 year.

(b) An allotment under subsection (a) of this section for the deduction of dues with respect to any employee shall terminate when —

(1) the agreement between the agency and the exclusive representative involved ceases to be applicable to the employee; or

(2) the employee is suspended or expelled from membership in the exclusive representative.

(c)(1) Subject to paragraph (2) of this subsection, if a petition has been filed with the Authority by a labor organization alleging that 10 percent of the employees in an appropriate unit in an agency have membership in the labor organization, the Authority shall investigate the petition to determine its validity. Upon certification by the Authority of the validity of the petition, the agency shall have a duty to negotiate with the labor organization solely concerning the deduction of dues of the labor organization from the pay of the members of the labor organization who are employees in the unit and who make a voluntary allotment for such purpose.

(2)(A) The provisions of paragraph (1) of this subsection shall not apply in the case of any appropriate unit for which there is an exclusive representative.

(B) Any agreement under paragraph (1) of this subsection between a labor organization and an agency with respect to an appropriate unit shall be null and void upon the certification of an exclusive representative of the unit.

Sec. 7116. Unfair labor practices

(a) For the purpose of this chapter, it shall be an unfair labor practice for an agency —

(1) to interfere with, restrain, or coerce any employee in the exercise by the employee of any right under this chapter;

(2) to encourage or discourage membership in any labor organization by discrimination in connection with hiring, tenure, promotion, or other conditions of employment;

(3) to sponsor, control, or otherwise assist any labor organization, other than to furnish, upon request, customary and routine services and facilities if the services and facilities are also furnished on an impartial basis to other labor organizations having equivalent status;

(4) to discipline or otherwise discriminate against an employee because the employee has filed a complaint, affidavit, or petition, or has given any information or testimony under this chapter;

(5) to refuse to consult or negotiate in good faith with a labor organization as required by this chapter;

(6) to fail or refuse to cooperate in impasse procedures and impasse decisions as required by this chapter;

(7) to enforce any rule or regulation (other than a rule or regulation implementing section 2302 of this title) which is in conflict with any applicable collective bargaining agreement if the agreement was in effect before the date the rule or regulation was prescribed; or

(8) to otherwise fail or refuse to comply with any provision of this chapter.

(b) For the purpose of this chapter, it shall be an unfair labor practice for a labor organization —

(1) to interfere with, restrain, or coerce any employee in the exercise by the employee of any right under this chapter;

(2) to cause or attempt to cause an agency to discriminate against any employee in the exercise by the employee of any right under this chapter;

(3) to coerce, discipline, fine, or attempt to coerce a member of the labor organization as punishment, reprisal, or for the purpose of hindering or impeding the member's work performance or productivity as an employee or the discharge of the member's duties as an employee;

(4) to discriminate against an employee with regard to the terms or conditions of membership in the labor organization on the basis of race, color, creed, national origin, sex, age, preferential or non-preferential civil service status, political affiliation, marital status, or handicapping condition;

(5) to refuse to consult or negotiate in good faith with an agency as required by this chapter;

(6) to fail or refuse to cooperate in impasse procedures and impasse decisions as required by this chapter;

(7)(A) to call, or participate in, a strike, work stoppage, or slowdown, or picketing of an agency in a labor-management dispute if such picketing interferes with an agency's operations, or

(B) to condone any activity described in subparagraph (A) of this paragraph by failing to take action to prevent or stop such activity; or

(8) to otherwise fail or refuse to comply with any provision of this chapter.

Nothing in paragraph (7) of this subsection shall result in any informational picketing which does not interfere with an agency's operations being considered as an unfair labor practice.

(c) For the purpose of this chapter it shall be an unfair labor practice for an exclusive representative to deny membership to any employee in the appropriate unit represented by such exclusive representative except for failure —

(1) to meet reasonable occupational standards uniformly required for admission, or

(2) to tender dues uniformly required as a condition of acquiring and retaining membership.

This subsection does not preclude any labor organization from enforcing discipline in accordance with procedures under its constitution or bylaws to the extent consistent with the provisions of this chapter.

(d) Issues which can properly be raised under an appeals procedure may not be raised as unfair labor practices prohibited under this section. Except for matters wherein, under section 7121(e) and (f) of this title, an employee has an option of using the negotiated grievance procedure or an appeals procedure, issues which can be raised under a grievance procedure may, in the discretion of the aggrieved party, be raised under the grievance procedure or as an unfair labor practice under this section, but not under both procedures.

(e) The expression of any personal view, argument, opinion or the making of any statement which —

(1) publicizes the fact of a representational election and encourages employees to exercise their right to vote in such election,

(2) corrects the record with respect to any false or misleading statement made by any person, or

(3) informs employees of the Government's policy relating to labor-management relations and representation,

shall not, if the expression contains no threat of reprisal or force or promise of benefit or was not made under coercive conditions, (A) constitute an unfair labor practice under any provision of this chapter, or (B) constitute grounds for the setting aside of any election conducted under any provisions of this chapter.

Sec. 7117. Duty to bargain in good faith; compelling need; duty to consult

(a)(1) Subject to paragraph (2) of this subsection, the duty to bargain in good faith shall, to the extent not inconsistent with any Federal law or any Government-wide rule or regulation, extend to matters which are the subject of any rule or regulation only if the rule or regulation is not a Government-wide rule or regulation.

(2) The duty to bargain in good faith shall, to the extent not inconsistent with Federal law or any Government-wide rule or regulation, extend to matters which are the subject of any agency rule or regulation referred to in paragraph (3) of this subsection only if the Authority has determined under subsection (b) of this section that no compelling need (as determined under regulations prescribed by the Authority) exists for the rule or regulation.

(3) Paragraph (2) of the subsection applies to any rule or regulation issued by any agency or issued by any primary national subdivision of such agency, unless an exclusive representative represents an appropriate unit including not less than a majority of the employees in the issuing agency or primary national subdivision, as the case may be, to whom the rule or regulation is applicable.

(b)(1) In any case of collective bargaining in which an exclusive representative alleges that no compelling need exists for any rule or regulation referred to in subsection (a)(3) of this section which is then in effect and which governs any matter at issue in such collective bargaining, the Authority shall determine under paragraph (2) of this subsection, in accordance with regulations prescribed by the Authority, whether such a compelling need exists.

(2) For the purpose of this section, a compelling need shall be determined not to exist for any rule or regulation only if —

(A) the agency, or primary national subdivision, as the case may be, which issued the rule or regulation informs the Authority in writing that a compelling need for the rule or regulation does not exist; or

(B) the Authority determines that a compelling need for a rule or regulation does not exist.

(3) A hearing may be held, in the discretion of the Authority, before a determination is made under this subsection. If a hearing is held, it shall be expedited to the extent practicable and shall not include the General Counsel as a party.

(4) The agency, or primary national subdivision, as the case may be, which issued the rule or regulation shall be a necessary party at any hearing under this subsection.

(c)(1) Except in any case to which subsection (b) of this section applies, if an agency involved in collective bargaining with an exclusive representative alleges that the duty to bargain in good faith does not extend to any matter, the exclusive representative may appeal the allegation to the Authority in accordance with the provisions of this subsection.

(2) The exclusive representative may, on or before the 15th day after the date on which the agency first makes the allegation referred to in paragraph (1) of this subsection, institute an appeal under this subsection by —

(A) filing a petition with the Authority; and

(B) furnishing a copy of the petition to the head of the agency.

(3) On or before the 30th day after the date of the receipt by the head of the agency of the copy of the petition under paragraph (2)(B) of this subsection, the agency shall —

(A) file with the Authority a statement —

(i) withdrawing the allegation; or

(ii) setting forth in full its reasons supporting the allegation; and

(B) furnish a copy of such statement to the exclusive representative.

(4) On or before the 15th day after the date of the receipt by the exclusive representative of a copy of a statement under paragraph (3)(B) of this subsection, the exclusive representative shall file with the Authority its response to the statement.

(5) A hearing may be held in the discretion of the Authority, before a determination is made under this subsection. If a hearing is held, it shall not include the General Counsel as a party.

(6) The Authority shall expedite proceedings under this subsection to the extent practicable and shall issue to the exclusive representative and to the agency a written decision on the allegation and specific reasons therefore at the earliest practicable date.

(d)(1) A labor organization which is the exclusive representative of a substantial number of employees, determined in accordance with criteria prescribed by the Authority, shall be granted consultation rights by any agency with respect to any Government-wide rule or regulation issued by the agency effecting any substantive change in any condition of employment. Such consultation rights shall terminate when the labor organization no longer meets the criteria prescribed by the Authority. Any issue relating to a labor organization's eligibility for, or continuation of, such consultation rights shall be subject to determination by the Authority.

(2) A labor organization having consultation rights under paragraph (1) of this subsection shall —

(A) be informed of any substantive change in conditions of employment proposed by the agency, and

(B) shall be permitted reasonable time to present its views and recommendations regarding the changes.

(3) If any views or recommendations are presented under paragraph (2) of this subsection to an agency by any labor organization —

(A) the agency shall consider the views or recommendations before taking final action on any matter with respect to which the views or recommendations are presented; and

(B) the agency shall provide the labor organization a written statement of the reasons for taking the final action.

Sec. 7118. Prevention of unfair labor practices

(a)(1) If any agency or labor organization is charged by any person with having engaged in or engaging in an unfair labor practice, the General Counsel shall investigate the charge and may issue and cause to be served upon the agency or labor organization a complaint. In any case in which the General Counsel does not issue a complaint because the charge fails to state an unfair labor practice, the General Counsel shall provide the person making the charge a written statement of the reasons for not issuing a complaint.

(2) Any complaint under paragraph (1) of this subsection shall contain a notice —

(A) of the charge;

(B) that a hearing will be held before the Authority (or any member thereof or before an individual employed by the authority and designated for such purpose); and

(C) of the time and place fixed for the hearing.

(3) The labor organization or agency involved shall have the right to file an answer to the original and any amended complaint and to appear in person or otherwise and give testimony at the time and place fixed in the complaint for the hearing.

(4)(A) Except as provided in subparagraph (B) of this paragraph, no complaint shall be issued based on any alleged unfair labor practice which occurred more than 6 months before the filing of the charge with the Authority.

(B) If the General Counsel determines that the person filing any charge was prevented from filing the charge during the 6-month period referred to in subparagraph (A) of this paragraph by reason of —

(i) any failure of the agency or labor organization against which the charge is made to perform a duty owed to the person, or

(ii) any concealment which prevented discovery of the alleged unfair labor practice during the 6-month period,

the General Counsel may issue a complaint based on the charge if the charge was filed during the 6-month period beginning on the day of the discovery by the person of the alleged unfair labor practice.

(5) The General Counsel may prescribe regulations providing for informal methods by which the alleged unfair labor practice may be resolved prior to the issuance of a complaint.

(6) The Authority (or any member thereof or any individual employed by the Authority and designated for such purpose) shall conduct a hearing on the complaint not earlier than 5 days after the date on which the complaint is served. In the discretion of the individual or individuals conducting the hearing, any person involved may be allowed to intervene in the hearing and to present testimony. Any such hearing shall, to the extent practicable, be conducted in accordance with the provisions of subchapter II of chapter 5 of this title, except that the parties shall not be bound by rules of evidence, whether statutory, common law, or adopted by a court. A transcript shall be kept of the hearing. After such a hearing the Authority, in its discretion, may upon notice receive further evidence or hear argument.

(7) If the Authority (or any member thereof or any individual employed by the Authority and designated for such purpose) determines after any hearing on a complaint under paragraph (5) of this subsection that the preponderance of the evidence received demonstrates that the agency or labor organization named in the complaint has engaged in or is engaging in an unfair labor practice, then the individual or individuals conducting the hearing shall state in writing their findings of fact and shall issue and cause to be served on the agency or labor organization an order —

(A) to cease and desist from any such unfair labor practice in which the agency or labor organization is engaged;

(B) requiring the parties to renegotiate a collective bargaining agreement in accordance with the order of the Authority and requiring that the agreement, as amended, be given retroactive effect;

(C) requiring reinstatement of an employee with backpay in accordance with section 5596 of this title; or

(D) including any combination of the actions described in subparagraphs (A) through (C) of this paragraph or such other action as will carry out the purpose of this chapter.

If any such order requires reinstatement of an employee with backpay, backpay may be required of the agency (as provided in section 5596 of this title) or of the labor organization, as the case may be, which is found to have engaged in the unfair labor practice involved.

(8) If the individual or individuals conducting the hearing determine that the preponderance of the evidence received fails to demonstrate that the agency or labor organization named in the complaint has engaged in or is engaging in an unfair labor practice, the individual or individuals shall state in writing their findings of fact and shall issue an order dismissing the complaint.

(b) In connection with any matter before the Authority in any proceeding under this section, the Authority may request, in accordance with the provisions of section 7105(i) of this title, from the Director of the Office of Personnel Management an advisory opinion concerning the proper interpretation of rules, regulations, or other policy directives issued by the Office of Personnel Management.

Sec. 7119. Negotiation impasses; Federal Service Impasses Panel

(a) The Federal Mediation and Conciliation Service shall provide services and assistance to agencies and exclusive representatives in the resolution of negotiation impasses. The Service shall determine under what circumstances and in what manner it shall provide services and assistance.

(b) If voluntary arrangements, including the services of the Federal Mediation and Conciliation Service or any other third-party mediation, fail to resolve a negotiation impasse -

(1) either party may request the Federal Service Impasses Panel to consider the matter, or

(2) the parties may agree to adopt a procedure for binding arbitration of the negotiation impasse, but only if the procedure is approved by the Panel.

(c)(1) The Federal Service Impasses Panel is an entity within the Authority, the function of which is to provide assistance in resolving negotiation impasses between agencies and exclusive representatives.

(2) The Panel shall be composed of a Chairman and at least six other members, who shall be appointed by the President, solely on the basis of fitness to perform the duties and functions involved, from among individuals who are familiar with Government operations and knowledgeable in labor-management relations.

(3) Of the original members of the Panel, 2 members shall be appointed for a term of 1 year, 2 members shall be appointed for a term of 3 years, and the Chairman and the remaining members shall be appointed for a term of 5 years. Thereafter each member shall be appointed for a term of 5 years, except that an individual chosen to fill a vacancy shall be appointed for the unexpired term of the member replaced. Any member of the Panel may be removed by the President.

(4) The Panel may appoint an Executive Director and any other individuals it may from time to time find necessary for the proper performance of its duties. Each member of the Panel who is not an employee (as defined in section 2105 of this title) is entitled to pay at a rate equal to the daily equivalent of the maximum annual rate of basic pay then currently paid under the General Schedule for each day he is engaged in the performance of official business of the Panel, including travel time, and is entitled to travel expenses as provided under section 5703 of this title.

(5)(A) The Panel or its designee shall promptly investigate any impasse presented to it under subsection (b) of this section. The Panel shall consider the impasse and shall either —

(i) recommend to the parties procedures for the resolution of the impasse; or

(ii) assist the parties in resolving the impasse through whatever methods and procedures, including factfinding and recommendations, it may consider appropriate to accomplish the purpose of this section.

(B) If the parties do not arrive at a settlement after assistance by the Panel under subparagraph (A) of this paragraph, the Panel may —

(i) hold hearings;

(ii) administer oaths, take the testimony or deposition of any person under oath, and issue subpenas as provided in section 7132 of this title; and

(iii) take whatever action is necessary and not inconsistent with this chapter to resolve the impasse.

(C) Notice of any final action of the Panel under this section shall be promptly served upon the parties, and the action shall be binding on such parties during the term of the agreement, unless the parties agree otherwise.

Sec. 7120. Standards of conduct for labor organizations

(a) An agency shall only accord recognition to a labor organization that is free from corrupt influences and influences opposed to basic democratic principles. Except as provided in subsection (b) of this section, an organization is not required to prove that it is free from such influences if it is subject to governing requirements adopted by the organization or by a national or international labor organization or federation of labor organizations with which it is affiliated, or in which it participates, containing explicit and detailed provisions to which it subscribes calling for —

(1) the maintenance of democratic procedures and practices including provisions for periodic elections to be conducted subject to recognized safeguards and provisions defining and securing the right of individual members to participate in the affairs of the organization, to receive fair and equal treatment under the governing rules of the organization, and to receive fair process in disciplinary proceedings;

(2) the exclusion from office in the organization of persons affiliated with communist or other totalitarian movements and persons identified with corrupt influences;

(3) the prohibition of business or financial interests on the part of organization officers and agents which conflict with their duty to the organization and its members; and

(4) the maintenance of fiscal integrity in the conduct of the affairs of the organization, including provisions for accounting and financial controls and regular financial reports or summaries to be made available to members.

(b) Notwithstanding the fact that a labor organization has adopted or subscribed to standards of conduct as provided in subsection (a) of this section, the organization is required to furnish evidence of its freedom from corrupt influences or influences opposed to basic democratic principles if there is reasonable cause to believe that —

(1) the organization has been suspended or expelled from, or is subject to other sanction, by a parent labor organization, or federation of organizations with which it had been affiliated, because it has demonstrated an unwillingness or inability to comply with governing requirements comparable in purpose to those required by subsection (a) of this section; or

(2) the organization is in fact subject to influences that would preclude recognition under this chapter.

(c) A labor organization which has or seeks recognition as a representative of employees under this chapter shall file financial and other reports with the Assistant Secretary of Labor for Labor Management Relations, provide for bonding of officials and employees of the organization, and comply with trusteeship and election standards.

(d) The Assistant Secretary shall prescribe such regulations as are necessary to carry out the purposes of this section. Such regulations shall conform generally to the principles applied to labor organizations in the private sector. Complaints of violations of this section shall be filed with the Assistant Secretary. In any matter arising under this section, the Assistant Secretary may require a labor organization to cease and desist from violations of this section and require it to take such actions as he considers appropriate to carry out the policies of this section.

(e) This chapter does not authorize participation in the management of a labor organization or acting as a representative of a labor organization by a management official, a supervisor, or a confidential employee, except as specifically provided in this chapter, or by an employee if the participation or activity would result in a conflict or apparent conflict of interest or would otherwise be incompatible with law or with the official duties of the employee.

(f) In the case of any labor organization which by omission or commission has willfully and intentionally, with regard to any strike, work stoppage, or slowdown, violated section 7116(b)(7) of this title, the Authority shall, upon an appropriate finding by the Authority of such violation —

(1) revoke the exclusive recognition status of the labor organization, which shall then immediately cease to be legally entitled and obligated to represent employees in the unit; or

(2) take any other appropriate disciplinary action.

SUBCHAPTER III - GRIEVANCES, APPEALS, AND REVIEW

Sec. 7121. Grievance procedures

(a)(1) Except as provided in paragraph (2) of this subsection, any collective bargaining agreement shall provide procedures for the settlement of grievances, including questions of arbitrability. Except as provided in subsections (d), (e), and (g) of this section, the procedures shall be the exclusive administrative procedures for resolving grievances which fall within its coverage.

(2) Any collective bargaining agreement may exclude any matter from the application of the grievance procedures which are provided for in the agreement.

(b)(1) Any negotiated grievance procedure referred to in subsection (a) of this section shall —

(A) be fair and simple,

(B) provide for expeditious processing, and

(C) include procedures that —

(i) assure an exclusive representative the right, in its own behalf or on behalf of any employee in the unit represented by the exclusive representative, to present and process grievances;

(ii) assure such an employee the right to present a grievance on the employee's own behalf, and assure the exclusive representative the right to be present during the grievance proceeding; and

(iii) provide that any grievance not satisfactorily settled under the negotiated grievance procedure shall be subject to binding arbitration which may be invoked by either the exclusive representative or the agency.

(2)(A) The provisions of a negotiated grievance procedure providing for binding arbitration in accordance with paragraph (1)(C)(iii) shall, if or to the extent that an alleged prohibited personnel practice is involved, allow the arbitrator to order —

(i) a stay of any personnel action in a manner similar to the manner described in section 1221(c) with respect to the Merit Systems Protection Board; and

(ii) the taking, by an agency, of any disciplinary action identified under section 1215(a)(3) that is otherwise within the authority of such agency to take.

(B) Any employee who is the subject of any disciplinary action ordered under subparagraph (A)(ii) may appeal such action to the same extent and in the same manner as if the agency had taken the disciplinary action absent arbitration.

(c) The preceding subsections of this section shall not apply with respect to any grievance concerning —

(1) any claimed violation of subchapter III of chapter 73 of this title (relating to prohibited political activities);

(2) retirement, life insurance, or health insurance;

(3) a suspension or removal under section 7532 of this title;

(4) any examination, certification, or appointment; or

(5) the classification of any position which does not result in the reduction in grade or pay of an employee.

(d) An aggrieved employee affected by a prohibited personnel practice under section 2302(b)(1) of this title which also falls under the coverage of the negotiated grievance procedure may raise the matter under a statutory procedure or the negotiated procedure, but not both. An employee shall be deemed to have exercised his option under this subsection to raise the matter under either a statutory procedure or the negotiated procedure at such time as the employee timely initiates an action under the applicable statutory procedure or timely files a grievance in writing, in accordance with the provisions of the parties' negotiated procedure, whichever event occurs first. Selection of the negotiated procedure in no manner prejudices the right of an aggrieved employee to request the Merit Systems Protection Board to review the final decision pursuant to section 7702 of this title in the case of any personnel action that could have been appealed to the Board, or, where applicable, to request the Equal Employment Opportunity Commission to review a final decision in any other matter involving a complaint of discrimination of the type prohibited by any law administered by the Equal Employment Opportunity Commission.

(e)(1) Matters covered under sections 4303 and 7512 of this title which also fall within the coverage of the negotiated grievance procedure may, in the discretion of the aggrieved employee, be raised either under the appellate procedures of section 7701 of this title or under the negotiated grievance procedure, but not both. Similar matters which arise under other personnel systems applicable to employees covered by this chapter may, in the discretion of the aggrieved employee, be raised either under the appellate procedures, if any, applicable to those matters, or under the negotiated grievance procedure, but not both. An employee shall be deemed to have exercised his option under this subsection to raise a matter either under the applicable appellate procedures or under the negotiated grievance procedure at such time as the employee timely files a notice of appeal under the applicable appellate procedures or timely files a grievance in writing in accordance with the provisions of the parties' negotiated grievance procedure, whichever event occurs first.

(2) In matters covered under sections 4303 and 7512 of this title which have been raised under the negotiated grievance procedure in accordance with this section, an arbitrator shall be governed by section 7701(c)(1) of this title, as applicable.

(f) In matters covered under sections 4303 and 7512 of this title which have been raised under the negotiated grievance procedure in accordance with this section, section 7703 of this title pertaining to judicial review shall apply to the award of an arbitrator in the same manner and under the same conditions as if the matter had been decided by the Board. In matters similar to those covered under sections 4303 and 7512 of this title which arise under other personnel systems and which an aggrieved employee has raised under the negotiated grievance procedure, judicial review of an arbitrator's award may be obtained in the same manner and on the same basis as could be obtained of a final decision in such matters raised under applicable appellate procedures.

(g)(1) This subsection applies with respect to a prohibited personnel practice other than a prohibited personnel practice to which subsection (d) applies.

(2) An aggrieved employee affected by a prohibited personnel practice described in paragraph (1) may elect not more than one of the remedies described in paragraph (3) with respect thereto. For purposes of the preceding sentence, a determination as to whether a particular remedy has been elected shall be made as set forth under paragraph (4).

(3) The remedies described in this paragraph are as follows:

(A) An appeal to the Merit Systems Protection Board under section 7701.

(B) A negotiated grievance procedure under this section.

(C) Procedures for seeking corrective action under subchapters II and III of chapter 12.

(4) For the purpose of this subsection, a person shall be considered to have elected —

(A) the remedy described in paragraph (3)(A) if such person has timely filed a notice of appeal under the applicable appellate procedures;

(B) the remedy described in paragraph (3)(B) if such person has timely filed a grievance in writing, in accordance with the provisions of the parties' negotiated procedure; or

(C) the remedy described in paragraph (3)(C) if such person has sought corrective action from the Office of Special Counsel by making an allegation under section 1214(a)(1).

(h) Settlements and awards under this chapter shall be subject to the limitations in Section 5596(b)(4) of this title.

Sec. 7122. Exceptions to arbitral awards

(a) Either party to arbitration under this chapter may file with the Authority an exception to any arbitrator's award pursuant to the arbitration (other than an award relating to a matter described in section 7121(f) of this title). If upon review the Authority finds that the award is deficient —

(1) because it is contrary to any law, rule, or regulation; or

(2) on other grounds similar to those applied by Federal courts in private sector labor-management relations;

the Authority may take such action and make such recommendations concerning the award as it considers necessary, consistent with applicable laws, rules, or regulations.

(b) If no exception to an arbitrator's award is filed under subsection (a) of this section during the 30-day period beginning on the date the award is served on the party, the award shall be final and binding. An agency shall take the actions required by an arbitrator's final award. The award may include the payment of backpay (as provided in section 5596 of this title).

Sec. 7123. Judicial review; enforcement

(a) Any person aggrieved by any final order of the Authority other than an order under —

(1) section 7122 of this title (involving an award by an arbitrator), unless the order involves an unfair labor practice under section 7118 of this title, or

(2) section 7112 of this title (involving an appropriate unit determination),

may, during the 60-day period beginning on the date on which the order was issued, institute an action for judicial review of the Authority's order in the United States court of appeals in the circuit in which the person resides or transacts business or in the United States Court of Appeals for the District of Columbia.

(b) The Authority may petition any appropriate United States court of appeals for the enforcement of any order of the Authority and for appropriate temporary relief or restraining order.

(c) Upon the filing of a petition under subsection (a) of this section for judicial review or under subsection (b) of this section for enforcement, the Authority shall file in the court the record in the proceedings, as provided in section 2112 of Title 28. Upon the filing of the petition, the court shall cause notice thereof to be served to the parties involved, and thereupon shall have jurisdiction of the proceeding and of the question determined therein and may grant any temporary relief (including a temporary restraining order) it considers just and proper, and may make and enter a decree affirming and enforcing, modifying and enforcing as so modified, or setting aside in whole or in part the order of the Authority. The filing of a petition under subsection (a) or (b) of this section shall not operate as a stay of the Authority's order unless the court specifically orders the stay. Review of the Authority's order shall be on the record in accordance with section 706 of this title. No objection that has not been urged before the Authority, or its designee, shall be considered by the court, unless the failure or neglect to urge the objection is excused because of extraordinary circumstances. The findings of the Authority with respect to questions of fact, if supported by substantial evidence on the record considered as a whole, shall be conclusive. If any person applies to the court for leave to adduce additional evidence and shows to the satisfaction of the court that the additional evidence is material and that there were reasonable grounds for the failure to adduce the evidence in the hearing before the Authority, or its designee, the court may order the additional evidence to be taken before the Authority, or its designee, and to be made a part of the record. The Authority may modify its findings as to the facts, or make new findings by reason of additional evidence

so taken and filed. The Authority shall file its modified or new findings, which, with respect to questions of fact, if supported by substantial evidence on the record considered as a whole, shall be conclusive. The Authority shall file its recommendations, if any, for the modification or setting aside of its original order. Upon the filing of the record with the court, the jurisdiction of the court shall be exclusive and its judgment and decree shall be final, except that the judgment and decree shall be subject to review by the Supreme Court of the United States upon writ of certiorari or certification as provided in section 1254 of Title 28.

(d) The Authority may, upon issuance of a complaint as provided in section 7118 of this title charging that any person has engaged in or is engaging in an unfair labor practice, petition any United States district court within any district in which the unfair labor practice in question is alleged to have occurred or in which such person resides or transacts business for appropriate temporary relief (including a restraining order). Upon the filing of the petition, the court shall cause notice thereof to be served upon the person, and thereupon shall have jurisdiction to grant any temporary relief (including a temporary restraining order) it considers just and proper. A court shall not grant any temporary relief under this section if it would interfere with the ability of the agency to carry out its essential functions or if the Authority fails to establish probable cause that an unfair labor practice is being committed.

SUBCHAPTER IV - ADMINISTRATIVE AND OTHER PROVISIONS

Sec. 7131. Official time

(a) Any employee representing an exclusive representative in the negotiation of a collective bargaining agreement under this chapter shall be authorized official time for such purposes, including attendance at impasse proceeding, during the time the employee otherwise would be in a duty status. The number of employees for whom official time is authorized under this subsection shall not exceed the number of individuals designated as representing the agency for such purposes.

(b) Any activities performed by any employee relating to the internal business of a labor organization (including the solicitation of membership, elections of labor organization officials, and collection of dues) shall be performed during the time the employee is in a non-duty status.

(c) Except as provided in subsection (a) of this section, the Authority shall determine whether any employee participating for, or on behalf of, a labor organization in any phase of proceedings before the Authority shall be authorized official time for such purpose during the time the employee otherwise would be in a duty status.

(d) Except as provided in the preceding subsections of this section —

(1) any employee representing an exclusive representative, or

(2) in connection with any other matter covered by this chapter, any employee in an appropriate unit represented by an exclusive representative,

shall be granted official time in any amount the agency and the exclusive representative involved agree to be reasonable, necessary, and in the public interest.

Sec. 7132. Subpenas

(a) Any member of the Authority, the General Counsel, or the Panel, any administrative law judge appointed by the Authority under section 3105 of this title, and any employee of the Authority designated by the Authority may —

(1) issue subpenas requiring the attendance and testimony of witnesses and the production of documentary or other evidence from any place in the United States; and

(2) administer oaths, take or order the taking of depositions, order responses to written interrogatories, examine witnesses, and receive evidence.

No subpena shall be issued under this section which requires the disclosure of intramanagement guidance, advice, counsel, or training within an agency or between an agency and the Office of Personnel Management.

(b) In the case of contumacy or failure to obey a subpena issued under subsection (a)(1) of this section, the United States district court for the judicial district in which the person to whom the subpena is addressed resides or is served may issue an order requiring such person to appear at any designated place to testify or to produce documentary or other

evidence. Any failure to obey the order of the court may be punished by the court as a contempt thereof.

(c) Witnesses (whether appearing voluntarily or under subpena) shall be paid the same fee and mileage allowances which are paid subpenaed witnesses in the courts of the United States.

Sec. 7133. Compilation and publication of data

(a) The Authority shall maintain a file of its proceedings and copies of all available agreements and arbitration decisions, and shall publish the texts of its decisions and the actions taken by the Panel under section 7119 of this title.

(b) All files maintained under subsection (a) of this section shall be open to inspection and reproduction in accordance with the provisions of sections 552 and 552a of this title.

Sec. 7134. Regulations

The Authority, the General Counsel, the Federal Mediation and Conciliation Service, the Assistant Secretary of Labor for Labor Management Relations, and the Panel shall each prescribe rules and regulations to carry out the provisions of this chapter applicable to each of them, respectively. Provisions of subchapter II of chapter 5 of this title shall be applicable to the issuance, revision, or repeal of any such rule or regulation.

Sec. 7135. Continuation of existing laws, recognitions, agreements, and procedures

(a) Nothing contained in this chapter shall preclude —

(1) the renewal or continuation of an exclusive recognition, certification of an exclusive representative, or a lawful agreement between an agency and an exclusive representative of its employees, which is entered into before the effective date of this chapter; or

(2) the renewal, continuation, or initial according of recognition for units of management officials or supervisors represented by labor organizations which historically or traditionally represent management officials or supervisors in private industry and which hold exclusive recognition for units of such officials or supervisors in any agency on the effective date of this chapter.

(b) Policies, regulations, and procedures established under and decisions issued under Executive Orders 11491, 11616, 11636, 11787, and 11838, or under any other Executive order, as in effect on the effective date of this chapter, shall remain in full force and effect until revised or revoked by the President, or unless superseded by specific provisions of this chapter or by regulations or decisions issued pursuant to this chapter.

Immigration Reform and Control Act

U.S. Code, Title 8, Sections 1324a and 1324b

Sec.

1324a. Unlawful employment of aliens.

1324b. Unfair immigration-related employment practices.

IRCA IN A NUTSHELL

Enacted: 1986

Purpose: To prevent the employment of unauthorized aliens and to prohibit discrimination on the basis of citizenship or national origin

Responsible agencies: U.S. Immigration and Naturalization Service and U.S. Department of Justice

---

Sec. 1324a. Unlawful employment of aliens

(a) Making employment of unauthorized aliens unlawful

(1) In general

It is unlawful for a person or other entity —

(A) to hire, or to recruit or refer for a fee, for employment in the United States an alien knowing the alien is an unauthorized alien (as defined in subsection (h)(3) of this section) with respect to such employment, or

(B) (i) to hire for employment in the United States an individual without complying with the requirements of subsection (b) of this section or (ii) if the person or entity is an agricultural association, agricultural employer, or farm labor contractor (as defined in section 1802 of Title 29), to hire, or to recruit or refer for a fee, for employment in the United States an individual without complying with the requirements of subsection (b) of this section.

(2) Continuing employment

It is unlawful for a person or other entity, after hiring an alien for employment in accordance with paragraph (1), to continue to employ the alien in the United States knowing the alien is (or has become) an unauthorized alien with respect to such employment.

(3) Defense

A person or entity that establishes that it has complied in good faith with the requirements of subsection (b) of this section with respect to the hiring, recruiting, or referral for employment of an alien in the United States has established an affirmative defense that the person or entity has not violated paragraph (1)(A) with respect to such hiring, recruiting, or referral.

(4) Use of labor through contract

For purposes of this section, a person or other entity who uses a contract, subcontract, or exchange, entered into, renegotiated, or extended after November 6, 1986, to obtain the labor of an alien in the United States knowing that the alien is an unauthorized alien (as defined in subsection (h)(3) of this section) with respect to performing such labor, shall be considered to have hired the alien for employment in the United States in violation of paragraph (1)(A).

(5) Use of State employment agency documentation

For purposes of paragraphs (1)(B) and (3), a person or entity shall be deemed to have complied with the requirements of subsection (b) of this section with respect to the hiring of an individual who was referred for such employment by a State employment agency (as defined by the Attorney General), if the person or entity has and retains (for the period and in the manner described in subsection (b)(3) of this section) appropriate documentation of such referral by that agency, which documentation certifies that the agency has complied with the procedures specified in subsection (b) of this section with respect to the individual's referral.

(6) Treatment of documentation for certain employees

(A) In general

For purposes of this section, if —

(i) an individual is a member of a collective-bargaining unit and is employed, under a collective bargaining agreement entered into between one or more employee organizations and an association of two or more employers, by an employer that is a member of such association, and

(ii) within the period specified in subparagraph (B), another employer that is a member of the association (or an agent of such association on behalf of the employer) has complied with the requirements of subsection (b) of this section with respect to the employment of the individual,

the subsequent employer shall be deemed to have complied with the requirements of subsection (b) of this section with respect to the hiring of the employee and shall not be liable for civil penalties described in subsection (e)(5) of this section.

(B) Period

The period described in this subparagraph is 3 years, or, if less, the period of time that the individual is authorized to be employed in the United States.

(C) Liability

(i) In general

If any employer that is a member of an association hires for employment in the United States an individual and relies upon the provisions of subparagraph (A) to comply with the requirements of subsection (b) of this section and the individual is an alien not authorized to work in the United States, then for the purposes of paragraph (1)(A), subject to clause (ii), the employer shall be presumed to have known at the time of hiring or afterward that the individual was an alien not authorized to work in the United States.

(ii) Rebuttal of presumption

The presumption established by clause (i) may be rebutted by the employer only through the presentation of clear and convincing evidence that the employer did not know (and could not reasonably have known) that the individual at the time of hiring or afterward was an alien not authorized to work in the United States.

(iii) Exception

Clause (i) shall not apply in any prosecution under subsection (f)(1) of this section.

(7) Application to Federal Government

For purposes of this section, the term "entity" includes an entity in any branch of the Federal Government.

(b) Employment verification system

The requirements referred to in paragraphs (1)(B) and (3) of subsection (a) of this section are, in the case of a person or other entity hiring, recruiting, or referring an individual for employment in the United States, the requirements specified in the following three paragraphs:

(1) Attestation after examination of documentation

(A) In general

The person or entity must attest, under penalty of perjury and on a form designated or established by the Attorney General by regulation, that it has verified that the individual is not an unauthorized alien by examining —

(i) a document described in subparagraph (B), or

(ii) a document described in subparagraph (C) and a document described in subparagraph (D).

A person or entity has complied with the requirement of this paragraph with respect to examination of a document if the document reasonably appears on its face to be genuine. If an individual provides a document or combination of documents that reasonably appears on its face to be genuine and that is sufficient to meet the requirements of the first sentence of this paragraph, nothing in this paragraph shall be construed as requiring the person or entity to solicit the production of any other document or as requiring the individual to produce such another document.

(B) Documents establishing both employment authorization and identity

A document described in this subparagraph is an individual's —

(i) United States passport;

(ii) resident alien card, alien registration card, or other document designated by the Attorney General, if the document —

(I) contains a photograph of the individual and such other personal identifying information relating to the individual as the Attorney General finds, by regulation, sufficient for purposes of this subsection,

(II) is evidence of authorization of employment in the United States, and

(III) contains security features to make it resistant to tampering, counterfeiting, and fraudulent use.

(C) Documents evidencing employment authorization

A document described in this subparagraph is an individual's —

(i) social security account number card (other than such a card which specifies on the face that the issuance of the card does not authorize employment in the United States); or

(ii) other documentation evidencing authorization of employment in the United States which the Attorney General finds, by regulation, to be acceptable for purposes of this section.

(D) Documents establishing identity of individual

A document described in this subparagraph is an individual's —

(i) driver's license or similar document issued for the purpose of identification by a State, if it contains a photograph of the individual or such other personal identifying information relating to the individual as the Attorney General finds, by regulation, sufficient for purposes of this section; or

(ii) in the case of individuals under 16 years of age or in a State which does not provide for issuance of an identification document (other than a driver's license) referred to in clause (i), documentation of personal identity of such other type as the Attorney General finds, by regulation, provides a reliable means of identification.

(E) Authority to prohibit use of certain documents

If the Attorney General finds, by regulation, that any document described in subparagraph (B), (C), or (D) as establishing employment authorization or identity does not reliably establish such authorization or identity or is being used fraudulently to an unacceptable degree, the Attorney General may prohibit or place conditions on its use for purposes of this subsection.

(2) Individual attestation of employment authorization

The individual must attest, under penalty of perjury on the form designated or established for purposes of paragraph (1), that the individual is a citizen or national of the United States, an alien lawfully admitted for permanent residence, or an alien who is authorized under this chapter or by the Attorney General to be hired, recruited, or referred for such employment.

(3) Retention of verification form

After completion of such form in accordance with paragraphs (1) and (2), the person or entity must retain the form and make it available for inspection by officers of the Service, the Special Counsel for Immigration-Related Unfair Employment Practices, or the Department of Labor during a period beginning on the date of the hiring, recruiting, or referral of the individual and ending —

(A) in the case of the recruiting or referral for a fee (without hiring) of an individual, three years after the date of the recruiting or referral, and

(B) in the case of the hiring of an individual —

(i) three years after the date of such hiring, or

(ii) one year after the date the individual's employment is terminated,

whichever is later.

(4) Copying of documentation permitted

Notwithstanding any other provision of law, the person or entity may copy a document presented by an individual pursuant to this subsection and may retain the copy, but only (except as otherwise permitted under law) for the purpose of complying with the requirements of this subsection.

(5) Limitation on use of attestation form

A form designated or established by the Attorney General under this subsection and any information contained in or appended to such form, may not be used for purposes other than for enforcement of this chapter and sections 1001, 1028, 1546, and 1621 of Title 18.

(6) Good faith compliance

(A) In general

Except as provided in subparagraphs (B) and (C), a person or entity is considered to have complied with a requirement of this subsection notwithstanding a technical or procedural failure to meet such requirement if there was a good faith attempt to comply with the requirement.

(B) Exception if failure to correct after notice

Subparagraph (A) shall not apply if —

(i) the Service (or another enforcement agency) has explained to the person or entity the basis for the failure,

(ii) the person or entity has been provided a period of not less than 10 business days (beginning after the date of the explanation) within which to correct the failure, and

(iii) the person or entity has not corrected the failure voluntarily within such period.

(C) Exception for pattern or practice violators

Subparagraph (A) shall not apply to a person or entity that has or is engaging in a pattern or practice of violations of subsection (a)(1)(A) or (a)(2) of this section.

(c) No authorization of national identification cards

Nothing in this section shall be construed to authorize, directly or indirectly, the issuance or use of national identification cards or the establishment of a national identification card.

(d) Evaluation and changes in employment verification system

(1) Presidential monitoring and improvements in system

(A) Monitoring

The President shall provide for the monitoring and evaluation of the degree to which the employment verification system established under subsection (b) of this section provides a secure system to determine employment eligibility in the United States and shall examine the suitability of existing Federal and State identification systems for use for this purpose.

(B) Improvements to establish secure system

To the extent that the system established under subsection (b) of this section is found not to be a secure system to determine employment eligibility in the United States, the President shall, subject to paragraph (3) and taking into account the results of any demonstration projects conducted under paragraph (4), implement such changes in (including additions to) the requirements of subsection (b) of this section as may be necessary to establish a secure system to determine employment eligibility in the United States. Such changes in the system may be implemented only if the changes conform to the requirements of paragraph (2).

(2) Restrictions on changes in system

Any change the President proposes to implement under paragraph (1) in the verification system must be designed in a manner so the verification system, as so changed, meets the following requirements:

(A) Reliable determination of identity

The system must be capable of reliably determining whether —

(i) a person with the identity claimed by an employee or prospective employee is eligible to work, and

(ii) the employee or prospective employee is claiming the identity of another individual.

(B) Using of counterfeit-resistant documents

If the system requires that a document be presented to or examined by an employer, the document must be in a form which is resistant to counterfeiting and tampering.

(C) Limited use of system

Any personal information utilized by the system may not be made available to Government agencies, employers, and other persons except to the extent necessary to verify that an individual is not an unauthorized alien.

(D) Privacy of information

The system must protect the privacy and security of personal information and identifiers utilized in the system.

(E) Limited denial of verification

A verification that an employee or prospective employee is eligible to be employed in the United States may not be withheld or revoked under the system for any reason other than that the employee or prospective employee is an unauthorized alien.

(F) Limited use for law enforcement purposes

The system may not be used for law enforcement purposes, other than for enforcement of this chapter or sections 1001, 1028, 1546, and 1621 of Title 18.

(G) Restriction on use of new documents

If the system requires individuals to present a new card or other document (designed specifically for use for this purpose) at the time of hiring, recruitment, or referral, then such document may not be required to be presented for any purpose other than under this chapter (or enforcement of sections 1001, 1028, 1546, and 1621 of Title 18) nor to be carried on one's person.

(3) Notice to Congress before implementing changes

(A) In general

The President may not implement any change under paragraph (1) unless at least —

(i) 60 days,

(ii) one year, in the case of a major change described in subparagraph (D)(iii), or

(iii) two years, in the case of a major change described in clause (i) or (ii) of subparagraph (D),

before the date of implementation of the change, the President has prepared and transmitted to the Committee on the Judiciary of the House of Representatives and to the Committee on the Judiciary of the Senate a written report setting forth the proposed change. If the President proposes to make any change regarding social security account number cards, the President shall transmit to the Committee on Ways and Means of the House of Representatives and to the Committee on Finance of the Senate a written report setting forth the proposed change. The President promptly shall cause to have printed in the Federal Register the substance of any major change (described in subparagraph (D)) proposed and reported to Congress.

(B) Contents of report

In any report under subparagraph (A) the President shall include recommendations for the establishment of civil and criminal sanctions for unauthorized use or disclosure of the information or identifiers contained in such system.

(C) Congressional review of major changes

(i) Hearings and review

The Committees on the Judiciary of the House of Representatives and of the Senate shall cause to have printed in the Congressional Record the substance of any major change described in subparagraph (D), shall hold hearings respecting the feasibility and desirability of implementing such a change, and, within the two year period before implementation, shall report to their respective Houses findings on whether or not such a change should be implemented.

(ii) Congressional action

No major change may be implemented unless the Congress specifically provides, in an appropriations or other Act, for funds for implementation of the change.

(D) Major changes defined

As used in this paragraph, the term "major change" means a change which would —

(i) require an individual to present a new card or other document (designed specifically for use for this purpose) at the time of hiring, recruitment, or referral,

(ii) provide for a telephone verification system under which an employer, recruiter, or referrer must transmit to a Federal official information concerning the immigration status of prospective employees and the official transmits to the person, and the person must record, a verification code, or

(iii) require any change in any card used for accounting purposes under the Social Security Act (42 U.S.C. §301 et seq.), including any change requiring that the only social security account number cards which may be presented in order to comply with subsection (b)(1)(C)(i) of this section are such cards as are in a counterfeit-resistant form consistent with the second sentence of section 205(c)(2)(D) of the Social Security Act (42 U.S.C. §405(c)(2)(D)).

(E) General revenue funding of social security card changes

Any costs incurred in developing and implementing any change described in subparagraph (D)(iii) for purposes of this subsection shall not be paid for out of any trust fund established under the Social Security Act (42 U.S.C. §301 et seq.).

(4) Demonstration projects

(A) Authority

The President may undertake demonstration projects (consistent with paragraph (2)) of different changes in the requirements of subsection (b) of this section. No such project may extend over a period of longer than five years.

(B) Reports on projects

The President shall report to the Congress on the results of demonstration projects conducted under this paragraph.

(e) Compliance

(1) Complaints and investigations

The Attorney General shall establish procedures —

(A) for individuals and entities to file written, signed complaints respecting potential violations of subsection (a) or (g)(1) of this section,

(B) for the investigation of those complaints which, on their face, have a substantial probability of validity,

(C) for the investigation of such other violations of subsection (a) or (g)(1) of this section as the Attorney General determines to be appropriate, and

(D) for the designation in the Service of a unit which has, as its primary duty, the prosecution of cases of violations of subsection (a) or (g)(1) of this section under this subsection.

(2) Authority in investigations

In conducting investigations and hearings under this subsection —

(A) immigration officers and administrative law judges shall have reasonable access to examine evidence of any person or entity being investigated,

(B) administrative law judges, may, if necessary, compel by subpoena the attendance of witnesses and the production of evidence at any designated place or hearing, and

(C) immigration officers designated by the Commissioner may compel by subpoena the attendance of witnesses and the production of evidence at any designated place prior to the filing of a complaint in a case under paragraph (2).

In case of contumacy or refusal to obey a subpoena lawfully issued under this paragraph and upon application of the Attorney General, an appropriate district court of the United States may issue an order requiring compliance with such subpoena and any failure to obey such order may be punished by such court as a contempt thereof.

(3) Hearing

(A) In general

Before imposing an order described in paragraph (4), (5), or (6) against a person or entity under this subsection for a violation of subsection (a) or (g)(1) of this section, the Attorney General shall provide the person or entity with notice and, upon request made within a reasonable time (of not less than 30 days, as established by the Attorney General) of the date of the notice, a hearing respecting the violation.

(B) Conduct of hearing

Any hearing so requested shall be conducted before an administrative law judge. The hearing shall be conducted in accordance with the requirements of section 554 of Title 5. The hearing shall be held at the nearest practicable place to the place where the person or entity resides or of the place where the alleged violation occurred. If no hearing is so requested, the Attorney General's imposition of the order shall constitute a final and unappealable order.

(C) Issuance of orders

If the administrative law judge determines, upon the preponderance of the evidence received, that a person or entity named in the complaint has violated subsection (a) or (g)(1) of this section, the administrative law judge shall state his findings of fact and issue and cause to be served on such person or entity an order described in paragraph (4), (5), or (6).

(4) Cease and desist order with civil money penalty for hiring, recruiting, and referral violations

With respect to a violation of subsection (a)(1)(A) or (a)(2) of this section, the order under this subsection —

(A) shall require the person or entity to cease and desist from such violations and to pay a civil penalty in an amount of —

(i) not less than $250 and not more than $2,000 for each unauthorized alien with respect to whom a violation of either such subsection occurred,

(ii) not less than $2,000 and not more than $5,000 for each such alien in the case of a person or entity previously subject to one order under this paragraph, or

(iii) not less than $3,000 and not more than $10,000 for each such alien in the case of a person or entity previously subject to more

than one order under this paragraph; and

(B) may require the person or entity —

(i) to comply with the requirements of subsection (b) of this section (or subsection (d) of this section if applicable) with respect to individuals hired (or recruited or referred for employment for a fee) during a period of up to three years, and

(ii) to take such other remedial action as is appropriate.

In applying this subsection in the case of a person or entity composed of distinct, physically separate subdivisions each of which provides separately for the hiring, recruiting, or referring for employment, without reference to the practices of, and not under the control of or common control with, another subdivision, each such subdivision shall be considered a separate person or entity.

(5) Order for civil money penalty for paperwork violations

With respect to a violation of subsection (a)(1)(B) of this section, the order under this subsection shall require the person or entity to pay a civil penalty in an amount of not less than $100 and not more than $1,000 for each individual with respect to whom such violation occurred. In determining the amount of the penalty, due consideration shall be given to the size of the business of the employer being charged, the good faith of the employer, the seriousness of the violation, whether or not the individual was an unauthorized alien, and the history of previous violations.

(6) Order for prohibited indemnity bonds

With respect to a violation of subsection (g)(1) of this section, the order under this subsection may provide for the remedy described in subsection (g)(2) of this section.

(7) Administrative appellate review

The decision and order of an administrative law judge shall become the final agency decision and order of the Attorney General unless either (A) within 30 days, an official delegated by regulation to exercise review authority over the decision and order modifies or vacates the decision and order, or (B) within 30 days of the date of such a modification or vacation (or within 60 days of the date of decision and order of an administrative law judge if not so modified or vacated) the decision and order is referred to the Attorney General pursuant to regulations, in which case the decision and order of the Attorney General shall become the final agency decision and order under this subsection. The Attorney General may not delegate the Attorney General's authority under this paragraph to any entity which has review authority over immigration-related matters.

(8) Judicial review

A person or entity adversely affected by a final order respecting an assessment may, within 45 days after the date the final order is issued, file a petition in the Court of Appeals for the appropriate circuit for review of the order.

(9) Enforcement of orders

If a person or entity fails to comply with a final order issued under this subsection against the person or entity, the Attorney General shall file a suit to seek compliance with the order in any appropriate district court of the United States. In any such suit, the validity and appropriateness of the final order shall not be subject to review.

(f) Criminal penalties and injunctions for pattern or practice violations

(1) Criminal penalty

Any person or entity which engages in a pattern or practice of violations of subsection (a)(1)(A) or (a)(2) of this section shall be fined not more than $3,000 for each unauthorized alien with respect to whom such a violation occurs, imprisoned for not more than six months for the entire pattern or practice, or both, notwithstanding the provisions of any other Federal law relating to fine levels.

(2) Enjoining of pattern or practice violations

Whenever the Attorney General has reasonable cause to believe that a person or entity is engaged in a pattern or practice of employment, recruitment, or referral in violation of paragraph (1)(A) or (2) of subsection (a) of this section, the Attorney General may bring a civil action in the appropriate district court of the United States requesting such relief, including a permanent or temporary injunction, restraining order, or other order against the person or entity, as the Attorney General deems necessary.

(g) Prohibition of indemnity bonds

(1) Prohibition

It is unlawful for a person or other entity, in the hiring, recruiting, or referring for employment of any individual, to require the individual to post a bond or security, to pay or agree to pay an amount, or otherwise to provide a financial guarantee or indemnity, against any potential liability arising under this section relating to such hiring, recruiting, or referring of the individual.

(2) Civil penalty

Any person or entity which is determined, after notice and opportunity for an administrative hearing under subsection (e) of this section, to have violated paragraph (1) shall be subject to a civil penalty of $1,000 for each violation and to an administrative order requiring the return of any amounts received in violation of such paragraph to the employee or, if the employee cannot be located, to the general fund of the Treasury.

(h) Miscellaneous provisions

(1) Documentation

In providing documentation or endorsement of authorization of aliens (other than aliens lawfully admitted for permanent residence) authorized to be employed in the United States, the Attorney General shall provide that any limitations with respect to the period or type of employment or employer shall be conspicuously stated on the documentation or endorsement.

(2) Preemption

The provisions of this section preempt any State or local law imposing civil or criminal sanctions (other than through licensing and similar laws) upon those who employ, or recruit or refer for a fee for employment, unauthorized aliens.

(3) Definition of unauthorized alien

As used in this section, the term "unauthorized alien" means, with respect to the employment of an alien at a particular time, that the alien is not at that time either (A) an alien lawfully admitted for permanent residence, or (B) authorized to be so employed by this chapter or by the Attorney General.

Sec. 1324b. Unfair immigration-related employment practices

(a) Prohibition of discrimination based on national origin or citizenship status

(1) General rule

It is an unfair immigration-related employment practice for a person or other entity to discriminate against any individual (other than an unauthorized alien, as defined in section 1324a(h)(3) of this title) with respect to the hiring, or recruitment or referral for a fee, of the individual for employment or the discharging of the individual from employment —

(A) because of such individual's national origin, or

(B) in the case of a protected individual (as defined in paragraph (3)), because of such individual's citizenship status.

(2) Exceptions

Paragraph (1) shall not apply to —

(A) a person or other entity that employs three or fewer employees,

(B) a person's or entity's discrimination because of an individual's national origin if the discrimination with respect to that person or entity and that individual is covered under section 703 of the Civil Rights Act of 1964 (42 U.S.C. §2000e-2), or

(C) discrimination because of citizenship status which is otherwise required in order to comply with law, regulation, or executive order, or required by Federal, State, or local government contract, or which the Attorney General determines to be essential for an employer to do business with an agency or department of the Federal, State, or local government.

(3) "Protected individual" defined

As used in paragraph (1), the term "protected individual" means an individual who —

(A) is a citizen or national of the United States, or

(B) is an alien who is lawfully admitted for permanent residence, is granted the status of an alien lawfully admitted for temporary residence under section 1160(a) or 1255a(a)(1) of this title, is admitted as a refugee under section 1157 of this title, or is granted asylum under section 1158 of this title; but does not include (i) an alien who fails to apply for naturalization within six months of the date the alien first becomes eligible (by virtue of period of lawful permanent residence) to apply for naturalization or, if later, within six months after November 6, 1986, and (ii) an alien who has applied on a timely basis, but has not been naturalized as a citizen within 2 years after the date of the application, unless the alien can establish that the alien is actively pursuing naturalization, except that time consumed in the Service's processing the application shall not be counted toward the 2-year period.

(4) Additional exception providing right to prefer equally qualified citizens

Notwithstanding any other provision of this section, it is not an unfair immigration-related employment practice for a person or other entity to prefer to hire, recruit, or refer an individual who is a citizen or national of the United States over another individual who is an alien if the two individuals are equally qualified.

(5) Prohibition of intimidation or retaliation

It is also an unfair immigration-related employment practice for a person or other entity to intimidate, threaten, coerce, or retaliate against any individual for the purpose of interfering with any right or privilege secured under this section or because the individual intends to file or has filed a charge or a complaint, testified, assisted, or participated in any manner in an investigation, proceeding, or hearing under this section. An individual so intimidated, threatened, coerced, or retaliated against shall be considered, for purposes of subsections (d) and (g) of this section, to have been discriminated against.

(6) Treatment of certain documentary practices as employment practices

A person's or other entity's request, for purposes of satisfying the requirements of section 1324a(b) of this title, for more or different documents than are required under such section or refusing to honor documents tendered that on their face reasonably appear to be genuine shall be treated as an unfair immigration-related employment practice if made for the purpose or with the intent of discriminating against an individual in violation of paragraph (1).

(b) Charges of violations

(1) In general

Except as provided in paragraph (2), any person alleging that the person is adversely affected directly by an unfair immigration-related employment practice (or a person on that person's behalf) or an officer of the Service alleging that an unfair immigration-related employment practice has occurred or is occurring may file a charge respecting such practice or violation with the Special Counsel (appointed under subsection (c) of this section). Charges shall be in writing under oath or affirmation and shall contain such information as the Attorney General requires. The Special Counsel by certified mail shall serve a notice of the charge (including the date, place, and circumstances of the alleged unfair immigration-related employment practice) on the person or entity involved within 10 days.

(2) No overlap with EEOC complaints

No charge may be filed respecting an unfair immigration-related employment practice described in subsection (a)(1)(A) of this section if a charge with respect to that practice based on the same set of facts has been filed with the Equal Employment Opportunity Commission under Title VII of the Civil Rights Act of 1964 (42 U.S.C. §2000e et seq.), unless the charge is dismissed as being outside the scope of such title. No charge respecting an employment practice may be filed with the Equal Employment Opportunity Commission under such title if a charge with respect to such practice based on the same set of facts has been filed under this subsection, unless the charge is dismissed under this section as being outside the scope of this section.

(c) Special Counsel

(1) Appointment

The President shall appoint, by and with the advice and consent of the Senate, a Special Counsel for Immigration-Related Unfair Employment Practices (hereinafter in this section referred to as the "Special Counsel") within the Department of Justice to serve for a term of four years. In the case of a vacancy in the office of the Special Counsel the President may designate the officer or employee who shall act as Special Counsel during such vacancy.

(2) Duties

The Special Counsel shall be responsible for investigation of charges and issuance of complaints under this section and in respect of the prosecution of all such complaints before administrative law judges and the exercise of certain functions under subsection (j)(1) of this section.

(3) Compensation

The Special Counsel is entitled to receive compensation at a rate not to exceed the rate now or hereafter provided for grade GS-17 of the General Schedule, under section 5332 of Title 5.

(4) Regional offices

The Special Counsel, in accordance with regulations of the Attorney General, shall establish such regional offices as may be necessary to carry out his duties.

(d) Investigation of charges

(1) By Special Counsel

The Special Counsel shall investigate each charge received and, within 120 days of the date of the receipt of the charge, determine whether or not there is reasonable cause to believe that the charge is true and whether or not to bring a complaint with respect to the charge before an administrative law judge. The Special Counsel may, on his own initiative, conduct investigations respecting unfair immigration-related employment practices and, based on such an investigation and subject to paragraph (3), file a complaint before such a judge.

(2) Private actions

If the Special Counsel, after receiving such a charge respecting an unfair immigration-related employment practice which alleges knowing and intentional discriminatory activity or a pattern or practice of discriminatory activity, has not filed a complaint before an administrative law judge with respect to such charge within such 120-day period, the Special Counsel shall notify the person making the charge of the determination not to file such a complaint during such period and the person making the charge may (subject to paragraph (3)) file a complaint directly before such a judge within 90 days after the date of receipt of the notice. The Special Counsel's failure to file such a complaint within such 120-day period shall not affect the right of the Special Counsel to investigate the charge or to bring a complaint before an administrative law judge during such 90-day period.

(3) Time limitations on complaints

No complaint may be filed respecting any unfair immigration-related employment practice occurring more than 180 days prior to the date of the filing of the charge with the Special Counsel. This subparagraph shall not prevent the subsequent amending of a charge or complaint under subsection (e)(1) of this section.

(e) Hearings

(1) Notice

Whenever a complaint is made that a person or entity has engaged in or is engaging in any such unfair immigration-related employment practice, an administrative law judge shall have power to issue and cause to be served upon such person or entity a copy of the complaint and a notice of hearing before the judge at a place therein fixed, not less than five days after the serving of the complaint. Any such complaint may be amended by the judge conducting the hearing, upon the motion of the party filing the complaint, in the judge's discretion at any time prior to the issuance of an order based thereon. The person or entity so complained of shall have the right to file an answer to the original or amended complaint and to appear in person or otherwise and give testimony at the place and time fixed in the complaint.

(2) Judges hearing cases

Hearings on complaints under this subsection shall be considered before administrative law judges who are specially designated by the Attorney General as having special training respecting employment discrimination and, to the extent practicable, before such judges who only consider cases under this section.

(3) Complainant as party

Any person filing a charge with the Special Counsel respecting an unfair immigration-related employment practice shall be considered a party to any complaint before an administrative law judge respecting such practice and any subsequent appeal respecting that complaint. In the discretion of the judge conducting the hearing, any other person may be allowed to intervene in the proceeding and to present testimony.

(f) Testimony and authority of hearing officers

(1) Testimony

The testimony taken by the administrative law judge shall be reduced to writing. Thereafter, the judge, in his discretion, upon notice may provide for the taking of further testimony or hear argument.

(2) Authority of administrative law judges

In conducting investigations and hearings under this subsection and in accordance with regulations of the Attorney General, the Special Counsel and administrative law judges shall have reasonable access to examine evidence of any person or entity being investigated. The administrative law judges by subpoena may compel the attendance of witnesses and the production of evidence at any designated place or hearing. In case of contumacy or refusal to obey a subpoena lawfully issued under this paragraph and upon application of the administrative law judge, an appropriate district court of the United States may issue an order requiring compliance with such subpoena and any failure to obey such order may be punished by such court as a contempt thereof.

(g) Determinations

(1) Order

The administrative law judge shall issue and cause to be served on the parties to the proceeding an order, which shall be final unless appealed as provided under subsection (i) of this section.

(2) Orders finding violations

(A) In general

If, upon the preponderance of the evidence, an administrative law judge determines that any person or entity named in the complaint has engaged in or is engaging in any such unfair immigration-related employment practice, then the judge shall state his findings of fact and shall issue and cause to be served on such person or entity an order which requires such person or entity to cease and desist from such unfair immigration-related employment practice.

(B) Contents of order

Such an order also may require the person or entity —

(i) to comply with the requirements of section 1324a(b) of this title with respect to individuals hired (or recruited or referred for employment for a fee) during a period of up to three years;

(ii) to retain for the period referred to in clause (i) and only for purposes consistent with section 1324a(b)(5) of this title, the name and address of each individual who applies, in person or in writing, for hiring for an existing position, or for recruiting or referring for a fee, for employment in the United States;

(iii) to hire individuals directly and adversely affected, with or without back pay;

(iv)(I) except as provided in subclauses (II) through (IV), to pay a civil penalty of not less than $250 and not more than $2,000 for each individual discriminated against,

(II) except as provided in subclauses (III) and (IV), in the case of a person or entity previously subject to a single order under this paragraph, to pay a civil penalty of not less than $2,000 and not more than $5,000 for each individual discriminated against,

(III) except as provided in subclause (IV), in the case of a person or entity previously subject to more than one order under this paragraph, to pay a civil penalty of not less than $3,000 and not more than $10,000 for each individual discriminated against, and

(IV) in the case of an unfair immigration-related employment practice described in subsection (a)(6) of this section, to pay a civil penalty of not less than $100 and not more than $1,000 for each individual discriminated against;

(v) to post notices to employees about their rights under this section and employers' obligations under section 1324a of this title;

(vi) to educate all personnel involved in hiring and complying with this section or section 1324a of this title about the requirements of this section or such section;

(vii) to remove (in an appropriate case) a false performance review or false warning from an employee's personnel file; and

(viii) to lift (in an appropriate case) any restrictions on an employee's assignments, work shifts, or movements.

(C) Limitation on back pay remedy

In providing a remedy under subparagraph (B)(iii), back pay liability shall not accrue from a date more than two years prior to the date of the filing of a charge with the Special Counsel. Interim earnings or amounts earnable with reasonable diligence by the individual or individuals discriminated against shall operate to reduce the back pay otherwise allowable under such paragraph. No order shall require the hiring of an individual as an employee or the payment to an individual of any back pay, if the individual was refused employment for any reason other than discrimination on account of national origin or citizenship status.

(D) Treatment of distinct entities

In applying this subsection in the case of a person or entity composed of distinct, physically separate subdivisions each of which provides separately for the hiring, recruiting, or referring for employment, without reference to the practices of, and not under the control of or common control with, another subdivision, each such subdivision shall be considered a separate person or entity.

(3) Orders not finding violations

If upon the preponderance of the evidence an administrative law judge determines that the person or entity named in the complaint has not engaged and is not engaging in any such unfair immigration-related employment practice, then the judge shall state his findings of fact and shall issue an order dismissing the complaint.

(h) Awarding of attorney's fees

In any complaint respecting an unfair immigration-related employment practice, an administrative law judge, in the judge's discretion, may allow a prevailing party, other than the United States, a reasonable attorney's fee, if the losing party's argument is without reasonable foundation in law and fact.

(i) Review of final orders

(1) In general

Not later than 60 days after the entry of such final order, any person aggrieved by such final order may seek a review of such order in the United States court of appeals for the circuit in which the violation is alleged to have occurred or in which the employer resides or transacts business.

(2) Further review

Upon the filing of the record with the court, the jurisdiction of the court shall be exclusive and its judgment shall be final, except that the same shall be subject to review by the Supreme Court of the United States upon writ of certiorari or certification as provided in section 1254 of Title 28.

(j) Court enforcement of administrative orders

(1) In general

If an order of the agency is not appealed under subsection (i)(1) of this section, the Special Counsel (or, if the Special Counsel fails to act, the person filing the charge) may petition the United States district court for the district in which a violation of the order is alleged to have occurred, or in which the respondent resides or transacts business, for the enforcement of the order of the administrative law judge, by filing in such court a written petition praying that such order be enforced.

(2) Court enforcement order

Upon the filing of such petition, the court shall have jurisdiction to make and enter a decree enforcing the order of the administrative law judge. In such a proceeding, the order of the administrative law judge shall not be subject to review.

(3) Enforcement decree in original review

If, upon appeal of an order under subsection (i)(1) of this section, the United States court of appeals does not reverse such order, such court shall have the jurisdiction to make and enter a decree enforcing the order of the administrative law judge.

(4) Awarding of attorneys' fees

In any judicial proceeding under subsection (i) of this section or this subsection, the court, in its discretion, may allow a prevailing party, other than the United States, a reasonable attorney's fee as part of costs but only if the losing party's argument is without reasonable foundation in law and fact.

(k) Termination dates

(1) This section shall not apply to discrimination in hiring, recruiting, or referring, or discharging of individuals occurring after the date of any termination of the provisions of section 1324a of this title, under subsection (l) of that section.

(2) The provisions of this section shall terminate 30 calendar days after receipt of the last report required to be transmitted under section 1324a(j) of this title if —

(A) the Comptroller General determines, and so reports in such report that —

(i) no significant discrimination has resulted, against citizens or nationals of the United States or against any eligible workers seeking employment, from the implementation of section 1324a of this title, or

(ii) such section has created an unreasonable burden on employers hiring such workers; and

(B) there has been enacted, within such period of 30 calendar days, a joint resolution stating in substance that the Congress approves the findings of the Comptroller General contained in such report.

The provisions of subsections (m) and (n) of section 1324a of this title shall apply to any joint resolution under subparagraph (B) in the same manner as they apply to a joint resolution under subsection (l) of such section.

(l) Dissemination of information concerning anti-discrimination provisions

(1) Not later than 3 months after November 29, 1990, the Special Counsel, in cooperation with

the chairman of the Equal Employment Opportunity Commission, the Secretary of Labor, and the Administrator of the Small Business Administration, shall conduct a campaign to disseminate information respecting the rights and remedies prescribed under this section and under Title VII of the Civil Rights Act of 1964 (42 U.S.C. §2000e et seq.) in connection with unfair immigration-related employment practices. Such campaign shall be aimed at increasing the knowledge of employers, employees, and the general public concerning employer and employee rights, responsibilities, and remedies under this section and such title.

(2) In order to carry out the campaign under this subsection, the Special Counsel —

(A) may, to the extent deemed appropriate and subject to the availability of appropriations, contract with public and private organizations for outreach activities under the campaign, and

(B) shall consult with the Secretary of Labor, the chairman of the Equal Employment Opportunity Commission, and the heads of such other agencies as may be appropriate.

(3) There are authorized to be appropriated to carry out this subsection $10,000,000 for each fiscal year (beginning with fiscal year 1991).

Uniformed Services Employment and Reemployment Rights Act

U.S. Code, Title 38, Sections 4301 to 4333

USERRA IN A NUTSHELL

Enacted: 1994

Purpose To provide rights to members of the uniformed services to return to their jobs after such service is ended and to be free of discrimination because of their service

Coverage: Private and public sector employers

Responsible agency: U.S. Department of Labor Veterans' Employment and Training Service

Sec. 4301. Purposes; sense of Congress

(a) The purposes of this chapter are —

(1) to encourage noncareer service in the uniformed services by eliminating or minimizing the disadvantages to civilian careers and employment which can result from such service;

(2) to minimize the disruption to the lives of persons performing service in the uniformed services as well as to their employers, their fellow employees, and their communities, by providing for the prompt reemployment of such persons upon their completion of such service; and

(3) to prohibit discrimination against persons because of their service in the uniformed services.

(b) It is the sense of Congress that the Federal Government should be a model employer in carrying out the provisions of this chapter.

Sec. 4302. Relation to other law and plans or agreements

(a) Nothing in this chapter shall supersede, nullify or diminish any Federal or State law (including any local law or ordinance), contract, agreement, policy, plan, practice, or other matter that establishes a right or benefit that is more beneficial to, or is in addition to, a right or benefit provided for such person in this chapter.

(b) This chapter supersedes any State law (including any local law or ordinance), contract, agreement, policy, plan, practice, or other matter that reduces, limits, or eliminates in any manner any right or benefit provided by this chapter, including the establishment of additional prerequisites to the exercise of any such right or the receipt of any such benefit.

Sec. 4303. Definitions

For the purposes of this chapter —

(1) The term "Attorney General" means the Attorney General of the United States or any person designated by the Attorney General to carry out a responsibility of the Attorney General under this chapter.

(2) The term "benefit", "benefit of employment", or "rights and benefits" means any advantage, profit, privilege, gain, status, account, or interest (other than wages or salary for work performed) that accrues by reason of an employment contract or agreement or an employer policy, plan, or practice and includes rights and benefits under a pension plan, a health plan, an employee stock ownership plan, insurance coverage and awards, bonuses, severance pay, supplemental unemployment benefits, vacations, and the opportunity to select work hours or location of employment.

(3) The term "employee" means any person employed by an employer. Such term includes any person who is citizen, national, or permanent resident alien of the United States employed in a workplace in a foreign country by an employer

that is an entity incorporated or otherwise organized in the United States or that is controlled by an entity organized in the United States, within the meaning of section 4319(c) of this title.

(4)(A) Except as provided in subparagraphs (B) and (C), the term "employer" means any person, institution, organization, or other entity that pays salary or wages for work performed or that has control over employment opportunities, including —

    (i) a person, institution, organization, or other entity to whom the employer has delegated the performance of employment-related responsibilities;

    (ii) the Federal Government;

    (iii) a State;

    (iv) any successor in interest to a person, institution, organization, or other entity referred to in this subparagraph; and

    (v) a person, institution, organization, or other entity that has denied initial employment in violation of section 4311.

(B) In the case of a National Guard technician employed under section 709 of Title 32, the term "employer" means the adjutant general of the State in which the technician is employed.

(C) Except as an actual employer of employees, an employee pension benefit plan described in section 3(2) of the Employee Retirement Income Security Act of 1974 (29 U.S.C. §1002(2)) shall be deemed to be an employer only with respect to the obligation to provide benefits described in section 4318.

(5) The term "Federal executive agency" includes the United States Postal Service, the Postal Rate Commission, any nonappropriated fund instrumentality of the United States, any Executive agency (as that term is defined in section 105 of Title 5) other than an agency referred to in section 2302(a)(2)(C)(ii) of Title 5, and any military department (as that term is defined in section 102 of Title 5) with respect to the civilian employees of that department.

(6) The term "Federal Government" includes any Federal executive agency, the legislative branch of the United States, and the judicial branch of the United States.

(7) The term "health plan" means an insurance policy or contract, medical or hospital service agreement, membership or subscription contract, or other arrangement under which health services for individuals are provided or the expenses of such services are paid.

(8) The term "notice" means (with respect to subchapter II) any written or verbal notification of an obligation or intention to perform service in the uniformed services provided to an employer by the employee who will perform such service or by the uniformed service in which such service is to be performed.

(9) The term "qualified", with respect to an employment position, means having the ability to perform the essential tasks of the position.

(10) The term "reasonable efforts", in the case of actions required of an employer under this chapter, means actions, including training provided by an employer, that do not place an undue hardship on the employer.

(11) Notwithstanding section 101, the term "Secretary" means the Secretary of Labor or any person designated by such Secretary to carry out an activity under this chapter.

(12) The term "seniority" means longevity in employment together with any benefits of employment which accrue with, or are determined by, longevity in employment.

(13) The term "service in the uniformed services" means the performance of duty on a voluntary or involuntary basis in a uniformed service under competent authority and includes active duty, active duty for training, initial active duty for training, inactive duty training, full-time National Guard duty, and a period for which a person is absent from a position of employment for the purpose of an examination to determine the fitness of the person to perform any such duty.

(14) The term "State" means each of the several States of the United States, the District of Columbia, the Commonwealth of Puerto Rico, Guam, the Virgin Islands, and other territories of the United States (including the agencies and political subdivisions thereof).

(15) The term "undue hardship", in the case of actions taken by an employer, means actions requiring significant difficulty or expense, when considered in light of —

(A) the nature and cost of the action needed under this chapter;

(B) the overall financial resources of the facility or facilities involved in the provision of the action; the number of persons employed at such facility; the effect on expenses and resources, or the impact otherwise of such action upon the operation of the facility;

(C) the overall financial resources of the employer; the overall size of the business of an employer with respect to the number of its employees; the number, type, and location of its facilities; and

(D) the type of operation or operations of the employer, including the composition, structure, and functions of the work force of such employer; the geographic separateness, administrative, or fiscal relationship of the facility or facilities in question to the employer.

(16) The term "uniformed services" means the Armed Forces, the Army National Guard and the Air National Guard when engaged in active duty for training, inactive duty training, or full-time National Guard duty, the commissioned corps of the Public Health Service, and any other category of persons designated by the President in time of war or national emergency.

Sec. 4304. Character of service

A person's entitlement to the benefits of this chapter by reason of the service of such person in one of the uniformed services terminates upon the occurrence of any of the following events:

(1) A separation of such person from such uniformed service with a dishonorable or bad conduct discharge.

(2) A separation of such person from such uniformed service under other than honorable conditions, as characterized pursuant to regulations prescribed by the Secretary concerned.

(3) A dismissal of such person permitted under section 1161(a) of Title 10.

(4) A dropping of such person from the rolls pursuant to section 1161(b) of Title 10.

Sec. 4311. Discrimination against persons who serve in the uniformed services and acts of reprisal prohibited

(a) A person who is a member of, applies to be a member of, performs, has performed, applies to perform, or has an obligation to perform service in a uniformed service shall not be denied initial employment, reemployment, retention in employment, promotion, or any benefit of employment by an employer on the basis of that membership, application for membership, performance of service, application for service, or obligation.

(b) An employer may not discriminate in employment against or take any adverse employment action against any person because such person (1) has taken an action to enforce a protection afforded any person under this chapter, (2) has testified or otherwise made a statement in or in connection with any proceeding under this chapter, (3) has assisted or otherwise participated in an investigation under this chapter, or (4) has exercised a right provided for in this chapter. The prohibition in this subsection shall apply with respect to a person regardless of whether that person has performed service in the uniformed services.

(c) An employer shall be considered to have engaged in actions prohibited —

(1) under subsection (a), if the person's membership, application for membership, service, application for service, or obligation for service in the uniformed services is a motivating factor in the employer's action, unless the employer can prove that the action would have been taken in the absence of such membership, application for membership, service, application for service, or obligation for service; or

(2) under subsection (b), if the person's (A) action to enforce a protection afforded any person under this chapter, (B) testimony or making of a statement in or in connection with any proceeding under this chapter, (C) assistance or other participation in an investigation under this chapter, or (D) exercise of a right provided for in this chapter, is a motivating factor in the employer's action, unless the employer can prove that the action would have been taken in the absence of such person's enforcement action, testimony, statement, assistance, participation, or exercise of a right.

(d) The prohibitions in subsections (a) and (b) shall apply to any position of employment, includ-

ing a position that is described in section 4312(d)(1)(C) of this title.

Sec. 4312. Reemployment rights of persons who serve in the uniformed services

(a) Subject to subsections (b), (c), and (d) and to section 4304, any person whose absence from a position of employment is necessitated by reason of service in the uniformed services shall be entitled to the reemployment rights and benefits and other employment benefits of this chapter if —

(1) the person (or an appropriate officer of the uniformed service in which such service is performed) has given advance written or verbal notice of such service to such person's employer;

(2) the cumulative length of the absence and of all previous absences from a position of employment with that employer by reason of service in the uniformed services does not exceed five years; and

(3) except as provided in subsection (f), the person reports to, or submits an application for reemployment to, such employer accordance with the provisions of subsection (e).

(b) No notice is required under subsection (a)(1) if the giving of such notice is precluded by military necessity or, under all of the relevant circumstances, the giving of such notice is otherwise impossible or unreasonable. A determination of military necessity for the purposes of this subsection shall be made pursuant to regulations prescribed by the Secretary of Defense and shall not be subject to judicial review.

(c) Subsection (a) shall apply to a person who is absent from a position of employment by reason of service in the uniformed services if such person's cumulative period of service in the uniformed services, with respect to the employer relationship for which a person seeks reemployment, does not exceed five years, except that any such period of service shall not include any service —

(1) that is required, beyond five years, to complete an initial period of obligated service;

(2) during which such person was unable to obtain orders releasing such person from a period of service in the uniformed services before the expiration of such five-year period and such inability was through no fault of such person;

(3) performed as required pursuant to section 10147 of Title 10, under section 502(a) or 503 of Title 32, or to fulfill additional training requirements determined and certified in writing by the Secretary concerned, to be necessary for professional development, or for completion of skill training or retraining; or

(4) performed by a member of a uniformed service who is —

(A) ordered to or retained on active duty under section 688, 12301(a), 12301(g), 12302, 12304, or 12305 of Title 10 or under section 331, 332, 359, 360, 367, or 712 of Title 14;

(B) ordered to or retained on active duty (other than for training) under any provision of law because of a war or national emergency declared by the President or the Congress, as determined by the Secretary concerned;

(C) ordered to active duty (other than for training) in support, as determined by the Secretary concerned, of an operational mission for which personnel have been ordered to active duty under section 12304 of Title 10;

(D) ordered to active duty in support, as determined by the Secretary concerned, of a critical mission or requirement of the uniformed services; or

(E) called into Federal service as a member of the National Guard under chapter 15 of Title 10 or under section 12406 of Title 10.

(d)(1) An employer is not required to reemploy a person under this chapter if —

(A) the employer's circumstances have so changed as to make such reemployment impossible or unreasonable;

(B) in the case of a person entitled to reemployment under subsection (a)(3), (a)(4), or (b)(2)(B) of section 4313, such employment would impose an undue hardship on the employer; or

(C) the employment from which the person leaves to serve in the uniformed services is for a brief, nonrecurrent period and there is no reasonable expectation that such employment will continue indefinitely or for a significant period.

(2) In any proceeding involving an issue of whether —

(A) any reemployment referred to in paragraph (1) is impossible or unreasonable because of a change in an employer's circumstances,

(B) any accommodation, training, or effort referred to in subsection (a)(3), (a)(4), or (b)(2)(B) of section 4313 would impose an undue hardship on the employer, or

(C) the employment referred to in paragraph (1)(C) is for a brief, nonrecurrent period and there is no reasonable expectation that such employment will continue indefinitely or for a significant period,

the employer shall have the burden of proving the impossibility or unreasonableness, undue hardship, or the brief or nonrecurrent nature of the employment without a reasonable expectation of continuing indefinitely or for a significant period.

(e)(1) Subject to paragraph (2), a person referred to in subsection (a) shall, upon the completion of a period of service in the uniformed services, notify the employer referred to in such subsection of the person's intent to return to a position of employment with such employer as follows:

(A) In the case of a person whose period of service in the uniformed services was less than 31 days, by reporting to the employer —

(i) not later than the beginning of the first full regularly scheduled work period on the first full calendar day following the completion of the period of service and the expiration of eight hours after a period allowing for the safe transportation of the person from the place of that service to the person's residence; or

(ii) as soon as possible after the expiration of the eight-hour period referred to in clause (i), if reporting within the period referred to in such clause is impossible or unreasonable through no fault of the person.

(B) In the case of a person who is absent from a position of employment for a period of any length for the purposes of an examination to determine the person's fitness to perform service in the uniformed services, by reporting in the manner and time referred to in subparagraph (A).

(C) In the case of a person whose period of service in the uniformed services was for more than 30 days but less than 181 days, by submitting an application for reemployment with the employer not later than 14 days after the completion of the period of service or if submitting such application within such period is impossible or unreasonable through no fault of the person, the next first full calendar day when submission of such application becomes possible.

(D) In the case of a person whose period of service in the uniformed services was for more than 180 days, by submitting an application for reemployment with the employer not later than 90 days after the completion of the period of service.

(2)(A) A person who is hospitalized for, or convalescing from, an illness or injury incurred in, or aggravated during, the performance of service in the uniformed services shall, at the end of the period that is necessary for the person to recover from such illness or injury, report to the person's employer (in the case of a person described in subparagraph (A) or (B) of paragraph (1)) or submit an application for reemployment with such employer (in the case of a person described in subparagraph (C) or (D) of such paragraph). Except as provided in subparagraph (B), such period of recovery may not exceed two years.

(B) Such two-year period shall be extended by the minimum time required to accommodate the circumstances beyond such person's control which make reporting within the period specified in subparagraph (A) impossible or unreasonable.

(3) A person who fails to report or apply for employment or reemployment within the appropriate period specified in this subsection shall not automatically forfeit such person's entitlement to the rights and benefits referred to in subsection (a) but shall be subject to the conduct rules, established policy, and general practices of the employer pertaining to explanations and discipline with respect to absence from scheduled work.

(f)(1) A person who submits an application for reemployment in accordance with subparagraph (C) or (D) of subsection (e)(1) or subsection (e)(2) shall provide to the person's employer (upon the request of such employer) documentation to establish that —

(A) the person's application is timely;

(B) the person has not exceeded the service limitations set forth in subsection (a)(2) (except as permitted under subsection (c)); and

(C) the person's entitlement to the benefits under this chapter has not been terminated pursuant to section 4304.

(2) Documentation of any matter referred to in paragraph (1) that satisfies regulations prescribed by the Secretary shall satisfy the documentation requirements in such paragraph.

(3)(A) Except as provided in subparagraph (B), the failure of a person to provide documentation that satisfies regulations prescribed pursuant to paragraph (2) shall not be a basis for denying reemployment in accordance with the provisions of this chapter if the failure occurs because such documentation does not exist or is not readily available at the time of the request of the employer. If, after such reemployment, documentation becomes available that establishes that such person does not meet one or more of the requirements referred to in subparagraphs (A), (B), and (C) of paragraph (1), the employer of such person may terminate the employment of the person and the provision of any rights or benefits afforded the person under this chapter.

(B) An employer who reemploys a person absent from a position of employment for more than 90 days may require that the person provide the employer with the documentation referred to in subparagraph (A) before beginning to treat the person as not having incurred a break in service for pension purposes under section 4318(a)(2)(A).

(4) An employer may not delay or attempt to defeat a reemployment obligation by demanding documentation that does not then exist or is not then readily available.

(g) The right of a person to reemployment under this section shall not entitle such person to retention, preference, or displacement rights over any person with a superior claim under the provisions of Title 5, United States Code, relating to veterans and other preference eligibles.

(h) In any determination of a person's entitlement to protection under this chapter, the timing, frequency, and duration of the person's training or service, or the nature of such training or service (including voluntary service) in the uniformed services, shall not be a basis for denying protection of this chapter if the service does not exceed the limitations set forth in subsection (c) and the notice requirements established in subsection (a)(1) and the notification requirements established in subsection (e) are met.

Sec. 4313. Reemployment positions

(a) Subject to subsection (b) (in the case of any employee) and sections 4314 and 4315 (in the case of an employee of the Federal Government), a person entitled to reemployment under section 4312, upon completion of a period of service in the uniformed services, shall be promptly reemployed in a position of employment in accordance with the following order of priority:

(1) Except as provided in paragraphs (3) and (4), in the case of a person whose period of service in the uniformed services was for less than 91 days —

(A) in the position of employment in which the person would have been employed if the continuous employment of such person with the employer had not been interrupted by such service, the duties of which the person is qualified to perform; or

(B) in the position of employment in which the person was employed on the date of the commencement of the service in the uniformed services, only if the person is not qualified to perform the duties of the position referred to in subparagraph (A) after reasonable efforts by the employer to qualify the person.

(2) Except as provided in paragraphs (3) and (4), in the case of a person whose period of service in the uniformed services was for more than 90 days —

(A) in the position of employment in which the person would have been employed if the continuous employment of such person with the employer had not been interrupted by such service, or a position of like seniority, status and pay, the duties of which the person is qualified to perform; or

(B) in the position of employment in which the person was employed on the date of the commencement of the service in the uniformed

services, or a position of like seniority, status and pay, the duties of which the person is qualified to perform, only if the person is not qualified to perform the duties of a position referred to in subparagraph (A) after reasonable efforts by the employer to qualify the person.

(3) In the case of a person who has a disability incurred in, or aggravated during, such service, and who (after reasonable efforts by the employer to accommodate the disability) is not qualified due to such disability to be employed in the position of employment in which the person would have been employed if the continuous employment of such person with the employer had not been interrupted by such service —

(A) in any other position which is equivalent in seniority, status, and pay, the duties of which the person is qualified to perform or would become qualified to perform with reasonable efforts by the employer; or

(B) if not employed under subparagraph (A), in a position which is the nearest approximation to a position referred to in subparagraph (A) in terms of seniority, status, and pay consistent with circumstances of such person's case.

(4) In the case of a person who (A) is not qualified to be employed in (i) the position of employment in which the person would have been employed if the continuous employment of such person with the employer had not been interrupted by such service, or (ii) in the position of employment in which such person was employed on the date of the commencement of the service in the uniformed services for any reason (other than disability incurred in, or aggravated during, service in the uniformed services), and (B) cannot become qualified with reasonable efforts by the employer, in any other position which is the nearest approximation to a position referred to first in clause (A)(i) and then in clause (A)(ii) which such person is qualified to perform, with full seniority.

(b)(1) If two or more persons are entitled to reemployment under section 4312 in the same position of employment and more than one of them has reported for such reemployment, the person who left the position first shall have the prior right to reemployment in that position.

(2) Any person entitled to reemployment under section 4312 who is not reemployed in a position of employment by reason of paragraph (1) shall be entitled to be reemployed as follows:

(A) Except as provided in subparagraph (B), in any other position of employment referred to in subsection (a)(1) or (a)(2), as the case may be (in the order of priority set out in the applicable subsection), that provides a similar status and pay to a position of employment referred to in paragraph (1) of this subsection, consistent with the circumstances of such person's case, with full seniority.

(B) In the case of a person who has a disability incurred in, or aggravated during, a period of service in the uniformed services that requires reasonable efforts by the employer for the person to be able to perform the duties of the position of employment, in any other position referred to in subsection (a)(3) (in the order of priority set out in that subsection) that provides a similar status and pay to a position referred to in paragraph (1) of this subsection, consistent with circumstances of such person's case, with full seniority.

Sec. 4314. Reemployment by the Federal Government

(a) Except as provided in subsections (b), (c), and (d), if a person is entitled to reemployment by the Federal Government under section 4312, such person shall be reemployed in a position of employment as described in section 4313.

(b)(1) If the Director of the Office of Personnel Management makes a determination described in paragraph (2) with respect to a person who was employed by a Federal executive agency at the time the person entered the service from which the person seeks reemployment under this section, the Director shall —

(A) identify a position of like seniority, status, and pay at another Federal executive agency that satisfies the requirements of section 4313 and for which the person is qualified; and

(B) ensure that the person is offered such position.

(2) The Director shall carry out the duties referred to in subparagraphs (A) and (B) of paragraph (1) if the Director determines that —

(A) the Federal executive agency that employed the person referred to in such paragraph no

longer exists and the functions of such agency have not been transferred to another Federal executive agency; or

(B) it is impossible or unreasonable for the agency to reemploy the person.

(c) If the employer of a person described in subsection (a) was, at the time such person entered the service from which such person seeks reemployment under this section, a part of the judicial branch or the legislative branch of the Federal Government, and such employer determines that it is impossible or unreasonable for such employer to reemploy such person, such person shall, upon application to the Director of the Office of Personnel Management, be ensured an offer of employment in an alternative position in a Federal executive agency on the basis described in subsection (b).

(d) If the adjutant general of a State determines that it is impossible or unreasonable to reemploy a person who was a National Guard technician employed under section 709 of Title 32, such person shall, upon application to the Director of the Office of Personnel Management, be ensured an offer of employment in an alternative position in a Federal executive agency on the basis described in subsection (b).

Sec. 4315. Reemployment by certain Federal agencies

(a) The head of each agency referred to in section 2302(a)(2)(C)(ii) of Title 5 shall prescribe procedures for ensuring that the rights under this chapter apply to the employees of such agency.

(b) In prescribing procedures under subsection (a), the head of an agency referred to in that subsection shall ensure, to the maximum extent practicable, that the procedures of the agency for reemploying persons who serve in the uniformed services provide for the reemployment of such persons in the agency in a manner similar to the manner of reemployment described in section 4313.

(c)(1) The procedures prescribed under subsection (a) shall designate an official at the agency who shall determine whether or not the reemployment of a person referred to in subsection (b) by the agency is impossible or unreasonable.

(2) Upon making a determination that the reemployment by the agency of a person referred to in subsection (b) is impossible or unreasonable, the official referred to in paragraph (1) shall notify the person and the Director of the Office of Personnel Management of such determination.

(3) A determination pursuant to this subsection shall not be subject to judicial review.

(4) The head of each agency referred to in subsection (a) shall submit to the Select Committee on Intelligence and the Committee on Veterans' Affairs of the Senate and the Permanent Select Committee on Intelligence and the Committee on Veterans' Affairs of the House of Representatives on an annual basis a report on the number of persons whose reemployment with the agency was determined under this subsection to be impossible or unreasonable during the year preceding the report, including the reason for each such determination.

(d)(1) Except as provided in this section, nothing in this section, section 4313, or section 4325 shall be construed to exempt any agency referred to in subsection (a) from compliance with any other substantive provision of this chapter.

(2) This section may not be construed —

(A) as prohibiting an employee of an agency referred to in subsection (a) from seeking information from the Secretary regarding assistance in seeking reemployment from the agency under this chapter, alternative employment in the Federal Government under this chapter, or information relating to the rights and obligations of employee and Federal agencies under this chapter; or

(B) as prohibiting such an agency from voluntarily cooperating with or seeking assistance in or of clarification from the Secretary or the Director of the Office of Personnel Management of any matter arising under this chapter.

(e) The Director of the Office of Personnel Management shall ensure the offer of employment to a person in a position in a Federal executive agency on the basis described in subsection (b) if —

(1) the person was an employee of an agency referred to in section 2302(a)(2)(C)(ii) of Title 5 at the time the person entered the service from which the person seeks reemployment under this section;

(2) the appropriate officer of the agency determines under subsection (c) that reemployment of

the person by the agency is impossible or unreasonable; and

(3) the person submits an application to the Director for an offer of employment under this subsection.

Sec. 4316. Rights, benefits, and obligations of persons absent from employment for service in a uniformed service

(a) A person who is reemployed under this chapter is entitled to the seniority and other rights and benefits determined by seniority that the person had on the date of the commencement of service in the uniformed services plus the additional seniority and rights and benefits that such person would have attained if the person had remained continuously employed.

(b)(1) Subject to paragraphs (2) through (6), a person who is absent from a position of employment by reason of service in the uniformed services shall be —

(A) deemed to be on furlough or leave of absence while performing such service; and

(B) entitled to such other rights and benefits not determined by seniority as are generally provided by the employer of the person to employees having similar seniority, status, and pay who are on furlough or leave of absence under a contract, agreement, policy, practice, or plan in effect at the commencement of such service or established while such person performs such service.

(2)(A) Subject to subparagraph (B), a person who —

(i) is absent from a position of employment by reason of service in the uniformed services, and

(ii) knowingly provides written notice of intent not to return to a position of employment after service in the uniformed service,

is not entitled to rights and benefits under paragraph (1)(B).

(B) For the purposes of subparagraph (A), the employer shall have the burden of proving that a person knowingly provided clear written notice of intent not to return to a position of employment after service in the uniformed service and, in doing so, was aware of the specific rights and benefits to be lost under subparagraph (A).

(3) A person deemed to be on furlough or leave of absence under this subsection while serving in the uniformed services shall not be entitled under this subsection to any benefits to which the person would not otherwise be entitled if the person had remained continuously employed.

(4) Such person may be required to pay the employee cost, if any, of any funded benefit continued pursuant to paragraph (1) to the extent other employees on furlough or leave of absence are so required.

(5) The entitlement of a person to coverage under a health plan is provided for under section 4317.

(6) The entitlement of a person to a right or benefit under an employee pension benefit plan is provided for under section 4318.

(c) A person who is reemployed by an employer under this chapter shall not be discharged from such employment, except for cause —

(1) within one year after the date of such reemployment, if the person's period of service before the reemployment was more than 180 days; or

(2) within 180 days after the date of such reemployment, if the person's period of service before the reemployment was more than 30 days but less than 181 days.

(d) Any person whose employment with an employer is interrupted by a period of service in the uniformed services shall be permitted, upon request of that person, to use during such period of service any vacation, annual, or similar leave with pay accrued by the person before the commencement of such service. No employer may require any such person to use vacation, annual, or similar leave during such period of service.

Sec. 4317. Health plans

(a)(1) In any case in which a person (or the person's dependents) has coverage under a health plan in connection with the person's position of employment, including a group health plan (as defined in section 607(1) of the Employee Retirement Income Security Act of 1974), and such person is absent from such position of employment by reason of service in the uniformed services, the plan shall provide that the person may elect to continue such coverage as provided in this subsection. The maximum period of cover-

age of a person and the person's dependents under such an election shall be the lesser of —

(A) the 18-month period beginning on the date on which the person's absence begins; or

(B) the day after the date on which the person fails to apply for or return to a position of employment, as determined under section 4312(e).

(2) A person who elects to continue health-plan coverage under this paragraph may be required to pay not more than 102 percent of the full premium under the plan (determined in the same manner as the applicable premium under section 4980B(f)(4) of the Internal Revenue Code of 1986) associated with such coverage for the employer's other employees, except that in the case of a person who performs service in the uniformed services for less than 31 days, such person may not be required to pay more than the employee share, if any, for such coverage.

(3) In the case of a health plan that is a multi-employer plan, as defined in section 3(37) of the Employee Retirement Income Security Act of 1974, any liability under the plan for employer contributions and benefits arising under this paragraph shall be allocated —

(A) by the plan in such manner as the plan sponsor shall provide; or

(B) if the sponsor does not provide —

(i) to the last employer employing the person before the period served by the person in the uniformed services, or

(ii) if such last employer is no longer functional, to the plan.

(b)(1) Except as provided in paragraph (2), in the case of a person whose coverage under a health plan was terminated by reason of service in the uniformed services, an exclusion or waiting period may not be imposed in connection with the reinstatement of such coverage upon reemployment under this chapter if an exclusion or waiting period would not have been imposed under a health plan had coverage of such person by such plan not been terminated as a result of such service. This paragraph applies to the person who is reemployed and to any individual who is covered by such plan by reason of the reinstatement of the coverage of such person.

(2) Paragraph (1) shall not apply to the coverage of any illness or injury determined by the Secretary of Veterans Affairs to have been incurred in, or aggravated during, performance of service in the uniformed services.

Sec. 4318. Employee pension benefit plans

(a)(1)(A) Except as provided in subparagraph (B), in the case of a right provided pursuant to an employee pension benefit plan (including those described in sections 3(2) and 3(33) of the Employee Retirement Income Security Act of 1974) or a right provided under any Federal or State law governing pension benefits for governmental employees, the right to pension benefits of a person reemployed under this chapter shall be determined under this section.

(B) In the case of benefits under the Thrift Savings Plan, the rights of a person reemployed under this chapter shall be those rights provided in section 8432b of Title 5. The first sentence of this subparagraph shall not be construed to affect any other right or benefit under this chapter.

(2)(A) A person reemployed under this chapter shall be treated as not having incurred a break in service with the employer or employers maintaining the plan by reason of such person's period or periods of service in the uniformed services.

(B) Each period served by a person in the uniformed services shall, upon reemployment under this chapter, be deemed to constitute service with the employer or employers maintaining the plan for the purpose of determining the nonforfeitability of the person's accrued benefits and for the purpose of determining the accrual of benefits under the plan.

(b)(1) An employer reemploying a person under this chapter shall, with respect to a period of service described in subsection (a)(2)(B), be liable to an employee pension benefit plan for funding any obligation of the plan to provide the benefits described in subsection (a)(2) and shall allocate the amount of any employer contribution for the person in the same manner and to the same extent the allocation occurs for other employees during the period of service. For purposes of determining the amount of such liability and any obligation of the plan, earnings and forfeitures shall not be includ-

ed. For purposes of determining the amount of such liability and for purposes of section 515 of the Employee Retirement Income Security Act of 1974 or any similar Federal or State law governing pension benefits for governmental employees, service in the uniformed services that is deemed under subsection (a) to be service with the employer shall be deemed to be service with the employer under the terms of the plan or any applicable collective bargaining agreement. In the case of a multiemployer plan, as defined in section 3(37) of the Employee Retirement Income Security Act of 1974, any liability of the plan described in this paragraph shall be allocated —

(A) by the plan in such manner as the sponsor maintaining the plan shall provide; or

(B) if the sponsor does not provide —

(i) to the last employer employing the person before the period served by the person in the uniformed services, or

(ii) if such last employer is no longer functional, to the plan.

(2) A person reemployed under this chapter shall be entitled to accrued benefits pursuant to subsection (a) that are contingent on the making of, or derived from, employee contributions or elective deferrals (as defined in section 402(g)(3) of the Internal Revenue Code of 1986) only to the extent the person makes payment to the plan with respect to such contributions or deferrals. No such payment may exceed the amount the person would have been permitted or required to contribute had the person remained continuously employed by the employer throughout the period of service described in subsection (a)(2)(B). Any payment to the plan described in this paragraph shall be made during the period beginning with the date of reemployment and whose duration is three times the period of the person's service in the uniformed services, such payment period not to exceed five years.

(3) For purposes of computing an employer's liability under paragraph (1) or the employee's contributions under paragraph (2), the employee's compensation during the period of service described in subsection (a)(2)(B) shall be computed —

(A) at the rate the employee would have received but for the period of service described in subsection (a)(2)(B), or

(B) in the case that the determination of such rate is not reasonably certain, on the basis of the employee's average rate of compensation during the 12-month period immediately preceding such period (or, if shorter, the period of employment immediately preceding such period).

(c) Any employer who reemploys a person under this chapter and who is an employer contributing to a multiemployer plan, as defined in section 3(37) of the Employee Retirement Income Security Act of 1974, under which benefits are or may be payable to such person by reason of the obligations set forth in this chapter, shall, within 30 days after the date of such reemployment, provide information, in writing, of such reemployment to the administrator of such plan.

Sec. 4319. Employment and reemployment rights in foreign countries

(a) Liability of controlling United States employer of foreign entity

If an employer controls an entity that is incorporated or otherwise organized in a foreign country, any denial of employment, reemployment, or benefit by such entity shall be presumed to be by such employer.

(b) Inapplicability to foreign employer

This subchapter does not apply to foreign operations of an employer that is a foreign person not controlled by an United States employer.

(c) Determination of controlling employer

For the purpose of this section, the determination of whether an employer controls an entity shall be based upon the interrelations of operations, common management, centralized control of labor relations, and common ownership or financial control of the employer and the entity.

(d) Exemption

Notwithstanding any other provision of this subchapter, an employer, or an entity controlled by an employer, shall be exempt from compliance with any of sections 4311 through 4318 of this title with respect to an employee in a workplace in a foreign country, if compliance with that section would cause such employer, or such entity controlled by an employer, to violate the law of the foreign country in which the workplace is located.

Sec. 4321. Assistance in obtaining reemployment or other employment rights or benefits

The Secretary (through the Veterans' Employment and Training Service) shall provide assistance to any person with respect to the employment and reemployment rights and benefits to which such person is entitled under this chapter. In providing such assistance, the Secretary may request the assistance of existing Federal and State agencies engaged in similar or related activities and utilize the assistance of volunteers.

Sec. 4322. Enforcement of employment or reemployment rights

(a) A person who claims that —

(1) such person is entitled under this chapter to employment or reemployment rights or benefits with respect to employment by an employer; and

(2)(A) such employer has failed or refused, or is about to fail or refuse, to comply with the provisions of this chapter; or

(B) in the case that the employer is a Federal executive agency, such employer or the Office of Personnel Management has failed or refused, or is about to fail or refuse, to comply with the provisions of this chapter,

may file a complaint with the Secretary in accordance with subsection (b), and the Secretary shall investigate such complaint.

(b) Such complaint shall be in writing, be in such form as the Secretary may prescribe, include the name and address of the employer against whom the complaint is filed, and contain a summary of the allegations that form the basis for the complaint.

(c) The Secretary shall, upon request, provide technical assistance to a potential claimant with respect to a complaint under this subsection, and when appropriate, to such claimant's employer.

(d) The Secretary shall investigate each complaint submitted pursuant to subsection (a). If the Secretary determines as a result of the investigation that the action alleged in such complaint occurred, the Secretary shall attempt to resolve the complaint by making reasonable efforts to ensure that the person or entity named in the complaint complies with the provisions of this chapter.

(e) If the efforts of the Secretary with respect to any complaint filed under subsection (a) do not resolve the complaint, the Secretary shall notify the person who submitted the complaint of —

(1) the results of the Secretary's investigation; and

(2) the complainant's entitlement to proceed under the enforcement of rights provisions provided under section 4323 (in the case of a person submitting a complaint against a State or private employer) or section 4324 (in the case of a person submitting a complaint against a Federal executive agency or the Office of Personnel Management).

(f) This subchapter does not apply to any action relating to benefits to be provided under the Thrift Savings Plan under Title 5.

Sec. 4323. Enforcement of rights with respect to a State or private employer

(a) Action for relief

(1) A person who receives from the Secretary a notification pursuant to section 4322(e) of this title of an unsuccessful effort to resolve a complaint relating to a State (as an employer) or a private employer may request that the Secretary refer the complaint to the Attorney General. If the Attorney General is reasonably satisfied that the person on whose behalf the complaint is referred is entitled to the rights or benefits sought, the Attorney General may appear on behalf of, and act as attorney for, the person on whose behalf the complaint is submitted and commence an action for relief under this chapter for such person. In the case of such an action against a State (as an employer), the action shall be brought in the name of the United States as the plaintiff in the action.

(2) A person may commence an action for relief with respect to a complaint against a State (as an employer) or a private employer if the person—

(A) has chosen not to apply to the Secretary for assistance under section 4322(a) of this title;

(B) has chosen not to request that the Secretary refer the complaint to the Attorney General under paragraph (1); or

(C) has been refused representation by the Attorney General with respect to the complaint under such paragraph.

(b) Jurisdiction

(1) In the case of an action against a State (as an employer) or a private employer commenced by the United States, the district courts of the United States shall have jurisdiction over the action.

(2) In the case of an action against a State (as an employer) by a person, the action may be brought in a State court of competent jurisdiction in accordance with the laws of the State.

(3) In the case of an action against a private employer by a person, the district courts of the United States shall have jurisdiction of the action.

(c) Venue

(1) In the case of an action by the United States against a State (as an employer), the action may proceed in the United States district court for any district in which the State exercises any authority or carries out any function.

(2) In the case of an action against a private employer, the action may proceed in the United States district court for any district in which the private employer of the person maintains a place of business.

(d) Remedies

(1) In any action under this section, the court may award relief as follows:

(A) The court may require the employer to comply with the provisions of this chapter.

(B) The court may require the employer to compensate the person for any loss of wages or benefits suffered by reason of such employer's failure to comply with the provisions of this chapter.

(C) The court may require the employer to pay the person an amount equal to the amount referred to in subparagraph (B) as liquidated damages, if the court determines that the employer's failure to comply with the provisions of this chapter was willful.

(2)(A) Any compensation awarded under subparagraph (B) or (C) of paragraph (1) shall be in addition to, and shall not diminish, any of the other rights and benefits provided for under this chapter.

(B) In the case of an action commenced in the name of the United States for which the relief includes compensation awarded under subparagraph (B) or (C) of paragraph (1), such compensation shall be held in a special deposit account and shall be paid, on order of the Attorney General, directly to the person. If the compensation is not paid to the person because of inability to do so within a period of 3 years, the compensation shall be covered into the Treasury of the United States as miscellaneous receipts.

(3) A State shall be subject to the same remedies, including prejudgment interest, as may be imposed upon any private employer under this section.

(e) Equity powers

The court may use its full equity powers, including temporary or permanent injunctions, temporary restraining orders, and contempt orders, to vindicate fully the rights or benefits of persons under this chapter.

(f) Standing

An action under this chapter may be initiated only by a person claiming rights or benefits under this chapter under subsection (a) or by the United States under subsection (a)(1).

(g) Respondent

In any action under this chapter, only an employer or a potential employer, as the case may be, shall be a necessary party respondent.

(h) Fees, court costs

(1) No fees or court costs may be charged or taxed against any person claiming rights under this chapter.

(2) In any action or proceeding to enforce a provision of this chapter by a person under subsection (a)(2) who obtained private counsel for such action or proceeding, the court may award any such person who prevails in such action or proceeding reasonable attorney fees, expert witness fees, and other litigation expenses.

(i) Inapplicability of state statute of limitations

No State statute of limitations shall apply to any proceeding under this chapter.

(j) Definition

In this section, the term "private employer" includes a political subdivision of a State.

Sec. 4324. Enforcement of rights with respect to Federal executive agencies

(a)(1) A person who receives from the Secretary a notification pursuant to section 4322(e) may request that the Secretary refer the complaint for litigation before the Merit Systems Protection Board. The Secretary shall refer the complaint to the Office of Special Counsel established by section 1211 of Title 5.

(2)(A) If the Special Counsel is reasonably satisfied that the person on whose behalf a complaint is referred under paragraph (1) is entitled to the rights or benefits sought, the Special Counsel (upon the request of the person submitting the complaint) may appear on behalf of, and act as attorney for, the person and initiate an action regarding such complaint before the Merit Systems Protection Board.

(B) If the Special Counsel declines to initiate an action and represent a person before the Merit Systems Protection Board under subparagraph (A), the Special Counsel shall notify such person of that decision.

(b) A person may submit a complaint against a Federal executive agency or the Office of Personnel Management under this subchapter directly to the Merit Systems Protection Board if that person —

(1) has chosen not to apply to the Secretary for assistance under section 4322(a);

(2) has received a notification from the Secretary under section 4322(e);

(3) has chosen not to be represented before the Board by the Special Counsel pursuant to subsection (a)(2)(A); or

(4) has received a notification of a decision from the Special Counsel under subsection (a)(2)(B).

(c)(1) The Merit Systems Protection Board shall adjudicate any complaint brought before the Board pursuant to subsection (a)(2)(A) or (b), without regard to whether the complaint accrued before, on, or after October 13, 1994. A person who seeks a hearing or adjudication by submitting such a complaint under this paragraph may be represented at such hearing or adjudication in accordance with the rules of the Board.

(2) If the Board determines that a Federal executive agency or the Office of Personnel Management has not complied with the provisions of this chapter relating to the employment or reemployment of a person by the agency, the Board shall enter an order requiring the agency or Office to comply with such provisions and to compensate such person for any loss of wages or benefits suffered by such person by reason of such lack of compliance.

(3) Any compensation received by a person pursuant to an order under paragraph (2) shall be in addition to any other right or benefit provided for by this chapter and shall not diminish any such right or benefit.

(4) If the Board determines as a result of a hearing or adjudication conducted pursuant to a complaint submitted by a person directly to the Board pursuant to subsection (b) that such person is entitled to an order referred to in paragraph (2), the Board may, in its discretion, award such person reasonable attorney fees, expert witness fees, and other litigation expenses.

(d)(1) A person adversely affected or aggrieved by a final order or decision of the Merit Systems Protection Board under subsection (c) may petition the United States Court of Appeals for the Federal Circuit to review the final order or decision. Such petition and review shall be in accordance with the procedures set forth in section 7703 of Title 5.

(2) Such person may be represented in the Federal Circuit proceeding by the Special Counsel unless the person was not represented by the Special Counsel before the Merit Systems Protection Board regarding such order or decision.

Sec. 4325. Enforcement of rights with respect to certain Federal agencies

(a) This section applies to any person who alleges that —

(1) the reemployment of such person by an agency referred to in subsection (a) of section 4315 was not in accordance with procedures for the reemployment of such person under subsection (b) of such section; or

(2) the failure of such agency to reemploy the person under such section was otherwise wrongful.

(b) Any person referred to in subsection (a) may submit a claim relating to an allegation referred to in that subsection to the inspector general of the agency which is the subject of the allegation. The inspector general shall investigate and resolve the allegation pursuant to procedures prescribed by the head of the agency.

(c) In prescribing procedures for the investigation and resolution of allegations under subsection (b), the head of an agency shall ensure, to the maximum extent practicable, that the procedures are similar to the procedures for investigating and resolving complaints utilized by the Secretary under section 4322(d).

(d) This section may not be construed —

(1) as prohibiting an employee of an agency referred to in subsection (a) from seeking information from the Secretary regarding assistance in seeking reemployment from the agency under this chapter or information relating to the rights and obligations of employees and Federal agencies under this chapter; or

(2) as prohibiting such an agency from voluntarily cooperating with or seeking assistance in or of clarification from the Secretary or the Director of the Office of Personnel Management of any matter arising under this chapter.

Sec. 4326. Conduct of investigation; subpoenas

(a) In carrying out any investigation under this chapter, the Secretary's duly authorized representatives shall, at all reasonable times, have reasonable access to and the right to interview persons with information relevant to the investigation and shall have reasonable access to, for purposes of examination, and the right to copy and receive, any documents of any person or employer that the Secretary considers relevant to the investigation.

(b) In carrying out any investigation under this chapter, the Secretary may require by subpoena the attendance and testimony of witnesses and the production of documents relating to any matter under investigation. In case of disobedience of the subpoena or contumacy and on request of the Secretary, the Attorney General may apply to any district court of the United States in whose jurisdiction such disobedience or contumacy occurs for an order enforcing the subpoena.

(c) Upon application, the district courts of the United States shall have jurisdiction to issue writs commanding any person or employer to comply with the subpoena of the Secretary or to comply with any order of the Secretary made pursuant to a lawful investigation under this chapter and the district courts shall have jurisdiction to punish failure to obey a subpoena or other lawful order of the Secretary as a contempt of court.

(d) Subsections (b) and (c) shall not apply to the legislative branch or the judicial branch of the United States.

Sec. 4331. Regulations

(a) The Secretary (in consultation with the Secretary of Defense) may prescribe regulations implementing the provisions of this chapter with regard to the application of this chapter to States, local governments, and private employers.

(b)(1) The Director of the Office of Personnel Management (in consultation with the Secretary and the Secretary of Defense) may prescribe regulations implementing the provisions of this chapter with regard to the application of this chapter to Federal executive agencies (other than the agencies referred to in paragraph (2)) as employers. Such regulations shall be consistent with the regulations pertaining to the States as employers and private employers, except that employees of the Federal Government may be given greater or additional rights.

(2) The following entities may prescribe regulations to carry out the activities of such entities under this chapter:

(A) The Merit Systems Protection Board.

(B) The Office of Special Counsel.

(C) The agencies referred to in section 2303(a)(2)(C)(ii) of Title 5.

Sec. 4332. Reports

The Secretary shall, after consultation with the Attorney General and the Special Counsel referred to in section 4324(a)(1) and no later than February 1, 1996, and annually thereafter through 2000, transmit to the Congress, a report containing the following matters for the fiscal year ending before such February 1:

(1) The number of cases reviewed by the Department of Labor under this chapter during the fiscal year for which the report is made.

(2) The number of cases referred to the Attorney General or the Special Counsel pursuant to section 4323 or 4324, respectively, during such fiscal year.

(3) The number of complaints filed by the Attorney General pursuant to section 4323 during such fiscal year.

(4) The nature and status of each case reported on pursuant to paragraph (1), (2), or (3).

(5) An indication of whether there are any apparent patterns of violation of the provisions of this chapter, together with an explanation thereof.

(6) Recommendations for administrative or legislative action that the Secretary, the Attorney General, or the Special Counsel considers necessary for the effective implementation of this chapter, including any action that could be taken to encourage mediation, before claims are filed under this chapter, between employers and persons seeking employment or reemployment.

Sec. 4333. Outreach

The Secretary, the Secretary of Defense, and the Secretary of Veterans Affairs shall take such actions as such Secretaries determine are appropriate to inform persons entitled to rights and benefits under this chapter and employers of the rights, benefits, and obligations of such persons and such employers under this chapter.

Davis-Bacon Act

U.S. Code, Title 40, Sections 276a to 276a-7

Sec.

276a.   Rate of wages for laborers and mechanics.

276a-1.   Termination of work on failure to pay agreed wages; completion of work by Government.

276a-2.   Payment of wages by Comptroller General from withheld payments; listing contractors violating contracts.

276a-3.   Effect on other Federal laws.

276a-4.   Effective date of sections 276a to 276a-5.

276a-5.   Suspension of sections 276a to 276a-5 during emergency.

276a-6.   Omitted.

276a-7.   Application of Sections 276a to 276a-5 to contracts entered into without regard to section 5 of Title 41.

DAVIS-BACON IN A NUTSHELL

Enacted: 1931

Purpose: To require employers to pay locally prevailing wages and benefits

Coverage: Employers on federally financed or assisted construction projects

Responsible agency: U.S. Department of Labor Wage and Hour Division

Sec. 276a. Rate of wages for laborers and mechanics

(a) The advertised specifications for every contract in excess of $2,000, to which the United States or the District of Columbia is a party, for construction, alteration, and/or repair, including painting and decorating, of public buildings or public works of the United States or the District of Columbia within the geographical limits of the States of the Union or the District of Columbia, and which requires or involves the employment of mechanics and/or laborers shall contain a provision stating the minimum wages to be paid various classes of laborers and mechanics which shall be based upon the wages that will be determined by the Secretary of Labor to be prevailing for the corresponding classes of laborers and mechanics employed on projects of a character similar to the contract work in the city, town, village, or other civil subdivision of the State in which the work is to be performed, or in the District of Columbia if the work is to be performed there; and every contract based upon these specifications shall contain a stipulation that the contractor or his subcontractor shall pay all mechanics and laborers employed directly upon the site of the work, unconditionally and not less often than once a week, and without subsequent deduction or rebate on any account, the full amounts accrued at time of payment, computed at wage rates not less than those stated in the advertised specifications, regardless of any contractual relationship which may be alleged to exist between the contractor or subcontractor and such laborers and mechanics, and that the scale of wages to be paid shall be posted by the contractor in a prominent and easily accessible place at the site of the work; and the further stipulation that there may be withheld from the contractor so much of accrued payments as may be considered necessary by the contracting officer to pay to laborers and mechanics employed by the contractor or any subcontractor on the work the difference between the rates of wages required by the contract to be paid laborers and mechanics on the work and the rates of wages received by such laborers and mechanics and not refunded to the contractor, subcontractors, or their agents.

(b) As used in sections 276a to 276a-5 of this title the term "wages", "scale of wages", "wage rates", "minimum wages", and "prevailing wages" shall include —

(1) the basic hourly rate of pay; and

(2) the amount of —

(A) the rate of contribution irrevocably made by a contractor or subcontractor to a trustee or to a third person pursuant to a fund, plan, or program; and

(B) the rate of costs to the contractor or subcontractor which may be reasonably anticipated in providing benefits to laborers and mechanics pursuant to an enforcible commitment to carry out a financially responsible plan or program which was communicated in writing to the laborers and mechanics affected,

for medical or hospital care, pensions on retirement or death, compensation for injuries or illness resulting from occupational activity, or insurance to provide any of the foregoing, for unemployment benefits, life insurance, disability and sickness insurance, or accident insurance, for vacation and holiday pay, for defraying costs of apprenticeship or other similar programs, or for other bona fide fringe benefits, but only where the contractor or subcontractor is not required by other Federal, State, or local law to provide any of such benefits:

Provided, That the obligation of a contractor or subcontractor to make payment in accordance with the prevailing wage determinations of the Secretary of Labor, insofar as sections 276a to 276a-5 of this title and other Acts incorporating sections 276a to 276a-5 of this title by reference are concerned may be discharged by the making of payments in cash, by the making of contributions of a type referred to in paragraph (2)(A), or by the assumption of an enforcible commitment to bear the costs of a plan or program of a type referred to in paragraph (2)(B), or any combination thereof, where the aggregate of any such payments, contributions, and costs is not less than the rate of pay described in paragraph (1) plus the amount referred to in paragraph (2).

In determining the overtime pay to which the laborer or mechanic is entitled under any Federal law, his regular or basic hourly rate of pay (or

other alternative rate upon which premium rate of overtime compensation is computed) shall be deemed to be the rate computed under paragraph (1), except that where the amount of payments, contributions, or costs incurred with respect to him exceeds the prevailing wage applicable to him under sections 276a to 276a-5 of this title, such regular or basic hourly rate of pay (or such other alternative rate) shall be arrived at by deducting from the amount of payments, contributions, or costs actually incurred with respect to him, the amount of contributions or costs of the types described in paragraph (2) actually incurred with respect to him, or the amount determined under paragraph (2) but not actually paid, whichever amount is the greater.

Sec. 276a-1. Termination of work on failure to pay agreed wages; completion of work by Government

Every contract within the scope of sections 276a to 276a-5 of this title shall contain the further provision that in the event it is found by the contracting officer that any laborer or mechanic employed by the contractor or any subcontractor directly on the site of the work covered by the contract has been or is being paid a rate of wages less than the rate of wages required by the contract to be paid as aforesaid, the Government may, by written notice to the contractor, terminate his right to proceed with the work or such part of the work as to which there has been a failure to pay said required wages and to prosecute the work to completion by contract or otherwise, and the contractor and his sureties shall be liable to the Government for any excess costs occasioned the Government thereby.

Sec. 276a-2. Payment of wages by Comptroller General from withheld payments; listing contractors violating contracts

(a) The Comptroller General of the United States is authorized and directed to pay directly to laborers and mechanics from any accrued payments withheld under the terms of the contract any wages found to be due laborers and mechanics pursuant to sections 276a to 276a-5 of this title; and the Comptroller General of the United States is further authorized and is directed to distribute a list to all departments of the Government giving the names of persons or firms whom he has found to have disregarded their obligations to employees and subcontractors. No contract shall be awarded to the persons or firms appearing on this list or to any firm, corporation, partnership, or association in which such persons or firms have an interest until three years have elapsed from the date of publication of the list containing the names of such persons or firms.

(b) If the accrued payments withheld under the terms of the contract, as aforesaid, are insufficient to reimburse all the laborers and mechanics with respect to whom there has been a failure to pay the wages required pursuant to sections 276a to 276a-5 of this title, such laborers and mechanics shall have the right of action and/or of intervention against the contractor and his sureties conferred by law upon persons furnishing labor or materials, and in such proceedings it shall be no defense that such laborers and mechanics accepted or agreed to accept less than the required rate of wages or voluntarily made refunds.

Sec. 276a-3. Effect on other Federal laws

Sections 276a to 276a-5 of this title shall not be construed to supersede or impair any authority otherwise granted by Federal law to provide for the establishment of specific wage rates.

Sec. 276a-4. Effective date of sections 276a to 276a-5

Sections 276a to 276a-5 of this title shall take effect thirty days after August 30, 1935, but shall not affect any contract then existing or any contract that may thereafter be entered into pursuant to invitations for bids that are outstanding on August 30, 1935.

Sec. 276a-5. Suspension of sections 276a to 276a-5 during emergency

In the event of a national emergency the President is authorized to suspend the provisions of sections 276a to 276a-5 of this title.

Sec. 276a-6. Omitted

Sec. 276a-7. Application of sections 276a to 276a-5 to contracts entered into without regard to section 5 of Title 41

The fact that any contract authorized by any Act is entered into without regard to section 5 of Title 41, or upon a cost-plus-a-fixed-fee basis or otherwise without advertising for proposals, shall not be construed to render inapplicable the provisions of sections 276a to 276a-5 of this title, if such Act would otherwise be applicable to such contract.

Walsh-Healey Government Contracts Act

U.S. Code, Title 41, Sections 35 to 45

Sec.

WALSH-HEALEY IN A NUTSHELL

Enacted: 1936

Purpose: To insure the payment of prevailing wages on public contracts

Coverage: Contractors engaged in the manufacturing or furnishing of materials for the U.S. Government

Responsible agency: U.S. Department of Labor Wage and Hour Division

---

Sec. 35. Contracts for materials, etc., exceeding $10,000; representations and stipulations

In any contract made and entered into by any executive department, independent establishment, or other agency or instrumentality of the United States, or by the District of Columbia, or by any corporation all the stock of which is beneficially owned by the United States (all the foregoing being hereinafter designated as agencies of the United States), for the manufacture or furnishing of materials, supplies, articles, and equipment in any amount exceeding $10,000, there shall be included the following representations and stipulations:

(a) That all persons employed by the contractor in the manufacture or furnishing of the materials, supplies, articles, or equipment used in the performance of the contract will be paid, without subsequent deduction or rebate on any account, not less than the minimum wages as determined by the Secretary of Labor to be the prevailing minimum wages for persons employed on similar work or in the particular or similar industries or groups of industries currently operating in the locality in which the materials, supplies, articles, or equipment are to be manufactured or furnished under said contract;

(b) That no person employed by the contractor in the manufacture or furnishing of the materials, supplies, articles, or equipment used in the performance of the contract shall be permitted to work in excess of forty hours in any one week: *Provided,* That the provisions of this subsection shall not apply to any employer who shall have entered into an agreement with his employees pursuant to the provisions of paragraphs (1) or (2) of subsection (b) of section 207 of Title 29;

(c) That no male person under sixteen years of age and no female person under eighteen years of age and no convict labor will be employed by the contractor in the manufacture or production or furnishing of any of the materials, supplies, articles, or equipment included in such contract, except that this section, or any other law or Executive order containing similar prohibitions against purchase of goods by the Federal Government, shall not apply to convict labor which satisfies the conditions of section 1761(c) of Title 18; and

(d) That no part of such contract will be performed nor will any of the materials, supplies, articles, or equipment to be manufactured or furnished under said contract be manufactured or fabricated in any plants, factories, buildings, or surroundings or under working conditions which are unsanitary or hazardous or dangerous to the health and safety of employees engaged in the performance of said contract. Compliance with the safety, sanitary, and factory inspection laws of the State in which the work or part thereof is to be performed shall be prima-facie evidence of compliance with this subsection.

Sec. 36. Liability for contract breach; cancellation; completion by Government agency; employee's wages

Any breach or violation of any of the representations and stipulations in any contract for the purposes set forth in section 35 of this title shall render the party responsible therefor liable to the United States of America for liquidated damages, in addition to damages for any other breach of such contract, the sum of $10 per day for each male person under sixteen years of age or each female person under eighteen years of age, or each convict laborer knowingly employed in the performance of such contract, and a sum equal to the amount of any deductions, rebates, refunds, or underpayment of wages due to any employee engaged in the performance of such contract; and, in addition, the agency of the United States entering into such contract shall have the right to cancel same and to make open-market purchases or enter into other contracts for the completion of the original contract, charging any additional cost to the original contractor. Any sums of money due to the United States of America by reason of any violation of any of the representations and stipulations of said contract set forth in section 35 of this title may be withheld from any amounts due on any such contracts or may be recovered in suits brought in the name of the United States of America by the Attorney General thereof. All sums withheld or recovered as deductions, rebates, refunds, or underpayments of wages shall be held in a special deposit account and shall be paid, on order of the Secretary of Labor, directly to the employees who have been paid less than minimum rates of pay as set forth in such contracts and on whose account such sums were withheld or recovered: *Provided,* That no claims by employees for such payments shall be entertained unless made within one year from the date of actual notice to the contractor of the withholding or recovery of such sums by the United States of America.

Sec. 37. Distribution of list of persons breaching contract; future contracts prohibited

The Comptroller General is authorized and directed to distribute a list to all agencies of the United States containing the names of persons or firms found by the Secretary of Labor to have breached any of the agreements or representations required by sections 35 to 45 of this title. Unless the Secretary of Labor otherwise recommends no contracts shall be awarded to such persons or firms or to any firm, corporation, partnership, or association in which such persons or firms have a controlling interest until three years have elapsed from the date the Secretary of Labor determines such breach to have occurred.

Sec. 38. Administration of Walsh-Healey provisions; officers and employees; appointment; investigations; rules and regulations

The Secretary of Labor is authorized and directed to administer the provisions of sections 35 to 45 of this title and to utilize such Federal officers and employees and, with the consent of the State, such State and local officers and employees as he may find necessary to assist in the administration of said sections and to prescribe rules and regulations with respect thereto. The Secretary shall appoint, subject to chapter 51 and subchapter III of chapter 53 of Title 5, an administrative officer, and such attorneys and experts, and other employees with regard to existing laws applicable to the employment and compensation of officers and employees of the United States, as he may from time to time find necessary for the administration of sections 35 to 45 of this title. The Secretary of Labor or his authorized representatives shall have power to make investigations and findings as provided in sections 35 to 45 of this title, and prosecute any inquiry necessary to his functions in any part of the United States. The Secretary of Labor shall have authority from time to time to make, amend, and rescind such rules and regulations as may be necessary to carry out the provisions of sections 35 to 45 of this title.

Sec. 39. Hearings on Walsh-Healey provisions by Secretary of Labor; witness fees; failure to obey order; punishment

Upon his own motion or on application of any person affected by any ruling of any agency of the United States in relation to any proposal or contract involving any of the provisions of sections 35 to 45 of this title, and on complaint of a breach or violation of any representation or stipulation as provided in said sections, the Secretary of Labor, or an impartial representative designated by him, shall have the power to hold hearings and to issue orders requiring the attendance and testimony of witnesses and the production of evidence under oath. Witnesses shall be paid the same fees and mileage that are paid witnesses in the courts of the United States. In case of contumacy, failure, or refusal of any person to obey such an order, any District Court of the United States or of any Territory or possession within the jurisdiction of which the inquiry is carried on, or within the jurisdiction of which said person who is guilty of contumacy, failure, or refusal is found, or resides or transacts business, upon the application by the Secretary of Labor or representative designated by him, shall have jurisdiction to issue to such person an order requiring such person to appear before

him or representative designated by him, to produce evidence if, as, and when so ordered, and to give testimony relating to the matter under investigation or in question; and any failure to obey such order of the court may be punished by said court as a contempt thereof; and shall make findings of fact after notice and hearing, which findings shall be conclusive upon all agencies of the United States, and if supported by the preponderance of the evidence, shall be conclusive in any court of the United States; and the Secretary of Labor or authorized representative shall have the power, and is authorized, to make such decisions, based upon findings of fact, as are deemed to be necessary to enforce the provisions of sections 35 to 45 of this title.

Sec. 40. Exceptions from Walsh-Healey provisions; modification of contracts; variations; overtime; suspension of representations and stipulations

Upon a written finding by the head of the contracting agency or department that the inclusion in the proposal or contract of the representations or stipulations set forth in section 35 of this title will seriously impair the conduct of Government business, the Secretary of Labor shall make exceptions in specific cases or otherwise when justice or public interest will be served thereby. Upon the joint recommendation of the contracting agency and the contractor, the Secretary of Labor may modify the terms of an existing contract respecting minimum rates of pay and maximum hours of labor as he may find necessary and proper in the public interest or to prevent injustice and undue hardship. The Secretary of Labor may provide reasonable limitations and may make rules and regulations allowing reasonable variations, tolerances, and exemptions to and from any or all provisions of sections 35 to 45 of this title respecting minimum rates of pay and maximum hours of labor or the extent of the application of said sections to contractors, as hereinbefore described. Whenever the Secretary of Labor shall permit an increase in the maximum hours of labor stipulated in the contract, he shall set a rate of pay for any overtime, which rate shall be not less than one and one-half times the basic hourly rate received by any employee affected: *Provided*, That whenever in his judgment such course is in the public interest, the President is authorized to suspend any or all of the representations and stipulations contained in section 35 of this title.

Sec. 41. "Person" defined in Walsh-Healey provisions

Whenever used in sections 35 to 45 of this title, the word "person" includes one or more individuals, partnerships, associations, corporations, legal representatives, trustees, trustees in cases under Title 11, or receivers.

Sec. 42. Effect of Walsh-Healey provisions on other laws

The provisions of sections 35 to 45 of this title shall not be construed to modify or amend Title III of the act entitled "An Act making appropriations for the Treasury and Post Office Departments for the fiscal year ending June 30, 1934, and for other purposes", approved May 3, 1933 (commonly known as the Buy American Act) (41 U.S.C. §10a et seq.), nor shall the provisions of sections 35 to 45 of this title be construed to modify or amend the Act entitled "An Act relating to the rate of wages for laborers and mechanics employed on public buildings of the United States and the District of Columbia by contractors and subcontractors, and for other purposes", approved March 3, 1931 (commonly known as the Bacon-Davis Act), as amended from time to time (40 U.S.C. §276a et seq.), nor the labor provisions of Title II of the National Industrial Recovery Act, approved June 16, 1933, as extended, or of section 7 of the Emergency Relief Appropriation Act, approved April 8, 1935; nor shall the provisions of sections 35 to 45 of this title be construed to modify or amend chapter 307 and section 4162 of Title 18.

Sec. 43. Walsh-Healey provisions not applicable to certain contracts

Sections 35 to 45 of this title shall not apply to purchases of such materials, supplies, articles, or equipment as may usually be bought in the open market; nor shall they apply to perishables, including dairy, livestock and nursery products, or to agricultural or farm products processed for first sale by the original producers; nor to any contracts made by the Secretary of Agriculture for the purchase of agricultural commodities or the products thereof. Nothing in said sections shall be construed to apply to carriage of freight or personnel by vessel, airplane, bus, truck, express, or railway line where published tariff rates are in effect or to

common carriers subject to the Communications Act of 1934 (47 U.S.C. §151 et seq.).

Sec. 43a. Administrative procedure provisions

(a) Applicability

Notwithstanding any provision of section 553 of Title 5, subchapter II of chapter 5, and chapter 7, of Title 5 shall be applicable in the administration of sections 35 to 39 and 41 to 43 of this title.

(b) Wage determination; administrative review

All wage determinations under section 35(a) of this title shall be made on the record after opportunity for a hearing. Review of any such wage determination, or of the applicability of any such wage determination, may be had within ninety days after such determination is made in the manner provided in chapter 7 of Title 5 by any person adversely affected or aggrieved thereby, who shall be deemed to include any supplier of materials, supplies, articles or equipment purchased or to be purchased by the Government from any source, who is in any industry to which such wage determination is applicable.

(c) Judicial review

Notwithstanding the inclusion of any stipulations required by any provision of sections 35 to 45 of this title in any contract subject to said sections, any interested person shall have the right of judicial review of any legal question which might otherwise be raised, including, but not limited to, wage determinations and the interpretation of the terms "locality" and "open market".

Sec. 43b. Manufacturers and regular dealers

(a) Secretary of Labor to determine

The Secretary of Labor may prescribe in regulations the standards for determining whether a contractor is a manufacturer of or a regular dealer in materials, supplies, articles, or equipment to be manufactured or used in the performance of a contract entered into by any executive department, independent establishment, or other agency or instrumentality of the United States, or by the District of Columbia, or by any corporation all the stock of which is beneficially owned by the United States, for the manufacture or furnishing of materials, supplies, articles, and equipment.

(b) Judicial review

Any interested person shall have the right of judicial review of any legal question regarding the interpretation of the terms "regular dealer" and "manufacturer", as defined pursuant to subsection (a) of this section.

Sec. 44. Separability of Walsh-Healey provisions

If any provision of sections 35 to 45 of this title, or the application thereof to any persons or circumstances, is held invalid, the remainder of said sections, and the application of such provisions to other persons or circumstances, shall not be affected thereby.

Sec. 45. Effective date of Walsh-Healey provisions; exception as to representations with respect to minimum wages

Sections 35 to 45 of this title shall apply to all contracts entered into pursuant to invitations for bids issued on or after ninety days from June 30, 1936: *Provided, however,* That the provisions requiring the inclusion of representations with respect to minimum wages shall apply only to purchases or contracts relating to such industries as have been the subject matter of a determination by the Secretary of Labor.

Drug-Free Workplace Act

U.S. Code, Title 41, Sections 701 to 707

DRUG-FREE WORKPLACE ACT IN A NUTSHELL

Enacted: 1988

Purpose: To encourage employee anti-drug programs

Coverage: Persons and employers who are awarded contracts by the federal government for the procurement of property or services in an amount greater than $100,000 and federal grantees

Sec. 701. Drug-free workplace requirements for Federal contractors

(a) Drug-free workplace requirement

(1) Requirement for persons other than individuals

No person, other than an individual, shall be considered a responsible source, under the meaning of such term as defined in section 403(8) of this title, for the purposes of being awarded a contract for the procurement of any property or services of a value greater than the simplified acquisition threshold (as defined in section 403(11) of this title) by any Federal agency, other than a contract for the procurement of commercial items as defined in section 403(12) of this title, unless such person agrees to provide a drug-free workplace by —

(A) publishing a statement notifying employees that the unlawful manufacture, distribution, dispensation, possession, or use of a controlled substance is prohibited in the person's workplace and specifying the actions that will be taken against employees for violations of such prohibition;

(B) establishing a drug-free awareness program to inform employees about —

(i) the dangers of drug abuse in the workplace;

(ii) the person's policy of maintaining a drug-free workplace;

(iii) any available drug counseling, rehabilitation, and employee assistance programs; and

(iv) the penalties that may be imposed upon employees for drug abuse violations;

(C) making it a requirement that each employee to be engaged in the performance of such contract be given a copy of the statement required by subparagraph (A);

(D) notifying the employee in the statement required by subparagraph (A), that as a condition of employment on such contract, the employee will —

(i) abide by the terms of the statement; and

[215]

(ii) notify the employer of any criminal drug statute conviction for a violation occurring in the workplace no later than 5 days after such conviction;

(E) notifying the contracting agency within 10 days after receiving notice under subparagraph (D)(ii) from an employee or otherwise receiving actual notice of such conviction;

(F) imposing a sanction on, or requiring the satisfactory participation in a drug abuse assistance or rehabilitation program by, any employee who is so convicted, as required by section 703 of this title; and

(G) making a good faith effort to continue to maintain a drug-free workplace through implementation of subparagraphs (A), (B), (C), (D), (E), and (F).

(2) Requirement for individuals

No Federal agency shall enter into a contract with an individual unless such individual agrees that the individual will not engage in the unlawful manufacture, distribution, dispensation, possession, or use of a controlled substance in the performance of the contract.

(b) Suspension, termination, or debarment of contractor

(1) Grounds for suspension, termination, or debarment

Each contract awarded by a Federal agency shall be subject to suspension of payments under the contract or termination of the contract, or both, and the contractor thereunder or the individual who entered the contract with the Federal agency, as applicable, shall be subject to suspension or debarment in accordance with the requirements of this section if the head of the agency determines that —

(A) the contractor violates the requirements of subparagraph (A), (B), (C), (D), (E), or (F) of subsection (a)(1) of this section; or

(B) such a number of employees of such contractor have been convicted of violations of criminal drug statutes for violations occurring in the workplace as to indicate that the contractor has failed to make a good faith effort to provide a drug-free workplace as required by subsection (a) of this section.

(2) Conduct of suspension, termination, and debarment proceedings

(A) If a contracting officer determines, in writing, that cause for suspension of payments, termination, or suspension or debarment exists, an appropriate action shall be initiated by a contracting officer of the agency, to be conducted by the agency concerned in accordance with the Federal Acquisition Regulation and applicable agency procedures.

(B) The Federal Acquisition Regulation shall be revised to include rules for conducting suspension and debarment proceedings under this subsection, including rules providing notice, opportunity to respond in writing or in person, and such other procedures as may be necessary to provide a full and fair proceeding to a contractor or individual in such proceeding.

(3) Effect of debarment

Upon issuance of any final decision under this subsection requiring debarment of a contractor or individual, such contractor or individual shall be ineligible for award of any contract by any Federal agency, and for participation in any future procurement by any Federal agency, for a period specified in the decision, not to exceed 5 years.

Sec. 702. Drug-free workplace requirements for Federal grant recipients

(a) Drug-free workplace requirement

(1) Persons other than individuals

No person, other than an individual, shall receive a grant from any Federal agency unless such person agrees to provide a drug-free workplace by —

(A) publishing a statement notifying employees that the unlawful manufacture, distribution, dispensation, possession, or use of a controlled substance is prohibited in the grantee's workplace and specifying the actions that will be taken against employees for violations of such prohibition;

(B) establishing a drug-free awareness program to inform employees about —

(i) the dangers of drug abuse in the workplace;

(ii) the grantee's policy of maintaining a drug-free workplace;

(iii) any available drug counseling, rehabilitation, and employee assistance programs; and

(iv) the penalties that may be imposed upon employees for drug abuse violations;

(C) making it a requirement that each employee to be engaged in the performance of such grant be given a copy of the statement required by subparagraph (A);

(D) notifying the employee in the statement required by subparagraph (A), that as a condition of employment in such grant, the employee will —

(i) abide by the terms of the statement; and

(ii) notify the employer of any criminal drug statute conviction for a violation occurring in the workplace no later than 5 days after such conviction;

(E) notifying the granting agency within 10 days after receiving notice of a conviction under subparagraph (D)(ii) from an employee or otherwise receiving actual notice of such conviction;

(F) imposing a sanction on, or requiring the satisfactory participation in a drug abuse assistance or rehabilitation program by, any employee who is so convicted, as required by section 703 of this title; and

(G) making a good faith effort to continue to maintain a drug-free workplace through implementation of subparagraphs (A), (B), (C), (D), (E), and (F).

(2) Individuals

No Federal agency shall make a grant to any individual unless such individual agrees as a condition of such grant that the individual will not engage in the unlawful manufacture, distribution, dispensation, possession, or use of a controlled substance in conducting any activity with such grant.

(b) Suspension, termination, or debarment of grantee

(1) Grounds for suspension, termination, or debarment

Each grant awarded by a Federal agency shall be subject to suspension of payments under the grant or termination of the grant, or both, and the grantee

thereunder shall be subject to suspension or debarment, in accordance with the requirements of this section if the agency head of the granting agency or his official designee determines, in writing, that —

(A) the grantee violates the requirements of subparagraph (A), (B), (C), (D), (E), (F), or (G) of subsection (a)(1) of this section; or

(B) such a number of employees of such grantee have been convicted of violations of criminal drug statutes for violations occurring in the workplace as to indicate that the grantee has failed to make a good faith effort to provide a drug-free workplace as required by subsection (a)(1) of this section.

(2) Conduct of suspension, termination, and debarment proceedings

A suspension of payments, termination, or suspension or debarment proceeding subject to this subsection shall be conducted in accordance with applicable law, including Executive Order 12549 or any superseding Executive order and any regulations promulgated to implement such law or Executive order.

(3) Effect of debarment

Upon issuance of any final decision under this subsection requiring debarment of a grantee, such grantee shall be ineligible for award of any grant from any Federal agency and for participation in any future grant from any Federal agency for a period specified in the decision, not to exceed 5 years.

Sec. 703. Employee sanctions and remedies

A grantee or contractor shall, within 30 days after receiving notice from an employee of a conviction pursuant to section 701(a)(1)(D)(ii) or 702(a)(1)(D)(ii) of this title —

(1) take appropriate personnel action against such employee up to and including termination; or

(2) require such employee to satisfactorily participate in a drug abuse assistance or rehabilitation program approved for such purposes by a Federal, State, or local health, law enforcement, or other appropriate agency.

Sec. 704. Waiver

(a) In general

A termination, suspension of payments, or suspension or debarment under this chapter may be waived by the head of an agency with respect to a particular contract or grant if —

(1) in the case of a waiver with respect to a contract, the head of the agency determines under section 701(b)(1) of this title, after the issuance of a final determination under such section, that suspension of payments, or termination of the contract, or suspension or debarment of the contractor, or refusal to permit a person to be treated as a responsible source for a contract, as the case may be, would severely disrupt the operation of such agency to the detriment of the Federal Government or the general public; or

(2) in the case of a waiver with respect to a grant, the head of the agency determines that suspension of payments, termination of the grant, or suspension or debarment of the grantee would not be in the public interest.

(b) Exclusive authority

The authority of the head of an agency under this section to waive a termination, suspension, or debarment shall not be delegated.

Sec. 705. Regulations

Not later than 90 days after November 18, 1988, the governmentwide regulations governing actions under this chapter shall be issued pursuant to the Office of Federal Procurement Policy Act (41 U.S.C. 401 et seq.).

Sec. 706. Definitions

For purposes of this chapter —

(1) the term "drug-free workplace" means a site for the performance of work done in connection with a specific grant or contract described in section 701 or 702 of this title of an entity at which employees of such entity are prohibited from engaging in the unlawful manufacture, distribution, dispensation, possession, or use of a controlled substance in accordance with the requirements of this Act;

(2) the term "employee" means the employee of a grantee or contractor directly engaged in the performance of work pursuant to the provisions of the grant or contract described in section 701 or 702 of this title;

(3) the term "controlled substance" means a controlled substance in schedules I through V of section 812 of Title 21;

(4) the term "conviction" means a finding of guilt (including a plea of nolo contendere) or imposition of sentence, or both, by any judicial body charged with the responsibility to determine violations of the Federal or State criminal drug statutes;

(5) the term "criminal drug statute" means a criminal statute involving manufacture, distribution, dispensation, use, or possession of any controlled substance;

(6) the term "grantee" means the department, division, or other unit of a person responsible for the performance under the grant;

(7) the term "contractor" means the department, division, or other unit of a person responsible for the performance under the contract; and

(8) the term "Federal agency" means an agency as that term is defined in section 552(f) of Title 5.

Sec. 707. Construction of chapter

Nothing in this chapter shall be construed to require law enforcement agencies, if the head of the agency determines it would be inappropriate in connection with the agency's undercover operations, to comply with the provisions of this chapter.

Title VII of the Civil Rights Act of 1964

U.S. Code, Title 42, Sections 2000e to 2000e-17

TITLE VII IN A NUTSHELL

Enacted: 1964

Purpose: To prevent employment discrimination on the basis of race, color, gender, nationality, or religion.

Coverage: Private sector employers with 15 or more employees, public agencies, employment agencies, labor unions with 25 or more members

Responsible agency: Equal Employment Opportunity Commission

Sec. 2000e. Definitions

For the purposes of this subchapter —

(a) The term "person" includes one or more individuals, governments, governmental agencies, political subdivisions, labor unions, partnerships, associations, corporations, legal representatives, mutual companies, joint-stock companies, trusts, unincorporated organizations, trustees, trustees in cases under Title 11, or receivers.

(b) The term "employer" means a person engaged in an industry affecting commerce who has fifteen or more employees for each working day in each of twenty or more calendar weeks in the current or preceding calendar year, and any agent of such a person, but such term does not include (1) the United States, a corporation wholly owned by the Government of the United States, an Indian tribe, or any department or agency of the District of Columbia subject by statute to procedures of the competitive service (as defined in section 2102 of Title 5), or (2) a bona fide private membership club (other than a labor organization) which is exempt from taxation under section 501(c) of Title 26, except that during the first year after March 24, 1972, persons having fewer than twenty-five employees (and their agents) shall not be considered employers.

(c) The term "employment agency" means any person regularly undertaking with or without compensation to procure employees for an employer or to procure for employees opportunities to work for an employer and includes an agent of such a person.

(d) The term "labor organization" means a labor organization engaged in an industry affecting commerce, and any agent of such an organization, and includes any organization of any kind, any agency, or employee representation committee, group, association, or plan so engaged in which employees participate and which exists for the purpose, in whole or in part, of dealing with employers concerning grievances, labor disputes, wages, rates of pay, hours, or other terms or conditions of employment, and any conference, general committee, joint or system board, or joint council so engaged which is subordinate to a national or international labor organization.

(e) A labor organization shall be deemed to be engaged in an industry affecting commerce if (1) it maintains or operates a hiring hall or hiring office which procures employees for an employer or procures for employees opportunities to work for an employer, or (2) the number of its members (or, where it is a labor organization composed of other labor organizations or their representatives, if the aggregate number of the members of such other labor organization) is (A) twenty-five or more during the first year after March 24, 1972, or (B) fifteen or more thereafter, and such labor organization —

(1) is the certified representative of employees under the provisions of the National Labor Relations Act, as amended (29 U.S.C. §151 et seq.), or the Railway Labor Act, as amended (45 U.S.C. §151 et seq.);

(2) although not certified, is a national or international labor organization or a local labor organization recognized or acting as the representative of employees of an employer or employers engaged in an industry affecting commerce; or

(3) has chartered a local labor organization or subsidiary body which is representing or actively seeking to represent employees of employers within the meaning of paragraph (1) or (2); or

(4) has been chartered by a labor organization representing or actively seeking to represent employees within the meaning of paragraph (1) or (2) as the local or subordinate body through which such employees may enjoy membership or become affiliated with such labor organization; or

(5) is a conference, general committee, joint or system board, or joint council subordinate to a national or international labor organization, which includes a labor organization engaged in an industry affecting commerce within the meaning of any of the preceding paragraphs of this subsection.

(f) The term "employee" means an individual employed by an employer, except that the term "employee" shall not include any person elected to public office in any State or political subdivision of any State by the qualified voters thereof, or any person chosen by such officer to be on such officer's personal staff, or an appointee on the policy making level or an immediate adviser with respect to the exercise of the constitutional or legal powers of the office. The exemption set forth in the preceding sentence shall not include employees subject to the civil service laws of a State government, governmental agency or political subdivision. With respect to employment in a foreign country, such term includes an individual who is a citizen of the United States.

(g) The term "commerce" means trade, traffic, commerce, transportation, transmission, or communication among the several States; or between a State and any place outside thereof; or within the District of Columbia, or a possession of the United States; or between points in the same State but through a point outside thereof.

(h) The term "industry affecting commerce" means any activity, business, or industry in commerce or in which a labor dispute would hinder or obstruct commerce or the free flow of commerce and includes any activity or industry "affecting commerce" within the meaning of the Labor-Management Reporting and Disclosure Act of 1959 (29 U.S.C. §401 et seq.), and further includes any governmental industry, business, or activity.

(i) The term "State" includes a State of the United States, the District of Columbia, Puerto Rico, the Virgin Islands, American Samoa, Guam, Wake Island, the Canal Zone, and Outer Continental Shelf lands defined in the Outer Continental Shelf Lands Act (43 U.S.C. §1331 et seq.).

(j) The term "religion" includes all aspects of religious observance and practice, as well as belief, unless an employer demonstrates that he is unable to reasonably accommodate to an employee's or prospective employee's religious observance or practice without undue hardship on the conduct of the employer's business.

(k) The terms "because of sex" or "on the basis of sex" include, but are not limited to, because of or on the basis of pregnancy, childbirth, or related medical conditions; and women affected by pregnancy, childbirth, or related medical conditions shall be treated the same for all employment-related purposes, including receipt of benefits under fringe benefit programs, as other persons not so affected but similar in their ability or inability to work, and nothing in section 2000e-2(h) of this title shall be interpreted to permit otherwise. This subsection shall not require an employer to pay for health insurance benefits for abortion, except where the life of the mother would be endangered if the fetus were carried to term, or except where medical complications have arisen from an abortion: *Provided*, That nothing herein shall preclude an employer from providing abortion benefits or otherwise affect bargaining agreements in regard to abortion.

(*l*) The term "complaining party" means the Commission, the Attorney General, or a person who may bring an action or proceeding under this subchapter.

(m) The term "demonstrates" means meets the burdens of production and persuasion.

(n) The term "respondent" means an employer, employment agency, labor organization, joint labor-management committee controlling apprenticeship or other training or retraining program,

including an on-the-job training program, or Federal entity subject to section 2000e-16 of this title.

Sec. 2000e-1. Applicability to foreign and religious employment

(a) Inapplicability of subchapter to certain aliens and employees of religious entities

This subchapter shall not apply to an employer with respect to the employment of aliens outside any State, or to a religious corporation, association, educational institution, or society with respect to the employment of individuals of a particular religion to perform work connected with the carrying on by such corporation, association, educational institution, or society of its activities.

(b) Compliance with statute as violative of foreign law

It shall not be unlawful under section 2000e-2 or 2000e-3 of this title for an employer (or a corporation controlled by an employer), labor organization, employment agency, or joint labor-management committee controlling apprenticeship or other training or retraining (including on-the-job training programs) to take any action otherwise prohibited by such section, with respect to an employee in a workplace in a foreign country if compliance with such section would cause such employer (or such corporation), such organization, such agency, or such committee to violate the law of the foreign country in which such workplace is located.

(c) Control of corporation incorporated in foreign country

(1) If an employer controls a corporation whose place of incorporation is a foreign country, any practice prohibited by section 2000e-2 or 2000e-3 of this title engaged in by such corporation shall be presumed to be engaged in by such employer.

(2) Sections 2000e-2 and 2000e-3 of this title shall not apply with respect to the foreign operations of an employer that is a foreign person not controlled by an American employer.

(3) For purposes of this subsection, the determination of whether an employer controls a corporation shall be based on —

(A) the interrelation of operations;

(B) the common management;

(C) the centralized control of labor relations; and

(D) the common ownership or financial control,

of the employer and the corporation.

Sec. 2000e-2. Unlawful employment practices

(a) Employer practices

It shall be an unlawful employment practice for an employer —

(1) to fail or refuse to hire or to discharge any individual, or otherwise to discriminate against any individual with respect to his compensation, terms, conditions, or privileges of employment, because of such individual's race, color, religion, sex, or national origin; or

(2) to limit, segregate, or classify his employees or applicants for employment in any way which would deprive or tend to deprive any individual of employment opportunities or otherwise adversely affect his status as an employee, because of such individual's race, color, religion, sex, or national origin.

(b) Employment agency practices

It shall be an unlawful employment practice for an employment agency to fail or refuse to refer for employment, or otherwise to discriminate against, any individual because of his race, color, religion, sex, or national origin, or to classify or refer for employment any individual on the basis of his race, color, religion, sex, or national origin.

(c) Labor organization practices

It shall be an unlawful employment practice for a labor organization —

(1) to exclude or to expel from its membership, or otherwise to discriminate against, any individual because of his race, color, religion, sex, or national origin;

(2) to limit, segregate, or classify its membership or applicants for membership, or to classify or fail or refuse to refer for employment any individual, in any way which would deprive or tend to deprive any individual of employment opportuni-

ties, or would limit such employment opportunities or otherwise adversely affect his status as an employee or as an applicant for employment, because of such individual's race, color, religion, sex, or national origin; or

(3) to cause or attempt to cause an employer to discriminate against an individual in violation of this section.

(d) Training programs

It shall be an unlawful employment practice for any employer, labor organization, or joint labor-management committee controlling apprenticeship or other training or retraining, including on-the-job training programs to discriminate against any individual because of his race, color, religion, sex, or national origin in admission to, or employment in, any program established to provide apprenticeship or other training.

(e) Businesses or enterprises with personnel qualified on basis of religion, sex, or national origin; educational institutions with personnel of particular religion

Notwithstanding any other provision of this subchapter, (1) it shall not be an unlawful employment practice for an employer to hire and employ employees, for an employment agency to classify, or refer for employment any individual, for a labor organization to classify its membership or to classify or refer for employment any individual, or for an employer, labor organization, or joint labor-management committee controlling apprenticeship or other training or retraining programs to admit or employ any individual in any such program, on the basis of his religion, sex, or national origin in those certain instances where religion, sex, or national origin is a bona fide occupational qualification reasonably necessary to the normal operation of that particular business or enterprise, and (2) it shall not be an unlawful employment practice for a school, college, university, or other educational institution or institution of learning to hire and employ employees of a particular religion if such school, college, university, or other educational institution or institution of learning is, in whole or in substantial part, owned, supported, controlled, or managed by a particular religion or by a particular religious corporation, association, or society, or if the curriculum of such school, college, university, or other educational institution or institution of learning is directed toward the propagation of a particular religion.

(f) Members of Communist Party or Communist-action or Communist-front organizations

As used in this subchapter, the phrase "unlawful employment practice" shall not be deemed to include any action or measure taken by an employer, labor organization, joint labor-management committee, or employment agency with respect to an individual who is a member of the Communist Party of the United States or of any other organization required to register as a Communist-action or Communist-front organization by final order of the Subversive Activities Control Board pursuant to the Subversive Activities Control Act of 1950 (50 U.S.C. §781 et seq.).

(g) National security

Notwithstanding any other provision of this subchapter, it shall not be an unlawful employment practice for an employer to fail or refuse to hire and employ any individual for any position, for an employer to discharge any individual from any position, or for an employment agency to fail or refuse to refer any individual for employment in any position, or for a labor organization to fail or refuse to refer any individual for employment in any position, if ——

(1) the occupancy of such position, or access to the premises in or upon which any part of the duties of such position is performed or is to be performed, is subject to any requirement imposed in the interest of the national security of the United States under any security program in effect pursuant to or administered under any statute of the United States or any Executive order of the President; and

(2) such individual has not fulfilled or has ceased to fulfill that requirement.

(h) Seniority or merit system; quantity or quality of production; ability tests; compensation based on sex and authorized by minimum wage provisions

Notwithstanding any other provision of this subchapter, it shall not be an unlawful employment practice for an employer to apply different standards of compensation, or different terms, condi-tions, or privileges of employment pursuant to a bona fide seniority or merit system, or a system which measures earnings by quantity or quality of production or to employees who work in different locations, provided that such differences are not the result of an intention to discriminate because of race, color, religion, sex, or national origin, nor shall it be an unlawful employment practice for an employer to give and to act upon the results of any professionally developed ability test provided that such test, its administration or action upon the results is not designed, intended or used to discriminate because of race, color, religion, sex or national origin. It shall not be an unlawful employment practice under this subchapter for any employer to differentiate upon the basis of sex in determining the amount of the wages or compensation paid or to be paid to employees of such employer if such differentiation is authorized by the provisions of section 206(d) of Title 29.

(i) Businesses or enterprises extending preferential treatment to Indians

Nothing contained in this subchapter shall apply to any business or enterprise on or near an Indian reservation with respect to any publicly announced employment practice of such business or enterprise under which a preferential treatment is given to any individual because he is an Indian living on or near a reservation.

(j) Preferential treatment not to be granted on account of existing number or percentage imbalance

Nothing contained in this subchapter shall be interpreted to require any employer, employment agency, labor organization, or joint labor-management committee subject to this subchapter to grant preferential treatment to any individual or to any group because of the race, color, religion, sex, or national origin of such individual or group on account of an imbalance which may exist with respect to the total number or percentage of persons of any race, color, religion, sex, or national origin employed by any employer, referred or classified for employment by any employment agency or labor organization, admitted to membership or classified by any labor organization, or admitted to, or employed in, any apprenticeship or other training program, in comparison with the total number or percentage of persons of such race, color, religion, sex, or national origin in any community, State, section, or other area, or in the available work force in any community, State, section, or other area.

(k) Burden of proof in disparate impact cases

(1)(A) An unlawful employment practice based on disparate impact is established under this subchapter only if —

(i) a complaining party demonstrates that a respondent uses a particular employment practice that causes a disparate impact on the basis of race, color, religion, sex, or national origin and the respondent fails to demonstrate that the challenged practice is job related for the position in question and consistent with business necessity; or

(ii) the complaining party makes the demonstration described in subparagraph (C) with respect to an alternative employment practice and the respondent refuses to adopt such alternative employment practice.

(B)(i) With respect to demonstrating that a particular employment practice causes a disparate impact as described in subparagraph (A)(i), the complaining party shall demonstrate that each particular challenged employment practice causes a disparate impact, except that if the complaining party can demonstrate to the court that the elements of a respondent's decisionmaking process are not capable of separation for analysis, the decisionmaking process may be analyzed as one employment practice.

(ii) If the respondent demonstrates that a specific employment practice does not cause the disparate impact, the respondent shall not be required to demonstrate that such practice is required by business necessity.

(C) The demonstration referred to by subparagraph (A)(ii) shall be in accordance with the law as it existed on June 4, 1989, with respect to the concept of "alternative employment practice".

(2) A demonstration that an employment practice is required by business necessity may not be used as a defense against a claim of intentional discrimination under this subchapter.

(3) Notwithstanding any other provision of this subchapter, a rule barring the employment of an individual who currently and knowingly uses or possesses a controlled substance, as defined in schedules I and II of section 102(6) of the Controlled Substances Act (21 U.S.C. §802(6)), other than the use or possession of a drug taken under the supervision of a licensed health care professional, or any other use or possession authorized by the Controlled Substances Act (21 U.S.C. §801 et seq.) or any other provision of Federal law, shall be considered an unlawful employment practice under this subchapter only if such rule is adopted or applied with an intent to discriminate because of race, color, religion, sex, or national origin.

(l) Prohibition of discriminatory use of test scores

It shall be an unlawful employment practice for a respondent, in connection with the selection or referral of applicants or candidates for employment or promotion, to adjust the scores of, use different cutoff scores for, or otherwise alter the results of, employment related tests on the basis of race, color, religion, sex, or national origin.

(m) Impermissible consideration of race, color, religion, sex, or national origin in employment practices

Except as otherwise provided in this subchapter, an unlawful employment practice is established when the complaining party demonstrates that race, color, religion, sex, or national origin was a motivating factor for any employment practice, even though other factors also motivated the practice.

(n) Resolution of challenges to employment practices implementing litigated or consent judgments or orders

(1)(A) Notwithstanding any other provision of law, and except as provided in paragraph (2), an employment practice that implements and is within the scope of a litigated or consent judgment or order that resolves a claim of employment discrimination under the Constitution or Federal civil rights laws may not be challenged under the circumstances described in subparagraph (B).

(B) A practice described in subparagraph (A) may not be challenged in a claim under the Constitution or Federal civil rights laws —

(i) by a person who, prior to the entry of the judgment or order described in subparagraph (A), had —

(I) actual notice of the proposed judgment or order sufficient to apprise such person that such judgment or order might adversely affect the interests and legal rights of such person and that an opportunity was available to present objections to such judgment or order by a future date certain; and

(II) a reasonable opportunity to present objections to such judgment or order; or

(ii) by a person whose interests were adequately represented by another person who had previously challenged the judgment or order on the same legal grounds and with a similar factual situation, unless there has been an intervening change in law or fact.

(2) Nothing in this subsection shall be construed to —

(A) alter the standards for intervention under rule 24 of the Federal Rules of Civil Procedure or apply to the rights of parties who have successfully intervened pursuant to such rule in the proceeding in which the parties intervened;

(B) apply to the rights of parties to the action in which a litigated or consent judgment or order was entered, or of members of a class represented or sought to be represented in such action, or of members of a group on whose behalf relief was sought in such action by the Federal Government;

(C) prevent challenges to a litigated or consent judgment or order on the ground that such judgment or order was obtained through collusion or fraud, or is transparently invalid or was entered by a court lacking subject matter jurisdiction; or

(D) authorize or permit the denial to any person of the due process of law required by the Constitution.

(3) Any action not precluded under this subsection that challenges an employment consent judgment or order described in paragraph (1)

shall be brought in the court, and if possible before the judge, that entered such judgment or order. Nothing in this subsection shall preclude a transfer of such action pursuant to section 1404 of Title 28.

Sec. 2000e-3. Other unlawful employment practices

(a) Discrimination for making charges, testifying, assisting, or participating in enforcement proceedings

It shall be an unlawful employment practice for an employer to discriminate against any of his employees or applicants for employment, for an employment agency, or joint labor-management committee controlling apprenticeship or other training or retraining, including on-the-job training programs, to discriminate against any individual, or for a labor organization to discriminate against any member thereof or applicant for membership, because he has opposed any practice made an unlawful employment practice by this subchapter, or because he has made a charge, testified, assisted, or participated in any manner in an investigation, proceeding, or hearing under this subchapter.

(b) Printing or publication of notices or advertisements indicating prohibited preference, limitation, specification, or discrimination; occupational qualification exception

It shall be an unlawful employment practice for an employer, labor organization, employment agency, or joint labor-management committee controlling apprenticeship or other training or retraining, including on-the-job training programs, to print or publish or cause to be printed or published any notice or advertisement relating to employment by such an employer or membership in or any classification or referral for employment by such a labor organization, or relating to any classification or referral for employment by such an employment agency, or relating to admission to, or employment in, any program established to provide apprenticeship or other training by such a joint labor-management committee, indicating any preference, limitation, specification, or discrimination, based on race, color, religion, sex, or national origin, except that such a notice or advertisement may indicate a preference, limitation, specification, or discrimination based on religion, sex, or national origin when religion, sex, national origin is a bona fide occupational qualification for employment.

Sec. 2000e-4. Equal Employment Opportunity Commission

(a) Creation; composition; political representation; appointment; term; vacancies; Chairman and Vice Chairman; duties of Chairman; appointment of personnel; compensation of personnel

There is hereby created a Commission to be known as the Equal Employment Opportunity Commission, which shall be composed of five members, not more than three of whom shall be members of the same political party. Members of the Commission shall be appointed by the President by and with the advice and consent of the Senate for a term of five years. Any individual chosen to fill a vacancy shall be appointed only for the unexpired term of the member whom he shall succeed, and all members of the Commission shall continue to serve until their successors are appointed and qualified, except that no such member of the Commission shall continue to serve (1) for more than sixty days when the Congress is in session unless a nomination to fill such vacancy shall have been submitted to the Senate, or (2) after the adjournment sine die of the session of the Senate in which such nomination was submitted. The President shall designate one member to serve as Chairman of the Commission, and one member to serve as Vice Chairman. The Chairman shall be responsible on behalf of the Commission for the administrative operations of the Commission, and, except as provided in subsection (b) of this section, shall appoint, in accordance with the provisions of Title 5 governing appointments in the competitive service, such officers, agents, attorneys, administrative law judges, and employees as he deems necessary to assist it in the performance of its functions and to fix their compensation in accordance with the provisions of chapter 51 and subchapter III of chapter 53 of Title 5, relating to classification and General Schedule pay rates: *Provided,* That assignment, removal, and compensation of administrative law judges shall be in accordance with sections 3105, 3344, 5372, and 7521 of Title 5.

(b) General Counsel; appointment; term; duties; representation by attorneys and Attorney General

(1) There shall be a General Counsel of the Commission appointed by the President, by and with the advice and consent of the Senate, for a term of four years. The General Counsel shall have responsibility for the conduct of litigation as provided in sections 2000e-5 and 2000e-6 of this Title. The General Counsel shall have such other duties as the Commission may prescribe or as may be provided by law and shall concur with the Chairman of the Commission on the appointment and supervision of regional attorneys. The General Counsel of the Commission on the effective date of this Act shall continue in such position and perform the functions specified in this subsection until a successor is appointed and qualified.

(2) Attorneys appointed under this section may, at the direction of the Commission, appear for and represent the Commission in any case in court, provided that the Attorney General shall conduct all litigation to which the Commission is a party in the Supreme Court pursuant to this subchapter.

(c) Exercise of powers during vacancy; quorum

A vacancy in the Commission shall not impair the right of the remaining members to exercise all the powers of the Commission and three members thereof shall constitute a quorum.

(d) Seal; judicial notice

The Commission shall have an official seal which shall be judicially noticed.

(e) Reports to Congress and the President

The Commission shall at the close of each fiscal year report to the Congress and to the President concerning the action it has taken and the moneys it has disbursed. It shall make such further reports on the cause of and means of eliminating discrimination and such recommendations for further legislation as may appear desirable.

(f) Principal and other offices

The principal office of the Commission shall be in or near the District of Columbia, but it may meet or exercise any or all its powers at any other place. The Commission may establish such regional or State offices as it deems necessary to accomplish the purpose of this subchapter.

(g) Powers of Commission

The Commission shall have power —

(1) to cooperate with and, with their consent, utilize regional, State, local, and other agencies, both public and private, and individuals;

(2) to pay to witnesses whose depositions are taken or who are summoned before the Commission or any of its agents the same witness and mileage fees as are paid to witnesses in the courts of the United States;

(3) to furnish to persons subject to this subchapter such technical assistance as they may request to further their compliance with this subchapter or an order issued thereunder;

(4) upon the request of (i) any employer, whose employees or some of them, or (ii) any labor organization, whose members or some of them, refuse or threaten to refuse to cooperate in effectuating the provisions of this subchapter, to assist in such effectuation by conciliation or such other remedial action as is provided by this subchapter;

(5) to make such technical studies as are appropriate to effectuate the purposes and policies of this subchapter and to make the results of such studies available to the public;

(6) to intervene in a civil action brought under section 2000e-5 of this Title by an aggrieved party against a respondent other than a government, governmental agency or political subdivision.

(h) Cooperation with other departments and agencies in performance of educational or promotional activities; outreach activities

(1) The Commission shall, in any of its educational or promotional activities, cooperate with other departments and agencies in the performance of such educational and promotional activities.

(2) In exercising its powers under this subchapter, the Commission shall carry out educational and outreach activities (including dissemination of information in languages other than English) targeted to —

(A) individuals who historically have been victims of employment discrimination and have not been equitably served by the Commission; and

(B) individuals on whose behalf the Commission has authority to enforce any other law prohibiting employment discrimination,

concerning rights and obligations under this subchapter or such law, as the case may be.

(i) Personnel subject to political activity restrictions

All officers, agents, attorneys, and employees of the Commission shall be subject to the provisions of section 7324 of Title 5, notwithstanding any exemption contained in such section.

(j) Technical Assistance Training Institute

(1) The Commission shall establish a Technical Assistance Training Institute, through which the Commission shall provide technical assistance and training regarding the laws and regulations enforced by the Commission.

(2) An employer or other entity covered under this subchapter shall not be excused from compliance with the requirements of this subchapter because of any failure to receive technical assistance under this subsection.

(3) There are authorized to be appropriated to carry out this subsection such sums as may be necessary for fiscal year 1992.

(k) EEOC Education, Technical Assistance, and Training Revolving Fund

(1) There is hereby established in the Treasury of the United States a revolving fund to be known as the "EEOC Education, Technical Assistance, and Training Revolving Fund" (hereinafter in this subsection referred to as the "Fund") and to pay the cost (including administrative and personnel expenses) of providing education, technical assistance, and training relating to laws administered by the Commission. Monies in the Fund shall be available without fiscal year limitation to the Commission for such purposes.

(2)(A) The Commission shall charge fees in accordance with the provisions of this paragraph to offset the costs of education, technical assistance, and training provided with monies in the Fund. Such fees for any education, technical assistance, or training —

(i) shall be imposed on a uniform basis on persons and entities receiving such education, assistance, or training,

(ii) shall not exceed the cost of providing such education, assistance, and training, and

(iii) with respect to each person or entity receiving such education, assistance, or training, shall bear a reasonable relationship to the cost of providing such education, assistance, or training to such person or entity.

(B) Fees received under subparagraph (A) shall be deposited in the Fund by the Commission.

(C) The Commission shall include in each report made under subsection (e) of this section information with respect to the operation of the Fund, including information, presented in the aggregate, relating to —

(i) the number of persons and entities to which the Commission provided education, technical assistance, or training with monies in the Fund, in the fiscal year for which such report is prepared,

(ii) the cost to the Commission to provide such education, technical assistance, or training to such persons and entities, and

(iii) the amount of any fees received by the Commission from such persons and entities for such education, technical assistance, or training.

(3) The Secretary of the Treasury shall invest the portion of the Fund not required to satisfy current expenditures from the Fund, as determined by the Commission, in obligations of the United States or obligations guaranteed as to principal by the United States. Investment proceeds shall be deposited in the Fund.

(4) There is hereby transferred to the Fund $1,000,000 from the Salaries and Expenses appropriation of the Commission.

Sec. 2000e-5. Enforcement provisions

(a) Power of Commission to prevent unlawful employment practices

The Commission is empowered, as hereinafter provided, to prevent any person from engaging in any unlawful employment practice as set forth in section 2000e-2 or 2000e-3 of this Title.

(b) Charges by persons aggrieved or member of Commission of unlawful employment practices by employers, etc.; filing; allegations; notice to respondent; contents of notice; investigation by Commission; contents of charges; prohibition on disclosure of charges; determination of reasonable cause; conference, conciliation, and persuasion for elimination of unlawful practices; prohibition on disclosure of informal endeavors to end unlawful practices; use of evidence in subsequent proceedings; penalties for disclosure of information; time for determination of reasonable cause

Whenever a charge is filed by or on behalf of a person claiming to be aggrieved, or by a member of the Commission, alleging that an employer, employment agency, labor organization, or joint labor-management committee controlling apprenticeship or other training or retraining, including on-the-job training programs, has engaged in an unlawful employment practice, the Commission shall serve a notice of the charge (including the date, place and circumstances of the alleged unlawful employment practice) on such employer, employment agency, labor organization, or joint labor-management committee (hereinafter referred to as the "respondent") within ten days, and shall make an investigation thereof. Charges shall be in writing under oath or affirmation and shall contain such information and be in such form as the Commission requires. Charges shall not be made public by the Commission. If the Commission determines after such investigation that there is not reasonable cause to believe that the charge is true, it shall dismiss the charge and promptly notify the person claiming to be aggrieved and the respondent of its action. In determining whether reasonable cause exists, the Commission shall accord substantial weight to final findings and orders made by State or local authorities in proceedings commenced under State or local law pursuant to the requirements of subsections (c) and (d) of this section. If the Commission determines after such investigation that there is reasonable cause to believe that the charge is true, the Commission shall endeavor to eliminate any such alleged unlawful employment practice by informal methods of conference, conciliation, and persuasion. Nothing said or done during and as a part of such informal endeavors may be made public by the Commission, its officers or employees, or used as evidence in a subsequent proceeding without the written consent of the persons concerned. Any person who makes public information in violation of this subsection shall be fined not more than $1,000 or imprisoned for not more than one year, or both. The Commission shall make its determination on reasonable cause as promptly as possible and, so far as practicable, not later than one hundred and twenty days from the filing of the charge or, where applicable under subsection (c) or (d) of this section, from the date upon which the Commission is authorized to take action with respect to the charge.

(c) State or local enforcement proceedings; notification of State or local authority; time for filing charges with Commission; commencement of proceedings

In the case of an alleged unlawful employment practice occurring in a State, or political subdivision of a State, which has a State or local law prohibiting the unlawful employment practice alleged and establishing or authorizing a State or local authority to grant or seek relief from such practice or to institute criminal proceedings with respect thereto upon receiving notice thereof, no charge may be filed under subsection (a) of this section by the person aggrieved before the expiration of sixty days after proceedings have been commenced under the State or local law, unless such proceedings have been earlier terminated, provided that such sixty-day period shall be extended to one hundred and twenty days during the first year after the effective date of such State or local law. If any requirement for the commencement of such proceedings is imposed by a State or local authority other than a requirement of the filing of a written and signed statement of the facts upon which the proceeding is based, the proceeding shall be deemed to have been commenced for the purposes of this subsection at the time such statement is sent by registered mail to the appropriate State or local authority.

(d) State or local enforcement proceedings; notification of State or local authority; time for action on charges by Commission

In the case of any charge filed by a member of the Commission alleging an unlawful employment practice occurring in a State or political subdivision of a State which has a State or local law prohibiting the practice alleged and establishing or authorizing a State or local authority to grant or seek relief from such practice or to institute criminal proceedings with respect thereto upon receiving notice thereof, the Commission shall, before taking any action with respect to such charge, notify the appropriate State or local officials and, upon request, afford them a reasonable time, but not less than sixty days (provided that such sixty-day period shall be extended to one hundred and twenty days during the first year after the effective day of such State or local law), unless a shorter period is requested, to act under such State or local law to remedy the practice alleged.

(e) Time for filing charges; time for service of notice of charge on respondent; filing of charge by Commission with State or local agency; seniority system

(1) A charge under this section shall be filed within one hundred and eighty days after the alleged unlawful employment practice occurred and notice of the charge (including the date, place and circumstances of the alleged unlawful employment practice) shall be served upon the person against whom such charge is made within ten days thereafter, except that in a case of an unlawful employment practice with respect to which the person aggrieved has initially instituted proceedings with a State or local agency with authority to grant or seek relief from such practice or to institute criminal proceedings with respect thereto upon receiving notice thereof, such charge shall be filed by or on behalf of the person aggrieved within three hundred days after the alleged unlawful employment practice occurred, or within thirty days after receiving notice that the State or local agency has terminated the proceedings under the State or local law, whichever is earlier, and a copy of such charge shall be filed by the Commission with the State or local agency.

(2) For purposes of this section, an unlawful employment practice occurs, with respect to a seniority system that has been adopted for an intentionally discriminatory purpose in violation of this subchapter (whether or not that discriminatory purpose is apparent on the face of the seniority provision), when the seniority system is adopted, when an individual becomes subject to the seniority system, or when a person aggrieved is injured by the application of the seniority system or provision of the system.

(f) Civil action by Commission, Attorney General, or person aggrieved; preconditions; procedure; appointment of attorney; payment of fees, costs, or security; intervention; stay of Federal proceedings; action for appropriate temporary or preliminary relief pending final disposition of charge; jurisdiction and venue of United States courts; designation of judge to hear and determine case; assignment of case for hearing; expedition of case; appointment of master

(1) If within thirty days after a charge is filed with the Commission or within thirty days after expiration of any period of reference under subsection (c) or (d) of this section, the Commission has been unable to secure from the respondent a conciliation agreement acceptable to the Commission, the Commission may bring a civil action against any respondent not a government, governmental agency, or political subdivision named in the charge. In the case of a respondent which is a government, governmental agency, or political subdivision, if the Commission has been unable to secure from the respondent a conciliation agreement acceptable to the Commission, the Commission shall take no further action and shall refer the case to the Attorney General who may bring a civil action against such respondent in the appropriate United States district court. The person or persons aggrieved shall have the right to intervene in a civil action brought by the Commission or the Attorney General in a case involving a government, governmental agency, or political subdivision. If a charge filed with the Commission pursuant to subsection (b) of this section, is dismissed by the Commission, or if within one hundred and eighty days from the filing of such charge or the expiration of any period of reference under subsection (c) or (d) of this section, whichever is later, the Commission has not filed a civil action under this section or the Attorney General has not filed a civil action in a case involving a government, governmental agency, or political subdivision, or the Commission has not entered into a conciliation agreement to which the person aggrieved is a party, the Commission, or

the Attorney General in a case involving a government, governmental agency, or political subdivision, shall so notify the person aggrieved and within ninety days after the giving of such notice a civil action may be brought against the respondent named in the charge (A) by the person claiming to be aggrieved or (B) if such charge was filed by a member of the Commission, by any person whom the charge alleges was aggrieved by the alleged unlawful employment practice. Upon application by the complainant and in such circumstances as the court may deem just, the court may appoint an attorney for such complainant and may authorize the commencement of the action without the payment of fees, costs, or security. Upon timely application, the court may, in its discretion, permit the Commission, or the Attorney General in a case involving a government, governmental agency, or political subdivision, to intervene in such civil action upon certification that the case is of general public importance. Upon request, the court may, in its discretion, stay further proceedings for not more than sixty days pending the termination of State or local proceedings described in subsection (c) or (d) of this section or further efforts of the Commission to obtain voluntary compliance.

(2) Whenever a charge is filed with the Commission and the Commission concludes on the basis of a preliminary investigation that prompt judicial action is necessary to carry out the purposes of this Act, the Commission, or the Attorney General in a case involving a government, governmental agency, or political subdivision, may bring an action for appropriate temporary or preliminary relief pending final disposition of such charge. Any temporary restraining order or other order granting preliminary or temporary relief shall be issued in accordance with rule 65 of the Federal Rules of Civil Procedure. It shall be the duty of a court having jurisdiction over proceedings under this section to assign cases for hearing at the earliest practicable date and to cause such cases to be in every way expedited.

(3) Each United States district court and each United States court of a place subject to the jurisdiction of the United States shall have jurisdiction of actions brought under this subchapter. Such an action may be brought in any judicial district in the State in which the unlawful employment practice is alleged to have been committed, in the judicial district in which the employment records relevant to such practice are maintained and administered, or in the judicial district in which the aggrieved person would have worked but for the alleged unlawful employment practice, but if the respondent is not found within any such district, such an action may be brought within the judicial district in which the respondent has his principal office. For purposes of sections 1404 and 1406 of Title 28, the judicial district in which the respondent has his principal office shall in all cases be considered a district in which the action might have been brought.

(4) It shall be the duty of the chief judge of the district (or in his absence, the acting chief judge) in which the case is pending immediately to designate a judge in such district to hear and determine the case. In the event that no judge in the district is available to hear and determine the case, the chief judge of the district, or the acting chief judge, as the case may be, shall certify this fact to the chief judge of the circuit (or in his absence, the acting chief judge) who shall then designate a district or circuit judge of the circuit to hear and determine the case.

(5) It shall be the duty of the judge designated pursuant to this subsection to assign the case for hearing at the earliest practicable date and to cause the case to be in every way expedited. If such judge has not scheduled the case for trial within one hundred and twenty days after issue has been joined, that judge may appoint a master pursuant to rule 53 of the Federal Rules of Civil Procedure.

(g) Injunctions; appropriate affirmative action; equitable relief; accrual of back pay; reduction of back pay; limitations on judicial orders

(1) If the court finds that the respondent has intentionally engaged in or is intentionally engaging in an unlawful employment practice charged in the complaint, the court may enjoin the respondent from engaging in such unlawful employment practice, and order such affirmative action as may be appropriate, which may include, but is not limited to, reinstatement or hiring of employees, with or without back pay (payable by the employer, employment agency, or labor organization, as the case may be, responsible for the unlawful employment practice), or any other

equitable relief as the court deems appropriate. Back pay liability shall not accrue from a date more than two years prior to the filing of a charge with the Commission. Interim earnings or amounts earnable with reasonable diligence by the person or persons discriminated against shall operate to reduce the back pay otherwise allowable.

(2)(A) No order of the court shall require the admission or reinstatement of an individual as a member of a union, or the hiring, reinstatement, or promotion of an individual as an employee, or the payment to him of any back pay, if such individual was refused admission, suspended, or expelled, or was refused employment or advancement or was suspended or discharged for any reason other than discrimination on account of race, color, religion, sex, or national origin or in violation of section 2000e-3(a) of this Title.

(B) On a claim in which an individual proves a violation under section 2000e-2(m) of this Title and a respondent demonstrates that the respondent would have taken the same action in the absence of the impermissible motivating factor, the court —

(i) may grant declaratory relief, injunctive relief (except as provided in clause (ii)), and attorney's fees and costs demonstrated to be directly attributable only to the pursuit of a claim under section 2000e-2(m) of this Title; and

(ii) shall not award damages or issue an order requiring any admission, reinstatement, hiring, promotion, or payment, described in subparagraph (A).

(h) Provisions of chapter 6 of Title 29 not applicable to civil actions for prevention of unlawful practices

The provisions of chapter 6 of Title 29 shall not apply with respect to civil actions brought under this section.

(i) Proceedings by Commission to compel compliance with judicial orders

In any case in which an employer, employment agency, or labor organization fails to comply with an order of a court issued in a civil action brought under this section, the Commission may commence proceedings to compel compliance with such order.

(j) Appeals

Any civil action brought under this section and any proceedings brought under subsection (i) of this section shall be subject to appeal as provided in sections 1291 and 1292, Title 28.

(k) Attorney's fee; liability of Commission and United States for costs

In any action or proceeding under this subchapter the court, in its discretion, may allow the prevailing party, other than the Commission or the United States, a reasonable attorney's fee (including expert fees) as part of the costs, and the Commission and the United States shall be liable for costs the same as a private person.

Sec. 2000e-6. Civil actions by the Attorney General

(a) Complaint

Whenever the Attorney General has reasonable cause to believe that any person or group of persons is engaged in a pattern or practice of resistance to the full enjoyment of any of the rights secured by this subchapter, and that the pattern or practice is of such a nature and is intended to deny the full exercise of the rights herein described, the Attorney General may bring a civil action in the appropriate district court of the United States by filing with it a complaint (1) signed by him (or in his absence the Acting Attorney General), (2) setting forth facts pertaining to such pattern or practice, and (3) requesting such relief, including an application for a permanent or temporary injunction, restraining order or other order against the person or persons responsible for such pattern or practice, as he deems necessary to insure the full enjoyment of the rights herein described.

(b) Jurisdiction; three-judge district court for cases of general public importance: hearing, determination, expedition of action, review by Supreme Court; single judge district court: hearing, determination, expedition of action

The district courts of the United States shall have and shall exercise jurisdiction of proceedings insti-

tuted pursuant to this section, and in any such proceeding the Attorney General may file with the clerk of such court a request that a court of three judges be convened to hear and determine the case. Such request by the Attorney General shall be accompanied by a certificate that, in his opinion, the case is of general public importance. A copy of the certificate and request for a three-judge court shall be immediately furnished by such clerk to the chief judge of the circuit (or in his absence, the presiding circuit judge of the circuit) in which the case is pending. Upon receipt of such request it shall be the duty of the chief judge of the circuit or the presiding circuit judge, as the case may be, to designate immediately three judges in such circuit, of whom at least one shall be a circuit judge and another of whom shall be a district judge of the court in which the proceeding was instituted, to hear and determine such case, and it shall be the duty of the judges so designated to assign the case for hearing at the earliest practicable date, to participate in the hearing and determination thereof, and to cause the case to be in every way expedited. An appeal from the final judgment of such court will lie to the Supreme Court.

In the event the Attorney General fails to file such a request in any such proceeding, it shall be the duty of the chief judge of the district (or in his absence, the acting chief judge) in which the case is pending immediately to designate a judge in such district to hear and determine the case. In the event that no judge in the district is available to hear and determine the case, the chief judge of the district, or the acting chief judge, as the case may be, shall certify this fact to the chief judge of the circuit (or in his absence, the acting chief judge) who shall then designate a district or circuit judge of the circuit to hear and determine the case.

It shall be the duty of the judge designated pursuant to this section to assign the case for hearing at the earliest practicable date and to cause the case to be in every way expedited.

(c) Transfer of functions, etc., to Commission; effective date; prerequisite to transfer; execution of functions by Commission

Effective two years after March 24, 1972, the functions of the Attorney General under this section shall be transferred to the Commission, together with such personnel, property, records, and unexpended balances of appropriations, allocations, and other funds employed, used, held, available, or to be made available in connection with such functions unless the President submits, and neither House of Congress vetoes, a reorganization plan pursuant to chapter 9 of Title 5, inconsistent with the provisions of this subsection. The Commission shall carry out such functions in accordance with subsections (d) and (e) of this section.

(d) Transfer of functions, etc., not to affect suits commenced pursuant to this section prior to date of transfer

Upon the transfer of functions provided for in subsection (c) of this section, in all suits commenced pursuant to this section prior to the date of such transfer, proceedings shall continue without abatement, all court orders and decrees shall remain in effect, and the Commission shall be substituted as a party for the United States of America, the Attorney General, or the Acting Attorney General, as appropriate.

(e) Investigation and action by Commission pursuant to filing of charge of discrimination; procedure

Subsequent to March 24, 1972, the Commission shall have authority to investigate and act on a charge of a pattern or practice of discrimination, whether filed by or on behalf of a person claiming to be aggrieved or by a member of the Commission. All such actions shall be conducted in accordance with the procedures set forth in section 2000e-5 of this title.

Sec. 2000e-7. Effect on State laws

Nothing in this subchapter shall be deemed to exempt or relieve any person from any liability, duty, penalty, or punishment provided by any present or future law of any State or political subdivision of a State, other than any such law which purports to require or permit the doing of any act which would be an unlawful employment practice under this subchapter.

Sec. 2000e-8. Investigations

(a) Examination and copying of evidence related to unlawful employment practices

In connection with any investigation of a charge filed under section 2000e-5 of this title, the Commission or its designated representative shall at all reasonable times have access to, for the purposes of examination, and the right to copy any evidence of any person being investigated or proceeded against that relates to unlawful employment practices covered by this subchapter and is relevant to the charge under investigation.

(b) Cooperation with State and local agencies administering State fair employment practices laws; participation in and contribution to research and other projects; utilization of services; payment in advance or reimbursement; agreements and rescission of agreements

The Commission may cooperate with State and local agencies charged with the administration of State fair employment practices laws and, with the consent of such agencies, may, for the purpose of carrying out its functions and duties under this subchapter and within the limitation of funds appropriated specifically for such purpose, engage in and contribute to the cost of research and other projects of mutual interest undertaken by such agencies, and utilize the services of such agencies and their employees, and, notwithstanding any other provision of law, pay by advance or reimbursement such agencies and their employees for services rendered to assist the Commission in carrying out this subchapter. In furtherance of such cooperative efforts, the Commission may enter into written agreements with such State or local agencies and such agreements may include provisions under which the Commission shall refrain from processing a charge in any cases or class of cases specified in such agreements or under which the Commission shall relieve any person or class of persons in such State or locality from requirements imposed under this section. The Commission shall rescind any such agreement whenever it determines that the agreement no longer serves the interest of effective enforcement of this subchapter.

(c) Execution, retention, and preservation of records; reports to Commission; training program records; appropriate relief from regulation or order for undue hardship; procedure for exemption; judicial action to compel compliance

Every employer, employment agency, and labor organization subject to this subchapter shall (1) make and keep such records relevant to the determinations of whether unlawful employment practices have been or are being committed, (2) preserve such records for such periods, and (3) make such reports therefrom as the Commission shall prescribe by regulation or order, after public hearing, as reasonable, necessary, or appropriate for the enforcement of this subchapter or the regulations or orders thereunder. The Commission shall, by regulation, require each employer, labor organization, and joint labor-management committee subject to this subchapter which controls an apprenticeship or other training program to maintain such records as are reasonably necessary to carry out the purposes of this subchapter, including, but not limited to, a list of applicants who wish to participate in such program, including the chronological order in which applications were received, and to furnish to the Commission upon request, a detailed description of the manner in which persons are selected to participate in the apprenticeship or other training program. Any employer, employment agency, labor organization, or joint labor-management committee which believes that the application to it of any regulation or order issued under this section would result in undue hardship may apply to the Commission for an exemption from the application of such regulation or order, and, if such application for an exemption is denied, bring a civil action in the United States district court for the district where such records are kept. If the Commission or the court, as the case may be, finds that the application of the regulation or order to the employer, employment agency, or labor organization in question would impose an undue hardship, the Commission or the court, as the case may be, may grant appropriate relief. If any person required to comply with the provisions of this subsection fails or refuses to do so, the United States district court for the district in which such person is found, resides, or transacts business, shall, upon application of the Commission, or the Attorney General in a case involving a government, governmental agency or political subdivision, have jurisdiction to issue to such person an order requiring him to comply.

(d) Consultation and coordination between Commission and interested State and Federal agencies in prescribing record-keeping and reporting requirements; availability of information furnished pursuant to recordkeeping and reporting requirements; conditions on availability

In prescribing requirements pursuant to subsection (c) of this section, the Commission shall consult with other interested State and Federal agencies and shall endeavor to coordinate its requirements with those adopted by such agencies. The Commission shall furnish upon request and without cost to any State or local agency charged with the administration of a fair employment practice law information obtained pursuant to subsection (c) of this section from any employer, employment agency, labor organization, or joint labor-management committee subject to the jurisdiction of such agency. Such information shall be furnished on condition that it not be made public by the recipient agency prior to the institution of a proceeding under State or local law involving such information. If this condition is violated by a recipient agency, the Commission may decline to honor subsequent requests pursuant to this subsection.

(e) Prohibited disclosures; penalties

It shall be unlawful for any officer or employee of the Commission to make public in any manner whatever any information obtained by the Commission pursuant to its authority under this section prior to the institution of any proceeding under this subchapter involving such information. Any officer or employee of the Commission who shall make public in any manner whatever any information in violation of this subsection shall be guilty, of a misdemeanor and upon conviction thereof, shall be fined not more than $1,000, or imprisoned not more than one year.

Sec. 2000e-9. Conduct of hearings and investigations pursuant to section 161 of Title 29

For the purpose of all hearings and investigations conducted by the Commission or its duly authorized agents or agencies, section 161 of Title 29 shall apply.

Sec. 2000e-10. Posting of notices; penalties

(a) Every employer, employment agency, and labor organization, as the case may be, shall post and keep posted in conspicuous places upon its premises where notices to employees, applicants for employment, and members are customarily posted a notice to be prepared or approved by the Commission setting forth excerpts, from or, summaries of, the pertinent provisions of this subchapter and information pertinent to the filing of a complaint.

(b) A willful violation of this section shall be punishable by a fine of not more than $100 for each separate offense.

Sec. 2000e-11. Veterans' special rights or preference

Nothing contained in this subchapter shall be construed to repeal or modify any Federal, State, territorial, or local law creating special rights or preference for veterans.

Sec. 2000e-12. Regulations; conformity of regulations with administrative procedure provisions; reliance on interpretations and instructions of Commission

(a) The Commission shall have authority from time to time to issue, amend, or rescind suitable procedural regulations to carry out the provisions of this subchapter. Regulations issued under this section shall be in conformity with the standards and limitations of subchapter II of chapter 5 of Title 5.

(b) In any action or proceeding based on any alleged unlawful employment practice, no person shall be subject to any liability or punishment for or on account of (1) the commission by such person of an unlawful employment practice if he pleads and proves that the act or omission complained of was in good faith, in conformity with, and in reliance on any written interpretation or opinion of the Commission, or (2) the failure of such person to publish and file any information required by any provision of this subchapter if he pleads and proves that he failed to publish and file such information in good faith, in conformity with the instructions of the Commission issued under this subchapter regarding the filing of such information. Such a defense, if established, shall be a bar to the action or proceeding, notwithstanding that (A) after such act or omission, such interpretation or opinion is modified or rescinded or is determined by judicial authority to be invalid or of no legal effect, or (B) after publishing or filing the description and annual reports, such publication or filing is determined by judicial authority not to be in conformity with the requirements of this subchapter.

Sec. 2000e-13. Application to personnel of Commission of sections 111 and 1114 of Title 18; punishment for violation of section 1114 of Title 18

The provisions of sections 111 and 1114, Title 18, shall apply to officers, agents, and employees of the Commission in the performance of their official duties. Notwithstanding the provisions of sections 111 and 1114 of Title 18, whoever in violation of the provisions of section 1114 of such Title kills a person while engaged in or on account of the performance of his official functions under this Act shall be punished by imprisonment for any term of years or for life.

Sec. 2000e-14. Equal Employment Opportunity Coordinating Council; establishment; composition; duties; report to President and Congress

The Equal Employment Opportunity Commission shall have the responsibility for developing and implementing agreements, policies and practices designed to maximize effort, promote efficiency, and eliminate conflict, competition, duplication and inconsistency among the operations, functions and jurisdictions of the various departments, agencies and branches of the Federal Government responsible for the implementation and enforcement of equal employment opportunity legislation, orders, and policies. On or before October 1 of each year, the Equal Employment Opportunity Commission shall transmit to the President and to the Congress a report of its activities, together with such recommendations for legislative or administrative changes as it concludes are desirable to further promote the purposes of this section.

Sec. 2000e-15. Presidential conferences; acquaintance of leadership with provisions for employment rights and obligations; plans for fair administration; membership

The President shall, as soon as feasible after July 2, 1964, convene one or more conferences for the purpose of enabling the leaders of groups whose members will be affected by this subchapter to become familiar with the rights afforded and obligations imposed by its provisions, and for the purpose of making plans which will result in the fair and effective administration of this subchapter when all of its provisions become effective. The President shall invite the participation in such conference or conferences of (1) the members of the President's Committee on Equal Employment Opportunity, (2) the members of the Commission on Civil Rights, (3) representatives of State and local agencies engaged in furthering equal employment opportunity, (4) representatives of private agencies engaged in furthering equal employment opportunity, and (5) representatives of employers, labor organizations, and employment agencies who will be subject to this subchapter.

Sec. 2000e-16. Employment by Federal Government

(a) Discriminatory practices prohibited; employees or applicants for employment subject to coverage

All personnel actions affecting employees or applicants for employment (except with regard to aliens employed outside the limits of the United States) in military departments as defined in section 102 of Title 5, in executive agencies as defined in section 105 of Title 5 (including employees and applicants for employment who are paid from nonappropriated funds), in the United States Postal Service and the Postal Rate Commission, in those units of the Government of the District of Columbia having positions in the competitive service, and in those units of the judicial branch of the Federal Government having positions in the competitive service, in the Smithsonian Institution, and in the Government Printing Office, the General Accounting Office, and the Library of Congress shall be made free from any discrimination based on race, color, religion, sex, or national origin.

(b) Equal Employment Opportunity Commission; enforcement powers; issuance of rules, regulations, etc.; annual review and approval of national and regional equal employment opportunity plans; review and evaluation of equal employment opportunity programs and publication of progress reports; consultations with interested parties; compliance with rules, regulations, etc.; contents of national and regional equal employment opportunity plans; authority of Librarian of Congress

Except as otherwise provided in this subsection, the Equal Employment Opportunity Commission shall have authority to enforce the provisions of subsection (a) of this section through appropriate remedies, including reinstatement or hiring of employees with or without back pay, as will effec-

tuate the policies of this section, and shall issue such rules, regulations, orders and instructions as it deems necessary and appropriate to carry out its responsibilities under this section. The Equal Employment Opportunity Commission shall —

(1) be responsible for the annual review and approval of a national and regional equal employment opportunity plan which each department and agency and each appropriate unit referred to in subsection (a) of this section shall submit in order to maintain an affirmative program of equal employment opportunity for all such employees and applicants for employment;

(2) be responsible for the review and evaluation of the operation of all agency equal employment opportunity programs, periodically obtaining and publishing (on at least a semiannual basis) progress reports from each such department, agency, or unit; and

(3) consult with and solicit the recommendations of interested individuals, groups, and organizations relating to equal employment opportunity.

The head of each such department, agency, or unit shall comply with such rules, regulations, orders, and instructions which shall include a provision that an employee or applicant for employment shall be notified of any final action taken on any complaint of discrimination filed by him thereunder. The plan submitted by each department, agency, and unit shall include, but not be limited to —

(1) provision for the establishment of training and education programs designed to provide a maximum opportunity for employees to advance so as to perform at their highest potential; and

(2) a description of the qualifications in terms of training and experience relating to equal employment opportunity for the principal and operating officials of each such department, agency, or unit responsible for carrying out the equal employment opportunity program and of the allocation of personnel and resources proposed by such department, agency, or unit to carry out its equal employment opportunity program.

With respect to employment in the Library of Congress, authorities granted in this subsection to the Equal Employment Opportunity Commission shall be exercised by the Librarian of Congress.

(c) Civil action by employee or applicant for employment for redress of grievances; time for bringing of action; head of department, agency, or unit as defendant

Within 90 days of receipt of notice of final action taken by a department, agency, or unit referred to in subsection (a) of this section, or by the Equal Employment Opportunity Commission upon an appeal from a decision or order of such department, agency, or unit on a complaint of discrimination based on race, color, religion, sex or national origin, brought pursuant to subsection (a) of this section, Executive Order 11478 or any succeeding Executive orders, or after one hundred and eighty days from the filing of the initial charge with the department, agency, or unit or with the Equal Employment Opportunity Commission on appeal from a decision or order of such department, agency, or unit until such time as final action may be taken by a department, agency, or unit, an employee or applicant for employment, if aggrieved by the final disposition of his complaint, or by the failure to take final action on his complaint, may file a civil action as provided in section 2000e-5 of this title, in which civil action the head of the department, agency, or unit, as appropriate, shall be the defendant.

(d) Section 2000e-5(f) through (k) of this Title applicable to civil actions

The provisions of section 2000e-5(f) through (k) of this title, as applicable, shall govern civil actions brought hereunder, and the same interest to compensate for delay in payment shall be available as in cases involving nonpublic parties.

(e) Government agency or official not relieved of responsibility to assure nondiscrimination in employment or equal employment opportunity

Nothing contained in this Act shall relieve any Government agency or official of its or his primary responsibility to assure nondiscrimination in employment as required by the Constitution and statutes or of its or his responsibilities under Executive Order 11478 relating to equal employment opportunity in the Federal Government.

Sec. 2000e-17. Procedure for denial, withholding, termination, or suspension of Government contract subsequent to acceptance by Government of affirmative action plan of employer; time of acceptance of plan

No Government contract, or portion thereof, with any employer, shall be denied, withheld, terminated, or suspended, by any agency or officer of the United States under any equal employment opportunity law or order, where such employer has an affirmative action plan which has previously been accepted by the Government for the same facility within the past twelve months without first according such employer full hearing and adjudication under the provisions of section 554 of Title 5, and the following pertinent sections: *Provided*, That if such employer has deviated substantially from such previously agreed to affirmative action plan, this section shall not apply: *Provided further*, That for the purposes of this section an affirmative action plan shall be deemed to have been accepted by the Government at the time the appropriate compliance agency has accepted such plan unless within forty-five days thereafter the Office of Federal Contract Compliance has disapproved such plan.

Americans with Disabilities Act
Subchapter I (Employment) and
Subchapter IV (Miscellaneous Provisions)

U.S. Code, Title 42, Sections 12101 to 12117 and 12201 to 12213)

ADA IN A NUTSHELL

Enacted: 1990

Purpose: To prevent discrimination against qualified persons with disabilities

Coverage: Private, state, and local government employers with 15 or more employees

Responsible agency: Equal Employment Opportunity Commission

Sec. 12101. Congressional findings and purposes

(a) Findings

The Congress finds that —

(1) some 43,000,000 Americans have one or more physical or mental disabilities, and this number is increasing as the population as a whole is growing older;

(2) historically, society has tended to isolate and segregate individuals with disabilities, and, despite some improvements, such forms of discrimination against individuals with disabilities continue to be a serious and pervasive social problem;

(3) discrimination against individuals with disabilities persists in such critical areas as employment, housing, public accommodations, education, transportation, communication, recreation, institutionalization, health services, voting, and access to public services;

(4) unlike individuals who have experienced discrimination on the basis of race, color, sex, national origin, religion, or age, individuals who have experienced discrimination on the basis of disability have often had no legal recourse to redress such discrimination;

(5) individuals with disabilities continually encounter various forms of discrimination, including outright intentional exclusion, the discriminatory effects of architectural, transportation, and communication barriers, overprotective rules and policies, failure to make modifications to existing facilities and practices, exclusionary qualification standards and criteria, segregation, and relegation to lesser services, programs, activities, benefits, jobs, or other opportunities;

(6) census data, national polls, and other studies have documented that people with disabilities, as a group, occupy an inferior status in our society, and are severely disadvantaged socially, vocationally, economically, and educationally;

(7) individuals with disabilities are a discrete and insular minority who have been faced with restrictions and limitations, subjected to a history of purposeful unequal treatment, and relegated to a position of political powerlessness in our society, based on characteristics that are beyond the control of such individuals and resulting from stereotypic assumptions not truly indicative of the individual ability of such individuals to participate in, and contribute to, society;

(8) the Nation's proper goals regarding individuals with disabilities are to assure equality of opportunity, full participation, independent living, and economic self-sufficiency for such individuals; and

(9) the continuing existence of unfair and unnecessary discrimination and prejudice denies people with disabilities the opportunity to compete on an equal basis and to pursue those opportunities for which our free society is justifiably famous, and costs the United States billions of dollars in unnecessary expenses resulting from dependency and nonproductivity.

(b) Purpose

It is the purpose of this Act —

(1) to provide a clear and comprehensive national mandate for the elimination of discrimination against individuals with disabilities;

(2) to provide clear, strong, consistent, enforceable standards addressing discrimination against individuals with disabilities;

(3) to ensure that the Federal Government plays a central role in enforcing the standards established in this chapter on behalf of individuals with disabilities; and

(4) to invoke the sweep of congressional authority, including the power to enforce the fourteenth amendment and to regulate commerce, in order to address the major areas of discrimination faced day-to-day by people with disabilities.

Sec. 12102. Definitions

As used in this Act:

(1) Auxiliary aids and services

The term "auxiliary aids and services" includes —

(A) qualified interpreters or other effective methods of making aurally delivered materials available to individuals with hearing impairments;

(B) qualified readers, taped texts, or other effective methods of making visually delivered materials available to individuals with visual impairments;

(C) acquisition or modification of equipment or devices; and

(D) other similar services and actions.

(2) Disability

The term "disability" means, with respect to an individual —

(A) a physical or mental impairment that substantially limits one or more of the major life activities of such individual;

(B) a record of such an impairment; or

(C) being regarded as having such an impairment.

(3) State

The term "State" means each of the several States, the District of Columbia, the Commonwealth of Puerto Rico, Guam, American Samoa, the Virgin Islands, the Trust Territory of the Pacific Islands, and the Commonwealth of the Northern Mariana Islands.

SUBCHAPTER I: EMPLOYMENT

Sec. 12111. Definitions

As used in this subchapter:

(1) Commission

The term "Commission" means the Equal Employment Opportunity Commission established by section 2000e-4 of this title.

(2) Covered entity

The term "covered entity" means an employer, employment agency, labor organization, or joint labor-management committee.

(3) Direct threat

The term "direct threat" means a significant risk to the health or safety of others that cannot be eliminated by reasonable accommodation.

(4) Employee

The term "employee" means an individual employed by an employer. With respect to employment in a foreign country, such term includes an individual who is a citizen of the United States.

(5) Employer

(A) In general

The term "employer" means a person engaged in an industry affecting commerce who has 15 or more employees for each working day in each of 20 or more calendar weeks in the current or preceding calendar year, and any agent of such person, except that, for two years following the effective date of this subchapter, an employer means a person engaged in an industry affecting commerce who has 25 or more employees for each working day in each of 20 or more calendar weeks in the current or preceding year, and any agent of such person.

(B) Exceptions

The term "employer" does not include —

(i) the United States, a corporation wholly owned by the government of the United States, or an Indian tribe; or

(ii) a bona fide private membership club (other than a labor organization) that is exempt from taxation under section 501(c) of Title 26.

(6) Illegal use of drugs

(A) In general

The term "illegal use of drugs" means the use of drugs, the possession or distribution of which is unlawful under the Controlled Substances Act (21 U.S.C. §801 et seq.). Such term does not include the use of a drug taken under supervision by a licensed health care professional, or other uses authorized by the Controlled Substances Act or other provisions of Federal law.

(B) Drugs

The term "drug" means a controlled substance, as defined in schedules I through V of section 202 of the Controlled Substances Act (21 U.S.C. §812).

(7) Person, etc.

The terms "person", "labor organization", "employment agency", "commerce", and "industry affecting commerce", shall have the same meaning given such terms in section 2000e of this title.

(8) Qualified individual with a disability

The term "qualified individual with a disability" means an individual with a disability who, with or without reasonable accommodation, can perform the essential functions of the employment position that such individual holds or desires. For the purposes of this subchapter, consideration shall be given to the employer's judgment as to what functions of a job are essential, and if an employer has prepared a written description before advertising or interviewing applicants for the job, this description shall be considered evidence of the essential functions of the job.

(9) Reasonable accommodation

The term "reasonable accommodation" may include —

(A) making existing facilities used by employees readily accessible to and usable by individuals with disabilities; and

(B) job restructuring, part-time or modified work schedules, reassignment to a vacant position, acquisition or modification of equipment or devices, appropriate adjustment or modifications of examinations, training materials or policies, the provision of qualified readers or interpreters, and other similar accommodations for individuals with disabilities.

(10) Undue hardship

(A) In general

The term "undue hardship" means an action requiring significant difficulty or expense, when considered in light of the factors set forth in subparagraph (B).

(B) Factors to be considered

In determining whether an accommodation would impose an undue hardship on a covered entity, factors to be considered include —

(i) the nature and cost of the accommodation needed under this chapter;

(ii) the overall financial resources of the facility or facilities involved in the provision of the reasonable accommodation; the number of persons employed at such facility; the effect on expenses and resources, or the impact otherwise of such accommodation upon the operation of the facility;

(iii) the overall financial resources of the covered entity; the overall size of the business of a covered entity with respect to the number of its employees; the number, type, and location of its facilities; and

(iv) the type of operation or operations of the covered entity, including the composition, structure, and functions of the workforce of such entity; the geographic separateness, administrative, or fiscal relationship of the facility or facilities in question to the covered entity.

Sec. 12112. Discrimination

(a) General rule

No covered entity shall discriminate against a qualified individual with a disability because of the disability of such individual in regard to job application procedures, the hiring, advancement, or discharge of employees, employee compensation, job training, and other terms, conditions, and privileges of employment.

(b) Construction

As used in subsection (a) of this section, the term "discriminate" includes —

(1) limiting, segregating, or classifying a job applicant or employee in a way that adversely affects the opportunities or status of such applicant or employee because of the disability of such applicant or employee;

(2) participating in a contractual or other arrangement or relationship that has the effect of subjecting a covered entity's qualified applicant or employee with a disability to the discrimination prohibited by this subchapter (such relationship includes a relationship with an employment or referral agency, labor union, an organization providing fringe benefits to an employee of the covered entity, or an organization providing training and apprenticeship programs);

(3) utilizing standards, criteria, or methods of administration —

(A) that have the effect of discrimination on the basis of disability; or

(B) that perpetuate the discrimination of others who are subject to common administrative control;

(4) excluding or otherwise denying equal jobs or benefits to a qualified individual because of the known disability of an individual with whom the qualified individual is known to have a relationship or association;

(5)(A) not making reasonable accommodations to the known physical or mental limitations of an otherwise qualified individual with a disability who is an applicant or employee, unless such covered entity can demonstrate that the accommodation would impose an undue hardship on the operation of the business of such covered entity; or

(B) denying employment opportunities to a job applicant or employee who is an otherwise qualified individual with a disability, if such denial is based on the need of such covered entity to make reasonable accommodation to the physical or mental impairments of the employee or applicant;

(6) using qualification standards, employment tests or other selection criteria that screen out or tend to screen out an individual with a disability or a class of individuals with disabilities unless the standard, test or other selection criteria, as used by the covered entity, is shown to be job-related for the position in question and is consistent with business necessity; and

(7) failing to select and administer tests concerning employment in the most effective manner to ensure that, when such test is administered to a job applicant or employee who has a disability that impairs sensory, manual, or speaking skills, such test results accurately reflect the skills, aptitude, or whatever other factor of such applicant or employee that such test purports to measure, rather than reflecting the impaired sensory, manual, or speaking skills of such employee or applicant (except where such skills are the factors that the test purports to measure).

(c) Covered entities in foreign countries

(1) In general

It shall not be unlawful under this section for a covered entity to take any action that constitutes discrimination under this section with respect to an employee in a workplace in a foreign country if compliance with this section would cause such covered entity to violate the law of the foreign country in which such workplace is located.

(2) Control of corporation

(A) Presumption

If an employer controls a corporation whose place of incorporation is a foreign country, any practice that constitutes discrimination under this section and is engaged in by such corporation shall be presumed to be engaged in by such employer.

(B) Exception

This section shall not apply with respect to the foreign operations of an employer that is a foreign person not controlled by an American employer.

(C) Determination

For purposes of this paragraph, the determination of whether an employer controls a corporation shall be based on —

(i) the interrelation of operations;

(ii) the common management;

(iii) the centralized control of labor relations; and

(iv) the common ownership or financial control,

of the employer and the corporation.

(d) Medical examinations and inquiries

(1) In general

The prohibition against discrimination as referred to in subsection (a) of this section shall include medical examinations and inquiries.

(2) Preemployment

(A) Prohibited examination or inquiry

Except as provided in paragraph (3), a covered entity shall not conduct a medical examination or make inquiries of a job applicant as to whether such applicant is an individual with a disability or as to the nature or severity of such disability.

(B) Acceptable inquiry

A covered entity may make preemployment inquiries into the ability of an applicant to perform job-related functions.

(3) Employment entrance examination

A covered entity may require a medical examination after an offer of employment has been made to a job applicant and prior to the commencement of the employment duties of such applicant, and may condition an offer of employment on the results of such examination, if —

(A) all entering employees are subjected to such an examination regardless of disability;

(B) information obtained regarding the medical condition or history of the applicant is collected and maintained on separate forms and in separate medical files and is treated as a confidential medical record, except that —

(i) supervisors and managers may be informed regarding necessary restrictions on the work or duties of the employee and necessary accommodations;

(ii) first aid and safety personnel may be informed, when appropriate, if the disability might require emergency treatment; and

(iii) government officials investigating compliance with this chapter shall be provided relevant information on request; and

(C) the results of such examination are used only in accordance with this subchapter.

(4) Examination and inquiry

(A) Prohibited examinations and inquiries

A covered entity shall not require a medical examination and shall not make inquiries of an employee as to whether such employee is an individual with a disability or as to the nature or severity of the disability, unless such examination or inquiry is shown to be job-related and consistent with business necessity.

(B) Acceptable examinations and inquiries

A covered entity may conduct voluntary medical examinations, including voluntary medical histories, which are part of an employee health program available to employees at that work site. A covered entity may make inquiries into the ability of an employee to perform job-related functions.

(C) Requirement

Information obtained under subparagraph (B) regarding the medical condition or history of any employee are subject to the requirements of subparagraphs (B) and (C) of paragraph (3).

Sec. 12113. Defenses

(a) In general

It may be a defense to a charge of discrimination under this chapter that an alleged application of qualification standards, tests, or selection criteria that screen out or tend to screen out or otherwise deny a job or benefit to an individual with a disability has been shown to be job-related and consistent with business necessity, and such performance cannot be accomplished by reasonable accommodation, as required under this subchapter.

(b) Qualification standards

The term "qualification standards" may include a requirement that an individual shall not pose a direct threat to the health or safety of other individuals in the workplace.

(c) Religious entities

(1) In general

This subchapter shall not prohibit a religious corporation, association, educational institution, or society from giving preference in employment to individuals of a particular religion to perform work connected with the carrying on by such corporation, association, educational institution, or society of its activities.

(2) Religious tenets requirement

Under this subchapter, a religious organization may require that all applicants and employees conform to the religious tenets of such organization.

(d) List of infectious and communicable diseases

(1) In general

The Secretary of Health and Human Services, not later than 6 months after July 26, 1990, shall —

(A) review all infectious and communicable diseases which may be transmitted through handling the food supply;

(B) publish a list of infectious and communicable diseases which are transmitted through handling the food supply;

(C) publish the methods by which such diseases are transmitted; and

(D) widely disseminate such information regarding the list of diseases and their modes of transmissability to the general public.

Such list shall be updated annually.

(2) Applications

In any case in which an individual has an infectious or communicable disease that is transmitted to others through the handling of food, that is included on the list developed by the Secretary of Health and Human Services under paragraph (1), and which cannot be eliminated by reasonable accommodation, a covered entity may refuse to assign or continue to assign such individual to a job involving food handling.

(3) Construction

Nothing in this chapter shall be construed to preempt, modify, or amend any State, county, or local law, ordinance, or regulation applicable to food handling which is designed to protect the public health from individuals who pose a significant risk to the health or safety of others, which cannot be eliminated by reasonable accommodation, pursuant to the list of infectious or communicable diseases and the modes of transmissability

published by the Secretary of Health and Human Services.

Sec. 12114. Illegal use of drugs and alcohol

(a) Qualified individual with a disability

For purposes of this subchapter, the term "qualified individual with a disability" shall not include any employee or applicant who is currently engaging in the illegal use of drugs, when the covered entity acts on the basis of such use.

(b) Rules of construction

Nothing in subsection (a) of this section shall be construed to exclude as a qualified individual with a disability an individual who —

(1) has successfully completed a supervised drug rehabilitation program and is no longer engaging in the illegal use of drugs, or has otherwise been rehabilitated successfully and is no longer engaging in such use;

(2) is participating in a supervised rehabilitation program and is no longer engaging in such use; or

(3) is erroneously regarded as engaging in such use, but is not engaging in such use;

except that it shall not be a violation of this chapter for a covered entity to adopt or administer reasonable policies or procedures, including but not limited to drug testing, designed to ensure that an individual described in paragraph (1) or (2) is no longer engaging in the illegal use of drugs.

(c) Authority of covered entity

A covered entity —

(1) may prohibit the illegal use of drugs and the use of alcohol at the workplace by all employees;

(2) may require that employees shall not be under the influence of alcohol or be engaging in the illegal use of drugs at the workplace;

(3) may require that employees behave in conformance with the requirements established under the Drug-Free Workplace Act of 1988 (41 U.S.C. §701 et seq.);

(4) may hold an employee who engages in the illegal use of drugs or who is an alcoholic to the same qualification standards for employment or job performance and behavior that such entity holds other employees, even if any unsatisfactory performance or behavior is related to the drug use or alcoholism of such employee; and

(5) may, with respect to Federal regulations regarding alcohol and the illegal use of drugs, require that —

(A) employees comply with the standards established in such regulations of the Department of Defense, if the employees of the covered entity are employed in an industry subject to such regulations, including complying with regulations (if any) that apply to employment in sensitive positions in such an industry, in the case of employees of the covered entity who are employed in such positions (as defined in the regulations of the Department of Defense);

(B) employees comply with the standards established in such regulations of the Nuclear Regulatory Commission, if the employees of the covered entity are employed in an industry subject to such regulations, including complying with regulations (if any) that apply to employment in sensitive positions in such an industry, in the case of employees of the covered entity who are employed in such positions (as defined in the regulations of the Nuclear Regulatory Commission); and

(C) employees comply with the standards established in such regulations of the Department of Transportation, if the employees of the covered entity are employed in a transportation industry subject to such regulations, including complying with such regulations (if any) that apply to employment in sensitive positions in such an industry, in the case of employees of the covered entity who are employed in such positions (as defined in the regulations of the Department of Transportation).

(d) Drug testing

(1) In general

For purposes of this subchapter, a test to determine the illegal use of drugs shall not be considered a medical examination.

(2) Construction

Nothing in this subchapter shall be construed to encourage, prohibit, or authorize the conducting of drug testing for the illegal use of drugs by job

applicants or employees or making employment decisions based on such test results.

(e) Transportation employees

Nothing in this subchapter shall be construed to encourage, prohibit, restrict, or authorize the otherwise lawful exercise by entities subject to the jurisdiction of the Department of Transportation of authority to —

(1) test employees of such entities in, and applicants for, positions involving safety-sensitive duties for the illegal use of drugs and for on-duty impairment by alcohol; and

(2) remove such persons who test positive for illegal use of drugs and on-duty impairment by alcohol pursuant to paragraph (1) from safety-sensitive duties in implementing subsection (c) of this section.

Sec. 12115. Posting notices

Every employer, employment agency, labor organization, or joint labor-management committee covered under this subchapter shall post notices in an accessible format to applicants, employees, and members describing the applicable provisions of this chapter, in the manner prescribed by section 2000e-10 of this title.

Sec. 12116. Regulations

Not later than 1 year after July 26, 1990, the Commission shall issue regulations in an accessible format to carry out this subchapter in accordance with subchapter II of chapter 5 of Title 5.

Sec. 12117. Enforcement

(a) Powers, remedies, and procedures

The powers, remedies, and procedures set forth in sections 2000e-4, 2000e-5, 2000e-6, 2000e-8, and 2000e-9 of this title shall be the powers, remedies, and procedures this subchapter provides to the Commission, to the Attorney General, or to any person alleging discrimination on the basis of disability in violation of any provision of this chapter, or regulations promulgated under section 12116 of this title, concerning employment.

(b) Coordination

The agencies with enforcement authority for actions which allege employment discrimination under this subchapter and under the Rehabilitation Act of 1973 (29 U.S.C. §701 et seq.) shall develop procedures to ensure that administrative complaints filed under this subchapter and under the Rehabilitation Act of 1973 are dealt with in a manner that avoids duplication of effort and prevents imposition of inconsistent or conflicting standards for the same requirements under this subchapter and the Rehabilitation Act of 1973. The Commission, the Attorney General, and the Office of Federal Contract Compliance Programs shall establish such coordinating mechanisms (similar to provisions contained in the joint regulations promulgated by the Commission and the Attorney General at part 42 of Title 28 and part 1691 of Title 29, Code of Federal Regulations, and the Memorandum of Understanding between the Commission and the Office of Federal Contract Compliance Programs dated January 16, 1981 (46 Fed. Reg. 7435, January 23, 1981)) in regulations implementing this subchapter and Rehabilitation Act of 1973 not later than 18 months after July 26, 1990.

SUBCHAPTER IV: MISCELLANEOUS PROVISIONS

Sec. 12201. Construction

(a) In general

Except as otherwise provided in this chapter, nothing in this chapter shall be construed to apply a lesser standard than the standards applied under title V of the Rehabilitation Act of 1973 (29 U.S.C. §790 et seq.) or the regulations issued by Federal agencies pursuant to such title.

(b) Relationship to other laws

Nothing in this chapter shall be construed to invalidate or limit the remedies, rights, and procedures of any Federal law or law of any State or political subdivision of any State or jurisdiction that provides greater or equal protection for the rights of individuals with disabilities than are afforded by this chapter. Nothing in this chapter shall be construed to preclude the prohibition of, or the imposition of restrictions on, smoking in places of employment covered by subchapter I of this chapter, in transportation covered by subchapter II or III of this chapter, or in places of public accommodation covered by subchapter III of this chapter.

(c) Insurance

Subchapters I through III of this chapter and title IV of this Act shall not be construed to prohibit or restrict —

(1) an insurer, hospital or medical service company, health maintenance organization, or any agent, or entity that administers benefit plans, or similar organizations from underwriting risks, classifying risks, or administering such risks that are based on or not inconsistent with State law; or

(2) a person or organization covered by this chapter from establishing, sponsoring, observing or administering the terms of a bona fide benefit plan that are based on underwriting risks, classifying risks, or administering such risks that are based on or not inconsistent with State law; or

(3) a person or organization covered by this chapter from establishing, sponsoring, observing or administering the terms of a bona fide benefit plan that is not subject to State laws that regulate insurance.

Paragraphs (1), (2), and (3) shall not be used as a subterfuge to evade the purposes of subchapter I and III of this chapter.

(d) Accommodations and services

Nothing in this chapter shall be construed to require an individual with a disability to accept an accommodation, aid, service, opportunity, or benefit which such individual chooses not to accept.

Sec. 12202. State immunity

A State shall not be immune under the eleventh amendment to the Constitution of the United States from an action in Federal or State court of competent jurisdiction for a violation of this chapter. In any action against a State for a violation of the requirements of this chapter, remedies (including remedies both at law and in equity) are available for such a violation to the same extent as such remedies are available for such a violation in an action against any public or private entity other than a State.

Sec. 12203. Prohibition against retaliation and coercion

(a) Retaliation

No person shall discriminate against any individual because such individual has opposed any act or practice made unlawful by this chapter or because such individual made a charge, testified, assisted, or participated in any manner in an investigation, proceeding, or hearing under this chapter.

(b) Interference, coercion, or intimidation

It shall be unlawful to coerce, intimidate, threaten, or interfere with any individual in the exercise or enjoyment of, or on account of his or her having exercised or enjoyed, or on account of his or her having aided or encouraged any other individual in the exercise or enjoyment of, any right granted or protected by this chapter.

(c) Remedies and procedures

The remedies and procedures available under sections 12117, 12133, and 12188 of this title shall be available to aggrieved persons for violations of subsections (a) and (b) of this section, with respect to subchapter I, subchapter II and subchapter III of this chapter, respectively.

Sec. 12205. Attorney's fees

In any action or administrative proceeding commenced pursuant to this chapter, the court or agency, in its discretion, may allow the prevailing party, other than the United States, a reasonable attorney's fee, including litigation expenses, and costs, and the United States shall be liable for the foregoing the same as a private individual.

Sec. 12206. Technical assistance

(a) Plan for assistance

(1) In general

Not later than 180 days after July 26, 1990, the Attorney General, in consultation with the Chair of the Equal Employment Opportunity Commission, the Secretary of Transportation, the Chair of the Architectural and Transportation Barriers Compliance Board, and the Chairman of the Federal Communications Commission, shall develop a plan to assist entities covered under this chapter, and other Federal agencies, in understanding the responsibility of such entities and agencies under this chapter.

(2) Publication of plan

The Attorney General shall publish the plan referred to in paragraph (1) for public comment in accordance with subchapter II of chapter 5 of Title 5 (commonly known as the Administrative Procedure Act).

(b) Agency and public assistance

The Attorney General may obtain the assistance of other Federal agencies in carrying out subsection (a) of this section, including the National Council on Disability, the President's Committee on Employment of People with Disabilities, the Small Business Administration, and the Department of Commerce.

(c) Implementation

(1) Rendering assistance

Each Federal agency that has responsibility under paragraph (2) for implementing this chapter may render technical assistance to individuals and institutions that have rights or duties under the respective subchapter or subchapters of this chapter for which such agency has responsibility.

(2) Implementation of subchapters

(A) Subchapter I

The Equal Employment Opportunity Commission and the Attorney General shall implement the plan for assistance developed under subsection (a) of this section, for subchapter I of this chapter.

(B) Subchapter II

(i) Part A

The Attorney General shall implement such plan for assistance for part A of subchapter II of this chapter.

(ii) Part B

The Secretary of Transportation shall implement such plan for assistance for part B of subchapter II of this chapter.

(C) Subchapter III

The Attorney General, in coordination with the Secretary of Transportation and the Chair of the Architectural Transportation Barriers Compliance Board, shall implement such plan for assistance for subchapter III of this chapter, except for section 12184 of this title, the plan for assistance for which shall be implemented by the Secretary of Transportation.

(D) Title IV

The Chairman of the Federal Communications Commission, in coordination with the Attorney General, shall implement such plan for assistance for title IV.

(3) Technical assistance manuals

Each Federal agency that has responsibility under paragraph (2) for implementing this chapter shall, as part of its implementation responsibilities, ensure the availability and provision of appropriate technical assistance manuals to individuals or entities with rights or duties under this chapter no later than six months after applicable final regulations are published under subchapters I, II, and III of this chapter and title IV.

(d) Grants and contracts

(1) In general

Each Federal agency that has responsibility under subsection (c)(2) of this section for implementing this chapter may make grants or award contracts to effectuate the purposes of this section, subject to the availability of appropriations. Such grants and contracts may be awarded to individuals, institutions not organized for profit and no part of the net earnings of which inures to the benefit of any private shareholder or individual (including educational institutions), and associations representing individuals who have rights or duties under this chapter. Contracts may be awarded to entities organized for profit, but such entities may not be the recipients or grants described in this paragraph.

(2) Dissemination of information

Such grants and contracts, among other uses, may be designed to ensure wide dissemination of information about the rights and duties established by this chapter and to provide information and technical assistance about techniques for effective compliance with this chapter.

(e) Failure to receive assistance

An employer, public accommodation, or other entity covered under this chapter shall not be excused from compliance with the requirements of this chapter because of any failure to receive technical assistance under this section, including any failure in the development or dissemination of any technical assistance manual authorized by this section.

Sec. 12208. Transvestites

For the purposes of this chapter, the term "disabled" or "disability" shall not apply to an individual solely because that individual is a transvestite.

Sec. 12209. Instrumentalities of Congress

The General Accounting Office, the Government Printing Office, and the Library of Congress shall be covered as follows:

(1) In general

The rights and protections under this chapter shall, subject to paragraph (2), apply with respect to the conduct of each instrumentality of the Congress.

(2) Establishment of remedies and procedures by instrumentalities

The chief official of each instrumentality of the Congress shall establish remedies and procedures to be utilized with respect to the rights and protections provided pursuant to paragraph (1).

(3) Report to Congress

The chief official of each instrumentality of the Congress shall, after establishing remedies and procedures for purposes of paragraph (2), submit to the Congress a report describing the remedies and procedures.

(4) Definition of instrumentalities

For purposes of this section, the term "instrumentality of the Congress" means the following: the General Accounting Office, the Government Printing Office, and the Library of Congress.

(5) Enforcement of employment rights

The remedies and procedures set forth in section 2000e-16 of this title shall be available to any employee of an instrumentality of the Congress who alleges a violation of the rights and protections under sections 12112 through 12114 of this title that are made applicable by this section, except that the authorities of the Equal Employment Opportunity Commission shall be exercised by the chief official of the instrumentality of the Congress.

(6) Enforcement of rights to public services and accommodations

The remedies and procedures set forth in section 2000e-16 of this title shall be available to any qualified person with a disability who is a visitor, guest, or patron of an instrumentality of Congress and who alleges a violation of the rights and protections under sections 12131 through 12150 of this title or section 12182 or 12183 of this title that are made applicable by this section, except that the authorities of the Equal Employment Opportunity Commission shall be exercised by the chief official of the instrumentality of the Congress.

(7) Construction

Nothing in this section shall alter the enforcement procedures for individuals with disabilities provided in the General Accounting Office Personnel Act of 1980 and regulations promulgated pursuant to that Act.

Sec. 12210. Illegal use of drugs

(a) In general

For purposes of this chapter, the term "individual with a disability" does not include an individual who is currently engaging in the illegal use of drugs, when the covered entity acts on the basis of such use.

(b) Rules of construction

Nothing in subsection (a) of this section shall be construed to exclude as an individual with a disability an individual who —

(1) has successfully completed a supervised drug rehabilitation program and is no longer engaging in the illegal use of drugs, or has otherwise been rehabilitated successfully and is no longer engaging in such use;

(2) is participating in a supervised rehabilitation program and is no longer engaging in such use; or

(3) is erroneously regarded as engaging in such use, but is not engaging in such use; except that it shall not be a violation of this chapter for a covered entity to adopt or administer reasonable policies or procedures, including but not limited to drug testing, designed to ensure that an individual described in paragraph (1) or (2) is no longer engaging in the illegal use of drugs; how-

ever, nothing in this section shall be construed to encourage, prohibit, restrict, or authorize the conducting of testing for the illegal use of drugs.

(c) Health and other services

Notwithstanding subsection (a) of this section and section 12211(b)(3) of this title, an individual shall not be denied health services, or services provided in connection with drug rehabilitation, on the basis of the current illegal use of drugs if the individual is otherwise entitled to such services.

(d) "Illegal use of drugs" defined

(1) In general

The term "illegal use of drugs" means the use of drugs, the possession or distribution of which is unlawful under the Controlled Substances Act (21 U.S.C. §801 et seq.). Such term does not include the use of a drug taken under supervision by a licensed health care professional, or other uses authorized by the Controlled Substances Act or other provisions of Federal law.

(2) Drugs

The term "drug" means a controlled substance, as defined in schedules I through V of section 202 of the Controlled Substances Act (21 U.S.C. §812).

Sec. 12211. Definitions

(a) Homosexuality and bisexuality

For purposes of the definition of "disability" in section 12102(2) of this title, homosexuality and bisexuality are not impairments and as such are not disabilities under this chapter.

(b) Certain conditions

Under this chapter, the term "disability" shall not include —

(1) transvestism, transsexualism, pedophilia, exhibitionism, voyeurism, gender identity disorders not resulting from physical impairments, or other sexual behavior disorders;

(2) compulsive gambling, kleptomania, or pyromania; or

(3) psychoactive substance use disorders resulting from current illegal use of drugs.

Sec. 12212. Alternative means of dispute resolution

Where appropriate and to the extent authorized by law, the use of alternative means of dispute resolution, including settlement negotiations, conciliation, facilitation, mediation, factfinding, minitrials, and arbitration, is encouraged to resolve disputes arising under this chapter.

Sec. 12213. Severability

Should any provision in this chapter be found to be unconstitutional by a court of law, such provision shall be severed from the remainder of the chapter, and such action shall not affect the enforceability of the remaining provisions of the chapter.

Railway Labor Act

U.S. Code, Title 45, Sections 151 to 188

Sec.

RLA IN A NUTSHELL

Enacted: 1926

Purpose: To guarantee self-organization and collective bargaining rights and to establish procedures to resolve labor disputes

Coverage: Railway and airline carriers

Responsible agencies:
- National Mediation Board
- National Railroad Adjustment Board

SUBCHAPTER I: GENERAL PROVISIONS

Sec. 151. Definitions; short title

When used in this chapter and for the purposes of this chapter —

First. The term "carrier" includes any railroad subject to the jurisdiction of the Surface Transportation Board, any express company that would have been subject to subtitle IV of Title 49, as of December 31, 1995, and any company which is directly or indirectly owned or controlled by or under common control with any carrier by railroad and which operates any equipment or facilities or performs any service (other than trucking service) in connection with the transportation, receipt, delivery, elevation, transfer in transit, refrigeration or icing, storage, and handling of property transported by railroad, and any receiver, trustee, or other individual or body, judicial or otherwise, when in the possession of the business of any such "carrier": *Provided, however,* That the term "carrier" shall not include any street, interurban, or suburban electric railway, unless such railway is operating as a part of a general steam-railroad system of transportation, but shall not exclude any part of the general steam-railroad system of transportation now or hereafter operated by any other motive power. The Surface Transportation Board is authorized and directed upon request of the Mediation Board or upon complaint of any party interested to determine after hearing whether any line operated by electric power falls within the terms of this proviso. The term "carrier" shall not include any company by reason of its being engaged in the mining of coal, the supplying of coal to a carrier where delivery is not beyond the mine tipple, and the operation of equipment or facilities therefor, or in any of such activities.

Second. The term "Adjustment Board" means the National Railroad Adjustment Board created by this chapter.

Third. The term "Mediation Board" means the National Mediation Board created by this chapter.

Fourth. The term "commerce" means commerce among the several States or between any State, Territory, or the District of Columbia and any foreign nation, or between any Territory or the District of Columbia and any State, or between any Territory and any other Territory, or between any Territory and the District of Columbia, or within any Territory or the District of Columbia, or between points in the same State but through any other State or any Territory or the District of Columbia or any foreign nation.

Fifth. The term "employee" as used herein includes every person in the service of a carrier (subject to its continuing authority to supervise and direct the manner of rendition of his service) who performs any work defined as that of an employee or subordinate official in the orders of the Surface Transportation Board now in effect, and as the same may be amended or interpreted by orders hereafter entered by the Board pursuant to the authority which is conferred upon it to enter orders amending or interpreting such existing orders: *Provided, however,* That no occupational classification made by order of the Surface Transportation Board shall be construed to define the crafts according to which railway employees may be organized by their voluntary action, nor shall the jurisdiction or powers of such employee organizations be regarded as in any way limited or defined by the provisions of this chapter or by the orders of the Board.

The term "employee" shall not include any individual while such individual is engaged in the physical operations consisting of the mining of coal, the preparation of coal, the handling (other than movement by rail with standard railroad locomotives) of coal not beyond the mine tipple, or the loading of coal at the tipple.

Sixth. The term "representative" means any person or persons, labor union, organization, or corporation designated either by a carrier or group of carriers or by its or their employees, to act for it or them.

Seventh. The term "district court" includes the United States District Court for the District of

Columbia; and the term "court of appeals" includes the United States Court of Appeals for the District of Columbia.

This chapter may be cited as the "Railway Labor Act."

Sec. 151a. General purposes

The purposes of the chapter are: (1) To avoid any interruption to commerce or to the operation of any carrier engaged therein; (2) to forbid any limitation upon freedom of association among employees or any denial, as a condition of employment or otherwise, of the right of employees to join a labor organization; (3) to provide for the complete independence of carriers and of employees in the matter of self-organization to carry out the purposes of this chapter; (4) to provide for the prompt and orderly settlement of all disputes concerning rates of pay, rules, or working conditions; (5) to provide for the prompt and orderly settlement of all disputes growing out of grievances or out of the interpretation or application of agreements covering rates of pay, rules, or working conditions.

Sec. 152. General duties

First. Duty of carriers and employees to settle disputes

It shall be the duty of all carriers, their officers, agents, and employees to exert every reasonable effort to make and maintain agreements concerning rates of pay, rules, and working conditions, and to settle all disputes, whether arising out of the application of such agreements or otherwise, in order to avoid any interruption to commerce or to the operation of any carrier growing out of any dispute between the carrier and the employees thereof.

Second. Consideration of disputes by representatives

All disputes between a carrier or carriers and its or their employees shall be considered, and, if possible, decided, with all expedition, in conference between representatives designated and authorized so to confer, respectively, by the carrier or carriers and by the employees thereof interested in the dispute.

Third. Designation of representatives

Representatives, for the purposes of this chapter, shall be designated by the respective parties without interference, influence, or coercion by either party over the designation of representatives by the other; and neither party shall in any way interfere with, influence, or coerce the other in its choice of representatives. Representatives of employees for the purposes of this chapter need not be persons in the employ of the carrier, and no carrier shall, by interference, influence, or coercion seek in any manner to prevent the designation by its employees as their representatives of those who or which are not employees of the carrier.

Fourth. Organization and collective bargaining; freedom from interference by carrier; assistance in organizing or maintaining organization by carrier forbidden; deduction of dues from wages forbidden

Employees shall have the right to organize and bargain collectively through representatives of their own choosing. The majority of any craft or class of employees shall have the right to determine who shall be the representative of the craft or class for the purposes of this chapter. No carrier, its officers, or agents shall deny or in any way question the right of its employees to join, organize, or assist in organizing the labor organization of their choice, and it shall be unlawful for any carrier to interfere in any way with the organization of its employees, or to use the funds of the carrier in maintaining or assisting or contributing to any labor organization, labor representative, or other agency of collective bargaining, or in performing any work therefor, or to influence or coerce employees in an effort to induce them to join or remain or not to join or remain members of any labor organization, or to deduct from the wages of employees any dues, fees, assessments, or other contributions payable to labor organizations, or to collect or to assist in the collection of any such dues, fees, assessments, or other contributions: *Provided,* That nothing in this chapter shall be construed to prohibit a carrier from permitting an employee, individually, or local representatives of employees from conferring with management during working hours without loss of time, or to prohibit a carrier from furnishing free transportation to its employees while engaged in the business of a labor organization.

Fifth. Agreements to join or not to join labor organizations forbidden

No carrier, its officers, or agents shall require any person seeking employment to sign any contract or agreement promising to join or not to join a labor organization; and if any such contract has been enforced prior to the effective date of this chapter, then such carrier shall notify the employees by an appropriate order that such contract has been discarded and is no longer binding on them in any way.

Sixth. Conference of representatives; time; place; private agreements

In case of a dispute between a carrier or carriers and its or their employees, arising out of grievances or out of the interpretation or application of agreements concerning rates of pay, rules, or working conditions, it shall be the duty of the designated representative or representatives of such carrier or carriers and of such employees, within ten days after the receipt of notice of a desire on the part of either party to confer in respect to such dispute, to specify a time and place at which such conference shall be held: *Provided*, (1) That the place so specified shall be situated upon the line of the carrier involved or as otherwise mutually agreed upon; and (2) that the time so specified shall allow the designated conferees reasonable opportunity to reach such place of conference, but shall not exceed twenty days from the receipt of such notice: *And provided further*, That nothing in this chapter shall be construed to supersede the provisions of any agreement (as to conferences) then in effect between the parties.

Seventh. Change in pay, rules, or working conditions contrary to agreement or to section 156 forbidden

No carrier, its officers, or agents shall change the rates of pay, rules, or working conditions of its employees, as a class, as embodied in agreements except in the manner prescribed in such agreements or in section 156 of this title.

Eighth. Notices of manner of settlement of disputes; posting

Every carrier shall notify its employees by printed notices in such form and posted at such times and places as shall be specified by the Mediation Board that all disputes between the carrier and its employees will be handled in accordance with the requirements of this chapter, and in such notices there shall be printed verbatim, in large type, the third, fourth, and fifth paragraphs of this section. The provisions of said paragraphs are made a part

of the contract of employment between the carrier and each employee, and shall be held binding upon the parties, regardless of any other express or implied agreements between them.

Ninth. Disputes as to identity of representatives; designation by Mediation Board; secret elections

If any dispute shall arise among a carrier's employees as to who are the representatives of such employees designated and authorized in accordance with the requirements of this chapter, it shall be the duty of the Mediation Board, upon request of either party to the dispute, to investigate such dispute and to certify to both parties, in writing, within thirty days after the receipt of the invocation of its services, the name or names of the individuals or organizations that have been designated and authorized to represent the employees involved in the dispute, and certify the same to the carrier. Upon receipt of such certification the carrier shall treat with the representative so certified as the representative of the craft or class for the purposes of this chapter. In such an investigation, the Mediation Board shall be authorized to take a secret ballot of the employees involved, or to utilize any other appropriate method of ascertaining the names of their duly designated and authorized representatives in such manner as shall insure the choice of representatives by the employees without interference, influence, or coercion exercised by the carrier. In the conduct of any election for the purposes herein indicated the Board shall designate who may participate in the election and establish the rules to govern the election, or may appoint a committee of three neutral persons who after hearing shall within ten days designate the employees who may participate in the election. The Board shall have access to and have power to make copies of the books and records of the carriers to obtain and utilize such information as may be deemed necessary by it to carry out the purposes and provisions of this paragraph.

Tenth. Violations; prosecution and penalties

The willful failure or refusal of any carrier, its officers or agents, to comply with the terms of the third, fourth, fifth, seventh, or eighth paragraph of this section shall be a misdemeanor, and upon conviction thereof the carrier, officer, or agent offending shall be subject to a fine of not less than

$1,000, nor more than $20,000, or imprisonment for not more than six months, or both fine and imprisonment, for each offense, and each day during which such carrier, officer, or agent shall willfully fail or refuse to comply with the terms of the said paragraphs of this section shall constitute a separate offense. It shall be the duty of any United States attorney to whom any duly designated representative of a carrier's employees may apply to institute in the proper court and to prosecute under the direction of the Attorney General of the United States, all necessary proceedings for the enforcement of the provisions of this section, and for the punishment of all violations thereof and the costs and expenses of such prosecution shall be paid out of the appropriation for the expenses of the courts of the United States: *Provided*, That nothing in this chapter shall be construed to require an individual employee to render labor or service without his consent, nor shall anything in this chapter be construed to make the quitting of his labor by an individual employee an illegal act; nor shall any court issue any process to compel the performance by an individual employee of such labor or service, without his consent.

Eleventh. Union security agreements; check-off

Notwithstanding any other provisions of this chapter, or of any other statute or law of the United States, or Territory thereof, or of any State, any carrier or carriers as defined in this chapter and a labor organization or labor organizations duly designated and authorized to represent employees in accordance with the requirements of this chapter shall be permitted —

(a) to make agreements, requiring, as a condition of continued employment, that within sixty days following the beginning of such employment, or the effective date of such agreements, whichever is the later, all employees shall become members of the labor organization representing their craft or class: *Provided*, That no such agreement shall require such condition of employment with respect to employees to whom membership is not available upon the same terms and conditions as are generally applicable to any other member or with respect to employees to whom membership was denied or terminated for any reason other than the failure of the employee to tender the periodic dues, initiation fees, and

assessments (not including fines and penalties) uniformly required as a condition of acquiring or retaining membership.

(b) to make agreements providing for the deduction by such carrier or carriers from the wages of its or their employees in a craft or class and payment to the labor organization representing the craft or class of such employees, of any periodic dues, initiation fees, and assessments (not including fines and penalties) uniformly required as a condition of acquiring or retaining membership: *Provided*, That no such agreement shall be effective with respect to any individual employee until he shall have furnished the employer with a written assignment to the labor organization of such membership dues, initiation fees, and assessments, which shall be revocable in writing after the expiration of one year or upon the termination date of the applicable collective agreement, whichever occurs sooner.

(c) The requirement of membership in a labor organization in an agreement made pursuant to subparagraph (a) of this paragraph shall be satisfied, as to both a present or future employee in engine, train, yard, or hostling service, that is, an employee engaged in any of the services or capacities covered in the First division of paragraph (h) of section 153 of this title defining the jurisdictional scope of the First Division of the National Railroad Adjustment Board, if said employee shall hold or acquire membership in any one of the labor organizations, national in scope, organized in accordance with this chapter and admitting to membership employees of a craft or class in any of said services; and no agreement made pursuant to subparagraph (b) of this paragraph shall provide for deductions from his wages for periodic dues, initiation fees, or assessments payable to any labor organization other than that in which he holds membership: *Provided, however*, That as to an employee in any of said services on a particular carrier at the effective date of any such agreement on a carrier, who is not a member of any one of the labor organizations, national in scope, organized in accordance with this chapter and admitting to membership employees of a craft or class in any of said services, such employee, as a condition of continuing his employment, may be required to become a member of the organization representing the craft in which he is employed on the effective date of the first agreement applicable to him: *Provided, further,* That nothing herein or in any such agreement or agreements shall prevent an employee from changing membership from one organization to another organization admitting to membership employees of a craft or class in any of said services.

(d) Any provisions in paragraphs Fourth and Fifth of this section in conflict herewith are to the extent of such conflict amended.

Sec. 153. National Railroad Adjustment Board

First. Establishment; composition; powers and duties; divisions; hearings and awards; judicial review

There is established a Board, to be known as the "National Railroad Adjustment Board", the members of which shall be selected within thirty days after June 21, 1934, and it is provided —

(a) That the said Adjustment Board shall consist of thirty-four members, seventeen of whom shall be selected by the carriers and seventeen by such labor organizations of the employees, national in scope, as have been or may be organized in accordance with the provisions of sections 151a and 152 of this title.

(b) The carriers, acting each through its board of directors or its receiver or receivers, trustee or trustees, or through an officer or officers designated for that purpose by such board, trustee or trustees, or receiver or receivers, shall prescribe the rules under which its representatives shall be selected and shall select the representatives of the carriers on the Adjustment Board and designate the division on which each such representative shall serve, but no carrier or system of carriers shall have more than one voting representative on any division of the Board.

(c) Except as provided in the second paragraph of subsection (h) of this section, the national labor organizations, as defined in paragraph (a) of this section, acting each through the chief executive or other medium designated by the organization or association thereof, shall prescribe the rules under which the labor members of the Adjustment Board shall be selected and shall select such members and designate the division on which each member shall serve; but no labor organization shall have more than one voting representative on any division of the Board.

(d) In case of a permanent or temporary vacancy on the Adjustment Board, the vacancy shall be filled by selection in the same manner as in the original selection.

(e) If either the carriers or the labor organizations of the employees fail to select and designate representatives to the Adjustment Board, as provided in paragraphs (b) and (c) of this section, respectively, within sixty days after June 21, 1934, in case of any original appointment to office of a member of the Adjustment Board, or in case of a vacancy in any such office within thirty days after such vacancy occurs, the Mediation Board shall thereupon directly make the appointment and shall select an individual associated in interest with the carriers or the group of labor organizations of employees, whichever he is to represent.

(f) In the event a dispute arises as to the right of any national labor organization to participate as per paragraph (c) of this section in the selection and designation of the labor members of the Adjustment Board, the Secretary of Labor shall investigate the claim of such labor organization to participate, and if such claim in the judgment of the Secretary of Labor has merit, the Secretary shall notify the Mediation Board accordingly, and within ten days after receipt of such advice the Mediation Board shall request those national labor organizations duly qualified as per paragraph (c) of this section to participate in the selection and designation of the labor members of the Adjustment Board to select a representative. Such representative, together with a representative likewise designated by the claimant, and a third or neutral party designated by the Mediation Board, constituting a board of three, shall within thirty days after the appointment of the neutral member, investigate the claims of the labor organization desiring participation and decide whether or not it was organized in accordance with sections 151a and 152 of this title and is otherwise properly qualified to participate in the selection of the labor members of the Adjustment Board, and the findings of such boards of three shall be final and binding.

(g) Each member of the Adjustment Board shall be compensated by the party or parties he is to represent. Each third or neutral party selected under the provisions of paragraph (f) of this section shall receive from the Mediation Board such compensation as the Mediation Board may fix, together with his necessary traveling expenses and expenses actually incurred for subsistence, or per diem allowance in lieu thereof, subject to the provisions of law applicable thereto, while serving as such third or neutral party.

(h) The said Adjustment Board shall be composed of four divisions, whose proceedings shall be independent of one another, and the said divisions as well as the number of their members shall be as follows:

First division: To have jurisdiction over disputes involving train- and yard-service employees of carriers; that is, engineers, firemen, hostlers, and outside hostler helpers, conductors, trainmen, and yard-service employees. This division shall consist of eight members, four of whom shall be selected and designated by the carriers and four of whom shall be selected and designated by the labor organizations, national in scope and organized in accordance with sections 151a and 152 of this title and which represent employees in engine, train, yard, or hostling service: *Provided, however,* That each labor organization shall select and designate two members on the First Division and that no labor organization shall have more than one vote in any proceedings of the First Division or in the adoption of any award with respect to any dispute submitted to the First Division: *Provided further, however,* That the carrier members of the First Division shall cast no more than two votes in any proceedings of the division or in the adoption of any award with respect to any dispute submitted to the First Division.

Second division: To have jurisdiction over disputes involving machinists, boilermakers, blacksmiths, sheet-metal workers, electrical workers, carmen, the helpers and apprentices of all the foregoing, coach cleaners, power-house employees, and railroad-shop laborers. This division shall consist of ten members, five of whom shall be selected by the carriers and five by the national labor organizations of the employees.

Third division: To have jurisdiction over disputes involving station, tower, and telegraph employees, train dispatchers, maintenance-of-way men, clerical employees, freight handlers, express, station, and store employees, signal men, sleeping-car conductors, sleeping-car porters, and maids and dining-car employees. This division shall consist of ten members, five of whom shall be selected by the carriers and five by the national labor organizations of employees.

Fourth division: To have jurisdiction over disputes involving employees of carriers directly or indirectly engaged in transportation of passengers or property by water, and all other employees of carriers over which jurisdiction is not given to the first, second, and third divisions. This division shall consist of six members, three of whom shall be selected by the carriers and three by the national labor organizations of the employees.

(i) The disputes between an employee or group of employees and a carrier or carriers growing out of grievances or out of the interpretation or application of agreements concerning rates of pay, rules, or working conditions, including cases pending and unadjusted on June 21, 1934, shall be handled in the usual manner up to and including the chief operating officer of the carrier designated to handle such disputes; but, failing to reach an adjustment in this manner, the disputes may be referred by petition of the parties or by either party to the appropriate division of the Adjustment Board with a full statement of the facts and all supporting data bearing upon the disputes.

(j) Parties may be heard either in person, by counsel, or by other representatives, as they may respectively elect, and the several divisions of the Adjustment Board shall give due notice of all hearings to the employee or employees and the carrier or carriers involved in any disputes submitted to them.

(k) Any division of the Adjustment Board shall have authority to empower two or more of its members to conduct hearings and make findings upon disputes, when properly submitted, at any place designated by the division: *Provided, however,* That except as provided in paragraph (h) of this section, final awards as to any such dispute must be made by the entire division as hereinafter provided.

(*l*) Upon failure of any division to agree upon an award because of a deadlock or inability to secure a majority vote of the division members, as provided in paragraph (n) of this section, then such division shall forthwith agree upon and select a neutral person, to be known as "referee", to sit with the division as a member thereof, and make an award. Should the division fail to agree upon and select a referee within ten days of the date of the deadlock or inability to secure a majority vote, then the division, or any member thereof, or the parties or either party to the dispute may certify that fact to the Mediation Board, which Board shall, within ten days from the date of receiving such certificate, select and name the referee to sit with the division as a member thereof and make an award. The Mediation Board shall be bound by the same provisions in the appointment of these neutral referees as are provided elsewhere in this chapter for the appointment of arbitrators and shall fix and pay the compensation of such referees.

(m) The awards of the several divisions of the Adjustment Board shall be stated in writing. A copy of the awards shall be furnished to the respective parties to the controversy, and the awards shall be final and binding upon both parties to the dispute. In case a dispute arises involving an interpretation of the award, the division of the board upon request of either party shall interpret the award in the light of the dispute.

(n) A majority vote of all members of the division of the Adjustment Board eligible to vote shall be competent to make an award with respect to any dispute submitted to it.

(o) In case of an award by any division of the Adjustment Board in favor of petitioner, the division of the Board shall make an order, directed to the carrier, to make the award effective and, if the award includes a requirement for the payment of money, to pay to the employee the sum to which he is entitled under the award on or before a day named. In the event any division determines that an award favorable to the petitioner should not be made in any dispute referred to it, the division shall make an order to the petitioner stating such determination.

(p) If a carrier does not comply with an order of a division of the Adjustment Board within the time limit in such order, the petitioner, or any person for whose benefit such order was made, may file in the District Court of the United States for the district in which he resides or in which is located the principal operating office of the carrier, or through which the carrier operates, a petition setting forth briefly the causes for which he claims relief, and the order of the division of the Adjustment Board in the premises. Such suit in the District Court of the United States shall proceed in all respects as other civil suits, except that on the trial of such suit the findings and order of the division of the Adjustment Board shall be conclusive on the parties, and except that the petitioner shall not be liable for costs in the district court nor for costs at any subsequent stage of the proceedings, unless they accrue upon his appeal, and such costs shall be paid out of the appropriation for the expenses of the courts of the United States. If the petitioner shall finally prevail he shall be allowed a reasonable attorney's fee, to be taxed and collected as a part of the costs of the suit. The district courts are empowered, under the rules of the court governing actions at law, to make such order and enter such judgment, by writ of mandamus or otherwise, as may be appropriate to enforce or set aside the order of the division of the Adjustment Board: *Provided, however,* That such order may not be set aside except for failure of the division to comply with the requirements of this chapter, for failure of the order to conform, or confine itself, to matters within the scope of the division's jurisdiction, or for fraud or corruption by a member of the division making the order.

(q) If any employee or group of employees, or any carrier, is aggrieved by the failure of any division of the Adjustment Board to make an award in a dispute referred to it, or is aggrieved by any of the terms of an award or by the failure of the division to include certain terms in such award, then such employee or group of employees or carrier may file in any United States district court in which a petition under paragraph (p) could be filed, a petition for review of the division's order. A copy of the petition shall be forthwith transmitted by the clerk of the court to the Adjustment Board. The Adjustment Board shall file in the court the record of the proceedings on which it based its action. The court shall have jurisdiction to affirm the order of the division, or to set it aside, in whole or in part, or it may remand the proceedings to the division for such further action as it may direct. On such review, the findings and order of the division shall be conclusive on the parties, except that the order of the division may be set aside, in whole or in part, or remanded to the division, for failure of the division to comply with the requirements of this chapter, for failure of the order to conform, or confine itself, to matters within the scope of the division's jurisdiction, or for fraud or corruption by a member of the division making the order. The judgment of the court shall be subject to review as provided in sections 1291 and 1254 of Title 28.

(r) All actions at law based upon the provisions of this section shall be begun within two years from the time the cause of action accrues under the award of the division of the Adjustment Board, and not after.

(s) The several divisions of the Adjustment Board shall maintain headquarters in Chicago, Illinois, meet regularly, and continue in session so long as there is pending before the division any matter within its jurisdiction which has been submitted for its consideration and which has not been disposed of.

(t) Whenever practicable, the several divisions or subdivisions of the Adjustment Board shall be supplied with suitable quarters in any Federal building located at its place of meeting.

(u) The Adjustment Board may, subject to the approval of the Mediation Board, employ and fix the compensations of such assistants as it deems necessary in carrying on its proceedings. The compensation of such employees shall be paid by the Mediation Board.

(v) The Adjustment Board shall meet within forty days after June 21, 1934, and adopt such rules as it deems necessary to control proceedings before the respective divisions and not in conflict with the provisions of this section. Immediately following the meeting of the entire Board and the adoption of such rules, the respective divisions shall meet and organize by the selection of a chairman, a vice chairman, and a secretary. Thereafter each division shall annually designate one of its members to act as chairman and one of its members to act as vice chairman: *Provided, however,* That the chairmanship and vice-chairmanship of any division shall alternate as between the groups, so that both the chairmanship and vice-chairmanship shall be held alternately by a representative of the carriers and a representative of the employees. In case of a vacancy, such vacancy shall be filled for the unexpired term by the selection of a successor from the same group.

(w) Each division of the Adjustment Board shall annually prepare and submit a report of its activities to the Mediation Board, and the substance of such report shall be included in the annual report of the Mediation Board to the Congress of the United States. The reports of each division of the Adjustment Board and the annual report of the Mediation Board shall state in detail all cases heard, all actions taken, the names, salaries, and duties of all agencies, employees, and officers receiving compensation from the United States under the authority of this chapter, and an account of all moneys appropriated by Congress pursuant to the authority conferred by this chapter and disbursed by such agencies, employees, and officers.

(x) Any division of the Adjustment Board shall have authority, in its discretion, to establish regional adjustment boards to act in its place and stead for such limited period as such division may determine to be necessary. Carrier members of such regional boards shall be designated in keeping with rules devised for this purpose by the carrier members of the Adjustment Board and the labor members shall be designated in keeping with rules devised for this purpose by the labor members of the Adjustment Board. Any such regional board shall, during the time for which it is appointed, have the same authority to conduct hearings, make findings upon disputes and adopt the same procedure as the division of the Adjustment Board appointing it, and its decisions shall be enforceable to the same extent and under the same processes. A neutral person, as referee, shall be appointed for service in connection with any such regional adjustment board in the same circumstances and manner as provided in paragraph (*l*) of this section, with respect to a division of the Adjustment Board.

Second. System, group, or regional boards: establishment by voluntary agreement; special adjustment boards: establishment, composition, designation of representatives by Mediation Board, neutral member, compensation, quorum, finality and enforcement of awards

Nothing in this section shall be construed to prevent any individual carrier, system, or group of carriers and any class or classes of its or their employees, all acting through their representatives, selected in accordance with the provisions of this chapter, from mutually agreeing to the establishment of system, group, or regional boards of adjustment for the purpose of adjusting and deciding disputes of the character specified in this section. In the event that either party to such a system, group, or regional board of adjustment is dissatisfied with such arrangement, it may upon ninety days' notice to the other party elect to come under the jurisdiction of the Adjustment Board.

If written request is made upon any individual carrier by the representative of any craft or class of employees of such carrier for the establishment of a special board of adjustment to resolve disputes otherwise referable to the Adjustment Board, or any dispute which has been pending before the Adjustment Board for twelve months from the date the dispute (claim) is received by the Board, or if any carrier makes such a request upon any such representative, the carrier or the representative upon whom such request is made shall join in an agreement establishing such a board within thirty days from the date such request is made. The cases which may be considered by such board shall be defined in the agreement establishing it. Such board shall consist of one person designated by the carrier and one person designated by the representative of the employees. If such carrier or such representative fails to agree upon the establishment of such a board as provided herein, or to exercise its rights to designate a member of the board, the carrier or representative making the request for the establishment of the special board may request the Mediation Board to designate a member of the special board on behalf of the carrier or representative upon whom such request was made. Upon receipt of a request for such designation the Mediation Board shall promptly make such designation and shall select an individual associated in interest with the carrier or representative he is to represent, who, with the member appointed by the carrier or representative requesting the establishment of the special board, shall constitute the board. Each member of the board shall be compensated by the party he is to represent. The members of the board so designated shall determine all matters not previously agreed upon by the carrier and the representative of the employees with respect to the establishment and jurisdiction of the board. If they are unable to agree such mat-

ters shall be determined by a neutral member of the board selected or appointed and compensated in the same manner as is hereinafter provided with respect to situations where the members of the board are unable to agree upon an award. Such neutral member shall cease to be a member of the board when he has determined such matters. If with respect to any dispute or group of disputes the members of the board designated by the carrier and the representative are unable to agree upon an award disposing of the dispute or group of disputes they shall by mutual agreement select a neutral person to be a member of the board for the consideration and disposition of such dispute or group of disputes. In the event the members of the board designated by the parties are unable, within ten days after their failure to agree upon an award, to agree upon the selection of such neutral person, either member of the board may request the Mediation Board to appoint such neutral person and upon receipt of such request the Mediation Board shall promptly make such appointment. The neutral person so selected or appointed shall be compensated and reimbursed for expenses by the Mediation Board. Any two members of the board shall be competent to render an award. Such awards shall be final and binding upon both parties to the dispute and if in favor of the petitioner, shall direct the other party to comply therewith on or before the day named. Compliance with such awards shall be enforcible by proceedings in the United States district courts in the same manner and subject to the same provisions that apply to proceedings for enforcement of compliance with awards of the Adjustment Board.

Sec. 154. National Mediation Board

First. Board of Mediation abolished; National Mediation Board established; composition; term of office; qualifications; salaries; removal

The Board of Mediation is abolished, effective thirty days from June 21, 1934, and the members, secretary, officers, assistants, employees, and agents thereof, in office upon June 21, 1934, shall continue to function and receive their salaries for a period of thirty days from such date in the same manner as though this chapter had not been passed. There is established, as an independent agency in the executive branch of the Government, a board to be known as the "National Mediation

Board", to be composed of three members appointed by the President, by and with the advice and consent of the Senate, not more than two of whom shall be of the same political party. Each member of the Mediation Board in office on January 1, 1965, shall be deemed to have been appointed for a term of office which shall expire on July 1 of the year his term would have otherwise expired. The terms of office of all successors shall expire three years after the expiration of the terms for which their predecessors were appointed; but any member appointed to fill a vacancy occurring prior to the expiration of the term for which his predecessor was appointed shall be appointed only for the unexpired term of his predecessor. Vacancies in the Board shall not impair the powers nor affect the duties of the Board nor of the remaining members of the Board. Two of the members in office shall constitute a quorum for the transaction of the business of the Board. Each member of the Board shall receive necessary traveling and subsistence expenses, or per diem allowance in lieu thereof, subject to the provisions of law applicable thereto, while away from the principal office of the Board on business required by this chapter. No person in the employment of or who is pecuniarily or otherwise interested in any organization of employees or any carrier shall enter upon the duties of or continue to be a member of the Board. Upon the expiration of his term of office a member shall continue to serve until his successor is appointed and shall have qualified.

All cases referred to the Board of Mediation and unsettled on June 21, 1934, shall be handled to conclusion by the Mediation Board.

A member of the Board may be removed by the President for inefficiency, neglect of duty, malfeasance in office, or ineligibility, but for no other cause.

Second. Chairman; principal office; delegation of powers; oaths; seal; report

The Mediation Board shall annually designate a member to act as chairman. The Board shall maintain its principal office in the District of Columbia, but it may meet at any other place whenever it deems it necessary so to do. The Board may designate one or more of its members to exercise the functions of the Board in mediation proceedings. Each member of the Board shall have power to administer oaths and affirmations. The Board shall have a seal which shall be judicially noticed. The Board shall make an annual report to Congress.

Third. Appointment of experts and other employees; salaries of employees; expenditures

The Mediation Board may (1) subject to the provisions of the civil service laws, appoint such experts and assistants to act in a confidential capacity and such other officers and employees as are essential to the effective transaction of the work of the Board; (2) in accordance with chapter 51 and subchapter III of chapter 53 of Title 5, fix the salaries of such experts, assistants, officers, and employees; and (3) make such expenditures (including expenditures for rent and personal services at the seat of government and elsewhere, for law books, periodicals, and books of reference, and for printing and binding, and including expenditures for salaries and compensation, necessary traveling expenses and expenses actually incurred for subsistence, and other necessary expenses of the Mediation Board, Adjustment Board, Regional Adjustment Boards established under paragraph (w) of section 153 of this title, and boards of arbitration, in accordance with the provisions of this section and sections 153 and 157 of this title, respectively), as may be necessary for the execution of the functions vested in the Board, in the Adjustment Board and in the boards of arbitration, and as may be provided for by the Congress from time to time. All expenditures of the Board shall be allowed and paid on the presentation of itemized vouchers therefore approved by the chairman.

Fourth. Delegation of powers and duties

The Mediation Board is authorized by its order to assign, or refer, any portion of its work, business, or functions arising under this chapter or any other Act of Congress, or referred to it by Congress or either branch thereof, to an individual member of the Board or to an employee or employees of the Board to be designated by such order for action thereon, and by its order at any time to amend, modify, supplement, or rescind any such assignment or reference. All such orders shall take effect forthwith and remain in effect until otherwise ordered by the Board. In conformity with and subject to the order or orders of the Mediation Board in the premises, (and) such individual member of the Board or employee designated shall have power and authority to act as to any of said work, business, or functions so assigned or referred to him for action by the Board.

Fifth. Transfer of officers and employees of Board of Mediation; transfer of appropriation

All officers and employees of the Board of Mediation (except the members thereof, whose offices are abolished) whose services in the judgment of the Mediation Board are necessary to the efficient operation of the Board are transferred to the Board, without change in classification or compensation; except that the Board may provide for the adjustment of such classification or compensation to conform to the duties to which such officers and employees may be assigned.

All unexpended appropriations for the operation of the Board of Mediation that are available at the time of the abolition of the Board of Mediation shall be transferred to the Mediation Board and shall be available for its use for salaries and other authorized expenditures.

Sec. 155. Functions of Mediation Board

First. Disputes within jurisdiction of Mediation Board

The parties, or either party, to a dispute between an employee or group of employees and a carrier may invoke the services of the Mediation Board in any of the following cases:

(a) A dispute concerning changes in rates of pay, rules, or working conditions not adjusted by the parties in conference.

(b) Any other dispute not referable to the National Railroad Adjustment Board and not adjusted in conference between the parties or where conferences are refused.

The Mediation Board may proffer its services in case any labor emergency is found by it to exist at any time.

In either event the said Board shall promptly put itself in communication with the parties to such controversy, and shall use its best efforts, by mediation, to bring them to agreement. If such efforts to bring about an amicable settlement through mediation shall be unsuccessful, the said Board

shall at once endeavor as its final required action (except as provided in paragraph third of this section and in section 160 of this title) to induce the parties to submit their controversy to arbitration, in accordance with the provisions of this chapter.

If arbitration at the request of the Board shall be refused by one or both parties, the Board shall at once notify both parties in writing that its mediatory efforts have failed and for thirty days thereafter, unless in the intervening period the parties agree to arbitration, or an emergency board shall be created under section 160 of this title, no change shall be made in the rates of pay, rules, or working conditions or established practices in effect prior to the time the dispute arose.

Second. Interpretation of agreement

In any case in which a controversy arises over the meaning or the application of any agreement reached through mediation under the provisions of this chapter, either party to the said agreement, or both, may apply to the Mediation Board for an interpretation of the meaning or application of such agreement. The said Board shall upon receipt of such request notify the parties to the controversy, and after a hearing of both sides give its interpretation within thirty days.

Third. Duties of Board with respect to arbitration of disputes; arbitrators; acknowledgment of agreement; notice to arbitrators; reconvening of arbitrators; filing contracts with Board; custody of records and documents

The Mediation Board shall have the following duties with respect to the arbitration of disputes under section 157 of this title:

(a) On failure of the arbitrators named by the parties to agree on the remaining arbitrator or arbitrators within the time set by section 157 of this title, it shall be the duty of the Mediation Board to name such remaining arbitrator or arbitrators. It shall be the duty of the Board in naming such arbitrator or arbitrators to appoint only those whom the Board shall deem wholly disinterested in the controversy to be arbitrated and impartial and without bias as between the parties to such arbitration. Should, however, the Board name an arbitrator or arbitrators not so disinterested and impartial, then, upon proper investigation and presentation of the facts, the Board shall promptly remove such arbitrator.

If an arbitrator named by the Mediation Board, in accordance with the provisions of this chapter, shall be removed by such Board as provided by this chapter, or if such an arbitrator refuses or is unable to serve, it shall be the duty of the Mediation Board, promptly, to select another arbitrator, in the same manner as provided in this chapter for an original appointment by the Mediation Board.

(b) Any member of the Mediation Board is authorized to take the acknowledgement of an agreement to arbitrate under this chapter. When so acknowledged, or when acknowledged by the parties before a notary public or the clerk of a district court or a court of appeals of the United States, such agreement to arbitrate shall be delivered to a member of said Board or transmitted to said Board, to be filed in its office.

(c) When an agreement to arbitrate has been filed with the Mediation Board, or with one of its members, as provided by this section, and when the said Board has been furnished the names of the arbitrators chosen by the parties to the controversy it shall be the duty of the Board to cause a notice in writing to be served upon said arbitrators, notifying them of their appointment, requesting them to meet promptly to name the remaining arbitrator or arbitrators necessary to complete the Board of Arbitration, and advising them of the period within which, as provided by the agreement to arbitrate, they are empowered to name such arbitrator or arbitrators.

(d) Either party to an arbitration desiring the reconvening of a board of arbitration to pass upon any controversy arising over the meaning or application of an award may so notify the Mediation Board in writing, stating in such notice the question or questions to be submitted to such reconvened Board. The Mediation Board shall thereupon promptly communicate with the members of the Board of Arbitration, or a subcommittee of such Board appointed for such purpose pursuant to a provision in the agreement to arbitrate, and arrange for the reconvening of said Board of Arbitration or subcommittee, and shall notify the respective parties to the controversy of the time and place at which the Board, or the subcommittee, will meet for hearings upon the matters in controversy to be submitted to it. No evidence other than that contained in the record filed with the original award shall be received or considered by such reconvened Board or subcommittee, except such evidence as may be necessary to illustrate the interpretations suggested by the parties. If any member of the original Board is unable or unwilling to serve on such reconvened Board or subcommittee thereof, another arbitrator shall be named in the same manner and with the same powers and duties as such original arbitrator.

(e) Within sixty days after June 21, 1934, every carrier shall file with the Mediation Board a copy of each contract with its employees in effect on the 1st day of April 1934, covering rates of pay, rules, and working conditions. If no contract with any craft or class of its employees has been entered into, the carrier shall file with the Mediation Board a statement of that fact, including also a statement of the rates of pay, rules, and working conditions applicable in dealing with such craft or class. When any new contract is executed or change is made in an existing contract with any class or craft of its employees covering rates of pay, rules, or working conditions, or in those rates of pay, rules, and working conditions of employees not covered by contract, the carrier shall file the same with the Mediation Board within thirty days after such new contract or change in existing contract has been executed or rates of pay, rules, and working conditions have been made effective.

(f) The Mediation Board shall be the custodian of all papers and documents heretofore filed with or transferred to the Board of Mediation bearing upon the settlement, adjustment, or determination of disputes between carriers and their employees or upon mediation or arbitration proceedings held under or pursuant to the provisions of any Act of Congress in respect thereto; and the President is authorized to designate a custodian of the records and property of the Board of Mediation until the transfer and delivery of such records to the Mediation Board and to require the transfer and delivery to the Mediation Board of any and all such papers and documents filed with it or in its possession.

Sec. 156. Procedure in changing rates of pay, rules, and working conditions

Carriers and representatives of the employees shall give at least thirty days' written notice of an intended change in agreements affecting rates of pay, rules, or working conditions, and the time and place for the beginning of conference between the representatives of the parties interested in such intended changes shall be agreed upon within ten days after the receipt of said notice, and said time shall be within the thirty days provided in the notice. In every case where such notice of intended change has been given, or conferences are being held with reference thereto, or the services of the Mediation Board have been requested by either party, or said Board has proffered its services, rates of pay, rules, or working conditions shall not be altered by the carrier until the controversy has been finally acted upon, as required by section 155 of this title, by the Mediation Board, unless a period of ten days has elapsed after termination of conferences without request for or proffer of the services of the Mediation Board.

Sec. 157. Arbitration

First. Submission of controversy to arbitration

Whenever a controversy shall arise between a carrier or carriers and its or their employees which is not settled either in conference between representatives of the parties or by the appropriate adjustment board or through mediation, in the manner provided in sections 151 - 156 of this title such controversy may, by agreement of the parties to such controversy, be submitted to the arbitration of a board of three (or, if the parties to the controversy so stipulate, of six) persons: *Provided, however,* That the failure or refusal of either party to submit a controversy to arbitration shall not be construed as a violation of any legal obligation imposed upon such party by the terms of this chapter or otherwise.

Second. Manner of selecting board of arbitration

Such board of arbitration shall be chosen in the following manner:

(a) In the case of a board of three the carrier or carriers and the representatives of the employees, parties respectively to the agreement to arbitrate, shall each name one arbitrator; the two arbitrators thus chosen shall select a third arbitrator. If the arbitrators chosen by the parties shall fail to name the third arbitrator within five days after their first meeting, such third arbitrator shall be named by the Mediation Board.

(b) In the case of a board of six the carrier or carriers and the representatives of the employees, parties respectively to the agreement to arbitrate, shall each name two arbitrators; the four arbitrators thus chosen shall, by a majority vote, select the remaining two arbitrators. If the arbitrators chosen by the parties shall fail to name the two arbitrators within fifteen days after their first meeting, the said two arbitrators, or as many of them as have not been named, shall be named by the Mediation Board.

Third. Board of arbitration; organization; compensation; procedure

(a) Notice of selection or failure to select arbitrators

When the arbitrators selected by the respective parties have agreed upon the remaining arbitrator or arbitrators, they shall notify the Mediation Board; and, in the event of their failure to agree upon any or upon all of the necessary arbitrators within the period fixed by this chapter, they shall, at the expiration of such period, notify the Mediation Board of the arbitrators selected, if any, or of their failure to make or to complete such selection.

(b) Organization of board; procedure

The board of arbitration shall organize and select its own chairman and make all necessary rules for conducting its hearings: *Provided, however,* That the board of arbitration shall be bound to give the parties to the controversy a full and fair hearing, which shall include an opportunity to present evidence in support of their claims, and an opportunity to present their case in person, by counsel, or by other representative as they may respectively elect.

(c) Duty to reconvene; questions considered

Upon notice from the Mediation Board that the parties, or either party, to an arbitration desire the reconvening of the board of arbitration (or a subcommittee of such board of arbitration appointed for such purpose pursuant to the agreement to arbitrate) to pass upon any controversy over the meaning or application of their award, the board, or its subcommittee, shall at once reconvene. No question other than, or in addition to, the questions relating to the meaning or application of the award, submitted by the party or parties in writing, shall be considered by the reconvened board of arbitration or its subcommittee.

Such rulings shall be acknowledged by such board or subcommittee thereof in the same manner, and filed in the same district court clerk's office, as the original award and become a part thereof.

(d) Competency of arbitrators

No arbitrator, except those chosen by the Mediation Board, shall be incompetent to act as an arbitrator because of his interest in the controversy to be arbitrated, or because of his connection with or partiality to either of the parties to the arbitration.

(e) Compensation and expenses

Each member of any board of arbitration created under the provisions of this chapter named by either party to the arbitration shall be compensated by the party naming him. Each arbitrator selected by the arbitrators or named by the Mediation Board shall receive from the Mediation Board such compensation as the Mediation Board may fix, together with his necessary traveling expenses and expenses actually incurred for subsistence, while serving as an arbitrator.

(f) Award; disposition of original and copies

The board of arbitration shall furnish a certified copy of its award to the respective parties to the controversy, and shall transmit the original, together with the papers and proceedings and a transcript of the evidence taken at the hearings, certified under the hands of at least a majority of the arbitrators, to the clerk of the district court of the United States for the district wherein the controversy arose or the arbitration is entered into, to be filed in said clerk's office as hereinafter provided. The said board shall also furnish a certified copy of its award, and the papers and proceedings, including testimony relating thereto, to the Mediation Board to be filed in its office; and in addition a certified copy of its award shall be filed in the office of the Interstate Commerce Commission: *Provided, however,* That such award shall not be construed to diminish or extinguish any of the powers or duties of the Interstate Commerce Commission, under subtitle IV of Title 49.

(g) Compensation of assistants to board of arbitration; expenses; quarters

A board of arbitration may, subject to the approval of the Mediation Board, employ and fix the compensation of such assistants as it deems necessary in carrying on the arbitration proceedings. The compensation of such employees, together with their necessary traveling expenses and expenses actually incurred for subsistence, while so employed, and the necessary expenses of boards of arbitration, shall be paid by the Mediation Board.

Whenever practicable, the board shall be supplied with suitable quarters in any Federal building located at its place of meeting or at any place where the board may conduct its proceedings or deliberations.

(h) Testimony before board; oaths; attendance of witnesses; production of documents; subpoenas; fees

All testimony before said board shall be given under oath or affirmation, and any member of the board shall have the power to administer oaths or affirmations. The board of arbitration, or any member thereof, shall have the power to require the attendance of witnesses and the production of such books, papers, contracts, agreements, and documents as may be deemed by the board of arbitration material to a just determination of the matters submitted to its arbitration, and may for that purpose request the clerk of the district court of the United States for the district wherein said arbitration is being conducted to issue the necessary subpoenas, and upon such request the said clerk or his duly authorized deputy shall be, and he is, authorized, and it shall be his duty, to issue such subpoenas.

Any witness appearing before a board of arbitration shall receive the same fees and mileage as witnesses in courts of the United States, to be paid by the party securing the subpoena.

Sec. 158. Agreement to arbitrate; form and contents; signatures and acknowledgment; revocation

The agreement to arbitrate —

(a) Shall be in writing;

(b) Shall stipulate that the arbitration is had under the provisions of this chapter;

(c) Shall state whether the board of arbitration is to consist of three or of six members;

(d) Shall be signed by the duly accredited representatives of the carrier or carriers and the employees, parties respectively to the agreement to arbitrate, and shall be acknowledged by said parties before a notary public, the clerk of a district court or court of appeals of the United States, or before a member of the Mediation Board, and, when so acknowledged, shall be filed in the office of the Mediation Board;

(e) Shall state specifically the questions to be submitted to the said board for decision; and that, in its award or awards, the said board shall confine itself strictly to decisions as to the questions so specifically submitted to it;

(f) Shall provide that the questions, or any one or more of them, submitted by the parties to the board of arbitration may be withdrawn from arbitration on notice to that effect signed by the duly accredited representatives of all the parties and served on the board of arbitration;

(g) Shall stipulate that the signatures of a majority of said board of arbitration affixed to their award shall be competent to constitute a valid and binding award;

(h) Shall fix a period from the date of the appointment of the arbitrator or arbitrators necessary to complete the board (as provided for in the agreement) within which the said board shall commence its hearings;

(i) Shall fix a period from the beginning of the hearings within which the said board shall make and file its award: *Provided,* That the parties may agree at any time upon an extension of this period;

(j) Shall provide for the date from which the award shall become effective and shall fix the period during which the award shall continue in force;

(k) Shall provide that the award of the board of arbitration and the evidence of the proceedings before the board relating thereto, when certified under the hands of at least a majority of the arbitrators, shall be filed in the clerk's office of the district court of the United States for the district wherein the controversy arose or the arbitration was entered into, which district shall be designated in the agreement; and, when so filed, such award and proceedings shall constitute the full and complete record of the arbitration;

(l) Shall provide that the award, when so filed, shall be final and conclusive upon the parties as to the facts determined by said award and as to the merits of the controversy decided;

(m) Shall provide that any difference arising as to the meaning, or the application of the provisions, of an award made by a board of arbitration shall be referred back for a ruling to the same board, or, by agreement, to a subcommittee of such board; and that such ruling, when acknowledged in the same manner, and filed in the same district court clerk's office, as the original award, shall be a part of and shall have the same force and effect as such original award; and

(n) Shall provide that the respective parties to the award will each faithfully execute the same.

The said agreement to arbitrate, when properly signed and acknowledged as herein provided, shall not be revoked by a party to such agreement: *Provided, however,* That such agreement to arbitrate may at any time be revoked and canceled by the written agreement of both parties, signed by their duly accredited representatives, and (if no board of arbitration has yet been constituted under the agreement) delivered to the Mediation Board or any member thereof; or, if the board of arbitration has been constituted as provided by this chapter, delivered to such board of arbitration.

Sec. 159. Award and judgment thereon; effect of chapter on individual employee

First. Filing of award

The award of a board of arbitration, having been acknowledged as herein provided, shall be filed in the clerk's office of the district court designated in the agreement to arbitrate.

Second. Conclusiveness of award; judgment

An award acknowledged and filed as herein provided shall be conclusive on the parties as to the merits and facts of the controversy submitted to arbitration, and unless, within ten days after the filing of the award, a petition to impeach the award, on the grounds hereinafter set forth, shall be filed in the clerk's office of the court in which the award has been filed, the court shall enter judgment on the award, which judgment shall be final and conclusive on the parties.

Third. Impeachment of award; grounds

Such petition for the impeachment or contesting of any award so filed shall be entertained by the court only on one or more of the following grounds:

(a) That the award plainly does not conform to the substantive requirements laid down by this chapter for such awards, or that the proceedings were not substantially in conformity with this chapter;

(b) That the award does not conform, nor confine itself, to the stipulations of the agreement to arbitrate; or

(c) That a member of the board of arbitration rendering the award was guilty of fraud or corruption; or that a party to the arbitration practiced fraud or corruption which fraud or corruption affected the result of the arbitration: *Provided, however,* That no court shall entertain any such petition on the ground that an award is invalid for uncertainty; in such case the proper remedy shall be a submission of such award to a reconvened board, or subcommittee thereof, for interpretation, as provided by this chapter: *Provided further,* That an award contested as herein provided shall be construed liberally by the court, with a view to favoring its validity, and that no award shall be set aside for trivial irregularity or clerical error, going only to form and not to substance.

Fourth. Effect of partial invalidity of award

If the court shall determine that a part of the award is invalid on some ground or grounds designated in this section as a ground of invalidity, but shall determine that apart of the award is valid, the court shall set aside the entire award: *Provided, however,* That, if the parties shall agree thereto, and if such valid and invalid parts are separable, the court shall set aside the invalid part, and order judgment to stand as to the valid part.

Fifth. Appeal; record

At the expiration of 10 days from the decision of the district court upon the petition filed as aforesaid, final judgment shall be entered in accordance with said decision, unless during said 10 days either party shall appeal therefrom to the court of appeals. In such case only such portion of the record shall be transmitted to the appellate court as is necessary to the proper understanding and consideration of the questions of law presented by said petition and to be decided.

Sixth. Finality of decision of court of appeals

The determination of said court of appeals upon said questions shall be final, and, being certified by the clerk thereof to said district court, judgment pursuant thereto shall thereupon be entered by said district court.

Seventh. Judgment where petitioner's contentions are sustained

If the petitioner's contentions are finally sustained, judgment shall be entered setting aside the award in whole or, if the parties so agree, in part; but in such case the parties may agree upon a judgment to be entered disposing of the subject matter of the controversy, which judgment when entered shall have the same force and effect as judgment entered upon an award.

Eighth. Duty of employee to render service without consent; right to quit

Nothing in this chapter shall be construed to require an individual employee to render labor or service without his consent, nor shall anything in this chapter be construed to make the quitting of his labor or service by an individual employee an illegal act; nor shall any court issue any process to compel the performance by an individual employee of such labor or service, without his consent.

Sec. 159a. Special procedure for commuter service

(a) Applicability of provisions

Except as provided in section 590(h) of this title, the provisions of this section shall apply to any dispute subject to this chapter between a publicly funded and publicly operated carrier providing rail commuter service (including the Amtrak Commuter Services Corporation) and its employees.

(b) Request for establishment of emergency board

If a dispute between the parties described in subsection (a) of this section is not adjusted under the foregoing provisions of this chapter and the President does not, under section 160 of this title, create an emergency board to investigate and report on such dispute, then any party to the dispute or the Governor of any State through which the service that is the subject of the dispute is operated may request the President to establish such an emergency board.

(c) Establishment of emergency board

(1) Upon the request of a party or a Governor under subsection (b) of this section, the President shall create an emergency board to investigate and report on the dispute in accordance with section 160 of this title. For purposes of this subsection, the period during which no change, except by agreement, shall be made by the parties in the conditions out of which the dispute arose shall be 120 days from the day of the creation of such emergency board.

(2) If the President, in his discretion, creates a board to investigate and report on a dispute between the parties described in subsection (a) of this section, the provisions of this section shall apply to the same extent as if such board had been created pursuant to paragraph (1) of this subsection.

(d) Public hearing by National Mediation Board upon failure of emergency board to effectuate settlement of dispute

Within 60 days after the creation of an emergency board under this section, if there has been no settlement between the parties, the National Mediation Board shall conduct a public hearing on the dispute at which each party shall appear and provide testimony setting forth the reasons it has not accepted the recommendations of the emergency board for settlement of the dispute.

(e) Establishment of second emergency board

If no settlement in the dispute is reached at the end of the 120-day period beginning on the date of the creation of the emergency board, any party to the dispute or the Governor of any State through which the service that is the subject of the dispute is operated may request the President to establish another emergency board, in which case the President shall establish such emergency board.

(f) Submission of final offers to second emergency board by parties

Within 30 days after creation of a board under subsection (e) of this section, the parties to the dispute shall submit to the board final offers for settlement of the dispute.

(g) Report of second emergency board

Within 30 days after the submission of final offers under subsection (f) of this section, the emergency board shall submit a report to the President setting forth its selection of the most reasonable offer.

(h) Maintenance of status quo during dispute period

From the time a request to establish a board is made under subsection (e) of this section until 60 days after such board makes its report under subsection (g) of this section, no change, except by agreement, shall be made by the parties in the conditions out of which the dispute arose.

(i) Work stoppages by employees subsequent to carrier offer selected; eligibility of employees for benefits

If the emergency board selects the final offer submitted by the carrier and, after the expiration of the 60-day period described in subsection (h) of this section, the employees of such carrier engage in any work stoppage arising out of the dispute, such employees shall not be eligible during the period of such work stoppage for benefits under the Railroad Unemployment Insurance Act (45 U.S.C. §351 et seq.).

(j) Work stoppages by employees subsequent to employees offer selected; eligibility of employer for benefits

If the emergency board selects the final offer submitted by the employees and, after the expiration of the 60-day period described in subsection (h) of this section, the carrier refuses to accept the final offer submitted by the employees and the employees of such carrier engage in any work stoppage arising out of the dispute, the carrier shall not participate in any benefits of any agreement between carriers which is designed to provide benefits to such carriers during a work stoppage.

Sec. 160. Emergency board

If a dispute between a carrier and its employees be not adjusted under the foregoing provisions of this chapter and should, in the judgment of the Mediation

Board, threaten substantially to interrupt interstate commerce to a degree such as to deprive any section of the country of essential transportation service, the Mediation Board shall notify the President, who may thereupon, in his discretion, create a board to investigate and report respecting such dispute. Such board shall be composed of such number of persons as to the President may seem desirable: *Provided, however,* That no member appointed shall be pecuniarily or otherwise interested in any organization of employees or any carrier. The compensation of the members of any such board shall be fixed by the President. Such board shall be created separately in each instance and it shall investigate promptly the facts as to the dispute and make a report thereon to the President within thirty days from the date of its creation.

There is authorized to be appropriated such sums as may be necessary for the expenses of such board, including the compensation and the necessary traveling expenses and expenses actually incurred for subsistence, of the members of the board. All expenditures of the board shall be allowed and paid on the presentation of itemized vouchers therefor approved by the chairman.

After the creation of such board and for thirty days after such board has made its report to the President, no change, except by agreement, shall be made by the parties to the controversy in the conditions out of which the dispute arose.

Sec. 161. Effect of partial invalidity of chapter

If any provision of this chapter, or the application thereof to any person or circumstance, is held invalid, the remainder of the chapter, and the application of such provision to other persons or circumstances, shall not be affected thereby.

Sec. 162. Authorization of appropriations

There is authorized to be appropriated such sums as may be necessary for expenditure by the Mediation Board in carrying out the provisions of this chapter.

Sec. 163. Repeal of prior legislation; exception

Chapters 6 and 7 of this title, providing for mediation, conciliation, and arbitration, and all Acts and parts of Acts in conflict with the provisions of this chapter are repealed, except that the members, secretary, officers, employees, and agents of the Railroad Labor Board, in office on May 20, 1926, shall receive their salaries for a period of 30 days

from such date, in the same manner as though this chapter had not been passed.

SUBCHAPTER II: CARRIERS BY AIR

Sec. 181. Application of subchapter I to carriers by air

All of the provisions of subchapter I of this chapter except section 153 of this title are extended to and shall cover every common carrier by air engaged in interstate or foreign commerce, and every carrier by air transporting mail for or under contract with the United States Government, and every air pilot or other person who performs any work as an employee or subordinate official of such carrier or carriers, subject to its or their continuing authority to supervise and direct the manner of rendition of his service.

Sec. 182. Duties, penalties, benefits, and privileges of subchapter I applicable

The duties, requirements, penalties, benefits, and privileges prescribed and established by the provisions of subchapter I of this chapter except section 153 of this title shall apply to said carriers by air and their employees in the same manner and to the same extent as though such carriers and their employees were specifically included within the definition of "carrier" and "employee", respectively, in section 151 of this title.

Sec. 183. Disputes within jurisdiction of Mediation Board

The parties or either party to a dispute between an employee or a group of employees and a carrier or carriers by air may invoke the services of the National Mediation Board and the jurisdiction of said Mediation Board is extended to any of the following cases:

(a) A dispute concerning changes in rates of pay, rules, or working conditions not adjusted by the parties in conference.

(b) Any other dispute not referable to an adjustment board, as hereinafter provided, and not adjusted in conference between the parties, or where conferences are refused.

The National Mediation Board may proffer its services in case any labor emergency is found by it to exist at any time.

The services of the Mediation Board may be invoked in a case under this subchapter in the same manner and to the same extent as are the disputes covered by section 155 of this title.

Sec. 184. System, group, or regional boards of adjustment

The disputes between an employee or group of employees and a carrier or carriers by air growing out of grievances, or out of the interpretation or application of agreements concerning rates of pay, rules, or working conditions, including cases pending and unadjusted on April 10, 1936 before the National Labor Relations Board, shall be handled in the usual manner up to and including the chief operating officer of the carrier designated to handle such disputes; but, failing to reach an adjustment in this manner, the disputes may be referred by petition of the parties or by either party to an appropriate adjustment board, as hereinafter provided, with a full statement of the facts and supporting data bearing upon the disputes.

It shall be the duty of every carrier and of its employees, acting through their representatives, selected in accordance with the provisions of this subchapter, to establish a board of adjustment of jurisdiction not exceeding the jurisdiction which may be lawfully exercised by system, group, or regional boards of adjustment, under the authority of section 153 of this title.

Such boards of adjustment may be established by agreement between employees and carriers either on any individual carrier, or system, or group of carriers by air and any class or classes of its or their employees; or pending the establishment of a permanent National Board of Adjustment as hereinafter provided. Nothing in this chapter shall prevent said carriers by air, or any class or classes of their employees, both acting through their representatives selected in accordance with provisions of this subchapter, from mutually agreeing to the establishment of a National Board of Adjustment of temporary duration and of similarly limited jurisdiction.

Sec. 185. National Air Transport Adjustment Board

When, in the judgment of the National Mediation Board, it shall be necessary to have a permanent national board of adjustment in order to provide for the prompt and orderly settlement of disputes between said carriers by air, or any of them, and its or their employees, growing out of grievances or out of the interpretation or application of agreements between said carriers by air or any of them, and any class or classes of its or their employees, covering rates of pay, rules, or working conditions, the National Mediation Board is empowered and directed, by its order duly made, published, and served, to direct the said carriers by air and such labor organizations of their employees, national in scope, as have been or may be recognized in accordance with the provisions of this chapter, to select and designate four representatives who shall constitute a board which shall be known as the "National Air Transport Adjustment Board." Two members of said National Air Transport Adjustment Board shall be selected by said carriers by air and two members by the said labor organizations of the employees, within thirty days after the date of the order of the National Mediation Board, in the manner and by the procedure prescribed by section 153 of this title for the selection and designation of members of the National Railroad Adjustment Board. The National Air Transport Adjustment Board shall meet within forty days after the date of the order of the National Mediation Board directing the selection and designation of its members and shall organize and adopt rules for conducting its proceedings, in the manner prescribed in section 153 of this title. Vacancies in membership or office shall be filled, members shall be appointed in case of failure of the carriers or of labor organizations of the employees to select and designate representatives, members of the National Air Transport Adjustment Board shall be compensated, hearings shall be held, findings and awards made, stated, served, and enforced, and the number and compensation of any necessary assistants shall be determined and the compensation of such employees shall be paid, all in the same manner and to the same extent as provided with reference to the National Railroad Adjustment Board by section 153 of this title. The powers and duties prescribed and established by the provisions of section 153 of this title with reference to the National Railroad Adjustment Board and the several divisions thereof are conferred upon and shall be exercised and performed in like manner and to the same extent by the said National Air Transport Adjustment Board, not exceeding, however, the jurisdiction conferred upon said National Air Transport Adjustment Board by the provisions of this subchapter. From and after the organization of the National Air Transport Adjustment Board, if any system, group, or regional board of adjustment established by any carrier or carriers by air and any class or classes of its or their employees is not satisfactory to either party thereto, the said party, upon ninety days' notice to the other party, may elect to come under the jurisdiction of the National Air Transport Adjustment Board.

Sec. 186. Omitted

Sec. 187. Separability

If any provision of this subchapter or application thereof to any person or circumstance is held invalid, the remainder of such sections and the application of such provision to other persons or circumstances shall not be affected thereby. Sec. 188. Authorization of appropriations There is authorized to be appropriated such sums as may be necessary for expenditure by the Mediation Board in carrying out the provisions of this chapter.

Sec. 188. Authorization of appropriations

There is authorized to be appropriated such sums as may be necessary for expenditure by the Mediation Board in carrying out the provisions of this chapter.

North American Agreement on Labor Cooperation

NAALC IN A NUTSHELL

Signed: 1993

Purpose: To supplement the North American Free Trade Agreement (NAFTA) by promoting improved labor conditions and the enforcement of the national labor laws in the United States, Canada, and Mexico.

Responsible agency: U.S. Labor Department Bureau of International Labor Affairs

---

PREAMBLE

The Government of the United States of America, the Government of Canada and the Government of the United Mexican States:

RECALLING their resolve in the North American Free Trade Agreement (NAFTA) to:

— create an expanded and secure market for the goods and services produced in their territories,

— enhance the competitiveness of their firms in global markets,

— create new employment opportunities and improve working conditions and living standards in their respective territories, and

— protect, enhance and enforce basic workers' rights;

AFFIRMING their continuing respect for each Party's constitution and law;

DESIRING to build on their respective international commitments and to strengthen their cooperation on labor matters;

RECOGNIZING that their mutual prosperity depends on the promotion of competition based on innovation and rising levels of productivity and quality;

SEEKING to complement the economic opportunities created by the NAFTA with the human resource development, labor-management cooperation and continuous learning that characterize high-productivity economies;

ACKNOWLEDGING that protecting basic workers' rights will encourage firms to adopt high-productivity competitive strategies;

RESOLVED to promote, in accordance with their respective laws, high-skill, high-productivity economic development in North America by:

— investing in continuous human resource development, including for entry into the workforce and during periods of unemployment;

— promoting employment security and career opportunities for all workers through referral and other employment services;

— strengthening labor-management cooperation to promote greater dialogue between worker organizations and employers and to foster creativity and productivity in the workplace;

— promoting higher living standards as productivity increases;

— encouraging consultation and dialogue between labor, business and government both in each country and in North America;

— fostering investment with due regard for the importance of labor laws and principles;

— encouraging employers and employees in each country to comply with labor laws and to work together in maintaining a progressive, fair, safe and healthy working environment;

BUILDING on existing institutions and mechanisms in Canada, Mexico and the United States to achieve the preceding economic and social goals; and

CONVINCED of the benefits to be gained from further cooperation between them on labor matters;

HAVE AGREED as follows:

PART ONE: OBJECTIVES

Article 1: Objectives

The objectives of this Agreement are to:

  a. improve working conditions and living standards in each Party's territory;

  b. promote, to the maximum extent possible, the labor principles set out in Annex 1;

  c. encourage cooperation to promote innovation and rising levels of productivity and quality;

  d. encourage publication and exchange of information, data development and coordination, and joint studies to enhance mutually beneficial understanding of the laws and institutions governing labor in each Party's territory;

  e. pursue cooperative labor-related activities on the basis of mutual benefit;

  f. promote compliance with, and effective enforcement by each Party of, its labor law; and

  g. foster transparency in the administration of labor law.

PART TWO: OBLIGATIONS

Article 2: Levels of Protection

Affirming full respect for each Party's constitution, and recognizing the right of each Party to establish its own domestic labor standards, and to adopt or modify accordingly its labor laws and regulations, each Party shall ensure that its labor laws and regulations provide for high labor standards, consistent with high quality and productivity workplaces, and shall continue to strive to improve those standards in that light.

Article 3: Government Enforcement Action

1. Each Party shall promote compliance with and effectively enforce its labor law through appropriate government action, subject to Article 42, such as:

  a. appointing and training inspectors;

  b. monitoring compliance and investigating suspected violations, including through on-site inspections;

  c. seeking assurances of voluntary compliance;

  d. requiring record keeping and reporting;

  e. encouraging the establishment of worker-management committees to address labor regulation of the workplace;

  f. providing or encouraging mediation, conciliation and arbitration services; or

  g. initiating, in a timely manner, proceedings to seek appropriate sanctions or remedies for violations of its labor law.

2. Each Party shall ensure that its competent authorities give due consideration in accordance with its law to any request by an employer, employee or their representatives, or other interested person, for an investigation of an alleged violation of the Party's labor law.

Article 4: Private Action

1. Each Party shall ensure that persons with a legally recognized interest under its law in a particular matter have appropriate access to administrative, quasi-judicial, judicial or labor tribunals for the enforcement of the Party's labor law.

2. Each Party's law shall ensure that such persons may have recourse to, as appropriate, procedures by which rights arising under:

  a. its labor law, including in respect of occupational safety and health, employment standards, industrial relations and migrant workers, and

  b. collective agreements, can be enforced.

Article 5: Procedural Guarantees

1. Each Party shall ensure that its administrative, quasi-judicial, judicial and labor tribunal proceedings for the enforcement of its labor law are fair, equitable and transparent and, to this end, each Party shall provide that:

a. such proceedings comply with due process of law;

b. any hearings in such proceedings are open to the public, except where the administration of justice otherwise requires;

c. the parties to such proceedings are entitled to support or defend their respective positions and to present information or evidence; and

d. such proceedings are not unnecessarily complicated and do not entail unreasonable charges or time limits or unwarranted delays.

2. Each Party shall provide that final decisions on the merits of the case in such proceedings are:

a. in writing and preferably state the reasons on which the decisions are based;

b. made available without undue delay to the parties to the proceedings and, consistent with its law, to the public; and

c. based on information or evidence in respect of which the parties were offered the opportunity to be heard.

3. Each Party shall provide, as appropriate, that parties to such proceedings have the right, in accordance with its law, to seek review and, where warranted, correction of final decisions issued in such proceedings.

4. Each Party shall ensure that tribunals that conduct or review such proceedings are impartial and independent and do not have any substantial interest in the outcome of the matter.

5. Each Party shall provide that the parties to administrative, quasi-judicial, judicial or labor tribunal proceedings may seek remedies to ensure the enforcement of their labor rights. Such remedies may include, as appropriate, orders, compliance agreements, fines, penalties, imprisonment, injunctions or emergency workplace closures.

6. Each Party may, as appropriate, adopt or maintain labor defense offices to represent or advise workers or their organizations.

7. Nothing in this Article shall be construed to require a Party to establish, or to prevent a Party from establishing, a judicial system for the enforcement of its labor law distinct from its system for the enforcement of laws in general.

8. For greater certainty, decisions by each Party's administrative, quasi-judicial, judicial or labor tribunals, or pending decisions, as well as related proceedings shall not be subject to revision or reopened under the provisions of this Agreement.

Article 6: Publication

1. Each Party shall ensure that its laws, regulations, procedures and administrative rulings of general application respecting any matter covered by this Agreement are promptly published or otherwise made available in such a manner as to enable interested persons and Parties to become acquainted with them.

2. When so established by its law, each Party shall:

a. publish in advance any such measure that it proposes to adopt; and

b. provide interested persons a reasonable opportunity to comment on such proposed measures.

Article 7: Public Information and Awareness

1. Each Party shall promote public awareness of its labor law, including by:

a. ensuring that public information is available related to its labor law and enforcement and compliance procedures; and

b. promoting public education regarding its labor law.

PART THREE: COMMISSION FOR LABOR COOPERATION

Article 8: The Commission

1. The Parties hereby establish the Commission for Labor Cooperation.

2. The Commission shall comprise a ministerial Council and a Secretariat. The Commission shall be assisted by the National Administrative Office of each Party.

Section A: The Council

Article 9: Council Structure and Procedures

1. The Council shall comprise labor ministers of the Parties or their designees.

2. The Council shall establish its rules and procedures.

3. The Council shall convene:

a. at least once a year in regular session, and

b. in special session at the request of any Party. Regular sessions shall be chaired successively by each Party.

4. The Council may hold public sessions to report on appropriate matters.

5. The Council may:

a. establish, and assign responsibilities to, committees, working groups or expert groups; and

b. seek the advice of independent experts.

6. All decisions and recommendations of the Council shall be taken by consensus, except as the Council may otherwise decide or as otherwise provided in this Agreement.

Article 10: Council Functions

1. The Council shall be the governing body of the Commission and shall:

a. oversee the implementation and develop recommendations on the further elaboration of this Agreement and, to this end, the Council shall, within four years after the date of entry into force of this Agreement, review its operation and effectiveness in the light of experience;

b. direct the work and activities of the Secretariat and of any committees or working groups convened by the Council;

c. establish priorities for cooperative action and, as appropriate, develop technical assistance programs on the matters set out in Article 11;

d. approve the annual plan of activities and budget of the Commission;

e. approve for publication, subject to such terms or conditions as it may impose, reports and studies prepared by the Secretariat, independent experts or working groups;

f. facilitate Party-to-Party consultations, including through the exchange of information;

g. address questions and differences that may arise between the Parties regarding the interpretation or application of this Agreement; and

h. promote the collection and publication of comparable data on enforcement, labor standards and labor market indicators.

2. The Council may consider any other matter within the scope of this Agreement and take such other action in the exercise of its functions as the Parties may agree.

Article 11: Cooperative Activities

1. The Council shall promote cooperative activities between the Parties, as appropriate, regarding:

a. occupational safety and health;

b. child labor;

c. migrant workers of the Parties;

d. human resource development;

e. labor statistics;

f. work benefits;

g. social programs for workers and their families;

h. programs, methodologies and experiences regarding productivity improvement;

i. labor-management relations and collective bargaining procedures;

j. employment standards and their implementation;

k. compensation for work-related injury or illness;

l. legislation relating to the formation and operation of unions, collective bargaining and the resolution of labor disputes, and its implementation;

m. the equality of women and men in the workplace;

n. forms of cooperation among workers, management and government;

o. the provision of technical assistance, at the request of a Party, for the development of its labor standards; and

p. such other matters as the Parties may agree.

2. In carrying out the activities referred to in paragraph 1, the Parties may, commensurate with the availability of resources in each Party, cooperate through:

a. seminars, training sessions, working groups and conferences;

b. joint research projects, including sectoral studies;

c. technical assistance; and

d. such other means as the Parties may agree.

3. The Parties shall carry out the cooperative activities referred to in paragraph 1 with due regard for the economic, social, cultural and legislative differences between them.

Section B: The Secretariat

Article 12: Secretariat Structure and Procedures

1. The Secretariat shall be headed by an Executive Director, who shall be chosen by the Council for a three-year term, which may be renewed by the Council for one additional three-year term. The position of Executive Director shall rotate consecutively between nationals of each Party. The Council may remove the Executive Director solely for cause.

2. The Executive Director shall appoint and supervise the staff of the Secretariat, regulate their powers and duties and fix their remuneration in accordance with general standards to be established by the Council. The general standards shall provide that:

a. staff shall be appointed and retained, and their conditions of employment shall be determined, strictly on the basis of efficiency, competence and integrity;

b. in appointing staff, the Executive Director shall take into account lists of candidates prepared by the Parties;

c. due regard shall be paid to the importance of recruiting an equitable proportion of the professional staff from among the nationals of each Party; and

d. the Executive Director shall inform the Council of all appointments.

3. The number of staff positions shall initially be set at 15 and may be changed thereafter by the Council.

4. The Council may decide, by a two-thirds vote, to reject any appointment that does not meet the general standards. Any such decision shall be made and held in confidence.

5. In the performance of their duties, the Executive Director and the staff shall not seek or receive instructions from any government or any other authority external to the Council. Each Party shall respect the international character of the responsibilities of the Executive Director and the staff and shall not seek to influence them in the discharge of their responsibilities.

6. The Secretariat shall safeguard:

a. from disclosure information it receives that could identify an organization or person if the person or organization so requests or the Secretariat otherwise considers it appropriate; and

b. from public disclosure any information it receives from any organization or person where the information is designated by that organization or person as confidential or proprietary.

7. The Secretariat shall act under the direction of the Council in accordance with Article 10(1)(b).

Article 13: Secretariat Functions

1. The Secretariat shall assist the Council in exercising its functions and shall provide such other support as the Council may direct.

2. The Executive Director shall submit for the approval of the Council the annual plan of activities and budget for the Commission, including provision for contingencies and proposed cooperative activities.

3. The Secretariat shall report to the Council annually on its activities and expenditures.

4. The Secretariat shall periodically publish a list of matters resolved under Part Four or referred to Evaluation Committees of Experts.

Article 14: Secretariat Reports and Studies

1. The Secretariat shall periodically prepare background reports setting out publicly available information supplied by each Party on:

a. labor law and administrative procedures;

b. trends and administrative strategies related to the implementation and enforcement of labor law;

c. labor market conditions such as employment rates, average wages and labor productivity; and

d. human resource development issues such as training and adjustment programs.

2. The Secretariat shall prepare a study on any matter as the Council may request. The Secretariat shall prepare any such study in accordance with terms of reference established by the Council, and may

a. consider any relevant information;

b. where it does not have specific expertise in the matter, engage one or more independent experts of recognized experience; and

c. include proposals on the matter.

3. The Secretariat shall submit a draft of any report or study that it prepares pursuant to paragraph 1 or 2 to the Council. If the Council considers that a report or study is materially inaccurate or otherwise deficient, the Council may remand it to the Secretariat for reconsideration or other disposition.

4. Secretariat reports and studies shall be made public 45 days after their approval by the Council, unless the Council otherwise decides.

Section C: National Administrative Offices

Article 15: National Administrative Office Structure

1. Each Party shall establish a National Administrative Office (NAO) at the federal government level and notify the Secretariat and the other Parties of its location.

2. Each Party shall designate a Secretary for its NAO, who shall be responsible for its administration and management.

3. Each Party shall be responsible for the operation and costs of its NAO.

Article 16: NAO Functions

1. Each NAO shall serve as a point of contact with:

a. governmental agencies of that Party;

b. NAOs of the other Parties; and

c. the Secretariat.

2. Each NAO shall promptly provide publicly available information requested by:

a. the Secretariat for reports under Article 14(1);

b. the Secretariat for studies under Article 14(2);

c. a NAO of another Party; and

d. an ECE.

3. Each NAO shall provide for the submission and receipt, and periodically publish a list, of public communications on labor law matters arising in the territory of another Party. Each NAO shall review such matters, as appropriate, in accordance with domestic procedures.

Section D: National Committees

Article 17: National Advisory Committee

Each Party may convene a national advisory committee, comprising members of its public, including representatives of its labor and business organizations and other persons, to advise it on the implementation and further elaboration of this Agreement.

Article 18: Governmental Committee

Each Party may convene a governmental committee, which may comprise or include representatives of federal and state or provincial governments, to advise it on the implementation and further elaboration of this Agreement.

Section E: Official Languages

Article 19: Official Languages

The official languages of the Commission shall be English, French and Spanish. The Council shall establish rules and procedures regarding interpretation and translation.

PART FOUR: COOPERATIVE CONSULTATIONS AND EVALUATIONS

Article 20: Cooperation

The Parties shall at all times endeavor to agree on the interpretation and application of this Agreement, and shall make every attempt through cooperation and consultations to resolve any matter that might affect its operation.

Section A: Cooperative Consultations

Article 21: Consultations between NAOs

1. A NAO may request consultations, to be conducted in accordance with the procedures set out in paragraph 2, with another NAO in relation to the other Party's labor law, its administration, or labor market conditions in its territory. The requesting NAO shall notify the NAOs of the other Parties and the Secretariat of its request.

2. In such consultations, the requested NAO shall promptly provide such publicly available data or information, including:

a. descriptions of its laws, regulations, procedures, policies or practices,

b. proposed changes to such procedures, policies or practices, and

c. such clarifications and explanations related to such matters, as may assist the consulting NAOs to better understand and respond to the issues raised.

3. Any other NAO shall be entitled to participate in the consultations on notice to the other NAOs and the Secretariat.

Article 22: Ministerial Consultations

1. Any Party may request in writing consultations with another Party at the ministerial level regarding any matter within the scope of this Agreement. The requesting Party shall provide specific and sufficient information to allow the requested Party to respond.

2. The requesting Party shall promptly notify the other Parties of the request. A third Party that considers it has a substantial interest in the matter shall be entitled to participate in the consultations on notice to the other Parties.

3. The consulting Parties shall make every attempt to resolve the matter through consultations under this Article, including through the exchange of sufficient publicly available information to enable a full examination of the matter.

Section B: Evaluations

Article 23: Evaluation Committee of Experts

1. If a matter has not been resolved after ministerial consultations pursuant to Article 22, any consulting Party may request in writing the establishment of an Evaluation Committee of Experts (ECE). The requesting Party shall deliver the request to the other Parties and to the Secretariat. Subject to paragraphs 3 and 4, the Council shall establish an ECE on delivery of the request.

2. The ECE shall analyze, in the light of the objectives of this Agreement and in a non-adversarial manner, patterns of practice by each Party in the enforcement of its occupational safety and health or other technical labor standards as they apply to the particular matter considered by the Parties under Article 22.

3. No ECE may be convened if a Party obtains a ruling under Annex 23 that the matter:

a. is not trade-related; or

b. is not covered by mutually recognized labor laws.

4. No ECE may be convened regarding any matter that was previously the subject of an ECE report in the absence of such new information as would warrant a further report.

Article 24: Rules of Procedure

1. The Council shall establish rules of procedure for ECEs, which shall apply unless the Council otherwise decides. The rules of procedure shall provide that:

a. an ECE shall normally comprise three members;

b. the chair shall be selected by the Council from a roster of experts developed in consultation with the ILO pursuant to Article 45 and, where possible, other members shall be selected from a roster developed by the Parties;

c. ECE members shall

i. have expertise or experience in labor matters or other appropriate disciplines,

ii. be chosen strictly on the basis of objectivity, reliability and sound judgment,

iii. be independent of, and not be affiliated with or take instructions from, any Party or the Secretariat, and

iv. comply with a code of conduct to be established by the Council;

d. an ECE may invite written submissions from the Parties and the public;

e. an ECE may consider, in preparing its report, any information provided by

    i. the Secretariat,

    ii. the NAO of each Party,

    iii. organizations, institutions and persons with relevant expertise, and

    iv. the public; and

f. each Party shall have a reasonable opportunity to review and comment on information that the ECE receives and to make written submissions to the ECE.

2. The Secretariat and the NAOs shall provide appropriate administrative assistance to an ECE, in accordance with the rules of procedure established by the Council under paragraph 1.

Article 25: Draft Evaluation Reports

1. Within 120 days after it is established, or such other period as the Council may decide, the ECE shall present a draft report for consideration by the Council, which shall contain:

a. a comparative assessment of the matter under consideration;

b. its conclusions; and

c. where appropriate, practical recommendations that may assist the Parties in respect of the matter.

2. Each Party may submit written views to the ECE on its draft report. The ECE shall take such views into account in preparing its final report.

Article 26: Final Evaluation Reports

1. The ECE shall present a final report to the Council within 60 days after presentation of the draft report, unless the Council otherwise decides.

2. The final report shall be published within 30 days after its presentation to the Council, unless the Council otherwise decides.

3. The Parties shall provide to each other and the Secretariat written responses to the recommendations contained in the ECE report within 90 days of its publication.

4. The final report and such written responses shall be tabled for consideration at the next regular session of the Council. The Council may keep the matter under review.

PART FIVE: RESOLUTION OF DISPUTES

Article 27: Consultations

1. Following presentation to the Council under Article 26(1) of an ECE final report that addresses the enforcement of a Party's occupational safety and health, child labor or minimum wage technical labor standards, any Party may request in writing consultations with any other Party regarding whether there has been a persistent pattern of failure by that other Party to effectively enforce such standards in respect of the general subject matter addressed in the report.

2. The requesting Party shall deliver the request to the other Parties and to the Secretariat.

3. Unless the Council otherwise provides in its rules and procedures established under Article 9(2), a third Party that considers it has a substantial interest in the matter shall be entitled to participate in the consultations on delivery of written notice to the other Parties and to the Secretariat.

4. The consulting Parties shall make every attempt to arrive at a mutually satisfactory resolution of the matter through consultations under this Article.

Article 28: Initiation of Procedures

1. If the consulting Parties fail to resolve the matter pursuant to Article 27 within 60 days of delivery of a request for consultations, or such other period as the consulting Parties may agree, any such Party may request in writing a special session of the Council.

2. The requesting Party shall state in the request the matter complained of and shall deliver the request to the other Parties and to the Secretariat.

3. Unless it decides otherwise, the Council shall convene within 20 days of delivery of the request and shall endeavor to resolve the dispute promptly.

4. The Council may:

a. call on such technical advisers or create such working groups or expert groups as it deems necessary,

b. have recourse to good offices, conciliation, mediation or such other dispute resolution procedures, or

c. make recommendations, as may assist the consulting Parties to reach a mutually satisfactory resolution of the dispute. Any such recommendations shall be made public if the Council, by a two-thirds vote, so decides.

5. Where the Council decides that a matter is more properly covered by another agreement or arrangement to which the consulting Parties are party, it shall refer the matter to those Parties for appropriate action in accordance with such other agreement or arrangement.

Article 29: Request for an Arbitral Panel

1. If the matter has not been resolved within 60 days after the Council has convened pursuant to Article 28, the Council shall, on the written request of any consulting Party and by a two-thirds vote, convene an arbitral panel to consider the matter where the alleged persistent pattern of failure by the Party complained against to effectively enforce its occupational safety and health, child labor or minimum wage technical labor standards is:

a. trade-related; and

b. covered by mutually recognized labor laws.

2. A third Party that considers it has a substantial interest in the matter shall be entitled to join as a complaining Party on delivery of written notice of its intention to participate to the disputing Parties and the Secretariat. The notice shall be delivered at the earliest possible time, and in any event no later than seven days after the date of the vote of the Council to convene a panel.

3. Unless otherwise agreed by the disputing Parties, the panel shall be established and perform its functions in a manner consistent with the provisions of this Part.

Article 30: Roster

1. The Council shall establish and maintain a roster of up to 45 individuals who are willing and able to serve as panelists. The roster members shall be appointed by consensus for terms of three years, and may be reappointed.

2. Roster members shall:

a. have expertise or experience in labor law or its enforcement, or in the resolution of disputes arising under international agreements, or other relevant scientific, technical or professional expertise or experience;

b. be chosen strictly on the basis of objectivity, reliability and sound judgment;

c. be independent of, and not be affiliated with or take instructions from, any Party or the Secretariat; and

d. comply with a code of conduct to be established by the Council.

Article 31: Qualifications of Panelists

1. All panelists shall meet the qualifications set out in Article 30.

2. Individuals may not serve as panelists for a dispute where:

a. they have participated pursuant to Article 28(4) or participated as members of an ECE that addressed the matter; or

b. they have, or a person or organization with which they are affiliated has, an interest in the matter, as set out in the code of conduct established under Article 30(2)(d).

Article 32: Panel Selection

1. Where there are two disputing Parties, the following procedures shall apply:

a. The panel shall comprise five members.

b. The disputing Parties shall endeavor to agree on the chair of the panel within 15 days after the Council votes to convene the panel. If the disputing Parties are unable to agree on the chair within this period, the disputing Party chosen by lot shall select within five days a chair who is not a citizen of that Party.

c. Within 15 days of selection of the chair, each disputing Party shall select two panelists who are citizens of the other disputing Party.

d. If a disputing Party fails to select its panelists within such period, such panelists shall be selected by lot from among the roster members who are citizens of the other disputing Party.

2. Where there are more than two disputing Parties, the following procedures shall apply:

a. The panel shall comprise five members.

b. The disputing Parties shall endeavor to agree on the chair of the panel within 15 days after the Council votes to convene the panel. If the disputing Parties are unable to agree on the chair within this period, the Party or Parties on the side of the dispute chosen by lot shall select within 10 days a chair who is not a citizen of such Party or Parties.

c. Within 30 days of selection of the chair, the Party complained against shall select two panelists, one of whom is a citizen of a complaining Party, and the other of whom is a citizen of another complaining Party. The complaining Parties shall select two panelists who are citizens of the Party complained against.

d. If any disputing Party fails to select a panelist within such period, such panelist shall be selected by lot in accordance with the citizenship criteria of subparagraph (c).

3. Panelists shall normally be selected from the roster. Any disputing Party may exercise a peremptory challenge against any individual not on the roster who is proposed as a panelist by a disputing Party within 30 days after the individual has been proposed.

4. If a disputing Party believes that a panelist is in violation of the code of conduct, the disputing Parties shall consult and, if they agree, the panelist shall be removed and a new panelist shall be selected in accordance with this Article.

Article 33: Rules of Procedure

1. The Council shall establish Model Rules of Procedure. The procedures shall provide:

a. a right to at least one hearing before the panel;

b. the opportunity to make initial and rebuttal written submissions; and

c. that no panel may disclose which panelists are associated with majority or minority opinions.

2. Unless the disputing Parties otherwise agree, panels convened under this Part shall be established and conduct their proceedings in accordance with the Model Rules of Procedure.

3. Unless the disputing Parties otherwise agree within 20 days after the Council votes to convene the panel, the terms of reference shall be:

"To examine, in light of the relevant provisions of the Agreement, including those contained in Part Five, whether there has been a persistent pattern of failure by the Party complained against to effectively enforce its occupational safety and health, child labor or minimum wage technical labor standards, and to make findings, determinations and recommendations in accordance with Article 36(2)."

Article 34: Third Party Participation

A Party that is not a disputing Party, on delivery of a written notice to the disputing Parties and the Secretariat, shall be entitled to attend all hearings, to make written and oral submissions to the panel and to receive written submissions of the disputing Parties.

Article 35: Role of Experts

On request of a disputing Party, or on its own initiative, the panel may seek information and technical advice from any person or body that it deems appropriate, provided that the disputing Parties so agree and subject to such terms and conditions as such Parties may agree.

Article 36: Initial Report

1. Unless the disputing Parties otherwise agree, the panel shall base its report on the submissions and arguments of the disputing Parties and on any information before it pursuant to Article 35.

2. Unless the disputing Parties otherwise agree, the panel shall, within 180 days after the last panelist is selected, present to the disputing Parties an initial report containing:

a. findings of fact;

b. its determination as to whether there has been a persistent pattern of failure by the Party complained against to effectively enforce its occupational safety and health, child labor or minimum wage technical labor standards in a matter that is trade-related and covered by mutually recognized labor laws, or any other determination requested in the terms of reference; and

c. in the event the panel makes an affirmative determination under subparagraph (b), its recommendations, if any, for the resolution of the dispute, which normally shall be that the Party complained against adopt and implement an action plan sufficient to remedy the pattern of non-enforcement.

3. Panelists may furnish separate opinions on matters not unanimously agreed.

4. A disputing Party may submit written comments to the panel on its initial report within 30 days of presentation of the report.

5. In such an event, and after considering such written comments, the panel, on its own initiative or on the request of any disputing Party, may:

    a. request the views of any participating Party;

    b. reconsider its report; and

    c. make any further examination that it considers appropriate.

Article 37: Final Report

1. The panel shall present to the disputing Parties a final report, including any separate opinions on matters not unanimously agreed, within 60 days of presentation of the initial report, unless the disputing Parties otherwise agree.

2. The disputing Parties shall transmit to the Council the final report of the panel, as well as any written views that a disputing Party desires to be appended, on a confidential basis within 15 days after it is presented to them.

3. The final report of the panel shall be published five days after it is transmitted to the Council.

Article 38: Implementation of Final Report

If, in its final report, a panel determines that there has been a persistent pattern of failure by the Party complained against to effectively enforce its occupational safety and health, child labor or minimum wage technical labor standards, the disputing Parties may agree on a mutually satisfactory action plan, which normally shall conform with the determinations and recommendations of the panel. The disputing Parties shall promptly notify the Secretariat and the Council of any agreed resolution of the dispute.

Article 39: Review of Implementation

1. If, in its final report, a panel determines that there has been a persistent pattern of failure by the Party complained against to effectively enforce its occupational safety and health, child labor or minimum wage technical labor standards, and:

    a. the disputing Parties have not agreed on an action plan under Article 38 within 60 days of the date of the final report, or

    b. the disputing Parties cannot agree on whether the Party complained against is fully implementing

        i. an action plan agreed under Article 38,

        ii. an action plan deemed to have been established by a panel under paragraph 2, or

        iii. an action plan approved or established by a panel under paragraph 4, any disputing Party may request that the panel be reconvened. The requesting Party shall deliver the request in writing to the other Parties and to the Secretariat. The Council shall reconvene the panel on delivery of the request to the Secretariat.

2. No Party may make a request under paragraph 1(a) earlier than 60 days, or later than 120 days, after the date of the final report. If the disputing Parties have not agreed to an action plan and if no request was made under paragraph 1(a), the last action plan, if any, submitted by the Party complained against to the complaining Party or Parties within 60 days of the date of the final report, or such other period as the disputing Parties may agree, shall be deemed to have been established by the panel 120 days after the date of the final report.

3. A request under paragraph 1(b) may be made no earlier than 180 days after an action plan has been:

    a. agreed under Article 38,

    b. deemed to have been established by a panel under paragraph 2, or

    c. approved or established by a panel under paragraph 4, and only during the term of any such action plan.

4. Where a panel has been reconvened under paragraph 1(a), it:

    a. shall determine whether any action plan proposed by the Party complained against is sufficient to remedy the pattern of non-enforcement and

        i. if so, shall approve the plan, or

        ii. if not, shall establish such a plan consistent with the law of the Party complained against, and

b. may, where warranted, impose a monetary enforcement assessment in accordance with Annex 39, within 90 days after the panel has been reconvened or such other period as the disputing Parties may agree.

5. Where a panel has been reconvened under paragraph 1(b), it shall determine either that:

a. the Party complained against is fully implementing the action plan, in which case the panel may not impose a monetary enforcement assessment, or

b. the Party complained against is not fully implementing the action plan, in which case the panel shall impose a monetary enforcement assessment in accordance with Annex 39, within 60 days after it has been reconvened or such other period as the disputing Parties may agree.

6. A panel reconvened under this Article shall provide that the Party complained against shall fully implement any action plan referred to in paragraph 4(a)(ii) or 5(b), and pay any monetary enforcement assessment imposed under paragraph 4(b) or 5(b), and any such provision shall be final.

Article 40: Further Proceeding

A complaining Party may, at any time beginning 180 days after a panel determination under Article 39(5)(b), request in writing that a panel be reconvened to determine whether the Party complained against is fully implementing the action plan. On delivery of the request to the other Parties and the Secretariat, the Council shall reconvene the panel. The panel shall make the determination within 60 days after it has been reconvened or such other period as the disputing Parties may agree.

Article 41: Suspension of Benefits

1. Subject to Annex 41A, where a Party fails to pay a monetary enforcement assessment within 180 days after it is imposed by a panel:

a. under Article 39(4)(b), or

b. under Article 39(5)(b), except where benefits may be suspended under paragraph 2(a), any complaining Party or Parties may suspend, in accordance with Annex 41B, the application to the Party complained against of NAFTA benefits in an amount no greater than that sufficient to collect the monetary enforcement assessment.

2. Subject to Annex 41A, where a panel has made a determination under Article 39(5)(b) and the panel:

a. has previously imposed a monetary enforcement assessment under Article 39(4)(b) or established an action plan under Article 39(4)(a)(ii), or

b. has subsequently determined under Article 40 that a Party is not fully implementing an action plan, the complaining Party or Parties may, in accordance with Annex 41B, suspend annually the application to the Party complained against of NAFTA benefits in an amount no greater than the monetary enforcement assessment imposed by the panel under Article 39(5)(b).

3. Where more than one complaining Party suspends benefits under paragraph 1 or 2, the combined suspension shall be no greater than the amount of the monetary enforcement assessment.

4. Where a Party has suspended benefits under paragraph 1 or 2, the Council shall, on the delivery of a written request by the Party complained against to the other Parties and the Secretariat, reconvene the panel to determine whether the monetary enforcement assessment has been paid or collected, or whether the Party complained against is fully implementing the action plan, as the case may be. The panel shall submit its report within 45 days after it has been reconvened. If the panel determines that the assessment has been paid or collected, or that the Party complained against is fully implementing the action plan, the suspension of benefits under paragraph 1 or 2, as the case may be, shall be terminated.

5. On the written request of the Party complained against, delivered to the other Parties and the Secretariat, the Council shall reconvene the panel to determine whether the suspension of benefits by the complaining Party or Parties pursuant to paragraph 1 or 2 is manifestly excessive. Within 45 days of the request, the panel shall present a report to the disputing Parties containing its determination.

PART SIX: GENERAL PROVISIONS

Article 42: Enforcement Principle

Nothing in this Agreement shall be construed to empower a Party's authorities to undertake labor law enforcement activities in the territory of another Party.

Article 43: Private Rights

No Party may provide for a right of action under its domestic law against any other Party on the ground that another Party has acted in a manner inconsistent with this Agreement.

Article 44: Protection of Information

1. If a Party provides confidential or proprietary information to another Party, including its NAO, the Council or the Secretariat, the recipient shall treat the information on the same basis as the Party providing the information.

2. Confidential or proprietary information provided by a Party to an ECE or a panel under this Agreement shall be treated in accordance with the rules of procedure established under Articles 24 and 33.

Article 45: Cooperation with the ILO

The Parties shall seek to establish cooperative arrangements with the ILO to enable the Council and Parties to draw on the expertise and experience of the ILO for purposes of implementing Article 24(1).

Article 46: Extent of Obligations

Annex 46 applies to the Parties specified in that Annex.

Article 47: Funding of the Commission

Each Party shall contribute an equal share of the annual budget of the Commission, subject to the availability of appropriated funds in accordance with the Party's legal procedures. No Party shall be obligated to pay more than any other Party in respect of an annual budget.

Article 48: Privileges and Immunities

The Executive Director and staff of the Secretariat shall enjoy in the territory of each of the Parties such privileges and immunities as are necessary for the exercise of their functions.

Article 49: Definitions

1. For purposes of this Agreement:

A Party has not failed to "effectively enforce its occupational safety and health, child labor or minimum wage technical labor standards" or comply with Article 3(1) in a particular case where the action or inaction by agencies or officials of that Party:

a. reflects a reasonable exercise of the agency's or the official's discretion with respect to investigatory, prosecutorial, regulatory or compliance matters; or

b. results from bona fide decisions to allocate resources to enforcement in respect of other labor matters determined to have higher priorities;

"labor law" means laws and regulations, or provisions thereof, that are directly related to:

a. freedom of association and protection of the right to organize;

b. the right to bargain collectively;

c. the right to strike;

d. prohibition of forced labor;

e. labor protections for children and young persons;

f. minimum employment standards, such as minimum wages and overtime pay, covering wage earners, including those not covered by collective agreements;

g. elimination of employment discrimination on the basis of grounds such as race, religion, age, sex, or other grounds as determined by each Party's domestic laws;

h. equal pay for men and women;

i. prevention of occupational injuries and illnesses;

j. compensation in cases of occupational injuries and illnesses;

k. protection of migrant workers;

"mutually recognized labor laws" means laws of both a requesting Party and the Party whose laws were the subject of ministerial consultations under Article 22 that address the same general subject matter in a manner that provides enforceable rights, protections or standards;

"pattern of practice" means a course of action or inaction beginning after the date of entry into force of the Agreement, and does not include a single instance or case;

"persistent pattern" means a sustained or recurring pattern of practice;

"province" means a province of Canada, and includes the Yukon Territory and the Northwest Territories and their successors;

"publicly available information" means information to which the public has a legal right under the statutory laws of the Party;

"technical labor standards" means laws and regulations, or specific provisions thereof, that are directly related to subparagraphs (d) through (k) of the definition of labor law. For greater certainty and consistent with the provisions of this Agreement, the setting of all standards and levels in respect of minimum wages and labor protections for children and young persons by each Party shall not be subject to obligations under this Agreement. Each Party's obligations under this Agreement pertain to enforcing the level of the general minimum wage and child labor age limits established by that Party;

"territory" means for a Party the territory of that Party as set out in Annex 49; and

"trade-related" means related to a situation involving workplaces, firms, companies or sectors that produce goods or provide services:

a. traded between the territories of the Parties; or

b. that compete, in the territory of the Party whose labor law was the subject of ministerial consultations under Article 22, with goods or services produced or provided by persons of another Party.

PART SEVEN: FINAL PROVISIONS

Article 50: Annexes

The Annexes to this Agreement constitute an integral part of the Agreement.

Article 51: Entry into Force

This Agreement shall enter into force on January 1, 1994, immediately after entry into force of the NAFTA, on an exchange of written notifications certifying the completion of necessary legal procedures.

Article 52: Amendments

1. The Parties may agree on any modification of or addition to this Agreement.

2. When so agreed, and approved in accordance with the applicable legal procedures of each Party, a modification or addition shall constitute an integral part of this Agreement.

Article 53: Accession

Any country or group of countries may accede to this Agreement subject to such terms and conditions as may be agreed between such country or countries and the Council and following approval in accordance with the applicable legal procedures of each country.

Article 54: Withdrawal

A Party may withdraw from this Agreement six months after it provides written notice of withdrawal to the other Parties. If a Party withdraws, the Agreement shall remain in force for the remaining Parties.

Article 55: Authentic Texts

The English, French and Spanish texts of this Agreement are equally authentic.

IN WITNESS WHEREOF, the undersigned, being duly authorized by the respective Governments, have signed this Agreement.

ANNEX 1: LABOR PRINCIPLES

The following are guiding principles that the Parties are committed to promote, subject to each Party's domestic law, but do not establish common minimum standards for their domestic law. They indicate broad areas of concern where the Parties have developed, each in its own way, laws, regulations, procedures and practices that protect the rights and interests of their respective workforces.

1. Freedom of association and protection of the right to organize

The right of workers exercised freely and without impediment to establish and join organizations of their own choosing to further and defend their interests.

2. The right to bargain collectively

The protection of the right of organized workers to freely engage in collective bargaining on matters concerning the terms and conditions of employment.

3. The right to strike

The protection of the right of workers to strike in order to defend their collective interests.

4. Prohibition of forced labor

The prohibition and suppression of all forms of forced or compulsory labor, except for types of compulsory work generally considered acceptable by the Parties, such as compulsory military service, certain civic obligations, prison labor not for private purposes and work exacted in cases of emergency.

5. Labor protections for children and young persons

The establishment of restrictions on the employment of children and young persons that may vary taking into consideration relevant factors likely to jeopardize the full physical, mental and moral development of young persons, including schooling and safety requirements.

6. Minimum employment standards

The establishment of minimum employment standards, such as minimum wages and overtime pay, for wage earners, including those not covered by collective agreements.

7. Elimination of employment discrimination

Elimination of employment discrimination on such grounds as race, religion, age, sex or other grounds, subject to certain reasonable exceptions, such as, where applicable, *bona fide occupational requirements or qualifications and established practices or rules governing retirement ages, and special measures of protection or assistance for particular groups designed to take into account the effects of discrimination.*

8. Equal pay for women and men

Equal wages for women and men by applying the principle of equal pay for equal work in the same establishment.

9. Prevention of occupational injuries and illnesses

Prescribing and implementing standards to minimize the causes of occupational injuries and illnesses.

10. Compensation in cases of occupational injuries and illnesses

The establishment of a system providing benefits and compensation to workers or their dependents in cases of occupational injuries, accidents or fatalities arising out of, linked with or occurring in the course of employment.

11. Protection of migrant workers

Providing migrant workers in a Party's territory with the same legal protection as the Party's nationals in respect of working conditions.

ANNEX 23: INTERPRETIVE RULING

1. Where a Party has requested the Council to convene an ECE, the Council shall, on the written request of any other Party, select an independent expert to make a ruling concerning whether the matter is:

a. trade-related; or

b. covered by mutually recognized labor laws.

2. The Council shall establish rules of procedure for the selection of the expert and for submissions by the Parties. Unless the Council decides otherwise, the expert shall present a ruling within 15 days after the expert is selected.

ANNEX 39: MONETARY ENFORCEMENT ASSESSMENTS

1. For the first year after the date of entry into force of this Agreement, any monetary enforcement assessment shall be no greater than 20 million dollars (U.S.) or its equivalent in the currency of the Party complained against. Thereafter, any monetary enforcement assessment shall be no greater than .007 percent of total trade in goods between the Parties during the most recent year for which data are available.

2. In determining the amount of the assessment, the panel shall take into account:

a. the pervasiveness and duration of the Party's persistent pattern of failure to effectively enforce its occupational safety and health, child labor or minimum wage technical labor standards;

b. the level of enforcement that could reasonably be expected of a Party given its resource constraints;

c. the reasons, if any, provided by the Party for not fully implementing an action plan;

d. efforts made by the Party to begin remedying the pattern of non-enforcement after the final report of the panel; and

e. any other relevant factors.

3. All monetary enforcement assessments shall be paid in the currency of the Party complained against into a fund established in the name of the Commission by the Council and shall be expended at the direction of the Council to improve or enhance the labor law enforcement in the Party complained against, consistent with its law.

ANNEX 41A: CANADIAN DOMESTIC ENFORCEMENT AND COLLECTION

1. For the purposes of this Annex, "panel determination" means:

a. a determination by a panel under Article 39(4)(b) or 5(b) that provides that Canada shall pay a monetary enforcement assessment; and

b. a determination by a panel under Article 39(5)(b) that provides that Canada shall fully implement an action plan where the panel:

i. has previously established an action plan under Article 39(4)(a)(ii) or imposed a monetary enforcement assessment under Article 39(4)(b); or

ii. has subsequently determined under Article 40 that Canada is not fully implementing an action plan.

2. Canada shall adopt and maintain procedures that provide that:

a. subject to subparagraph (b), the Commission, at the request of a complaining Party, may in its own name file in a court of competent jurisdiction a certified copy of a panel determination;

b. the Commission may file in court a panel determination that is a panel determination described in paragraph 1(a) only if Canada has failed to comply with the determination within 180 days of when the determination was made;

c. when filed, the panel determination, for purposes of enforcement, shall become an order of the court;

d. the Commission may take proceedings for enforcement of a panel determination that is

made an order of the court, in that court, against the person against whom the panel determination is addressed in accordance with paragraph 6 of Annex 46;

e. proceedings to enforce a panel determination that has been made an order of the court shall be conducted by way of summary proceedings;

f. in proceedings to enforce a panel determination that is a panel determination described in paragraph 1(b) and that has been made an order of the court, the court shall promptly refer any question of fact or any question of interpretation of the panel determination to the panel that made the panel determination, and the decision of the panel shall be binding on the court;

g. a panel determination that has been made an order of the court shall not be subject to domestic review or appeal; and

h. an order made by the court in proceedings to enforce a panel determination that has been made an order of the court shall not be subject to review or appeal.

3. Where Canada is the Party complained against, the procedures adopted and maintained by Canada under this Annex shall apply and the procedures set out in Article 41 shall not apply.

4. Any change by Canada to the procedures adopted and maintained by Canada under this Annex that have the effect of undermining the provisions of this Annex shall be considered a breach of this Agreement.

ANNEX 41B: SUSPENSION OF BENEFITS

1. Where a complaining Party suspends NAFTA tariff benefits in accordance with this Agreement, the Party may increase the rates of duty on originating goods of the Party complained against to levels not to exceed the lesser of:

a. the rate that was applicable to those goods immediately prior to the date of entry into force of the NAFTA, and

b. the Most-Favored-Nation rate applicable to those goods on the date the Party suspends such benefits, and such increase may be applied only for such time as is necessary to collect, through such increase, the monetary enforcement assessment.

2. In considering what tariff or other benefits to suspend pursuant to Article 41(1) or (2):

    a. a complaining Party shall first seek to suspend benefits in the same sector or sectors as that in respect of which there has been a persistent pattern of failure by the Party complained against to effectively enforce its occupational safety and health, child labor or minimum wage technical labor standards; and

    b. a complaining Party that considers it is not practicable or effective to suspend benefits in the same sector or sectors may suspend benefits in other sectors.

ANNEX 46: EXTENT OF OBLIGATIONS

1. On the date of signature of this Agreement, or of the exchange of written notifications under Article 51, Canada shall set out in a declaration a list of any provinces for which Canada is to be bound in respect of matters within their jurisdiction. The declaration shall be effective on delivery to the other Parties, and shall carry no implication as to the internal distribution of powers within Canada. Canada shall notify the other Parties six months in advance of any modification to its declaration.

2. Unless a communication relates to a matter that would be under federal jurisdiction if it were to arise within the territory of Canada, the Canadian NAO shall identify the province of residence or establishment of the author of any communication regarding the labor law of another Party that it forwards to the NAO of another Party. That NAO may choose not to respond if that province is not included in the declaration made under paragraph 1.

3. Canada may not request consultations under Article 22, the establishment of an Evaluation Committee of Experts under Article 23, consultations under Article 27, the initiation of procedures under Article 28 or the establishment of a panel or join as a complaining Party under Article 29 at the instance, or primarily for the benefit, of any government of a province not included in the declaration made under paragraph 1.

4. Canada may not request consultations under Article 22, the establishment of an Evaluation Committee of Experts under Article 23, consultations under Article 27, the initiation of procedures under Article 28 or the establishment of a panel or join as a complaining Party under Article 29, unless Canada states in writing that the matter would be under federal jurisdiction if it were to arise within the territory of Canada, or:

    a. Canada states in writing that the matter would be under provincial jurisdiction if it were to arise within the territory of Canada; and

    b. the federal government and the provinces included in the declaration account for at least 35 percent of Canada's labor force for the most recent year in which data are available, and

    c. where the matter concerns a specific industry or sector, at least 55 percent of the workers concerned are employed in provinces included in Canada's declaration under paragraph 1.

5. No other Party may request consultations under Article 22, the establishment of an Evaluation Committee of Experts under Article 23, consultations under Article 27, the initiation of procedures under Article 28 or the establishment of a panel or join as a complaining Party under Article 29, concerning a matter related to a labor law of a province unless that province is included in the declaration made under paragraph 1 and the requirements of subparagraphs 4(b) and (c) have been met.

6. Canada shall, no later than the date on which an arbitral panel is convened pursuant to Article 29 respecting a matter within the scope of paragraph 5 of this Annex, notify in writing the complaining Parties and the Secretariat of whether any monetary enforcement assessment or action plan imposed by a panel under Article 39(4) or (5) against Canada shall be addressed to Her Majesty in right of Canada or Her Majesty in right of the province concerned.

7. Canada shall use its best efforts to make the Agreement applicable to as many of its provinces as possible.

8. Two years after the date of entry into force of this Agreement, the Council shall review the operation of this Annex and, in particular, shall consider whether the Parties should amend the thresholds established in paragraph 4.

ANNEX 49: COUNTRY-SPECIFIC DEFINITIONS

For purposes of this Agreement:

"territory" means:

a. with respect to Canada, the territory to which its customs laws apply, including any areas beyond the territorial seas of Canada within which, in accordance with international law and its domestic law, Canada may exercise rights with respect to the seabed and subsoil and their natural resources;

b. with respect to Mexico,

i. the states of the Federation and the Federal District,

ii. the islands, including the reefs and keys, in adjacent seas,

iii. the islands of Guadalupe and Revillagigedo situated in the Pacific Ocean,

iv. the continental shelf and the submarine shelf of such islands, keys and reefs,

v. the waters of the territorial seas, in accordance with international law, and its interior maritime waters,

vi. the space located above the national territory, in accordance with international law, and

vii. any areas beyond the territorial seas of Mexico within which, in accordance with international law, including the United Nations Convention on the Law of the Sea, and its domestic law, Mexico may exercise rights with respect to the seabed and subsoil and their natural resources; and

c. with respect to the United States,

i. the customs territory of the United States, which includes the 50 states, the District of Columbia and Puerto Rico,

ii. the foreign trade zones located in the United States and Puerto Rico, and

iii. any areas beyond the territorial seas of the United States within which, in accordance with international law and its domestic law, the United States may exercise rights with respect to the seabed and subsoil and their natural resources.

Topic Finder

AIR CARRIER

Railway Labor Act

ALIENS

Immigration Reform and Control Act

ARMED FORCES

Uniformed Services Employment and Reemployment Rights Act

CHILD LABOR

Fair Labor Standards Act

COLLECTIVE BARGAINING

National Labor Relations Act

Federal Service Labor-Management Relations Act

Railway Labor Act

CONSTRUCTION INDUSTRY

Davis-Bacon Act

DISCRIMINATION

Age Discrimination in Employment Act

Title VII of The Civil Rights Act of 1964

Americans with Disabilities Act

DISABILITIES

Americans with Disabilities Act

EQUAL PAY

Fair Labor Standards Act

FEDERAL EMPLOYEES

Federal Service Labor-Management Relations Act

FEDERAL CONTRACTORS

Davis-Bacon Act

Walsh-Healey Government Contracts Act

GROUP HEALTH PLANS

Consolidated Omnibus Budget Reconciliation Act

HEALTH AND SAFETY

Occupational Safety and Health Act

INJUNCTIONS

Norris LaGuardia Anti-Injunction Act

MINIMUM WAGE

Fair Labor Standards Act

Davis-Bacon Act

Walsh-Healey Government Contracts Act

OVERTIME PAY

Fair Labor Standards Act

PLANT CLOSINGS

Worker Adjustment and Retraining Notification Act

POLYGRAPHS

Employee Polygraph Protection Act

RAILROADS

Railway Labor Act

SECONDARY BOYCOTTS

National Labor Relations Act

TRUSTEESHIPS

Labor-Management Reporting and Disclosure Act

UNFAIR LABOR PRACTICES

National Labor Relations Act

Federal Service Labor-Management Relations Act

UNION ELECTIONS

Labor-Management Reporting and Disclosure Act

UNION MEMBER RIGHTS

Labor-Management Reporting and Disclosure Act

VETERANS

Uniformed Services Employment and Reemployment Rights Act

ORDER FORM

Please send me:

———— copies of *How to Win Past Practice Grievances* by Robert M. Schwartz

———— copies of *The Legal Rights of Union Stewards* by Robert M. Schwartz (English edition)

———— copies of *Derechos Legales de los Delegados de Sindicato* (Spanish edition of *The Legal Rights of Union Stewards*) by Robert M. Schwartz

———— copies of *The FMLA Handbook: A Practical Guide to the Family and Medical Leave Act for Union Members and Stewards* by Robert M. Schwartz

All books are $9.95. For shipping add $3.00 for the first copy and $1.00 for each additional copy.

Total enclosed: $ ————————————————

——
name

——
address   *city*   *state zip*

Mail to: Work Rights Press
               Box 391887
               Cambridge, MA 02139

Bulk rates for orders of 25 or more available upon request.

Telephone: 1-800-576-4552